The Roots of Western Finance

The Roots of Western Finance

Power, Ethics, and Social Capital in the Ancient World

Thomas K. Park and James B. Greenberg

LEXINGTON BOOKS
Lanham • Boulder • New York • London

Cover image: Cuneiform tablet case impressed with four cylinder seals in Assyrian and Anatolian styles, for cuneiform tablet 66.245.17a: loan of silver. Old Assyrian Trading Colony, ca. twentieth to nineteenth century BC. The MET OACS collection accession 66.245.17b.

Published by Lexington Books
An imprint of The Rowman & Littlefield Publishing Group, Inc.
4501 Forbes Boulevard, Suite 200, Lanham, Maryland 20706
www.rowman.com

Unit A, Whitacre Mews, 26-34 Stannary Street, London SE11 4AB

Quotes in chapter 1 from Martha T. Roth, *Law Collections from Mesopotamia*. Atlanta: Society of Biblical Literature, 1997. Used with permission.

Quotes in chapter 3 from Miriam Lichtheim, *Ancient Egyptian Literature*, Volumes I–III. Oakland: University of California Press Books, 2006. Used with permission.

British Library Cataloguing in Publication Information Available

Library of Congress Cataloging-in-Publication Data

Names: Park, Thomas Kerlin, author. | Greenberg, James B., author.
Title: The roots of Western finance : power, ethics, and social capital in the ancient world / Thomas K. Park and James B. Greenberg.
Description: Lanham : Lexington Books, [2017] | Includes bibliographical references and index.
Identifiers: LCCN 2017016289 (print) | LCCN 2017006783 (ebook) | ISBN 9781498545822 (Electronic) | ISBN 9781498545815 (cloth : alk. paper)
Subjects: LCSH: Commerce—History—To 500. | Commerce—History—Medieval, 500-1500. | Finance—History—To 1500. | Economic history. | History, Ancient.
Classification: LCC HF357 (print) | LCC HF357 .P37 2017 (ebook) | DDC 332.093—dc23
LC record available at https://lccn.loc.gov/2017016289

™ The paper used in this publication meets the minimum requirements of American National Standard for Information Sciences—Permanence of Paper for Printed Library Materials, ANSI/NISO Z39.48-1992.

Printed in the United States of America

Contents

Acknowledgments

We would like to express our gratitude to all the scholars without whose work this book would have been impossible. Our particular thanks go as well to those who have commented on earlier drafts of these chapters. The decades of support by our families, friends, and the University of Arizona have also been of inestimable value.

Introduction

From an anthropological perspective, financial *activities* take place in a complex *milieu*, in which specific *parties*, with particular *motives,* achieve their goals using some form of *agency* (social, cultural, economic capital).[1] Understanding the roots of western finance requires attention to transformation and continuity in the technical details of the financial venture, the milieu in which it occurs, the characteristics of the parties to the transaction, the forms of capital which empower the relative returns to the parties, and the goals which motivate the financial undertaking. We take as our starting point Paul Feyerabend's observation on the roots of science:

> There is no idea, however ancient and absurd, that is not capable of improving our knowledge. The whole history of thought is absorbed into science and is used for improving every single theory.[2]

Debt and notions of justice can be shown to be fundamentally intertwined in financial thinking across the ages. Ethics, politics, and law develop slowly but take form in societies and then gradually influence the international trading sector. Similarly, loans tie parties of disparate wealth and influence together within specific milieu which differentially empower them and this has its influence on ethical and political systems. It is networks of capital (social, cultural, and economic) which provide the resources that to a significant degree decide contractual advantages and the biases of commercial law more generally.

We argue that the continual transformations which led to the modern financial system have been motivated by ethics and the networks of social capital which sustain financial inequalities. Recognizing this provides us better insight into ancient and historical economies than a traditional economic focus on markets or government policy. Our focus on finance, necessarily neglects many aspects of economic and urban history in order to argue more succinctly that an understanding even of historical markets or governments requires an understanding of ethics, viewed as a system of expectations and obligations, and as a key financial institution in its own right. As an Inupiaq father suggests, obligations and honor are basic to human society: "Always do what you say you are going to do, otherwise you break meaning." This is his advice to his son Gilbert.[3]

Oddly enough, these two concepts seem, in our view, to have been rarely emphasized[4] even in studies of ancient finance. In Jack Goody's work, *The Theft of History*, one of the chapters bears the interesting title "The theft of 'capitalism': Braudel and global comparison."[5] Goody's succinct critique of Eurocentric interpretations of history is not wholly original nor is his disparagement of claims that the European development of capitalism implies a "failure" of other civilizations. We agree that the case for such failures is unpersuasive and hope to provide new insights. Analyses of finance have tended to focus too narrowly on technical dimensions, leaving aside social, political, and cultural dimensions, and have even missed technical continuities that transcend cultural boundaries. Unfortunately, the anthropological literature on finance remains largely confined to studies of specific societies and is rarely historical or comparative. Our work is intended as an initial attempt to address this neglect.

We should acknowledge the hubris of proposing a different way of analyzing credit and finance in an area encompassing Mesopotamia, Greece, Rome, the Levant, south in Egypt to the first cataract of the Nile, and for the first half millennia of the Islamic world. That we propose to do this as a prelude to a second book so as to eventually cover a period from 4000 BC to 2008 AD may be regarded as preposterous. In our defense, so much has been written that we can build on the work of legions of great scholars. We would also note that any reading of the enormous scholarship for this topic leaves the impression that there is such strongly felt ownership of periods and regions that no Egyptologist would dare venture to write seriously about Mesopotamia, or vice versa, nor would a specialist in either region venture a professional opinion about classical Athens. At times, it seems that few specialists on Athens would even venture an opinion about the Early Republic of Rome. There are, it seems, comparisons begging to be made. Fortunately, our work spans an area and time for which our cultural and political knowledge are rich, and though we cannot do full justice to any area or period, we can argue that finance, like trade, connected a diversity of regions and provides an intellectual entry to a gamut of intercultural influences.

Still, before we proceed, we would like to acknowledge emphatically at the outset that this work is heavily dependent on the linguistic expertise of many brilliant scholars. Although we have competence in a number of languages, they are by no means as many as we might wish. It is important to make these inadequacies clear at the start. While we have run our ideas by scholars better versed in some of the key languages, we take responsibility for any remaining issues in our discussion of Ancient Mesopotamia, Ancient Egypt, the Greco-Roman world, the Judeo-Christian positions on finance, or the early financial history of the Islamic World.

Beyond acknowledging our debts to all the great scholars of the civilizations we discuss, and our reviewers, we need to make it clear at once that we take the position that theoretical ideas provide illumination for research and we are not persuaded that any particular wavelength of light has an exclusive patent on illumination.

We have used a number of scholars (who rely on various theories to explain the economies of selected civilizations), whose theories we have not found persuasive for the financial realm on which we focus, yet we do not want to pretend their work adds little of value. Quite the contrary, as we argue for the particular merits of a few specific wavelengths of light, we will briefly review their most interesting ideas in our chapters.

From an anthropological perspective, credit is not simply an economic transaction, it also depends on social relationships. Although some credit arrangements need only willing partners, most agreements require the presence of forms of power to work. Such power rests not just on the ability of authorities to enforce payments or mediate disputes, but, more importantly on the creation and maintenance of reputation or "credit worthiness" as we say today. Because credit is embedded in and influences social arrangements and financial institutions, the various forms credit may take, and the structures of financial arrangements themselves, reveal hidden interests that entail promises and notions of justice that arguably were more important to creditors than material returns on investment.

The argument we make is that to appreciate these hidden interests one must begin with the obligations and ethics that organize networks of social capital, as their logic provides a better basis for understanding ancient and historical economies than a focus on markets or government policy. Due in part to the vagaries of historical preservation and in part to our distaste for redundancy we have chosen to focus on different facets of finance, as here conceived, in each chapter: those facets most readily apparent in the historical and archaeological material.

Credit has at least three attributes that make it a particularly good vehicle with which to explore the internal logic of local social formations. First, because credit is a promise to repay the loan of goods or services in the future,[6] it not only creates enduring social bonds, but as the lender generally sets the terms of repayment, it is readily used as a tool to control people and resources, and even to capture regional economies.[7] Second, credit tends to leave more social tracings in the historical record than do cash transactions. Finally, credit is more than an asymmetrical form of exchange, a set of social relations, or what appears to be a commodity; its many forms are cultural products that are embedded in the specific social and jural mores of each society, each in their own unique way.[8]

A modern chauvinist in business may well be reluctant to promote women but, if there is such a thing as progress, the symbolic violence he may exercise will be viewed both by women and other men today in a different way than similar actions would have been viewed in ancient Attica. More generally, symbolic violence as a concept makes best sense within a cultural and symbolic landscape and these, inevitably, transform over time. While the imposition of a transhistorical understanding has uses, it should not be confused with an attempt to understand (in the *verstehen* sense) historical decision-making. In the ancient world, not only were there major differences in the legal and financial positions available to women and men (Athens lagged far behind even early Mesopotamia in this regard) or to poor and rich (Egypt was far ahead in this respect) but, perception of such relationships also evolved everywhere over time.

THEORETICAL PERSPECTIVES

Here, we outline in a necessarily initial way the key theoretical positions that contextualize our contribution to an already existing and inordinately complex discourse. By "hidden interests" we refer to something of a similar nature to social capital both as a personal construct (à la Bourdieu) and as societal infrastructure (à la R. Putnam[9] and others). Yet, we find this concept in both its renditions far too narrow. Bourdieu recognizes this when he talks of material, cultural and social capitals belonging to individuals who convert one or more of these forms of social capital into symbolic capital that becomes the basis for linguistic violence—the way humans impose processes to their own advantage on others. Bourdieu's conception is a little too agentive for our liking. By contrast, Putnam's suggestion that social capital consists of societal features such as trust, norms, and networks provides an infrastructural and behavioral version of social capital that tends to direct attention away from the ways social capital is individually constructed. We prefer to acknowledge that both Bourdieu's and Putnam's position have merit.

In our view, social networks are not only deliberately expanded with self-serving goals in mind, they are also pre-expanded for some people because past societies expected some types of people to fulfill particular roles and provide explicit approbation for this via social structure. Ethnic identities, race and social hierarchies are frequently a basis for such pre-expansions. Furthermore, like all complex systems, societies' social networks have implications for everyone including ones their constructors cannot foresee. The economic or financial fortunes of individuals and institutions depend on the combined activities of many within and outside society as conventionally conceived. While all may be fair in love or war, little is foreseen in either.

All societies institutionalize behaviors, preferring some over others, and these cultural or legal preferences are now understood to limit the opportunity sets of those not preferred. In the modern economic literature such constraints are referred to as inequality traps which prevent some types of individuals from realizing their capabilities.[10] Societies incorporate inequality traps of many kinds that may, viewed under another lens, be seen as hidden interests benefiting some at the expense of others. Yet, conceiving these as individual advantages rather than as well understood group, class, gender, ethnic or institutional advantages would be worse than anachronistic—Amartya Sen noted in 1977[11] that the prevailing economic conception of economic actors as social morons was indefensible. Later, a whole literature in economics developed that talked of post-autistic economics[12] as an antidote to the methodological individualist position Sen had criticized.

We start from the position that individuals are socio-historical products who place great stock, for a variety of cultural reasons, in their social networks and the esteem of their peers. The networks they invest in have had the admiration and opprobrium of significant segments of the public even as they have been acknowledged to institutionalize various forms of hierarchy. Perhaps the classical Greek view that ostracism was akin to death captures the importance of social ties in a way that is still more familiar to us than the modern Inupiaq view that failing to fulfill all one's promises is to destroy meaning. Some interests are hidden in the customs and laws of society, some in the promises individuals make, some in the long term working out of network potentials and some are developed and defended by vested interests such as ethnic groups, classes, and factions of all kinds and genders. Although hidden interests are never totally veiled and only a few can be inferred from the historical record, these few should be subject to analysis. We propose a close reading of that record to begin a broader reconstruction of the past from the partial record remaining to us.

The best early data on how a broad set of hidden interests can play a critical role in finance comes from the Republic of Rome,[13] but we find evidence for networks of social capital throughout the ancient world. Hidden interests are in part "hidden" because we moderns have hidden them from our understanding of the economy; by a mixture of concern that partiality and fraud are synonymous or the more general results of an ideological obsession. Many intellectuals are convinced that humans are individualistic maximizers, not intrinsically social beings with wide social ties. This misconception makes it difficult to appreciate the positive side of social capital writ broadly. That we regularly do symbolic violence to anyone expressing other than self-serving intentions would be bad enough, but some scholars go further and imagine that those living in an earlier age were similarly socially challenged.

Despite this, people continue to do what they have done; they network, move through revolving doors between government and the private sector, and make extensive use of their social capital to further their own affairs and those of their friends despite our claims that bureaucracies and society must be rational, meritocratic and individualistic. Presidents and other high officials have been members of Yale University's Skull and Bones Club, or other similarly oriented organizations, whose members, it is said, swear to always give preference to other members of their club—and never to judge a candidate only on merit. While there is indeed no evidence that such people have failed in these great oaths, their fulfillment of such oaths is a well kept secret symptomatic of our times. In the Republic of Rome partiality enhanced reputation.

The ghost of Max Weber, it seems, is everywhere and his notion that one should view modern bureaucracies as efficient institutions where needs are processed without regard to the status of the supplicant belies, as he knew, the real use of the rolodex and its digital heirs and predecessors. In the ancient world, bureaucracies provided some efficiencies but this should not be exaggerated; in Egypt the enormous importance attached to equal justice before the law had its shock value due to the norm in other areas: the inheritance of bureaucratic position and the importance of social connection at all levels of society.

Just as personal ties may be activated at particular times yet reflect an enduring reality so, too, many customs that have become so accepted as to be almost beyond scrutiny also reflect enduring relations of inequality that provide hidden advantages. Even the World Bank has suggested that long past colonial regimes instituted inequality traps that have enduring influence to this day.[14]

Our project aims to reconstruct the transformations in financial institutions with attention to these instituted (hidden) interests. These need not be so simple as different rates or laws for different classes of people for the entire fabric of social life is fair game. In Mesopotamia and Egypt grain storage by temples, communities, and states had regulations that provided potential advantages to institutions. We discuss these in more detail in the appropriate chapters, but an example that often escapes the modern scholar's eye is that the mere designation of where a loan of grain is received and returned can provide significant advantages to the lender. This is because when grain is poured into a container it takes up more space before than after it has settled during transport. This difference can be on the order of 15 percent or more.[15]

When we are also dealing with differences in quality between old stored (weevil damaged) grain and new freshly harvested grain the advantages are even more significant. That granaries also charged interest to some borrowers and not to others reflects a different set of inequalities in networks of social capital that also were probably just as infrequently questioned. Astonishingly, much of the scholarly literature on the classical and ancient economies anachronistically assumes that explicitly mentioned interest rates were the primary source of profit in lending even for grain. As we will see, the gradual development of loan instruments of greater and greater specificity suggests that people well understood the other sources of advantage.

A number of scholars of the ancient Mediterranean and Near East have been attracted by Polanyi's claims that ancient economies were socially embedded and that markets did not function as significant drivers of the economy. Polanyi's position was that markets dealt with a very finite set of goods with generally inefficient prices and the forces of competition in these markets did not extend to most key factors of production. Moses Finley,[16] most prominently, made such a claim for the Classical Greco-Roman economies. Vociferous debates, referred in anthropology as the formalist-substantivist debates,[17] had innumerable scholars taking each side. In retrospect, many arguments tended to trivialize Polanyi's distinctions and relied on little more than a caricature of the neoclassical economic model as both foil and trumpet. Even so, thin theory did not prevent first rate historical research. We can now say that economists largely recognize the near idiotic simplicity of the neoclassical model being pushed in the 1960s, and we need feel no obligation to defend it let alone foist it on the ancient or classical world. In our view, Polanyi's main error was to imagine capitalist economies as less embedded in social relations and less committed to ideological justifications for inequality.

A more promising start has been to suggest that elements of Keynesian analysis might be relevant, especially, to an understanding of the ancient Egyptian economy.[18] The key elements thought to be relevant have to do with the role of investment (viewed as Keynesian savings) in economic stimulation and the role of high employment in prosperity. While the details of Keynes' prescription and the relevance of WWII in ending the Great Depression are not important here, the general set of ideas relating government expenditures and savings (leading to private sector investment) as stimulus for the economy have implications for any study of past civilizations. This is true even if we have to modify these ideas to recognize that in economies without money the idea of monetary policy as tied to stimulus is almost irrelevant. Recent work has suggested that levels of economic inequality in the last two centuries have been in part a structural result tied to low growth in the economy and high returns on investment as well as due to the outcome of societal perspectives on social justice and the leveling impacts of wars.[19] Comparable elements can be found in the economies in the more distant past we are examining.

We will review this idea in more detail in the chapter on Egypt, but we feel it important here to note that Piero Sraffa's work, in particular his *Production of Commodities by Means of Commodities*,[20] provides an improved starting point over the Keynesian model for our purposes. Sraffa's model does not rely on a significant monetary system operating semi-autonomously from the production side of the economy. Instead, it imagines savings for investment as a socially negotiated extraction from the shares due to management and labor in all productive sectors.

We do not think a model of this sort can be adequate if it does not include the immaterial infrastructure and again point out that even Keynes well understood the psychological issues driving savings and investment. He phrased this in terms of propensity to consume or save and imagined factors that might sway individuals one way or the other. Lest we think such propensities are simply natural consider that whether someone invests in the education of their children or puts money in a bank for bankers to invest it is still investment that may well bear fruit, and yet economists and their banker cousins have an overwhelming propensity to consider only the latter as savings or investment. What counts as investment and why investment occurs is cultural not natural and we would be well advised to remember this when studying the past. Investments in temples for example were investments in productive facilities and salaries as well as in promotion of a belief system, but neither would long survive without the other. It is not at all clear that the construction of a pyramid and its attendant supporting infrastructure has the same resultant stream of annual societal returns as the construction of a major temple of the same initial cost, and this is surely relevant to understanding prosperity in ancient economies.

Put succinctly, our view of credit and finance considers that forms of credit involve both ideologies and institutionalization of hierarchy and privilege. These are empowered by networks of cultural, social, and economic capital and provide differential advantages that motivate agents to pursue socio-historically situated goals. Just as these cultural logics are intertwined within a society, the nature of international trade has systematically forced myriad encounters and negotiations which have stimulated the innovation and the increasing sophistication of financial systems writ broadly.

In this book, we focus on credit and finance in ancient societies, beginning with Sumer and ending around 1100 AD in the Islamic world. We attempt to provide insight into the deep structures, processes, and inner cultural logics that made ancient institutions and social relations work in distinctive ways, giving their economies their own particularity and dynamics. Our examination of the history of credit in early civilizations reveals that investments in social capital were a key component of early finance just as they are today. It also exposes the variety of ways hidden interests, who benefits or productive inequalities, show up in each civilization's financial structure. Even more critically it points to how important ethical discourse and notions of justice have been in shaping financial discourses in each society.

Our first two chapters canvas Mesopotamian financial history through the 1st millennium BC—examining the earliest urban formations and the various empires encompassing the region. The first chapter focuses on the intellectual, religious, and legal frameworks. The second explores the gradual development of increasingly sophisticated technologies of credit. Mesopotamia had precedence not only in urbanization but also in the development of explicit economic and financial accounting that gives us our earliest insights into ancient finances. Despite considerable turnover in polities, the continuity in the cuneiform record is extraordinary and lends itself to careful documentation of transformations in the institutional supports for credit. These sources make it clear that cultural constructs and material infrastructure are fundamental to the transformations that occur over time. Mesopotamian records provide many insights into credit and investment schemes implemented for millennia before the earliest true coins (made of electrum a natural amalgam of silver and gold) appeared in seventh century (BC) Lydia. Long before this Babylonian loans included explicit interest, initially through temple or palace regulation of interest rates. Complex loans and hidden interest in many forms served both to promote prosperity and to hold society together.

The third chapter examines the only slightly later pharaonic civilization on the Nile that also flourished without money though it elaborated a sophisticated economy based on administrative, religious, and private sector investments. Like Mesopotamia, Egypt managed to elaborate accounting practices to fit a grain based economy that needed careful accounting to track returns on large scale investments. Not surprisingly, these accounting techniques facilitate the extraction of surplus and its wise investment in remunerative activities. We argue that the peculiarities of the Nile flood guaranteed a greater surplus than a more regular regime could have afforded. The enormous continuity in polities controlling a core, well defined, geographic territory makes the Egyptian case more suitable for speculation about the factors affecting changes in national surplus and overall patterns of investment. We will argue, among other things, that Egyptian investment investment choices in the context of a chaotic flood regime produced a financial framework that was critical to long-term economic prosperity.

The fourth chapter, by virtue of the written record available, provides the most detailed illustration of our argument about social networks. In it, we focus on classical Athens and the Early Republic of Rome: where early reflections on lending at interest gave rise to an opprobrium that cast a long temporal shadow. We argue that subsequent developments, both in the Islamic world and Europe, borrowed heavily from Greco-Roman practice. The splendid scholarship available also makes it possible to sketch out in fairly convincing detail the ways in which hidden interests, social hierarchy and social capital were key to financial developments. The philosophical thought of the Greeks and the legal sophistication of the Romans combine to help us illustrate the enormous significance of social networks, ideas of honor and obligation, and practices which put social capital front and center in the financial structure.

The fifth chapter examines the Judeo-Christian tradition and with a focus on credit, lending and usury shows that it was built on a Mesopotamian legacy. Even so, Jewish moral reflection on lending provided the first purely moral analysis of lending at interest. Even as it borrowed heavily from Mesopotamian practice, Jewish reflections endorsed a distinction between Jews and others that might have been patterned after Mesopotamian class distinctions. The history of the opprobrium placed on usury in Europe and the Islamic world has roots in the philosophical thought of Plato and Aristotle as well as in quite separate ethical considerations derived from religious thinkers. In the west, the problem of what was fair and what constituted usury eventually led Aquinas and his followers to put forward ideas of opportunity cost.

Our sixth chapter on Islamic finance finds a plethora of evidence for commonality in financial practice suggesting continuity between the principles examined in the earlier chapters and those of Islamic society in the Eastern Mediterranean in the Early Middle ages. This chapter, in part, continues our discussion of Egypt. Not surprisingly, the elaboration of old practices, their refinement, and the enunciation of new principles in the Islamic world formed the basis of much financial history leading up to the modern period. In particular, we find that two technical paths, tied to two distinct ethical principles, first developed explicitly in classical Athens, form the basis of major differences between the development of finance in Europe and that of the Islamic world. We also discuss the significant continuities between social obligations linked to honor in the Early Republic and similar practices in the Islamic world. However, the major focus of this chapter is the extraordinary concern in Islamic financial practice and law for requiring contracts to make explicit everything that hitherto was happily hidden. Justice in lending thus could be said to become paramount in this period and, for the first time, tantamount to transparency in lending.

Our appendix, *Technologies of Power and the Metrology of Grain Storage*, addresses the sophisticated ways grain compression was recognized in metrological systems of both ancient Mesopotamia and dynastic Egypt. Since the metrology is different but focused narrowly in both cases and hitherto largely ignored by scholars it can be most efficiently addressed in a single place. The reality that grain compresses has been well understood historically as a means for differential advantage between lender and recipient of a loan. This major source of hidden interest is only briefly alluded to in the chapters on Mesopotamia and Egypt because the details are mathematical and a bit arcane.

NOTES

1. This pentad, which is derived from that used by Kenneth Burke in *A Grammar of Motives*, provides a useful way to focus on the larger picture of transformations in credit and financial undertakings. Burke's basic pentad; act, scene, agent, agency, purpose was designed for literary analysis but has long since been adopted to anthropological work.
2. Paul Feyerabend, *Against Method*, p. 47.
3. Cited in, Wales (Seward Peninsula), Alaska, BBC June 12, 2013, The other Wales, caption photo 17.
4. An exception that we draw from extensively in chapter 4 is Verboven, *The Economy of Friends*.
5. Chapter 7, Goody, *The Theft of History*.
6. Firth and Yamey. "Capital, Savings and Credit in Peasant Societies."
7. Biddick, "People and Things," 8.
8. Braudel, *The Structures of Everyday Life,* 477.
9. Putnam. *Bowling Alone*.
10. While Sen's writings figure prominently, for example, *The Idea of Justice*, the literature is enormous and we should mention in particular two other works: Crocker, *Ethics of Global Development*, as well as Wolff and De-Shalit, *Disadvantage*.
11. Sen, "Rational Fools."
12. The journal of *Post-Autistic Economics* has now been renamed the *Real-World Economics Review* and is supported by the Post-Autistic Economics Network.
13. Verboven 2002.
14. The World Bank. *World Development Report 2006; Equity and Development*, chapter 6. The now classic article on this is Acemoglu, Johnson, and Robinson, "The Colonial Origins of Comparative Development."

15. Kula, *Measures and Men,* devotes chapter 7 to grain compression. Medieval arguments were heated and focused not only on the dimensions of a bushel but also on the way in which grain was poured into the bushel: the difference between a bushel filled by pouring from the height deemed ethical (where the hands hang normally) and one poured from shoulder height, pressed and heaped was about 25 percent (p. 48). A quarter to half of this 25 percent might typically be in the "heap" but the heap depended very much on the width to depth ratio of the container and a "Byzantine" heap could represent between one sixth and half of the bushel (p. 66). While a wide shallow bushel could have a larger heap it would typically have correspondingly less compression. Hence some bushels of the same volume contained far more due to the regulations dealing with what counted as a full bushel. That a large granary would, due to grain compression, store more grain than its dimensions might suggest seems to have escaped the attention of scholars of the ancient world; as we observe in the chapters on Mesopotamia and Egypt.

16. Finley. *The Ancient Economy*. and *Studies in Land and Credit in Ancient Athens*. For an overview and extended discussion see, Scheidel and Von Reden, *The Ancient Economy*.For a decidedly unconvinced perspective see, Cohen, *Athenian Economy and Society*.

17. LeClair and Schneider, *Economic Anthropology* .Various contributions discuss the formalist-substantivist debate in detail.

18. Warburton. *State and Economy in Ancient Egypt.*

19. Picketty. *Capital in the Twenty-First Century*.

20. Sraffa. *Production of Commodities by Means of Commodities.* Perhaps the most important point Sraffa makes is that it is possible to construct a measure of value that is immune to inflation or depreciation in any particular commodity or set of commodities—assuming we want to talk about absolute change over time this is a necessary measure and something Ricardo long sought unsuccessfully. For us this is only important in the abstract in as much as it means it is logically coherent to speak of change in aggregate or specific values over time—even if for ancient economies we will never have the necessary date to construct such a standard commodity (basically a very specially weighted basket of commodities).

Chapter One

Mesopotamian Roots of the Modern Financial System

Before they were writing documents in southern Mesopotamia, Sumerians were doing accounting in an early script producing texts that revealed precious little about social structure. Yet, the absence of particular material in the early stages of writing does not imply any behavioral discontinuities are revealed when other data is included in later texts. If we measure in centuries, Sumerians and Akkadians quickly developed scripts to represent a much larger part of their language. Because Mesopotamians wrote their texts largely on baked (sun, kiln, or fired as buildings were burnt) clay tablets, they have survived in the arid ground of the region better than other writing materials used elsewhere, such as papyrus.[1]

The early role of Mesopotamia in financial thought has been both appreciated and misunderstood as the following attest:

> [Sir Isaac] Newton was not the first of the age of reason. He was the last of the magicians, the last of the Babylonians and Sumerians . . . Because he looked on the whole universe and all that is in it as a riddle, as a secret which could be read by applying pure thought to certain evidence, certain mystic clues which God had laid about the world to allow a sort of philosopher's treasure hunt . . . By pure thought, by concentration of the mind, the riddle, he believed, would be revealed to the initiate.[2]—John Maynard Keynes

> Newton was able to combine prodigious mental faculty with credulities and delusions that would disgrace a rabbit.[3]—George Bernard Shaw

> It was the need to coordinate various amounts and kinds of matter and information among the diversified Mesopotamian socio-economic units that militated for the growth of permanent cross-cutting networks of exchange and information.[4]—Norman Yoffee

While Keynes' characterization of Sir Isaac Newton reflects a reasonably accurate assessment of Mesopotamian proclivities for semiotic interpretations of Nature, Einstein said of Newton, "Nature to him was an open book, whose letters he could read without effort."[5] Shaw's assessment of Newton epitomizes a very modern distaste for religious arguments as well as an extraordinary faith in both science and modern rabbits. An important mystery we hope to clarify in this chapter is why it came to pass that the financing of trade and economic activities through credit should have appeared so early in Mesopotamia. Until contrary evidence is produced we have even to ask why it should have first appeared and been elaborated here rather than in other parts of the globe. This chapter addresses basic questions about the financial milieu and the purposes envisaged for credit while the next looks at the details of the financial instruments developed in Mesopotamia for they came to influence as well Egypt, the Eastern Mediterranean and in due course the Islamic World and Europe with consequences for the modern global economy.

We will try to bridge the gap between the modern viewpoint and the Mesopotamian to look at the origins of finance and credit, inspired by Yoffee's emphasis on the importance for Mesopotamian studies of "cross-cutting networks of exchange and information"—the latter viewed as generated by human or divine sources.

Before the mid-twentieth century, historians tended to equate history with written documents, and consequently found claims such as that "history begins with Sumer" reasonable approximations of the truth as they saw it.[6] Once a host of new scientific sources of data from archaeology became current along with the development of oral history, such claims became, at best, foolish and intolerably ethnocentric. To subscribe to such a position, would be like relying only on Athenian materials to describe attitudes toward women in the ancient world, when there is ample evidence that women's authority, status and economic clout in Sumer, Akkad, Ebla, and many Mesopotamian cities was far more substantial than in Athens.[7] Our focus on finance necessarily prohibits an adequate discussion of other issues so, for example, despite the urban origin of most financial thought we discuss the history of urbanism or political developments only as required for our arguments. Fortunately, many apposite works, in these and other areas, are easily available for consultation.

POLITICAL EXPANSION AND FINANCIAL DEVELOPMENT

The earlier archaeological record for the gradual appearance of towns in the 9000–4000 BC era in the Fertile Crescent is rich. Although much has been written based on these materials, there are still some astonishing gaps. Schol-

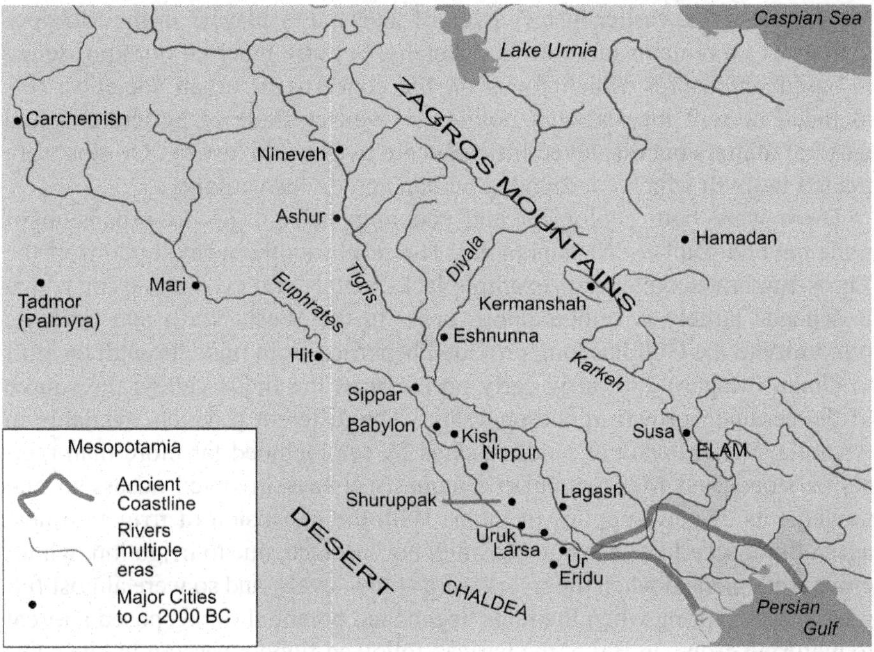

Map 1.1. Mesopotamia in the Ancient Period.
Data from Norman Bancroft Hunt. *Historical Atlas of Ancient Mesopotamia* (New York: Checkmark Books, 2004), 19.

ars presume the Sumerians either developed indigenously or came to southern Mesopotamia along the north coast of the Gulf. Although the earliest urban alliances seem to center around Eridu and Uruk in southern Mesopotamia, they owe much to agricultural innovations and town development within the broader Fertile Crescent, as well as to the productivity of flood recession agriculture in southern Mesopotamia.[8] Apparent social innovations suggest a gradual movement from communal values to increased pervasiveness of social differentiation. Even the idea of individual destinies, different for elites and commoners, can be found across the region; though these changes seem to accelerate the fastest in southern Mesopotamia.[9]

From 4000 BC on we know much more and we need not speculate about the origins of the Akkadians (whose language is Semitic) or that of various Amorite dynasties who replaced the Ur III dynasty, whose internal problems weakened it to the point it fell to the Elamites. Similarly we know enough about the Kassites (that they originated to the north and spoke a non-semitic language) who (c. 1590 BC) took advantage of the internal failures of the Old Babylonian dynasty centered in the middle Euphrates to establish a dynasty.

Nevertheless, the earlier history even of later major players in the Mesopotamian world remains more or less sketchy, because much of our knowledge is based on records which focus on the concerns of urban societies: this included current international politics as well as trade or agricultural and pastoral matters but displayed little concern over world history. Origins were treated in myth which confounded human and divine causality.

There were both ecological and economic advantages to expansion of trade beyond southern Mesopotamia. The fertile southern flood plains of the Tigris-Euphrates valley, for example lacks metals and even stone for which it depends largely on mountainous areas to the West, North and East. Its proximity to the Gulf has long provided benefited from trade through the gulf to Oman (Magan) and fairly early on as far as the Indus valley; the source of the sesame[10] grown in Mesopotamia. The different products available in Anatolia, Syria, Persia or lands reached by sea included far more than metals or stone, and Mesopotamian conquests always involved access to and movements of new supplies of labor. With the expansion of irrigation new agricultural schedules became possible. For instance, due to irrigation, winter crops were planted when the rivers were at low levels, and so were almost full grown in the spring when the rains began, and potential floods posed a threat to maturing crops. In Egypt the harvest followed flood recession in late summer; whereas, in some parts of the Levant and Syria harvest occurs in summer or early fall as it does in Europe. This pattern of grains ripening at different times in different places, meant grains were either cheap or expensive more than once a year.

Irrigation also entailed other sets of ecological challenges. Because for much of the year the water table stayed high enough for agriculture, salinization became an issue. Coping with salinization, by abandoning soils with high salinity, required the continual reworking of irrigation canal networks. Fortunately, this was facilitated in part by the regular changes in river courses. Unfortunately, changes in the course of the Tigris and the Euphrates and the gulf coastline also had obvious impacts on the prosperity of cities which are not movable and depended on agriculture. It is probable that such shifts contributed to the many political transformations that made Mesopotamian history so different from Egyptian history where the Nile flood and low off season water table neither caused significant salinization nor forced regular change in urban location.

The variety of crop schedules in the greater Mesopotamian region and the early importance of trade and finance contributed to the development of sophisticated methods for managing funds. The superb possibilities of navigation on the Euphrates, and to a lesser degree on the Tigris, also facilitated long distance trade that, at times stretching from the Indus to Egypt and Anatolia, may explain the success of many cities, including Ebla which even more than Sumer had few natural resources nearby.

Throughout this core area, the kings of ancient Mesopotamia, and religious leaders, urged warfare on their human servitors[11] taking divine concerns to heart—perhaps none more enthusiastically than the later Assyrians who flayed, decapitated and impaled their enemies and decorated their palaces with graphic depictions of their divinely ordained exploits. The political history of ancient Mesopotamia is so full of conquest, movement of captives to refurbish populations or to power agricultural production and expansion, that it might seem surprising that any cultural continuity could be found. Yet, not only was there considerable continuity in cosmology but even the basic structure of finance across the region, though modified, showed extraordinary continuity and steady refinement due to the continued use of the cuneiform script and gradual development of the accounting techniques with which it began. Our distance in time and its tendency to compress long periods of socio-economic prosperity to focus on briefer periods of political conquest distract us from seeing gradual and cumulative financial change.

Cuneiform writing, which was used for multiple languages, continued as the basis of literacy and science as well as religious and political record keeping late into the first millennium BC in some areas. The Sumerian language, which had its last resurgence as the official spoken language in the Ur III period, continued to be an important literary language across the greater Mesopotamian region even during the later Assyrian Empire, whose leaders continued to revere southern Mesopotamia as the center of culture and science. The library of Assyrian ruler Assurbanipal (reigned ca. 668–627 BC) in Nineveh, for example, encompassed many thousands of cuneiform tablets assiduously collected (taken) and copied and included at least one hundred bilingual Sumerian-Akkadian texts.[12]

Sumerian itself may have been overlooked as a possible reason for Mesopotamian enthusiasm for loaning at interest. Although linguists are quite reasonably reluctant to attribute extra-linguistic causality to language structures an argument can be made that the prejudice against lending at interest, as unnatural, expressed thousands of years later by Plato and Aristotle despite millennia of lending at interest, would have seemed as irrational to Mesopotamians as to moderns. In Sumerian grammar for perfect tense verbs (completed action), the "agent" producing the profit would have been the commodity, while the trader who had facilitated that increase became a facilitator of the "agent's" action. Subjects tied to perfect tense transitive verbs took, in Sumerian, an ergative case ending, while the direct object was declined as if it were in a nominative case. In short, the noun that would, in an imperfect tense, be in the nominative took a new declension (the ergative). Instead of a subject and an object this has been described as the subject giving its agency to the object. One gloss is that of a doctor and patient - the doctor empowers the patient to be healthy.[13] An alternative, and perhaps more fitting gloss might come from the financial realm: an investor establishes and empowers a loan.[14]

A trivial example would be that in a sentence such as "the King built the house" rather than placing "the King" in nominative case and "the house" in accusative case, as Sumerian does in the present or imperfect tense, in perfect tenses, Sumerian puts "The King" in ergative case (the noun has an "e" on the end) and leaves "the house" uninflected (it has no ending added) as it would be if it were in the Sumerian nominative case—as if the king has arranged

Photo 1.1 Cuneiform tablet: loan of silver. Old Assyrian Trading Colony, ca. twentieth–nineteenth century BC. (The cover image is the clay envelope for this tablet.)
Source: Gift of Mr. and Mrs. J. J. Klejman, 1966 to the Metropolitan Museum of Art, accession number 66.245.17a. www.metmuseum.org

for the house to house things. The house once built has agency and so merits the nominative case.[15]

A more revealing example has been translated as: "The king of Ur, the king of the four quarters, built the temple (where) honey, butter and wine in his place of sacrifice shall not cease." Sumerian grammar presents this concept though a grammatical construct in which the completed temple forever provides for the gods [due to the efforts of the king i.e. once built].[16]

It would be hard to exaggerate Sumerian concerns with the theme of continuity of action or clarity about the agency involved in setting something in motion. A typical inscription, *mu en ^{d}inanna maš-e i-pà* which may be translated as "the year the *en* of the god Inanna (unmarked) was chosen by omens (marked as ergative)," attributes empowerment to the omen in instituting the new priestess (*en*) of the goddess in her role, in which she henceforth acts (has agency).[17]

Structurally this construction parallels the investor-agent contract and the obligations humanity incurred to the superior gods who created them (see below). More importantly, perhaps, is that this perspective is general: once empowered agency follows. From this point of view the moral squeamishness about lent money being "naturally" unproductive, so enthusiastically endorsed by the Greeks, would be quite unnatural in a Sumerian context where a loan once made had grammatical as well as real world agency.[18]

WHEN MESOPOTAMIAN GODS COMMUNICATED PEOPLE PAID HEED: THE ORIGINS OF SEMIOTICS

The Torah and the Bible portray creation as the result of the one God making a series of entirely effective verbal proclamations. The most famous passages include; Genesis: "Then God said, "Let there be light, and there was light" as well as John 1: "In the beginning was the Word and the Word was with God, and the Word was God." These re-workings of earlier polytheistic proclamations are presented as the statements of an omnipotent creator. Sumerians viewed life through a lens of myths, about plural gods. Some myths explained humanity's place in the cosmos as a creation whose primary purpose was to nourish and honor humanity's creators who had grown tired of providing for themselves. Sumerian gods were thought to have made humanity in their own image, with similar intellect and psychology, though with less power and shorter life spans.

For several millennia, Mesopotamians thought some humans were clearly created with a destiny that could be ignored only with difficulty. They assumed the gods were in constant communication with the human world, but did not speak with one voice. Like humans, the gods could quarrel. And each, though all were immortal, was inclined to prefer their own prosperity over that of other gods, even if they concurred on the value of a more general concept of divine welfare and, usually, agreed on the value of humans in promoting it. Divine communications were transmitted in dreams, in the stars, and through the "media" of all aspects of the world from sheep intestines to earthquakes, winds, or droughts. The key was to understand the signs and make appropriate decisions. To this end, Mesopotamian science advocated acute empirical observation to discern from what has happened, what will happen. Anything odd was thought to be a certain, if cryptic, message from the gods. Specialists made enormous lists in an elaborate range of categories documenting completed events to facilitate a search for correlations in the past which might suggest the probable meaning of a recent event. They also engaged, for this purpose and other reasons, in considerable analytic effort in understanding mathematics both applied and theoretical.[19] In this sense, as Keynes noted, Isaac Newton was following the Mesopotamian approach.

During the reign of Nabonidus in the Neo-Babylonian period, the king looked for signs to decide on who should be appointed the *entu* priestess. The following account (c. 554 BC) has a number of typical Mesopotamian features:

> When Nanna desired an entu priestess . . . Namra-sit [an epithet of Nanna meaning Light Emission] made manifest his firm decision; to Nabonidus, the king of Babylon . . . Because of the desire for an entu priestess, in the month of Ululu, on the thirteenth day of the month "the work of the goddesses," the Fruit (i.e., Nanna) was eclipsed and set while eclipsed. "Sin desires an entu-priestess" was thus his sign and decision . . . I Nabonidus . . . did revere his firm command and became attentive . . . I sought out the sanctuaries of Shamash and Adad, the lords of divination (i.e., extispicy), and Shamash and Adad answered me with a firm "yes" . . . I repeated (the inquiry) and checked the message, and they answered me with an omen more favorable than before. I (then) performed an omen concerning the daughters of my relatives, but they answered me with a no. A third time I made an extispicy concerning a daughter of my (own) issue and they answered me with a favorable omen . . . I was attentive to the word of Sin, the exalted lord, the god who fashioned me, and the command of Shamash and Adad, the lords of divination, and installed a daughter of my own issue in the office of high priestess and named her En-nigaldi-Nanna.[20]

Mesopotamian civilization was premised on the existence of many gods who expressed themselves to the human world via signs and portents in the apparent world, such as an eclipse or extispicy (reading of entrails) or features of human dreams. Yet, rather than viewing divine communication as a statement about the inevitable or an effective utterance, the Mesopotamian experts viewed divine discourse as a fair warning about a probable future and castigated those who attempted to make key decisions without consulting the gods.[21] In the case of desired events such as victory in war, that probable future might not happen unless proper rituals were followed while, in the case of undesirable outcomes, the indicated future event would occur unless proper precautions were taken to avert "fate."

The much discussed example of the substitute king illustrates this latter case well. Portents suggesting the King is to die in the near future, perhaps in a particular way or place or time, elicited a Mesopotamian ruse: send the real King off to his summer residence and place a peasant or laborer on the throne (properly dressed, addressed, and honored) and then arrange for the false king to meet the fate predicted for the real king. This was seen as adroitly saving the real King from death and perfectly satisfying the requirements of the gods for a kingly death. In Mesopotamian mythology, the gods, like similarly immortal modern cartoon characters, regularly bamboozled each other.[22] Intellectual sophistication, as it is today, was low.

The main mandate from the gods was for humans to be productive, to irrigate and grow the crops and keep the livestock fertile and numerous so that the gods, via their temples, could be nourished physically and appropriately honored. Warfare was an instrument of expansion that benefited the god(s) whose people expanded, so warfare and fertility were early on combined in one female god, Inanna (Sumerian) or Ishtar (Akkadian). In the early city states, each state had its own primary god distinct from that of its competitors, as well as temples to multiple gods, but as empires developed centralized administrations a more coherent hierarchy of gods developed in tandem and expansion took on broader religious meanings.

New names, relations and precedence within the divine realm facilitated the justification of new power centers in the real world, but even the most violent first millennium BC Assyrian rulers continued to honor southern Mesopotamia as the center of learning and followed the empirical science developed originally in that region to understand the communications of the gods. This cosmological view, though it encouraged acute empirical observation and record keeping, was not premised on the existence of deterministic causality originating either from the gods or their human and animal proxies. It was not until the Greeks that the notion of a world of hidden causality (the Platonic realm) was significantly developed, even as classical Greek thought retained the ancient notion of both human and divine influence on events. In this sense, Newton and his age were even more Aristotelian than they were Babylonian.

Agency is a key to understanding the Sumerian outlook as it came to shape the broader Mesopotamian perspectives. Humans, as agents of the gods with approximate destinies, were merely exemplars of the more general situation:

the idea of destiny was extended to include plants and animals which themselves had agency most significantly expressed in their fertility or ability to serve as the embodiment of divine communications. Humans in all their variety were the agents that helped even domesticates fulfill their destinies. In a similar fashion, inanimate objects, such as wind or flood or astronomical constellations, had agency, in the sense of being divinely empowered, which could be expected to influence the world. This focus on intention driven events in the real world may be seen as a near reduction of cosmological causality to agents. Viewing the matter in Aristotelian terms, while recognizing final and material or instrumental causality, the Mesopotamian focus neglected efficient and formal causality in explanations of history. Thus, Mesopotamians understood that wars were won with people and equipment (or the weather) and the will of the gods, but did not really analyze history in terms of deterministic physics or environmental or social systems with interacting variables. Instead they assigned agency in areas where Aristotle, as well as Newton, and we, their intellectual heirs, tend to find less persuasive. Yet, the credulousness of the Mesopotamian mind can be overdone and the Mesopotamian financial legacy, for example, shows every evidence of being shaped by an assiduous effort to regulate human behavior and acquire natural resources to enhance society and the economy through purely mundane ways.

BRIEF SOCIO-POLITICAL CHRONOLOGY

Although we cannot in this chapter devote significant space to Mesopotamian political history, a few more precise dates may help.[23] Mesopotamian urban civilization was first established in the early fourth millennium BC, with cities developing in Elam and both Akkadian and Sumerian speaking areas of Mesopotamia. Urbanism began to flourish in the early third millennium BC, first in cities whose inhabitants spoke Sumerian in the adjacent lands of the two rivers north-west of the Sumerian heartland. Soon inhabitants of some cities upriver, such as Kish, came largely to speak Akkadian. Early cities also developed in western Syria where Eblaite (like Akkadian, a semitic language) was spoken though most records were kept in Sumerian. Though it appears that the Sumerians invented most of what made Mesopotamian civilization unique, including its writing system, both Sumerian and Semitic speakers were participants in a vibrant civilization by early in the third millennium BC.

Early city states developed from about 4000 BC but the period from 3500 BC to 2800 BC in Lower Mesopotamia provided what has been called an urban revolution, stamped by what archaeologists have called the Uruk culture.[24] Temples stored a "surplus" of grain produced by obligated labor.

Religious ideologies led both elites and dependents to provide significant productive labor to the temples of the gods associated with individual cities first and other divinities whose support seemed important to city welfare.

The second era of urbanization developed from 2800 BC to 2000 BC and might be said to involve broader forms of political solidarity embracing several adjacent cities and this urbanization developed not just in southern Mesopotamia but also in Elam (to the East), upper Mesopotamia, the Levant, and Anatolia. It also culminated in the formation of the first true states and empires. Most significantly from our point of view the development of associated financial instruments provides us our best documentation of the development of finance, as we have come to know it.

While we do not have particularly rich information on social structure for the early part of this period, it appears that societies continued to be organized as extended households including people (labor) of different status. Temples were imagined as a type of household and during this period palaces came to dominate even the temples and were themselves also described as households. Thus in Lagash around 2400 BC the ruler, Uru'inimgina, reorganized the city's "households" to consolidate many temples and estates under his control, placing for example his wife in charge of the temple to the goddess Bau which consolidated the estates and obligated labor of several temples (now collectively called household Bau-é-bau).[25] Obligated labor might include captives derived from conquest and free citizens. In later times such labor also included people obligated as pledges for debt. The early activities of temples included banking grains, financing the military, and lending or expending grains for the welfare of the temple.

Sargon I established an Akkadian speaking empire centered in Akkad and his dynasty endured for approximately 180 years (2334–2154 BC). Ur III, the last Sumerian dynasty was a state (2112–2004 BC) with provincial governors and an elaborate system of government finance and accounting. Toward the end of this period there was significant urban decline followed by new forms of urbanization.

In a third period of urbanization (2000–1200 BC), sometimes referred to as the regional system, trade with areas outside the core came into greater prominence. The Old Assyrian Period (2025–c. 1715 BC)[26] refers not to an empire but to an era in which trade between Assur, north west of Akkad, and Kanesh, in Anatolia, was elaborated and institutionalized. Assur became independent of Ur late in the Ur III period and continued at the apex of the Old Assyrian trade during the first three centuries of the second millennium BC. The Old Babylonian Period (c. 1894–1595 BC) included many dynasties controlling more than one city and many independent cities in the Babylonian region. Around 1761–59 BC, Hammurabi established what came to be a new empire (stretching from the SE to Mari a city on the intersection of trade routes to the NW and the SW. Hammurabi's conquests included areas formerly controlled by Elam, Rim-Sin of Larsa and Zimri-Lim of Mari. Other powers prevailed for a time in different parts of the greater Mesopotamian region, for example, Hittites (1650–1500 and 1360–1207 BC).

The period from 1200 BC to 750 BC is often called the Early Iron Age and was characterized by initial declines in the areas controlled and then the reestablishment through conquest of control over areas formerly owing allegiance. Thus, Assyria (1350–627 BC) quickly re-established control over the its entire territory but then fragmented (by 750 BC) under regional governors. Babylonia also had a period of glory (beginning with the reign of Nebuchadnezzar I (1125–1104 BC) and then suffered conquests from Elam and Assyria.

What is now referred to as the Assyrian Empire developed from the reign of Tigleth-pileser III (744–727 BC) and lasted until the reign of Assurbanipal (668–631 BC) in Nineveh after which twenty years of succession disputes brought it to a collapse. The Neo-Babylonian Period (c. 626–539 BC) is the period in which Nebuchadnezzar II exiled the Israelites and the period in which Babylon became a great metropolis. To round off the chronological guideposts, we might note that Persia then conquered Mesopotamia (525–331 BC) and much of the broader region including Egypt (525–404 BC, 343–332 BC). Alexander, too, conquered the entire area of Mesopotamia as well as Egypt (330–323 BC). Then came Rome.

A reasonable guess at the early causality of urban growth might begin with a focus on the high productivity of grain production for early agriculture in southern Mesopotamia and, later, of wool in the Syrian regions that sustained early cities, such as Ebla, in the second era of urbanization. The advantages and stimulus of trade between regions must also be mentioned.[27] Other key factors might include insecurities leading to fortification of urban areas, the enhancement of religious beliefs associated with productivity and military success and an initial political organization based on urban councils and religious elites. While ideological and economic fundamentals must have been partial drivers of Mesopotamian success, understanding the significance of cultural and religious influence requires an overview of political and economic change in the region over more than 3,500 years. We will focus our attention on religious and cultural factors that we feel are relevant to our financial analysis and this necessarily includes the institutionalization of justice and hierarchy.

There were a limited number of political and social paradigms starting with those of the city-states. The early city-states began with most major infrastructure (architectural and agricultural) tied to temples and in particular to the temple complex of a main city god or goddess. City assemblies of elites played significant roles both early in time and for millennia. Additional infrastructure devoted to secular administration and the development of a palace complex came after that of temples and the walled city and probably proceeded in tandem with the development of complex irrigation systems but preceded the development of significant empires.[28]

Empires often followed a common model with major campaigns to subdue increasingly distant lands to collect revenues for the palace complex and the continued support of temple complexes in the cities within the empire's dominion. Thus a capital, such as Akkad or later Ur III, would dominate a number of cities and a region. The king's palace could be in one city while a key religious center was in another. Thus, Ur with its temple to Nanna, Nippur with its temple to Enlil or the temple of Ninhursag at Kish and of Enki at Eridu were particularly critical in the early period.[29] Control of the main temples to the most important gods consistently conferred a measure of legitimacy necessary for claims of paramount status.

Regional centers might be headed by centrally appointed governors or local leaders (the Sumerian terms *lugal* and *en* were often used) while the top people in the religious temples could similarly be appointed by the paramount authority or from among local elites. Temples and cities had their own established sources of revenue but those flows were incorporated into a managed system when an empire or league was established. In the case of the region dominated by Ebla (the tell is located about 55 km south of Aleppo), it has been speculated that major decisions, such as succession, had to be confirmed by the king's mother, and that several "lugal" were women.[30]

The role of elites in governance had considerable institutional variability from the beginning. By the Old Assyrian Period, groups of elites regulated commerce in many towns along key trade routes in ways that seem complementary to the powers of local government.[31] Although we have excellent records for this period it is probable that the complementarity of the private and public sectors in regulating trade was not a radically new phenomena during the Old Assyrian Period even if it may have been more thoroughly developed in this period.

Records kept across the millennia gradually adapted over time to changes in language, to changing administrative needs, and to differences that reflect the vast geographical extent of the Mesopotamian cultural region. This extraordinarily detailed and lengthy record provides unmatched insights into the development of human civilization; and, due to the large proportion of records dealing with administration and finance, offers real possibilities for understanding the development and social significance of financial institutions in the development of early civilizations. In using these data, our most significant concern is to contribute to an understanding of financial history, particularly regarding the role of social capital and hidden interests; these are documented less explicitly in the earliest tablets, and only somewhat more clearly in the later tablets. While we do not assume that what was not explicitly discussed on cuneiform tablets was not present in practice, there are many reasons to suspect that as society became more complex it involved not just more complex agriculture but more elaborate financial interconnections, and that the increasing sophistication of financial accounting corresponds to some degree to a more ample calculus of benefits, obligations, and interests in the real world.

LEGAL REGULATION AND THE SOCIO-ECONOMICS OF DEBT

Scholars have suggested that what have been referred to as Mesopotamian law codes were really examples of case law showing a correspondence between two events in the real world: the social or material situation and the appropriate ruling. Consequently, they have begun to consider whether what was being practiced should be viewed as an approximation or a step toward an abstract morality or whether no abstract morality with absolute principles was envisaged and legal cases were presented merely as practical illustrations to help figure out how the gods would have people behave in order to facilitate the pursuit of human and divine destinies. If we impose strong rules of consistency, the laws are problematic; and, if we look for abstract conclusions about morality, they are hard to find.

From this perspective, it is best to assume that Mesopotamian empirical legal examples should be taken in the same sense as other Mesopotamian observational data—as a means to figure out and to illustrate the intentions of the gods. A case ruled a particular way in the context of a consequent prosperous ruler or state suggests the ruling is the appropriate response to the facts of the case. There is a human tendency to abstract and generalize that cannot long ignore a large set of carefully chosen examples. Many of the Old Testament ethical prescriptions, presented in the scriptures as ethical rules for all time, have clear connections to the Mesopotamian law cases which may not originally have been viewed in this way. The traditional translations of Mesopotamian legal cases refer to collections as the "Laws of . . ." or the "Code of . . ." but modern scholars suggest they might each better be viewed as "the legal cases or the judgments of . . ." This is how we propose to view the selections we find most illuminating.

While we only examine financial cases, relatively few of them have much to say about the specifics of credit. Nevertheless, those that do touch on credit also shed light on the specifics of social behavior and even social progress. In part, this is because labor was a key asset that could be obligated, loaned or even sold. The possibility of various liens on that labor, as well as the gender and social status (social class, free citizen, slave or foreigner) of that labor had always to be taken into consideration.[32] While many individual loan tablets survived from earlier periods, only from the second millennium BC are there a number of guides to financial practice within the legal cases such as those suggesting that grain was to be loaned by individuals at 33 percent while silver was to be loaned at 20 percent. The most relevant examples from the better known legal cases recorded on cuneiform tablets are: [33]

From the laws of Ur-Namma ca. 2100 BC

15. If a son-in-law [enters] the household of his father-in-law but subsequently the father-in-law [gives his wife to his (the son-in-law's) comrade], he (the father-in-law) shall [weigh and deliver to him (the jilted son-in-law)] twofold (the value of) the prestations [which he (the son-in-law) brought (when he entered the house)].

From the Laws of Lipit-Ishtar (5th ruler of the dynasty of Isin) ii 25–40 (1930 BC)

I imposed service (equally) on the household of a living father and on the undivided household (of brothers). I, Lipit-Ishtar, son of the god Enlil, obligated those in a household of a living father and in an undivided household of brothers to service for seventy (days per year). I obligated those in a household of dependent workers to service for ten days per month . . . the wife of a man. . . . the son of a man . . .[(more than two columns lost)]

From the Laws of X (2050–1880 BC): unknown ruler perhaps a fragment of the legal cases of Ur Namma

m. If a man [gives another man] 300 silas of grain as an interest bearing loan, its interest rate per annum is [100 silas of grain]

n. If a man [gives] another man 10 shekels of silver as an interest-bearing loan, its interest rate per annum is [2 shekels in silver].

From the Laws of Eshnunna, Old Babylonian Period (1770 BC)

4. If he (the adopted son) declares to his father and mother, "you are not my father," or "You are not my mother," he shall forfeit house, field, orchard, slaves, and possessions, and they shall sell him for silver (into slavery) for his full value.

16. The son of a man who has not yet received his inheritance share or a slave will not be advanced credit.

18A. Per 1 shekel (of silver) interest accrues at the rate of 36 barley corns (= 20 percent); per 300 silas (of grain) interest accrues at the rate of 100 silas (= 33 percent).

38. If, in a partnership, one intends to sell his share and his partner wishes to buy, he shall match any outside offer.

From the Code of Hammurabi, 6th ruler 1st Dynasty of Babylon (ca. 1750 BC)

40. a *naditu*, a merchant, or any holder of a field with a special service obligation may sell her or his field, orchard, or house; the buyer shall perform the service obligation on the field, orchard, or house which he purchases.

gap cc. If a man gives silver to another man for investment in a partnership venture, before the god they shall equally divide the profit or the loss.

100. If a merchant gives silver to a trading agent for conducting business transactions and sends him off on a business trip, the trading agent [shall . . .] while on the business trip; if he should realize [a profit] where he went, he shall calculate the total interest, per transaction and time elapsed, on as much silver as he took, and he shall satisfy the merchant.

101. If he should realize no profit where he went, the trading agent shall give to the merchant twofold the silver he took.

102. If a merchant should give silver to a trading agent for an investment venture, and he incurs a loss on his journeys, he shall return silver to the merchant in the amount of the capital sum.

103. If enemy forces should make him abandon whatever goods he is transporting while on his business trip, the trading agent shall swear an oath by the god and shall be released.

105. If the trading agent should be negligent and not take a sealed receipt for (each payment in) silver that he gives to the merchant, any silver that is not documented in a sealed receipt will not be included in the final accounting.

151. If a woman who is residing in a man's house should have her husband agree by binding contract that no creditor of her husband shall seize her (for his debts)—if that man has a debt incurred before marrying that woman, his creditors will not seize his wife; and if that woman has a debt incurred before entering the man's house, her creditors will not seize her husband.

u. If a man who has an interest-bearing loan does not have silver with which to repay it, he (the merchant) shall take grain and silver in accordance with the royal edict and the interest on it at the annual rate of 60 silas per 1 kur (= 20 percent); if the merchant should attempt to increase and collect the interest on the (silver) loan [up to the grain interest rate of 100 silas of grain) per kur (= 33 percent), [or any other way beyond] 36 barleycorns [per shekel (= 20 percent) of silver], he shall forfeit whatever he had given.

Old Hittite law cases (1650–1500 BC)

31. If a free man and a female slave are lovers and live together, and he takes her as his wife, and they make a house and children, but afterwards either they become estranged or they each find a new marriage partner, they shall divide the house equally, and the man shall take the children, with the woman taking one child.

32. If a male slave [takes] a [free] woman in marriage, [and they make a home and children, when they divide their house], they shall divide their possessions [equally, and the free woman shall take] most of [the children] with [the male slave taking] one child.

34. If a male slave pays a bride price for a woman and takes her as his wife, no one shall free her from slavery.

36. If a slave pays a bride price for a free young man and acquires him as a son-in-law, no one shall free him from slavery.

40. If a man who has a TUKUL-obligation defaults, and a man owing šaḫḫan-services has taken his place, the man owing šaḫḫan-services shall say: "This is my TUKUL-obligation, and this other is my obligation for šaḫḫan-services." He shall secure for himself a sealed deed concerning the land of the man having the TUKUL-obligation, he shall hold the TUKUL-obligation and perform the šaḫḫan-services.

48. A ḫipparaš-man renders the luzzi-services. Let no one transact business with a ḫipparaš-man. Let no one buy his child, his land, or his vineyard(s). Whoever transacts business with a ḫipparaš-man shall forfeit his purchase price, and the ḫipparaš-man shall take back whatever he sold.

55. When a delegation of Hittites, men owing šaḫḫan-services came, they did reverence to the father of the king, and said: "No one pays us a wage. They say to us: "You are men required to perform your jobs as a šaḫḫan-service !" The father of the king [stepped] into the assembly and declared under his seal: "You must continue to perform šaḫḫan-services just like your colleagues."

Middle Assyrian law cases (ca. 1076 BC)

A.29. If a woman should enter her husband's house, her dowry and whatever she brings with her from her father's house, and also whatever her father-in-law gave her upon her entering, are clear for her sons, her father-in-law's sons shall have no valid claim. But if her husband intends to take control of her, he shall give it to whichever of his sons he wishes.

A.35. If a widow should enter into a man's house, whatever she brings with her belongs to her (new) husband; and if a man should enter into a woman's house, whatever he brings with him belongs to the woman.

A.38. If a woman is residing in her own father's house and her husband divorces her, he shall take the valuables which he himself bestowed upon her; he shall have no claim to the bride wealth which he brought (to her father's house), it is clear for the woman.

A.44. If there is an Assyrian man or an Assyrian woman who is residing in a man's house as a pledge for a debt, for as much as his value, and he is taken for the full value (i.e., his value as pledge does not exceed that of the debt), he (the pledge holder) shall whip (the pledge), pluck out (the pledge's) hair, (or) mutilate or pierce (the pledge's) ears.

A.48. If a man <wants to give in marriage> his debtor's daughter who is residing in his house as a pledge, he shall ask permission of her father and then he shall give her to a husband. If her father does not agree, he shall not give her. If her father is dead, he shall ask permission of one of her brothers and the latter shall consult with her (other) brothers. If one brother so desires he shall declare, "I will redeem my sister within one month"; if he should not redeem her within one month, the creditor, if he so pleases, shall clear her of encumbrances and shall give her to a husband . . .

C.3. [If a man] sells into a foreign land [either a man's son] or a man's daughter who [is residing in his house] either for a silver (debt) or as a pledge, and they prove the charges against him and find him guilty, he shall forfeit his silver [. . .] he shall give his/its [. . .] to the owner of the property, they shall strike him [x blows with rods]; he shall perform the king's service for 40 days. But if the man whom he sells dies in the foreign land, he shall make full payment for a life. He may sell into a foreign land an Assyrian man or an Assyrian woman who had been taken for full value (i.e., the value as pledge does not exceed that of the debt).

O.3. If brothers [divide] the estate of their father, orchards and wells [in the plot of land . . . the oldest son shall select and take a double] share, [and his brothers shall select and take] shares one after the other; [the youngest son is the one who apportions whatever šilufjlu-personnel there are and all the associated] equipment in the field (to be divided). . .

Neo-Babylonian law cases (ca. 700 BC)

6. A man who sells a slave woman against whom a claim arises so that she is taken away-the seller shall give to the buyer the silver (of the purchase price) in its capital amount according to the sale document. Should she bear children (while in the possession of the buyer), he shall give half a shekel of silver for each.

8. A man who gives his daughter in marriage to a member of the amēlu-class, and the father (of the groom) commits certain properties in his tablet and awards them to his son, and the father-in-law commits the dowry of his daughter, and they write the tablets in mutual agreement-they will not alter the commitments of their respective tablets. The father will not make any reduction to the properties as written in the tablet to his son's benefit, which he showed to his in-law. Even should the father, whose wife fate carries away, then marry a second wife and should she then bear him sons, the sons of the second woman shall take one-third of the balance of his estate.

10. A man who gives a dowry to his daughter, and she has no so or daughter, and fate carries her away—her dowry shall revert to her paternal estate.

12. A wife whose husband takes her dowry, and who has no son or daughter, and whose husband fate carries away-a dowry equivalent to the dowry (which her husband had received) shall be given to her from her husband's estate. If her husband should award to her a marriage gift, she shall take her husband's marriage gift together with her dowry, and thus her claim is satisfied. If she has no dowry, a judge shall assess the value of her husband's estate, and shall give to her some property in accordance with the value of her husband's estate.

Many of the law cases cited above shed light on the imbrication of debt and social status: including the treatment of gender in matters of credit, the respective roles of individuals, and the relationship between households and the state where financial or labor obligations are concerned. *UN 15* focuses on the obligations entailed in arranging a marriage. In this case, the two parties are placed in the household of the intended wife's father but the marriage is not enacted because the father apparently finds a more advantageous placement for his daughter. The case indicates that this failure to proceed with the marriage of ones daughter to another's son entails a payment of two times the initial bride wealth brought into the intended wife's father's household. It is clear that this a pure example of a debt incurred by a promise of marriage accompanied by marriage goods—the honor of the daughter is not in question. *CH 151* provides a means of protecting spouses from the other's creditors as long as the debt pre-dates the marriage. Even as case *CH 151* provides protection for a wife from her husband's debts it also recognizes that she may have debts of her own.

Many later cases involving people also take into account social status; and, despite all indications that the locus of authority is in the head of a household, who is usually male, the cases across Mesopotamia exhibit considerable gender equality in legal consideration (*OH 31, 32, 34, 36, MA A.44, C.3, NB 12*). In these later cases the wives' rights to their dowry and gifts received from their husband seem to survive the marriage. A Middle Assyrian case (*MA A.38*) suggest that bride wealth stays where it was bestowed, while New Babylonian cases (*NB 10 12*) suggest dowry stays with the woman, and even if no dowry was paid, something comparable from the man's estate should be awarded if a wife survives her husband. In Syria (Late Bronze Age fourteen–twelfth century BC) while women usually were married off and received primarily a dowry they could, discretionarily, inherit as if they were a son since they were within the family circle from within which heirs had to come.[34]

Some of the earliest law cases cited, Lipit-Ishtar (*ii 25–40*), define the labor debts of citizens toward the state. Some of the laws cited protect the rights of individuals (*CH 103, 105*): the first protects a business that incurs losses due to warfare—he need only take an oath to that effect, and his debt is forgiven. The second similarly protects the business agent by insisting on the necessity of a written record in order for loans to be valid. Cases *CH 101* and *102* illustrate the protection of the interests of the lender against lack of entrepreneurial success on the part of his business agent. The first case holds the agent responsible for earning a profit: it makes a clear argument for the opportunity cost of money (silver). The second case provides some forgiveness for a demonstrable loss by insisting only on the repayment of the investment rather than of twice the investment. Case *CH 40* makes it clear that the prebendal system of specified income or services from lands accruing to the beneficiary of the prebend, who could be the state or a temple or an individual, does not prevent transactions in land. Cases *CH 38* and *CH gap cc* deal with partnerships rather than relationships between a lender and his agent. Case *CH 38* constrains the price of partnership shares sold between partners to that of the best outside bidder. Case *CH gap cc* confines partnership explicitly to those arrangements in which both profits and losses are equally shared.

Case *LE 16* simply notes that slaves and men who have not reached the age of majority, in the sense of inheriting their share of wealth, cannot receive loans. This prohibition against lending to sons before their majority, an edict that protects their fathers is, as we will see, still found in the Roman Republic. In most cases, the focus of the cases of the early second millennium BC is on loans by or to individuals while in the earliest periods loans of either grain or silver would have been entirely by institutions such as temples or cities to individuals and the institutions would have represented gods—and so had their own legal mandate. The most important light these cases shed on credit and hidden interest is that they show explicitly how even early Mesopotamian society provided both positive and negative sanctions above and beyond those enunciated in specific contracts. The simple point we wish to make here is that social customs as well as laws within which lending occurs are as much part of the financial system as the physical or environmental constraints on storage or trade.

The surviving Old Hittite, Middle Assyrian and Neo-Babylonian cases (like the Lipit-Ishtar case from 1930 BC) focus on loans and debts involving people, a definition that seems not to include slaves. The Old Hittite cases make it clear that it is not just debts between individuals that must be respected but also that many members of society owe service of one kind or another to the state (*OH 40, 48, 55*) and this service is debt that cannot be absolved. Some obligations (šaḫḫan-services) go with usufruct of a property and some go with a human skill set (TUKUL-obligation).[35]

Males and females can be pledged for debts and either can be sold if and only if they are pledged in full (*MA A.44 C.3*)—in other words if the debt for which they are pledged is greater than or equal to the value of the pledge. A debtor's daughter (*MA A.48*) given as a pledge can be married off with permission of her father, but if he is dead, only if the debtors sons are given one month to redeem their sister and fail to do so. Marriage is, more generally, clearly portrayed as a portfolio of mutual debts that stop being co-mingled at death or divorce and then have to be sorted according to both customary expectations and individual additional obligations (*MA A.29, A35, A.38*). Gifts turn out to be loans that are recalled if the conditions on which they were premised are no longer valid while legal commitments (*NB 8*) by either family made at marriage and recorded on tablets cannot be escaped as they were the very basis of the marriage. It may seem odd from a modern perspective, where many pretend that all humans are free actors engaging in bounded rationality, that most of these ancient cases that deal with debt focus on people, but this is merely anachronistic thinking that projects our own relatively brief historical period in which explicitly coerced labor is in disrepute onto the past.

There are a few of the ancient cases that do focus directly on interest rates for loans of specific commodities. The attempt to stabilize rates (*L of X m* and *n, LE 18A, CH u*) for merchant loans was undoubtedly less unproblematic than it might seem. In practice, issues of old grain versus new and compressed or uncompressed grain are left either to custom or to subsidiary agreements. The potential for obfuscation was probably greater with grain than silver, and this may have been the prime determinant of its higher interest rate. Since there are many opportunities for hidden interest, any particular interest rate, for example, 20 percent or 33 percent, may or may not represent all of the rate being paid by the debtor or the benefit gained by the lender. While rates established by edict are unlikely to have been designed to be prohibitory or, exclusively, to facilitate the lender's position in a transaction, it is clear that in Mesopotamia rates were high and are likely to have facilitated the flow of resources into the hands of the lending class as well as into the treasuries and granaries of lending institutions. In the course of time, as we will see, loan contracts began to take into consideration hitherto hidden interests more explicitly.

Case *CH 100* that deals with a trading partner describes a standard arrangement whereby a merchant lends money to a partner who travels with it, and is obliged in due course to return the principle lent with a specific interest. The period of loan was apparently only calculated up to the date commodities were purchased with it. One might presume that upon return the transport costs might be recorded and deducted. The traveling partner is clearly allowed to retain profits over and above any promised interest. Cases (*CH 101, 102, 103*) illustrate how risks were allocated between partners, and how the various contingencies of loss were treated. In case *CH 101*, the traveling partner goes to a place and fails to make a profit. Clearly, here the onus was on the traveling partner to make a profit, and if he failed to do so, this was treated as a failure to performed his duty, and he was expected to repay twice the sum lent him.

By contrast, in *CH Case 102* the traveling partner incurs a loss of goods during the journey and, while he still bears all the risk, he is obliged to only repay the principle. In *Case CH 103*, the traveling partner is robbed during his journey, and the goods entrusted to him are stolen. In this case, the lender bears the risks, and as long as the traveling partner swore an oath by his god that this was the truth, he was held harmless, and was not obliged to repay the loan. *CH gap cc* provides a case for a presumably local partnership in which profits and losses are equally divided and one party is not at risk from long distance travel.

The legal cases, taken as a whole, illustrate the broad social character of debt and the intertwining of the interests of states and households as they impact individuals of different classes, genders and nationalities. They also map out at one level major historical transformations in credit instruments. Debts in Mesopotamia knew few boundaries and the basic institutions of household, city, temple, and state used both human and material assets to advance their affairs. The individual loan documents and temple accounts examined in the next chapter shed further light on the pervasiveness of hidden interest in credit and finance as well as better illustrate the gradual development of increasingly sophisticated lending instruments proceeding from those of early temples to the more standardized forms used by later merchants.

PRACTICAL ISSUES RELATED TO ANCIENT FINANCE: THE DEVELOPMENT OF ACCOUNTING

At least one of the earliest writing systems (cuneiform) seems to have originated as a means of keeping economic accounts and to have evolved in tandem with the evolution of accounting systems.[36] Early Mesopotamian bookkeeping, for example, led to sophisticated accounting recorded in a fairly standardized cuneiform script that remained in use for around three thousand years. Loans, deposits, and transfers to third parties' accounts became standard practice in ancient Mesopotamia and preceded coinage by at least a thousand years. The recent explosion of credit based forms of money obscures what otherwise might be obvious. Credit preceded "money stuff" just as using consumables such as grain or cattle as storehouses of value typically preceded the use of other selected objects for such purposes. Both long preceded the creation of real coinage. Ur III had recourse not only to grains and cattle to store value but also made use of silver coils, gold rings or other standardized objects of silver, copper and bronze for accounting purposes and as storehouses of value.[37]

Financial records are intrinsically tied to basic metrological systems. Sumerian accountants in archaic times (Uruk IVA, Uruk III, ca. 3400–3000 BC) were the first to develop a set of symbols for basic arithmetic that were adapted both to counting, *per se,* and to measuring. The earliest records, however, display a care to keep the measures for each product separate. Figure 1.1 illustrates the basic counting system as applied to barley.[38]

In figure 1.1, Row A represents a number (3*9000 + 1*900 + 6*30 + 1*5 +1 = 28,086) of containers of barley (depicted below the number–each container had a volume of about 4.8 liters).[39] Row B begins with an encased

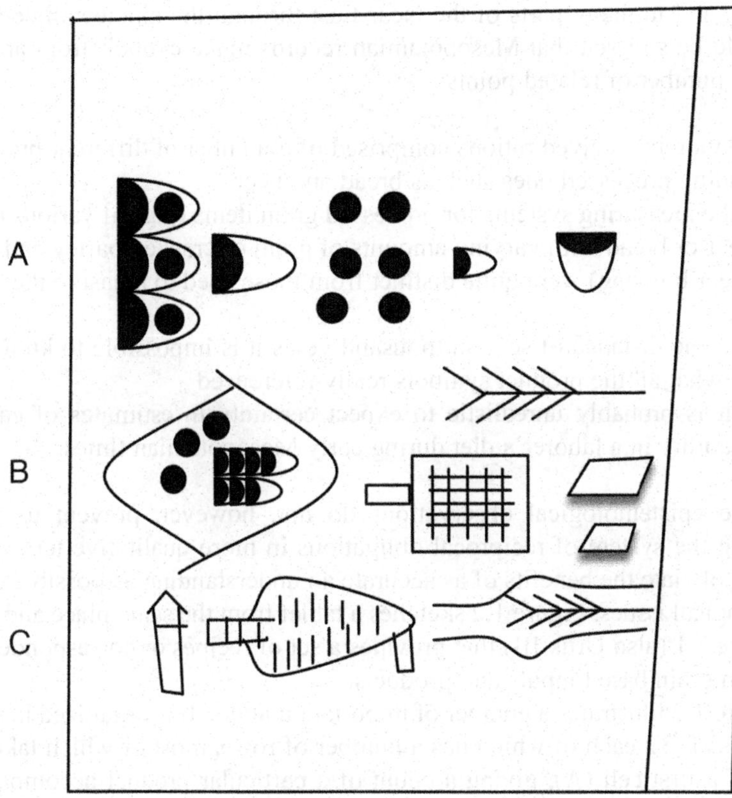

Figure 1.1. Archaic Mesopotamian account (Uruk III).
Original drawing by Thomas Park. Original Source: Nissan et al, p. 37.

number (37) from a different numbering system counting the months included in the record. Here the smaller bullet shape equals one not five: note that six fives carry over to a thirty in the first system while ten ones carry over to a ten in the second. The remaining symbols (the last two were deliberately effaced) may provide some indication of the function of the record, but scholars are unsure of their meaning.

Row C has two initial symbols that provide the name of the responsible official (Ku Šim); and, a final symbol that may reference how the barley was obtained. It is apparent that even in this simple account a measure of grain volume and of days require two separate, if obviously related, counting systems. This concern to have separate measures for each product (e.g., jars of beer of different sizes, breads of different compositions, different measures for grains, and grain products like cracked barley [for beer], or malt) is already explicit by the archaic period in Mesopotamia. A similar lack of commensurability in measures and valuation can be found in the feudal period of Europe, and in many parts of the Near East through the nineteenth century. It should be stressed that Mesopotamian records make explicit from archaic times a number of related points:

- that laborers received rations comprised of a number of different products including processed ones such as bread and beer
- that the measuring systems for processed grain items (jugs of various types of beer or bread with varying amounts of grain or cracked barley and malt for beer brewing) were quite distinct from those used to measure the grain harvest
- that at the distance of several thousand years it is impossible to know exactly what all the product symbols really referenced
- that it is probably unrealistic to expect certainty in estimates of caloric availability in a laborer's diet during early Mesopotamian times.

These epistemological observations do not, however, prevent us from studying the system of reciprocal obligations in more qualitative terms, nor do they obviate the benefits of as accurate an understanding as possible of all metrological issues. Figure 1.2 sketches a tablet from the same place and time as figure 1.1 (also Uruk III) that provides a set of recipes or correspondences between grain based inputs and products.

Figure 1.2 illustrates a number of important matters. It is organized in three columns (1–3), each of which has a number of rows, most of which take the form of a first cell (A), giving a count of a particular product accompanied by a symbol for the product, and a second cell (B) that gives the volume of inputs needed to produce the listed quantity of product. Column (2) begins

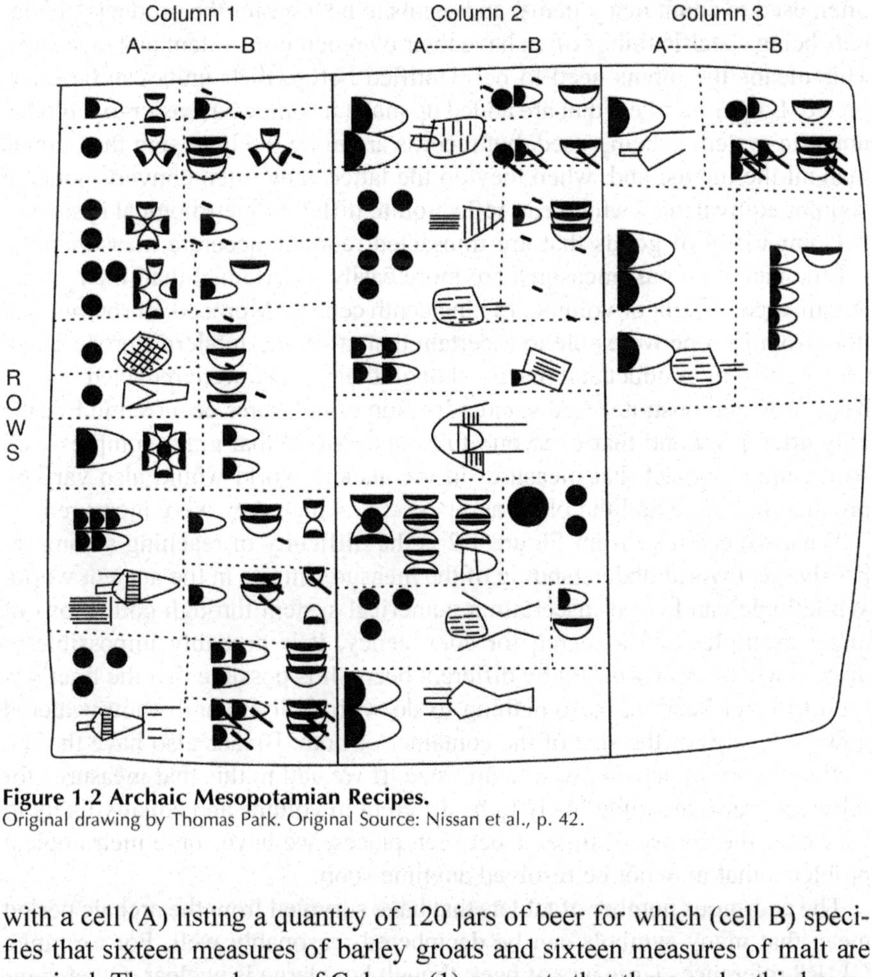

Figure 1.2 Archaic Mesopotamian Recipes.
Original drawing by Thomas Park. Original Source: Nissan et al., p. 42.

with a cell (A) listing a quantity of 120 jars of beer for which (cell B) specifies that sixteen measures of barley groats and sixteen measures of malt are required. The second row of Column (1) suggests that three and a third measures of groats produce ten of some grain product indicated by the symbol for a third suggesting the fraction serves as a measure of how much the inputs are "stretched." The third row down suggests five measures of groats will produce twenty of a grain product referenced by the sign for one quarter. The fourth row down of Column (1) shows 30 units of a cereal product produced from a given amount of barley groats (six?). From this record these units could be just about anything from bread to porridge.

The first entry Nissan *et al.* believe is an error that emphasizes the arbitrariness of the symbols. It suggests five measures of groats produce one grain product accompanied by the symbol for one half.[40] An important interpretive problem illustrated by this example is that while a sexagesimal system is often used to count many items, and seems to be used for the products, the inputs being specific things often have their own numeric system and measures. This means the inputs need to be identified before their units can be interpreted. Larger numbers that are added up make it somewhat easier to tell what numeric system is being used, but records are more likely to sum the outputs than all the inputs; and, when they do the latter, they often convert inputs to "output equivalents" which can reflect quite different metrological systems.

Comparison of goods that are transacted requires accurate measurement, yet the names of past measures are more easily ascertained than their actual length, area, weight or volume. In nineteenth century Morocco, observant visitors from Europe were able to ascertain that, as in pre-modern Europe, measures varied by product and place—though their names were recycled.[41] Kula has amply demonstrated that standardization of measures occurred in Europe only after 1789 and that everyone fully understood that grain compresses,[42] so we might expect that measures in the ancient world would also vary by product measured and the place and period in which they were measured.

What we can take from Figure 1.2 is the difficulty of reaching a comprehensive real world understanding of the measures in use in the ancient world. While logic can help us ascertain a numerical system through collections of many examples and a search for consistency, it is probably impossible to discern what is really meant by different beers. It is possible that the fractions used to label beers have something to do with their strength (how watered down they are) or the size of the container or both. Breads also have the potential to vary in density, weight and size. If we add to this that measures for different grains are quite likely to be different in volume and equally likely to vary over the course of time or between places, we have some metrological problems that may not be resolved anytime soon.

The enormous number of tablets that have survived from the archaic period mean that many symbols can be deciphered reasonably well. For example, C1, R8 references large jars of beer, though how large is unclear. Other symbols referring to jars of beer (C1, R9 or C2, R1) give no hint of the size of the jar or the type of beer (thick, thin, strong, weak, etc.). Thus, this tablet of inputs and outputs still leaves an accurate assessment of many phenomenological aspects of the outputs beyond reach.

We have quite a lot of metrological information for the archaic period but a full understanding of most ancient cuneiform records is hampered by the limited information recorded as well as by variation across space and time. In the Late Uruk period some basic equivalences of long duration were developed for weights: the load a man could carry; 1 talent = 60 mina = 3600 shekels and 1 shekel (weight) = 1 gur of grain = 6 minas of wool = 2 silas of sesame oil.[43] Capacity measures from late fourth millennium Uruk provide the following definitions: 1 granary = 2400 (great) *gur*, 1 (great) *gur* = 2 *lidga*, 1 *lidga* = 4 *bariga*, 1 *bariga* = 6 *ban*, 1 *ban* = 10 *sila* and Mesopotamia experts have estimated that 1 *sila* was approximately 1 liter in size. This would give a granary capacity of approximately 1,152,000 liters of grain and a great gur of 480 liters.[44]

In the mid-third millennium BC capacity measures had not changed significantly. A mathematical tablet (TSS 50) from Shuruppag (ca. 2600 BC) asks how many men can be provided from a granary if each man gets 7 sila of grain. This presumes a standard granary size and the calculations allow us to calculate that size.[45] The problem provides a calculation indicating that 164,571 men could be furnished 7 sila with 3 sila remaining. This provides an easy way to calculate the capacity of the granary as 1,152,018 sila. If we use the number of sila (480) from our late fourth millennium Uruk metrology list we get a granary capacity of 2400 (great, e.g., 480 *sila* or 8 *bariga*) *gur* in conformity with the granary capacity in that same late fourth millennium Uruk list. This suggests about 650 years of uniformity in measures of "granary capacity."

The problem from Shuruppag does not tell us how many days the 7 *sila* payment was to cover and the problem may presume a week's wages per man or the daily wages of a household headed by a man. The former seems more likely. Uruk III figures, as well as abundant later evidence, make it clear that workers also regularly received other products such as beer or porridge.[46] Since we do not have precise knowledge of the caloric contents per volume of these products it may be impossible to accurately estimate exact caloric components or composition of a worker's diet.[47] Since advanced mathematics had little to do with commerce or credit, it would seem clear that numerological systems themselves provided no significant constraints to any forms of credit whether they were unique to a commodity or generalized to many commodities. Numerological signs tended to be for record keeping, and most single calculations would be done in the head, or on an abacus or pebble board in Classic times, and their result recorded in writing—not the steps leading to the result (unlike long division in current primary schools).[48]

We might ask whether numerological systems have oriented societies' commercial activities in any way. A suggestion[49] that will be explored more fully later is that labor accounting practices based on two meals a day per laborer for each of the thirty days in a month oriented some Mesopotamian numerological systems to count in multiples of 6 and 10 as well as led to the expectation of loans at 1/60th per month—leading to 12/60 = 20 percent per year on loans of silver.

There were most likely other factors involved. It may not be amiss to recognize the possible imbrication of religious, calendrical, and production systems in the development of numerical notation. The fundamental nature of powers of both 6 and 10 in Mesopotamian numerological systems, and the absence of powers of 6, but the presence of powers of 10, in comparable age Egyptian numerical notation may derive from the use of differently conceived religious calendars. Early on, it is thought that the Mesopotamian year was conceived as two seasons each of six months lasting thirty days. Early temple rituals may have made six a religiously significant number. Ur III workdays were divided into sixty parts whose lengths varied through the seasons with the length of a day (as opposed to keeping hours a uniform length and having more daylight hours in different seasons).[50] Over time, base six system became less important in Mesopotamian numerical notation.[51]

IN BRIEF

The intellectual and religious developments in ancient Mesopotamia contributed to the development of a sophisticated financial sector of great utility to early states. Mesopotamian financial arrangements grew in sophistication over time, and the cuneiform documentation, despite its metrological complexity, provides an excellent window into that growth. In the next chapter, there are two further points we hope to make. We illustrate, if selectively, the ways in which lending became more sophisticated between the third and the first millennium, in the sense of taking explicitly into consideration an increasing number of relevant factors that explain why societies were so receptive to new credit technologies. This early evolutionary trajectory is important and, via inter-regional trade, influenced finance in other regions.

This wide influence spreading gradually with trade over many centuries also explains why the Mesopotamian financial trajectory has had such a lasting influence on the way finance has been done ever since. We examine the gradual evolution of financial contracts and the evidence for the early relevance of social capital to all forms of finance, though this topic is easier to study in later historical periods. The evolution of credit instruments from simple texts specifying very little to more sophisticated texts detailing many important considerations also helps us discern the, initially behind the scenes, financial influence of social networks and ethical frameworks. It is important to recognize that, unlike today, social influence on finance in the ancient world was a point of honor and not regarded as evidence of a socio-pathological condition.

NOTES

1. Stone, which is hard to work and even harder to carry around, has durability suitable for monuments but lacks general purpose utility for writing.

2. Keynes, *Newton, the Man*, 277.

3. Patch *Thirty Years with B.B.S.*, 235. Comments by George Bernard Shaw, at a 1930 banquet in honor of Einstein recorded by Shaw's secretary.

4. Yoffee "Decline and Rise of Mesopotamian civilization," 21.

5. E.N. Da C. Andrade, Isaac Newton, 275.

6. The term is associated with Kramer's *History Begins at Sumer*, but the idea that history begins with writing was a core assumption of Toynbee's *A Study of History* and was largely accepted by historians until Jan Vansina *De la Tradition Orale* began to be appreciated.

7. Chapter 6, "Gender and Mesopotamian History," Mieroop, *Cuneiform texts and the Writing of History* (138–160) provides an overview and ample evidence of the much greater religious, financial and political authority of women across the Mesopotamian world. The epic of Gilgamesh has major tutelary roles for two women, a prostitute and an inn keeper, and suggests the Uruk assembly devised a heroic quest of an unruly king to improve his education. The degree of gender equity may have been related to the equal prominence of male and female Mesopotamian gods. Prominent temples devoted to female gods, such as Innana/Ishtar the goddess of fertility and war, were most naturally staffed by women and headed by a priestess and, like, all temples may have begun as self-supporting, but gained the support of kings as palace administrations grew in strength. Durand, *La Femme dans le Proche-Orient antique*, and Bahrani, *Women of Babylon*, provide reviews of the status of women in ancient Mesopotamia including perspectives on female deities such as Ishtar and issues of gender and sexual desire.

8. Crawford, *Sumer and the Sumerians*, provides a useful overview of the archaeology of Sumer with a focus on style and institutional change. In particular, she notes (chapter 5) that the early settlements were dominated by temple complexes and only later developed secular government structures. Nissen, *Early History of the Ancient Near East*, 55–60 provides the case for flood recession agriculture, as the water level in southern Mesopotamia lowered and rich marsh land became available leading to the intensification of urbanization preceding any development of irrigation *per se*.

9. Akkermans and Schwarz, *Archaeology of Syria*, 179.

10. Postgate, *Early Mesopotamia*, 171–79. Cereal crops were planted in the fall when water was low in the Euphrates and Tigris and harvested in the Spring when water was reaching its highest—and ideally before any floods. Summer heat in southern Mesopotamia is too high for grains, but suitable for sesame, which appears to have been introduced in the Akkadian period.

11. Bahrani, *Rituals of War* provides a detailed and fascinating analysis of this celebration of violence in the service of the gods.

12. Mieroop, *A History of the Ancient Near East*, 245.

13. Hayes, *A Manual Sumerian Grammar and Texts,* 8–12. Sumerian is linguistically unrelated to Semitic, and has been referred to as a split ergative language.

Modern grammarians have suggested that the uninflected noun in Sumerian perfect tense sentences with direct objects may be said to be in the absolutive case even though it is simply unmarked—a feature in Sumerian of the nominative case. With transitive verbs in perfect tenses what we might see as the direct "object" takes on this unmarked character just as does the "nominative case" subject of the verb in any imperfect tense or with any intransitive verb.

14. Hayes, 9 suggests marking ergativity is like admitting that in a sentence such as "The boy rolled the ball down the hill" it is really the ball that is rolling and the boy who simply got it going.

15. In Latin by contrast, a sentence such as *Puer ab agricola amatus erat* (the boy had been loved by the farmer) recognizes the farmer as agent and puts him in the ablative case, has the boy in the nominative as the subject of the sentence and has the verb in the passive (past perfect). The boy, though the subject, is not an active subject and is merely the recipient of the farmer's love nor is the ablative case restricted to the perfect tenses in Latin.

16. A more literal rendition showing the ergative ending (e) and the unmarked ending (∅) would be"[The king of Ur, the king of the four quarters].e, [the temple (where) honey, butter and wine in his place of sacrifice shall not cease ∅].∅ [built].∅" Here, the king is ergative (e) case, the temple is unmarked (referred to by linguists as in the absolutive case) and the transitive past perfect tense verbal phrase is also unmarked. As an agglutinative language the king and his superlatives are glued together with a group ending implying they are not the subject of the sentence. Instead, agency with its unmarked ending is transferred to the temple by the completed action of the king. Because some cuneiform signs differ in meaning but not in pronunciation scholars have transliterated signs pronounced the same with different subscripts. The standard transcription is actually: [lugal-Urim5.a lugal.anub.da limmu.bi.ak].e [e2 lal3 inun u3 ĝeštin ki.siskur2.ak.ani.a **nu**. šilig.e(d). ∅].∅ mu.na.n.du3.∅]. Hayes, Ibid., 212.

17. U 3517, UET 3 no.1667, see Frayne, *Ur III Period*, 362.

18. While this claim amounts to a form of Whorf's hypothesis, cf. Hymes, *Language in Culture and Society,* 129–34 often this hypothesis is associated with extreme linguistic relativism. Brown, *Words and Things,* chapter VII, has suggested a much milder view wherein language simply makes more accessible, or not, particular categorizations. We would in no way suggest ergativity forced Sumerians to create loans of silver at interest but rather that it may have made profit bearing loans of sheep or silver seem quite comparable and ethically unproblematic.

19. Bottéro, *Mesopotamia*, chapter 8, "Divination and the Scientific Spirit."

20. Chavalas, *The Ancient Near East,* 394, 405n10.

21. An early example can be found in the Cutha legend where Naram-Sin fails three times to defeat enemies without consulting the gods and then wises up, as it were. Benjamin Studevent-Hickman and Christopher Morgan, "Old Akkadian Period Texts," In chavalas, 35–40. In mythology, one god, for example, Anu, held the "tablet of destinies" which functioned as a powerful spell which allowed that god to declare destinies yet even in fights among gods there were ways to defeat the holder of the tablet. Destinies were bindings of a form, more binding than decrees which had to be

supervised by the gods, but destinies were not all encompassing or forever determining. cf. Lambert's discussion in *Babylonian Creation Myths*, 448ff.

22. Bottéro, chapter 9, "The Substitute King and His Fate."

23. An excellent historical overview in which this chronology is better developed than space allows here is, Liverani, "Historical Overview," in Snell, *A Companion to the Ancient Near East.* 3–19.

24. In the period of city states, of which there were about thirty-five, the main cities from SE to NW (those mentioned in the Sumerian King list) were: Eridu, Ur, Larsa, Uruk, Bad-tibira, Lagash, Girsu, Shuruppak, Umma, Isin, Adab, Marad, Nippur, Dilbat, Abu Salabikh, Babylon, Kish, Jemdat Nasr, Sippar, and Akshak.

25. Mieroop, *A History*, 45.

26. Veenhof and Eidem, *Mesopotamia*, 24, suggests that the Old Assyrian Period can be said to end in the last quarter of the eighteenth century BC.

27. Gelb, Ebla, and Lagash: Environmental contrast, chapter in Gelb *Origins of Cities*. See also Marchesi, chapter 14, "Of Plants and Trees," in Matthiae and Marchetti, *Ebla and Its Landscape*, 274–5 who suggests that agriculture played a larger part in the economy than Gelb supposed.

28. Nissen, *The Early History,* 59 makes a strong case for the development of irrigation after that of urbanization.

29. Postgate, *Early Mesopotamia*, 34.

30. Pettinato, *Ebla*, 5, 41, 69–77, 169. The archaeology of the region has been ably summarized in, Matthiae and Marchetti, *Ebla and its Landscape.*

31. Veenhof and Eidem. In particular, see section 2.1, "Institutions" and the discussion of week eponyms, datu-payers, and 10-man boards, etc. pp. 76–79.

32. Wells and Magdalene, *Law from the Tigris to the Tiber* Vol. II: 179. Westbrook notes in "A Sumerian Freedman" that mixed status marriages such as between a freeman and a slave woman might have an obligatory payment to the slave's owner of one child.

33. Roth, *Law Collections from Mesopotamia and Asia Minor*. Note that brackets are Roth's glosses for more complex constructions or her clarifications. A sila is still about a liter in volume. The laws of Ur-Namma may in fact have been part of the administrative reforms implemented by Sulgi (Ur III).

34. Westbrook, in "Social Justice and Creative Jurisprudence in LBA Syria" discusses just such a case from the city of Emar. Wells and Magdalene, *Law from the Tigris to the Tiber*, Vol. II: 119.

35. Roth, 244–45 suggests that TUKUL-obligation originally derives from a Sumerian word gisTUKUL for weapon though in the OH context it seems to have more broadly involved skilled service. In contrast, šaḫḫan-services seems somewhat closer to the feudal services associate with serfs on agricultural lands.

36. Michalowski, "Mesopotamian Cuneiform" in Daniels and Bright, *World's Writing Systems*, 33–72. Englund, "Proto-Cuneiform Account Books and Journals." In Hudson and Wunsch, *Creating Economic Order*, 23–46.

37. The best study of the significance of "money stuff" in ancient Mesopotamia is Ouyang's *Monetary Role of Silver*. Ouyang focuses on objects that serve as storehouses of value or are used for accounting purposes. Recent understandings of money

focus on the role of the state in assuring value, a form of credit between the state and the end user. This role is clearly limited in the ancient world in so far as both end user and the state already agree on the intrinsic value of the "money stuff."

38. Redrawn from Nissen, Damerow, and Englund, *Archaic Bookkeeping*. Frontispiece and p. 37. Nissen et al also note the variation of measures by product and over space and time (77).

39. Nissen et al., 70, note that there is strong archaeological evidence and later textual evidence that the basic unit of measure for rationing barley may have been the archaeologically common "bevel rimmed bowl" which seems to have corresponded to a daily ration of 0.8 liters or a monthly ration of about 24 liters of barley (corresponding to the small horizontal basket symbol). They suggest that the unit accounting symbol (the taller upright basket) thus itself contained six rationing bowls. For comparative purposes we can estimate the ration in kg: a cubic meter of barley weighing 705 kg and 0.8 liters (0.0008 cubic meters) would correspond to 0.564 kg of barley per day. Yet later (82) Nissan et al. note that a ration record in the Old Sumerian period clearly states that laborers receive 1 barig 2 ban of barley each which corresponds to 72 liters a month (2.4 liters a day) or three times this much grain. Perhaps the smaller measures represent barley when they were supplemented by rations of other products.

40. Nissan et al., 43, think this might be an error and want a ten in the place of the one, on the pattern of the immediately subsequent entries, but this claim seems needlessly to suppose Mesopotamian accountants made trivial errors and is based on a stronger assumption that there is standardization in the measure of products than seems necessary. Maybe this recipe was assigned the symbol for a half for good reason—perhaps five measures of groats make one batch of porridge occupying twice the volume of the dry groats. The numbering system in the first column may be hexegesimal but the products are distinct and arbitrary: there is no accounting for taste.

41. Park and Boum, *Historical Dictionary of Morocco*, 353–55.

42. Kula, *Measures and Men*, chapter 7, notes (48) that in the medieval period it was well known that compression merely through shaking plus the common addition of a heap on top of the measure could add as much as 25 percent to the quantity measured. Elaborate precautions were taken to to define the construction of the measures themselves and to specify whether measures were heaped or "stricken", compressed either by transport, by the height (lowered or raised arm) from which the grain was poured or by being measured on the vibrating floors of mills. While this is better documented for medieval Europe it is clear that considerable knowledge of grain compression existed in the ancient world as well. For a detailed discussion see the Appendix on grain compression which considers this issue in both Mesopotamia and Egypt.

43. Mieroop, *A History*, 33.

44. Robson, "Mesopotamian Mathematics," in Katz, *Mathematics of Egypt, Mesopotamia, China, India, and Islam*, 74–5. Thus, 2400*2*4*6*10 = 1,152,000.

45. Robson in Katz, 74–5.

46. A more bourgeois diet shows up on a statue inscription from the UR III period as: two *sila* of bread two *sila* of date-syrup, one *sila* of wine, one *sila* of beer, one cut of mutton, the monthly assignment for the table of the god Enlil (Frayne, *Ur III*

Period, 315). This mention of prebendal benefits does show a broad range of staples. Approximately a liter of grain was a fairly standard daily ration in the ancient world, for example, the Greek *choinix* and the Babylonian *qû.* Powell, Weights and Measures. Freedman, *Anchor Bible Dictionary*, Vol 6: 905. Powell distinguishes four eras in Babylonian metrology: (1) to ca. 2200, (2) ca. 2200–1600, (3) ca. 1600–650 and (4) after 650 BC. By 2200 there was a fully integrated system of measures linking length, area, volume, capacity and weight. The unit of length and capacity was a cubit of about 50 centimeters. Between 1600 and 650 areal measures became based on units of capacity—this works equally well if we use the amount of seed or normal output as long as seed is sown in proportion to soil fertility.

47. Chrisomalis, *Numerical Notation*, 12–13, classified the world's numerological systems into six types based on three ways of portraying the values in each base (*cumulative*, *ciphered*, and *multiplicative*) and two ways of reckoning the sum of all the signs (*additive* and *positional*). A *positional* version of the *cumulative* system would be the Babylonian cuneiform which like Roman numerals repeats the signs in each power to indicate how many of each power, but since it relies on a single sign (a standard stylus mark) it uses *position* and patterned grouping to indicate which power is involved rather than a distinct sign for each power as in the Roman or Egyptian systems. Egyptian hieroglyphic numerals were decimal (powers of 10 up to 1,000,000) and cumulative-additive. They had different symbols for each power and repeated them to indicate up to nine of each. Many Mesopotamian numerologies include powers of 10 plus multiples of six (e.g., 6, 60, 600, 1200). Even though powers of 10 have been most common historically and dominate today, we still have 60 minute hours, 60 second minutes, and Rome used to have 360 day years until the calendar was reformed. The current use of binary or hexadecimal or other bases seem to be purely a matter of convenience (including the importance of modular arithmetic in various bases for cryptography).

48. Computational instruments like abaci and pebble boards (functioning similarly but without rods) were much in use as early as the fifth century BC in the Mediterranean (Chrisomalis, 144). Similar aids have been attested in early Mesopotamia and Egypt where scribes were taught elaborate algorithms for calculations of various sorts. The explicit use of these algorithms tends to show up only in texts intended for instruction. There seems to be no indication that the numerological systems involved inhibited the development of useful material or algorithmic aids to computation.

49. Michael Hudson, "Reconstructing the Origins of Interest-Bearing Debt and the Logic of Clean Slates," in Hudson and Mieroop, *Debt and Economic Renewal*, 23–24. Friberg, *Reallexikon der Assyriologie,* 570 notes that in the OB period the standard interest rate for silver or barley was 20 percent (e.g., 12 shekels per mina or 1 bariga per gur) but exceptionally for grain it was 33 1/3 percent (e.g., 10 ban per gur). In the time of Hammurabi, 33 1/3 percent seems to be the norm.

50. Proto-cuneiform had six different counting systems in each of which six was a base (two sexagesimal systems and four bi-sexagesimal systems). In the Ur III period, in addition to Ur itself, there seem to have been eighteen core provinces each with

a governor; and, there were three cities, including Ur, that had the status of capitals: Sharlach, *Provincial Taxation*, 8.

51. The politically similar city of Ebla used (ca. 2500–2350 BC) a numeric notation that had a special symbol for 60 but was otherwise purely decimal. Mari (twentieth to eighteenth centuries BC) on the Syrian border had a purely decimal notation with no special role for six despite still being firmly in the cuneiform world (Chrisomalis, 246, 254).

Chapter Two

Mesopotamian Financial Innovations

In this chapter we primarily focus on the application of increasingly sophisticated mathematical techniques to production, trade and finance in the Mesopotamian region especially between the Ur III period (ca. 2100 BC) and the establishment of the first deposit bank, the House of Egibi, in the seventh century BC. We look closely at the parties to these transactions and the evidence for social hierarchy and social capital as well. Grain in the core areas of the middle and lower Tigris-Euphrates river system was shipped via river and had to be accounted for in the various volumes it assumed on quayside, on boat and in granaries or other storage medium. Merchant and the state thus each had both metrological concerns and a need to accurately assess revenue streams. This provided a rich environment for accounting and financial innovations that increasingly took many factors into account:

> By the beginning of the second millennium—the Old Babylonian (hereafter OB) period—cribal education was producing what is now conventionally called Babylonian mathematics: the earliest known body of "pure" mathematics in history. There has been much research over the last seventy years into the computational techniques, conceptualization and terminology of OB maths, but little exploration of its place in society.[1]

Scholars of ancient land tenure note that many early records were inscribed on stone (*kuddurus*), despite stone's rarity in Mesopotamia. On the assumption that remaining records on stone or clay tablet are representative of the original body of records, they have been able to describe the evolution of important aspects of land tenure up to the UR III period. The best analyzed set of land tenure records covers the following periods: Uruk III (ca. 3100–2900 BC), Early dynastic I-II (2900–2600 BC), Early dynastic IIIa Fara (2600–

2400 BC), Early dynastic IIIb (Pre-Sargonic (2450–2340 BC), Sargonic (2340–2159 BC), and Ur III (2117–2008 BC).[2] The records on stone and clay tablet take the form of sale documents listing some or all of the following: sellers (often plural) and buyers (always singular individuals or households), the objects of sale, the price, location, rituals, additional payments, officials and witnesses. The objects of sale include orchards, humans, houses, animals and (prior to Ur III) fields. Additional payments are often listed but their intent is obscure in ancient records. More recent land tenure situations often involve people with ancillary rights; for example, seasonal rights to grazing or other usufruct or to portions of a harvest due to inheritance or credit.

In all ancient periods, women and men show up as both buyers and sellers (as well as objects of sale). The evidence suggests that in this ancient period private land holdings were larger and more common in the north, fewer and less numerous to the south, and perhaps non-existent in the far south of Mesopotamia. Sales or real estate tended to have multiple sellers in the Fara and Pre-Sargonic periods but there was a clear transition to single sellers by the Sargonic period. Scholars hypothesize that familial ownership was gradually replaced by individual tenure. The Sippar stone dating to the Sargonic period records twenty-three sales including fields whose areas are measured in volume of seed sown ranging from 15 quarts per iku up to 60 quarts suggesting that variations in soil quality, as one would expect, determine how much seed to plant per unit of area and figure in the value of the field.[3]

That the records from Ur III do not include fields complements the other evidence of the dominant economic role of the state by the Ur III period. Scholars have hypothesized therefor that private land tenure (ownership of fields *per se*) spread from north to south during the ancient period and have shown that their relative rarity in the south continued into Old Babylonian times. If we include extended households as private property owners an alternative inference is that private holdings existed in greater frequency than evidenced in the *kuddurus* but were more likely in the south to result from endowments originating from temples or the state than from transactions that would need documentation in the form of a sale.

UR III AND THE THIRD MILLENNIUM BC: IMBRICATION OF THE SOCIAL AND THE FINANCIAL

Shulgi established administrative reforms in Ur III that provided an early version of centralization in which city state governors were administratively under the central administration of the capital. High level administrative positions were heritable (father to son). Merchants of high social status flourished in the private sector, though their social status was less than that of high level administrators.[4] While we cannot discuss most of the fascinating details of Ur III social structure here we can focus on the financial aspects. We need to begin a bit earlier to appreciate the transformations. An example of an early loan with interest involving debt bondage (ca. 2600 BC) from Nippur is the following:

> Šuna received from Šeš-dada 7 shekels of silver (as a loan). In lieu of the interest, he placed uba'a his slave [woman] (with Šeš-dada). He (i.e., Šuna) swore by the name of the king to pay a daily wage of 5 liters (of barley), should she abstain from work. 3 witnesses. Date. Seal of Š[una], son of X-x.[5]

Clearly the loan in silver, here, is told from the debtor's perspective. As the text documents, the debtor's acknowledgment of the debt, is normally made with interest, and the pledge of labor is to serve instead of the interest, until the loan is repaid. Even more revealing is the alternative pledge, to provide a wage of 5 *sila* of barley if his slave does not work. An explanation is in order. The assumption could be either that the work could be expected to provide the equivalent in value of 5 liters of barley each day, or that a penalty premium is pledged over and above the slave's expected productivity should she refuse to work. Scholars have suggested another theory: that interest (and its equivalents) were intended to prevent the borrower from re-accessing the property handed over (in principle temporarily) in lieu of the interest.[6] Thus the goal was to set the rate high enough that permanent usufruct of the property was assured. Steinkeller has suggested that most loans in the Ur III period were made to accomplish goals other than obtaining the specified interest. For instance, if the use of the land or people pledged was the main objective, the intent of charging interest was to prolong or even make permanent that use. In such cases, what appears as security for a loan is in fact part of a bondage instrument intended to bind people or land to the lender's usage.[7]

If the borrower had to pay 5 *sila* a day[8] (1 *gur* = 300 *sila*) this would be the equivalent of 1 *gur* every two months. While this is not easily translated into silver value, which we would need to do in order to calculate a rate of interest in silver, it is possible to contextualize this amount to make it more intelligible. If 18 *iku* of land can produce 30 *gur* of grain then 6 *gur* (the annual figure) would require 18/5 = 3.6 *iku* or a field about 114 meters on a side.[9] While, in this particular case, the simpler alternative is the alienation of a slave's labor until the loan can be repaid, we may at least entertain the assumption that the two are roughly equivalent. We might assume that 7 shekels of silver need to be put to work to produce at least as much above the principle as a 114 meter-square field could produce to make the loan rational for a person in good financial health, though this is not strictly the case. If the man can do without the servant's work, he saves on her salary and needs only to make 7 shekels minus the salary to break even.

Given that ill treatment and death of the slave would probably also extinguish the debt of interest (be laid at the door of the lender of silver) it does seem that the loan could, in principle, be repaid—assuming the slave did her daily work, and the loan was put to productive use. Less optimistically, the borrower may have been in bad financial arrears, and have had no hope of redeeming the loan, which may even have been destined to repay debts, and his final desperate arrangement is to hock his servant or wife.[10] Such wide interpretive options seem to be the norm in Mesopotamian studies.

Given the multiple economic benefits to lenders, debt bondage may at most have been an incidental benefit from lending rather than its major goal either at the institutional or private level. The early general use of loans is illustrated by prebendal land itself being leased out, by the beneficiary, to a third party as early as Ur III times.[11] It is possible that compressible characteristics of grain may have contributed to a notion, in ancient Mesopotamia, that a 20 percent rate of interest on a commercial loan was a just amount,[12] but the rate of grain deterioration under storage may have played a role. It would be senseless to peg a specific rate on either factor in ancient Mesopotamia. Indeed, Hudson's view is that this figure is linked to Babylonian units of account. Thus temples estimated an average thirty-day month plus a two-meal day required 60 units into which they divided their monthly measures of expenditure. Southern Mesopotamia accordingly charged 1/60 interest per month on loans in silver which is 12/60 per year or 20 percent.[13]

This figure for a "normal" rate lasted in some areas for two thousand years, and was established before 2000 BC. In our view, while such considerations may have been contributing factors in making 20 percent seem a compelling figure, the undeniable 20 percent compressibility of grain within storage vessels as expressed in a typical Old Babylonian constant of storage is likely to have as authentic a genealogy. The two justifications are not incompatible as the latter reality may have made the former custom seem morally just, as well as convenient.

Understanding credit in its broad social context depends only marginally on knowledge of labor costs and worker nutrition. Yet the multiple ways in which hidden interest can be accumulated in an era of metrological variability should caution us against trying to draw transhistorical or trans-locational comparisons even when we have loans specifying particular rates of interest.

Another early example of interest bearing debt dates from a stela (ca. 2400 BC), and involves a "loan" of land from the city state of Lagash to that of Umma (land that both states claimed). Upon defeating the leader of Umma, Eanatum made him promise to use the land as an interest bearing loan. The initial assessed capital value was 518,400 liters of barley. During the reign of Eanatum's successor and brother, Enanatum I, the loan is assessed at a value of 11,833,454 gallons (44,789, 760 liters).[14] Only a tiny fraction of a percent of the loan had been paid but we do not have dates for any payments or details. On the basis of the standard 33 percent interest on loans of grain, the total said to be owed could have been reached in fifteen to sixteen years. The debt was enough to help cause a war, though the general conflict endured for 150 years. By the Old Akkadian period, northern Babylonian records include the earliest loans in the normal sense but it is unclear if they actually involve interest despite the presence of a term that is equated, in later lexical texts, with the Akkadian word for interest bearing loans (ḫubullum) and, eventually, with the word for interest itself.[15]

Scholars have shown that with the establishment of the Akkadian dynasty more sophisticated accounting techniques show up from Kish to Ebla. Earlier accounting was characterized by increasingly detailed specifics while during the Akkadian dynasty normal rates were worked out for yields on inputs for grain (e.g., beer, bread, or daily rations) as well as for labor productivity in specific tasks.[16] This allowed accounts to specify both inputs and expected outputs, and enabled administrators to farm out the work to a "supervisor" who they could hold responsible to deliver the expected quantities—thereby creating an incentive structure for the supervisor. Additionally this system shifted the risks of production from the lending institution to supervisor who had been advanced these inputs. By the Ur III period, accounts had become both detailed and sophisticated in calculating the relationship between inputs and outputs, and in setting standardized expectations.

GOVERNMENT ACCOUNTS, INCENTIVES, AND HIDDEN BENEFITS

A fascinating administrative account of female workers in a grain processing facility in Umma (table 2.1) during the archaic period (Ur III) may provide some insight into hidden benefits at the administrative level.

While the repayment correspondences between grain inputs (as grist for the mill) and grain outputs (flour, etc.) are implicit in the document, they are explicit in other texts from the period. The lack of uniformity in grain measures is clear even in the earlier pre-cuneiform Mesopotamian texts as we have seen. The real importance of this account, however, lies in its labor calculations. The account represents the labor and grain advanced as something that produces an appropriate return evaluated as processed products equal in value to the grain plus the full use of labor inputs. The detailed entries in the

Table 2.1. A Production Process Using Female Workers in Umma during Ur III Period

Ur-Šara, a foreman in the facility was advanced labor and grain inputs and then was expected to provide in return an appropriate number of outputs. Thus he was advanced inputs: 36 female laborers for a 314 day period (day 23 of month 3 to day 7 of next year's month 2), totaling 11,304 female labor days, plus the equivalents of 308 *gur,* 3 (*barig*) 3 (*bán*) 8 *sila* of barley (e.g., 8 +30 +180 +92,400 = 92,618 *sila* of barley): the actual advances were in various grains; wheat, spelt and emmer, as well as barley (had the measures been uniform the grain advances add up to 273 *gur* 2 *barig* 2 *bán* 9 *sila* but the use of uniform barley measures implies the actual measures for each grain were indeed different). Labor is noted as paid 3 *bán* per month (e.g., 30 *sila* or one *sila* per day). Total labor **advances** (11,304 female labor days) plus the grain **advanced** (92,618 *sila* of barley) was recorded as a **debt** along with an additional 31 10/60 female labor days specified as the work performance of the "free" days of a deceased laborer named Nin-hegal. This laborer died 187 days before the end of the period (note 187/6 is the 31 10/60 debt recorded for this missing labor).	The production side of the ledger,begins with a labor subtraction (minus 1,884 **free** days i.e., minus one-sixth). Including this figure the foreman itemizes 10,715 days of female labor producing grain value of 300 *gur,* 1 (*barig*), 1 (*bán*) 6 1/2 *sila* of barley equivalents. The grain products themselves amounted to 243 *gur* 1 *barig* 3 1/2 *bán* 7 1/2 *sila* of various flours and breads. The listed labor outputs also included winnowing barley, carrying straw to a temple, miscellaneous services, producing various types of flour, loading of barges, and weaving of textiles. The 10,715 days of female labor recorded as covered includes the 187 days of labor not provided by Nin-hegal due to her early demise. The foreman concludes with a specification of his **obligation: of advances minus his credited appropriate outputs / production**: 8 *gur,* 2 (*barig*) 2 (*bán*) 1 1/2 *sila* of barley (e.g., 1.5 + 20 + 120 + 2,400 = 2541.5 sila) and 620 10/60 female worker days. The grain deficit results from a simple subtraction of grain products credited (converted to the expected inputs needed) plus rations from the uniform barley measure of grain advanced while the labor deficit listed is in effect the result of subtracting 10,715 days from the sum of 11,304 and then adding 31 10/60. N.B. 620 days is about 5.5 percent of the total labor and the foreman gets one-sixth of output (approx 16.5 percent) so there is no issue of financial difficulty in the current account.
The INPUTS	The OUTPUTS

Source: Data from Nissen et al. *Archaic Bookkeeping*. Our interpretation of the data.

account (not shown here) make it clear both that shortfalls in grain products are calculated based on expected normal equivalents (e.g., between barley and barley flour, which might be seen as a unifying currency); and, that labor shortfalls are based on expectations of normal labor productivity (e.g., a day of milling by one female worker should produce a given amount of flour).

The account raises a number of interesting questions including what is meant by "free" days, and why the missing work and associated free days of the deceased woman's work are allocated the way they are on the two sides of the ledger. Nissan et al claim that "free" days are rest days, and even suggest that the typical amount calculated (one-sixth of female labor days and one-tenth of male labor days) is on the meager side from the perspective of recuperating from strenuous labor. [17] Their discussion of the allocation of the "free" days to the advances side of the ledger and that of 187 non-existent days to the production side indicates that their puzzlement perhaps was a result of this assumption.

In our analysis, we follow Eleanor Robson's general suggestion that such accounts represent labor obligations to institutions (state or temple households) that have been put under the direction of a supervisor who incurs a debt or obligation to return outputs to the institution providing the labor and other advances. This labor may have been part of the *bala* system (see below). Thus inputs include a specific number of days of labor for a specific number of laborers, and the supervisor's incurred obligation is a specific number of output products based on those inputs.[18] It thus makes sense to imagine an incentive structure in which the supervisor, if he produces an excess above the contracted obligation, can retain this surplus. On this interpretation, the example[19] suggests that the supervisor has an incentive to be productive and, interestingly, a disincentive to overwork the labor too much. In many historical cases, labor may well have been owed in much the same way feudal lords were owed tithes, a specified number of days per year, and killing off labor would have meant less labor available in future years. Though slave labor may have been available from time to time, the economy seems to have worked on a prebendal system where institutions were owed specific amounts of labor, and particular individuals or groups acquired the benefits thereof as a perk of office or a right of conquest.

The assumption that "free days" are vacation days is highly problematic. Does it really make sense that female laborers would have one sixth of the days in a year off and men only one tenth? Moreover, what would either eat while on vacation given their minimal ration? Instead, following Robson, we believe a more plausible explanation is that the "free" days are not vacation days, and instead the term refers to days for which the foreman does not have to pay back advances. On this assumption, the tablet is extremely interesting due to the death of a laborer.

The 187 days "not worked" also count toward production (i.e., show up on the output side of the account) because the foreman does not owe products for them; he gets credit on the output side of the account since the death is not attributed to negligence on his part. Assuming, the "free" days are incentives for the foreman to maximize production (each is an average day), the foreman keeps for himself one-sixth of average production for the female workdays he supervises. Thus the return expected to the provider of the inputs is five-sixths of the total production, and the ratios of expected output to inputs are setup accordingly. Adding in the full 187 missed days on the output side of the ledger in the labor category allows the foreman to write off those days—which he never received. Entering one-sixth of the "free" days (31 10/60) for the deceased laborer into the final calculation of inputs as "owed" (see left column) makes sense since the foreman already has been given credit for those days in the initial subtraction (top of second column) that defines his benefits, so this avoids any "double deduction." Both the foreman and the owner lose from the death, and the account clearly documents the foreman's loss by also putting his missed benefit of one-sixth of the 187 days on the input side of the ledger. Thus five-sixths are allowed on the output side as if they were accounted for in outputs and one-sixth is placed on the input side to facilitate the foreman's calculation of his personal rates of return and the full 187 days are accounted for in the ledger.

If the one-sixth of the total female days referred to as "free" days were rest days, rather than days free of obligation, we would have to join Nissan *et al* in puzzlement over why one-sixth of the missing days due to a death would be itemized as advances on the input side rather than the account deducting the entire 187 days as credited production, that is, shown entirely as a credit on the production side. Recognizing the foreman's typical share of the production, his incentive package, the accounting makes complete sense: The foreman is shown in the accounts as getting the one sixth he deserves (as a separate input) for that worker and not owing the five-sixths of the 187 days because the laborer died before providing those days: thus no complaints by either party are justifiable from this account.

In other ledgers the implication is that the comparable fraction for male workers is one tenth of the average production for the male work days supervised.[20] Robson's interpretation implies that the state assumed men were more productive than women. Actually this may be entirely due to the respective prices of male and female labor products not to the physical productivity of men or women but either way there is no need to assume that men got less vacation than women. Most likely, we can infer that the state tried to provide a comparable incentive for supervising either male or female labor.

It is well worth noting that if state revenues depended on high production levels, then providing serious incentives for high production makes a great deal of sense.[21] It is also worth noting that there is no explicit extra credit for the grain paid to the workers. Because the net grain owed is calculated by subtracting rations from the total grain provided, the total non "free" days advanced is simply five-sixths of the total number of days of female work advanced. The input-output algorithm used was thus something like X amount of grain and Y amount of labor (paid 3 *bán* a month by the state) should produce a *net* Z amount of products owed by the foreman (consumption of grain by labor seems to come out of the advances to the foreman). Deficits thus were reckoned in grain product equivalents and number of labor days not employed productively. If we assume the foreman put the extra grain (2,541 *sila* of barley) and labor (his one-sixth or 1,884 days plus the labor deficit giving the 620 one-sixth days the account shows) to work productively (his own production not shown in the official ledger), he would have been in an excellent position to pay his assessed deficit.

If on the contrary we assume with Nissan *et al.* that the foreman was simply in arrears he would owe the equivalent of 620 + 2,541 *sila* of grain (at one *sila* a day for rations) this would be 3,161 days of rations or more than 8.6 years of a single laborer's daily rations. This is hardly a viable career. Assuming instead that he ran his own business at least as well as he did the institution's, we could simply use the labor figure to make a crude estimate of his private benefits, and note that the net total (11,304–187) divided by six is 1,852.83 days. Subtracting the 620.167 days (for which he must still compensate the state) this leaves us with 1,232.67 days of labor whose average production he could keep. As a proportion of the total labor, this is 11 percent, suggesting that his overall personal profits may have been a bit over 11 percent of the total state revenues from his production facility.[22]

That even this crude figure is near the theoretical 10 percent for men suggests that the use of one-sixth for female free days may well have provided comparability in terms of incentives for supervising male and female labor. This account of the grain processing facility thus can be seen as an illustration of the way state production in the archaic period was run on a mixture of credit and hidden interest. Even though state production was conceived as a system of debits and credits, both the state and the foremen had an incentive to exploit labor to the maximum short of grievously harming the laborers.

We can use this example to reflect on the consequences of a worker dying (to fatigue or disease). In the case in question, once a female laborer is made available to the foreman he can expect to get approximately sixty-one days of average labor per year for himself from her if she does not die. If labor is scarce and she dies he risks losing this labor for following years. On the other hand, if his production levels are lower than the norm (indicated by high enough deficits to jeopardize repayment), he may risk getting fewer laborers next time around. In any case, for each day left in the year after a laborer dies the foreman loses one-sixth (or if male one-tenth) of a day of labor so he has a strong incentive not to kill off his labor force. Because he also has just as strong an incentive to maximize production and meet his quotas,[23] from a management perspective, the system is well optimized.

GOVERNANCE AND CREDIT: THE BALA SYSTEM IN UR III

One of the key administrative arrangements in the Ur III state (ca. 2112–2004 BC), was an elaborate set of mutual obligations called the *Bala* system, [24] which means "turn or rotation" that redistributed resources between regions.[25] Under this system (which replaced a simple pyramidal system of provincial taxation), the crown sent assessors to each of the eighteen regions to assess its needs each month. Depending on this assessment, each province provided or received certain resources to or from the crown. However, rather than each region providing and receiving set quotas, recognizing seasonal and annual variations in supply and receipts, crown allocations were for specific purposes: ranging from provisions for particular individuals and specific expeditions up to larger allocations for garrisons and armies. Core regions specialized in providing specific commodities such as livestock, reeds, or timber.

Outside the core areas a "tax of the provinces" (*gún ma-da*) paid in livestock was assessed on military personnel—with the amount paid based on rank. Presumably the military obtained those livestock from their own assessments on the population. This broad territory includes some ninety settlements stretching at least from Assur in the northwest to Susa in the southeast. The periphery also paid other taxes such as the *šu-gíd* and *máš-da-ri-a* which could be paid in silver, timber, sesame, wine, or other products. There is evidence that Ur III had a small private sector relative to the activities sponsored by government or temple organizations.[26]

There is clear evidence that livestock were usually delivered to the town of Puzriš Dagan and that the crown regularly distributed livestock to several regions.[27] In some cases this merely involved deductions from the provincial account that listed its obligations to the crown, implying perhaps that the livestock could stay in the province, while in other cases accounts indicate flows that seem to be (at least net) from one province to another. Since the system was rotational with different commodities and regions involved in different months, the record seems to suggest something much more complex than a simple *quid pro quo*. Thus, while a region in effect had a debt to the system (and most prominently the crown), the system itself had institutionalized obligations for disbursement to both individuals and regions the full extent of which can only be surmised.

Flows of labor were also part of the *bala* system, and at least for this period in part explain the proliferation of texts recording loans of labor and the conditions tied to such loans, as in the processing system discussed above or the loan of barley to the military discussed below. Recent work has shown that manual labor in Ur III was of two distinct types: (a) *éren* or conditionally freed labor such as soldiers or native community labor and (b) UN.IL or menial labor. The former worked half time in return for compensation in kind and in the form of sustenance fields and their labor was considered provision of *bala* while the latter worked full time in return for rations including barley, oil, wool and garments and, rarely, access to land. The half time labor category included supervisors and applied to women, largely doing textile work, as well as men.[28]

Text *RA 4.78* provides an account of two months of *bala* of Ur-Lamma the provincial governor of Girsu that itemizes what has been received and what deficits remain:[29]

> 2150 gur, 76 2/3 sila grain,
> the extra (from) the account, month of Akiti, Year S44.
> 3 gur, 235 sila wheat, which entered the storehouse,
> via Lu-utu, foreman of the mill.
> 252 gur, 20 sila bran, Šulgi-aamu.
> (text breaks)
> [ ] bran,
> [ ] regular quality [ ]
> Deficit: 1217 gur, 86 1/3 sila grain.
> 1544 gur, 103 2/3 sila bran
> 7746 5/6 female workers for one day.
> 43 talents, 6 ma-na willow wood.
> 17,571 reed bundles,
> it is the deficit.

The notion that the *bala* for this period could be in deficit exactly 7,746 and five-sixths female worker days makes most sense if, as discussed above, foremen who supervise the female labor themselves benefit from one-sixth of the labor (7,746 itself is evenly divisible by six). It would appear that the state receives labor and someone uses it to prepare the *bala* the state is expected to provide. In this case, bran obviously is a by-product of milling grain and there is a deficit of both bran and the labor force to mill it listed, so it may be that the governor planned to contract for more milling of grain and, with some bran already in hand, can calculate his deficit both of bran and labor.

Bureaucratic institutions are associated with the earliest examples of explicitly elaborated loans in Mesopotamia. While most scholars, following Weber's influential work, associate bureaucracy with efficiency or even narrow-minded bureaucratic perspectives this may be seriously anachronistic when applied to Ur III. Modern organization theory suggests that some docility, in the sense of willingness to learn from one's coworkers, promotes productivity. Yet it is not clear, during the early periods, how many bureaucrats were exclusively devoted to their organizations. In later Islamic times, it might have been almost impossible to find a bureaucrat who did not also have his own private entrepreneurial activities. Not to have such activities was considered problematic in many senses. Beyond this, it is not clear that all organizations had only narrow sets of goals, let alone pure devotion to optimizing intakes and outputs—surely a prerequisite for consistent narrow-mindedness. There is evidence of some degree of specialization as we know that during the Ur III period bureaucrats were generically called *dub-sar* (scribes) and were required to pass through the scribal academy (*eduba*) so they were probably all literate though this cannot be said to preclude private financial activities.[30]

The temples served a number of key charitable functions such as taking care of war orphans and widows, and received revenues from their own lands, as well as subsidies from the state, though temples paid taxes. Their lending would have been seen as both socially beneficial and of business value.[31] Hidden or implicit interest occurs in many forms, but in Mesopotamia early records suggest that it first took the form of several key types of returns to temple loans based both on repayment, sometimes with interest, and the productive activities of obligated labor. Urbanization is thought to increase the need for some form of currency, because urban dwellers tend to buy smaller quantities, and to do so much more frequently than rural dwellers (e.g., a piece of meat versus a whole sheep). Before the advent of cash, an early alternative may have been that most people belonged to large households or were dependencies of institutions. In an urbanizing society, such as that of ancient Mesopotamia, trade provided multiple opportunities for profit, but the destitute may have largely depended on selling their labor in return for payments in staples and lodging.

Benefits on a loan might involve specifying that the borrower provide labor to the lender during the period of the loan. This would only work for large loans if the borrower controlled a labor force. The following loan in the Ur III period between the administration of Umma and the royal military has been interpreted in this way:

> 90,000 liters of barley, a lo[an], (its interest is to be paid by) harvesting barley; for each 60 liters (of the loan) 1 iku of land is to be harvested; That he will not sue (regarding this transaction), (and) to repay the barley (of the loan at the

> time of) the harvest, and to return it to its (original) silo, (and), if the barley (of the field in question) is not harvested, in that field, as much as it gets destroyed (because it was not harvested), to replace the (spoiled) barley, he (i.e., Šarrum-ili) swore by the name of the king. From the governor of Umma Šarrum-ili, the colonel of the conscripts of Girsu, received (this barley loan). Date. Seal of Šarrum-ili, the colonel of the conscripts, son of Tulta, the colonel.[32]

Cuneiform textual translations often include material interpolated to explain the actual annotations. Despite the enormous amount of brilliant work done on cuneiform texts, many texts are abbreviated, and translators regularly interpolate material to explain the cursory material actually included on the tablets. Steinkeller correctly infers that this loan implies 1,500 *iku* of land to be harvested, and goes on to explain the text by interpolating a variety of material and attempting to calculate a rate of interest implied in the loan.[33] Other examples of the period suggest that a 9.5 *iku* field might take 132 persons days to harvest, so at that rate a 1 *iku* field would take approximately fourteen person days.[34]

Yet, given a daily rate of 6 liters (*sila*) per person the 60 liters mentioned implies ten person days per *iku* should suffice for the harvest. The loan provides 60 liters to harvest each *iku*, and for 1500 *iku* it provides 90,000 liters. This means that the borrower would get, in terms of labor value, exactly the required cost of harvesting the 1500 *iku* (90,000 liters of barley) leaving no room for profit on the loan, while being obliged to repay the principle, unless some profit is taken from the harvest. This suggests an alternative interpretation is possible: the loan may simply be an advance without interest specifying merely that 90,000 liters be restored to the silo, from which the advance was taken after the harvest, that the recipient commits to doing the entire harvest and is responsible for any harvest losses. This implies either that there is an implausibly well understood expectation of the amount to be harvested and no profit allowed or, more likely, a well understood amount of harvest to return and that any excess, as with tax farming, accrues to the borrower responsible for the harvest.

Many other possibilities are apparent despite the brevity of the text, and may provide potential hidden interest. It is possible that some or all of the conscripts rations are available to the commander from some other source, providing some profit through the 60 liters per *iku* allowance, or that the conscripts are slaves and can be heavily worked and therefore provide profit.[35] There may well have been labor shortages during some periods of Ur III; and, if so the conscripts (whose number is not stated) may have provided significant additional benefits to the commander on other lands and this consignment of labor, with its potential benefits, may have been very welcome in return for the relatively minor service requested.[36]

The document indicates the borrower should repay the loan at the upcoming harvest. However, if the conscripts provide labor both on land that the borrower cultivated for his own profit, and on the lands where he used the conscript labor to implement the 90,000 liter loan, then his control of the conscripts (which can be withdrawn when the state is providing the loan whether due the *Bala* system or conquest) acts as collateral for the loan itself as well as the guarantee for the completion of the harvest. Because unspoiled grain must be returned to the original silo, transportation costs, as usual, are born by the borrower, and the lender obviously also benefits from getting new grain for old. These clear benefits to the lender suggest there may also be hidden benefits to the recipient even if the text does not clearly specify them.

Antichretic loans involve the receipt of funds in exchange for the temporary transfer of lands to the lender (interim revenue serves as interest on the loan). An example of this form of loan is provided by a chief shepherd to a military figure during Ur III who accepts income from three plots in the place of interest on a loan (obviously the principle is still due):

> 1/2 mina of silver as a loan from SI.A-a, Puzur-Haya, [son? of] [Š]u?-Enlil?, the colonel received (extending) from the hamlet, that of Apilanum up to the feeder-canal is the šuku plot of a unit of 10 (soldiers), the subordinates of Ennum-ili; (extending) from the feeder-canal up to the Dula dike is the šuku plot of 36 iku, (the land of) a unit of 10 (soldiers, (under) Kuruda; (extending) from the feeder-canal up to the Dula dike is the šuku plot of 18 iku, (the land of) a unit of 10 (soldiers), under Iddin-Er ra. Puzur-Haya has [pledged?] (this land in lieu of the loan) [to] SI.A-a[37]

The three plots listed presumably had provided income to the thirty soldiers and perhaps others. We do not know if the cultivators were the soldiers before or under the loan. We can safely assume that Puzur-Haya's pledging of the lands in return for a loan in silver must have transferred some or all of the lands' revenue to the lender (SI.A.). The document does not provide enough detail to calculate how this can be boiled down to an equivalent rate of return on the loan.

If the soldiers provided all the labor during the harvest season, the loan could transfer all the revenue to the lender by indirectly pledging both the land and the labor for the period of the loan, or it could be pledging merely the revenue normally accruing to the soldiers from other people's work on their lands. Since labor is not mentioned, it is most probable that, whoever was involved, the labor went with the land. If all revenues from the land accrued to the lender, the benefit perceived would have been the production plus the prevailing cost of labor. Alternatively, benefits to the lender might have amounted to production minus the normal cost of labor. As we do not know if these plots were normally expected to provide fully for the soldiers, or if soldiers also had other revenues, it would be rash to speculate further.

Even during the Ur III period, there were many variations on this type of loan. For example, there were partial antichretic loans. Typically, in such cases only a portion of the revenue from the land in the hands of the lender might be made available to him, and the remainder of the revenue (minus costs of production) would be returned to the landowner (borrower of funds).[38]

This variation is not particularly different in principle, but it radically transforms the opportunities for antichretic loans because the revenue from the land does not have to correspond in value to an expected interest income from the amount lent. It merely needs to be sufficient not equivalent. Nevertheless, partial antichretic loans are clearly more complex to supervise and implement, and so might not be particularly desirable if they involve ceding management of an important piece of land. Land might be also used simply as a pledge for a loan; allowing the lender in case of default on its terms to take over the land until such time as the loan principle and interest are repaid.

OLD ASSYRIAN TRADERS

We have particularly rich records for the Old Assyrian traders many of whom originated from Assur and worked largely out of Kanesh (in Anatolia) during the 1912–1830 BC period.[39] When interest on loans was specified it was usually 30 percent between Assyrians in Kanesh but apparently more when Assyrians loaned to Anatolians. Various forms of security were normal including pledges, guarantors, joint liability (especially of spouses) and a form of general mortgage on the assets of the borrower.[40]

Lending to individuals seems to have taken similar forms to that of earlier Mesopotamian dynasties; and, the prebendal system continued to be practiced though in a gradually more sophisticated way. Labor was regularly bound to individuals, not just institutions, in this period though this is unlikely to have been a novelty. A common commercial partnership, *be 'ulātum*, was a type of short term work contract binding a worker to a contractor. The other common partnership, set up as a *naruqqu*-contract, proved to have amazing longevity and became, in more sophisticated form, a staple of long distance trade.[41]

Historical developments in Assyrian territory changed many aspects of government and the financial system, though inheriting a great deal from the past, developed significantly new levels of sophistication. There were standard partnerships (*tappa 'ūtum*) in which partners had full liability, money lenders, and bearers checks and, as befit an entrepôt for trade between Anatolia and Mesopotamia, a complex set of ways, some of dubious legal standing, by traders from each area to secure their debts.[42] From the perspective of the evolution of finance there was also something seemingly new: an Old Assyrian merchant *naruqqu*-contract from Assur reads in part:[43]

> In all 30 minas of gold, Amur-Ištar's partnership capital. Reckoned from the year named after Susaya he will trade for 12 years. He will enjoy a third of the profit. He will be responsible for a third. Whoever gets his money back before the completion of his term must take the silver at the rate of 4 minas of silver for 1 mina of gold. He will not get any of the profit.

This *naruqqu* contract creates a partnership having at least thirteen shareholders and lists their proportion (weight) of the investment (*šipkātum*: varying between 1 and 4 minas of gold). It implies that they will share proportionally in two thirds of the profit accruing to the trade, unless they ask for their funds back early, while their active agent, Amur-Ištar, will have the remaining third and is responsible/liable only for a third. Early withdrawal earns no profit and the exchange rate between gold and silver is specified to avoid disputes in the event partners are repaid in silver.

This contract is particularly interesting because it approaches the form of the later Islamic *commenda;* in that the mobile trader has a specified "share in that profit" (*šalšātum* or thirds) along with the investors, who do not travel; profits are shared in proportion to their investment, but only after the conclusion of the period specified. Most telling, in the sense of a step forward, is that the traveling partner has diminished liability. This is considerably more sophisticated than the partnership implied in the century later Code of Hammurabi (*CH 100, 102*: c.1750 BC) which holds the agent responsible for a specified rate of return and, in case of outright loss, liable for the full return of the principle.

A more typical *commenda* contract during the Islamic period would allow the trader to have a 50 percent share in the profits; and, would also involve agreements about liability; either explicitly or implicitly (based on standard legal understandings) recognizing no liability on the part of the traveling partner unless he used the funds in demonstrably improper ways, from a business consensus or legal point of view. The *naruqqu* contract implies the losses, and profits, are to be split between the investors and the trader in the same ratio. This is a significant improvement in liability from the perspective of the traveling partner and seems to point directly toward the later form of the *commenda.*

There are examples from the Old Assyrian period of transferring outstanding debts into shares in a *naruqqu*-contract (i.e., converting a sum owed to one into an additional share of profit at the conclusion of the contract agreed to by the debtor—without contributing new funds). Letters and judicial records suggest that such contracts could have shares that were fully negotiable or inheritable, indicating that Old Assyrian traders had gone some distance toward the development of sophisticated "company law."[44] Other legal records of a financial nature document transfers of property titles, private legal actions against debtors whose creditors could dun the families and wives of debtors, and even obtain the right to borrow from a moneylender the amount due from a creditor at the expense of the debtor. There is also a record of an Anatolian contract dealing with the acquisition of a field as an antichretic pledge in view of facilitating the later conveyance of the field to a third party.[45]

FINANCIAL SPREADSHEETS AND NEW LOAN CONDITIONS IN THE OLD BABYLONIAN PERIOD

The survival of very large numbers of personal loan documents from second millennium BC Mesopotamia is a bit of a puzzle. Because the loan was considered transferable, loans were sealed by the debtor and handed over to the creditor, so upon their repayment debtors usually were at great pains to recover and destroy them. Litigation over (failed) repayment of loans survives from the Old Babylonian period between a creditor, Erib-Sin, and two partners that mentions a double payment penalty clause but no joint liability for the two debtors.[46] The survival of so many intact loan documents suggests that either countless loans were never repaid, or perhaps archival copies were retained. Some scholars have suggested that the real purpose of loans in the ancient world was to create obligations or a form of indentured labor rather than to generate profit through the loan itself.[47] This idea seems to require some way, possibly high interest rates, to assure that loans cannot be repaid. Based on the evidence available, it is not at all clear that this was the case; and, the extensive record of debt forgiveness via edicts also argues against this explanation. It may simply be that debts recorded on documents that had been subsequently forgiven by edict did not have to be destroyed—the edict took precedence. The existence of abnormally large numbers of debt documents from periods immediately preceding edicts would, indeed, support such a position.[48]

Perhaps the earliest spreadsheet known dates to 1822 BC, and uses a mixed numerical counting and metrological system for grain. The amounts recorded in table 2.2 use standard grain metrology (*gur, barig, ban,* and *sila*) up to a point but larger amounts of *gur* are prefixed by a widely used (by this time) discrete counting system (numbers are simply recorded in a place system in which the rightmost place represents multiples of 60 (in this case of *gur*) the next to the left is a further multiple of 10, then a further multiple of 60 then

Table 2.2. An Early Spreadsheet Summing Up Grain Assets in 1822 BC for Towns in the Kingdom of Larsa. Source: YBC 4721. Grice 1919, no. 103.

Grain assets	*For Ur*	*For [...]*	*For Larsa*	*Total*	*Its name*
5ğ 1.0.0	5ğ 1.0.0			5ğ 1.0.0	Lipit-Suen
5ğ 1.0.0		3ğ 34.4.4, 5	1ğ 26.0.1, 5	5ğ 1.0.0	Nur-Dagan
4ğ 56.0.0	3ğ gur	N/A	56.0.0	4ğ 56.0.0	Ili-ériba
4ğ 37.3.2			4ğ 37.3.2	4ğ 37.3.2	Šamaš-kima-ilišu
From 23.[1.4 sila of Šamaš-kima-ilišu's] workers					
1 9ğ 36.0.2 gur	8ğ 1.0.0	3ğ 34.4.4, 5	8ğ gur 0.1.3, 5 sila	1 9ğ 36.0.2 gur	
From the grain of Lu-. . . . And from 23.1.4 sila of Šamaš-kima-ilišu's workers					
Month 1, 7th day, Year that Rim-Sin became king: 1822 BC					

Source: Modified from Robson, *Mathematics in Ancient Iraq*, 166. Notes: Abbreviations: ğ = ğeš = 60; 1 9 = 1 ğešu 9 ğeš = 1*10 + 9 = 19 ğeš; 34.4.4, 5 = 34 gur 4 barig 4 ban, 5 sila = 34*300 + 4*60 + 4*10 + 5 sila; sila = approx. a liter of grain. Note that the metrological system for grain here goes up to the gur and then gur get counted in the numerical system.

again a further multiple of 10). The grain in this account only avails itself of two places (60 then 10) and the account adds up both columns and rows like a spreadsheet:[49]

While this early spreadsheet does use standard numbers for large amounts, it retains the grain metrological system until it has to sum up many "*gur*." It is worth noting that by this time there is clear evidence that scribes used intermediary calculations on erasable surfaces to reckon the figures they had to put in reports; and, so could easily convert from a metrological system tailored to a product to a more standardized set of figures to be included in a report.

Bureaucracy relies on efficient accounting for its advantage. As we have seen this accounting initially involved careful counting systems in which different numerical systems were tied to distinctive metrology for each type of product. Over time Mesopotamian counting and metrological systems became somewhat less complex. Presumably this facilitated clarity in accounts.

While credit undoubtedly pre-dates bureaucratic institutions, detailed written contracts appear first with bureaucratic institutions listed as the creditors. There are several reasons for this chronology, but the most important is tied to the exigencies of bookkeeping in the ancient world. Initially, no simple money was available, market prices were unreliably connected to the investment value of a product and profits were ensured by access to coerced or highly exploited labor, rather than stable market prices for land or labor providing a stable basis for returns on investment. Inputs generated a return through seasonal speculations or through a prebendal system, not through some efficient price structure for land, labor, or outputs created by a market. Typically, accounts would have been kept for each commodity while monitoring exchange rates between commodities would be useful only when sales or exchanges were contemplated. Bureaucratic institutions, such as temples, were the first to have the means to adequately manage finances, and the legitimacy required to regulate loans and impose sanctions.

Before their appearance in Mesopotamia, private loans of goats or sheep initially motivated by risk management considerations[50] undoubtedly had implicit interest bearing characteristics, but as in earlier or more recent pastoral societies (e.g., half of the offspring belong to the lender), such terms might have been specified orally and in qualitative terms. Such a vague prototypical loan could have been quickly transformed into the precursors of modern credit once bureaucratic institutions with sanctioning powers appeared. More elaborate forms of credit involving bureaucratic institutions would have preceded elaborate forms initiated by private parties.[51]

From a social point of view even a structured pair of cash transactions may be better seen not as two independent transactions but as a pair of linked transactions forming an implicit credit arrangement. One such pair that has shown perhaps the greatest robustness around the globe has already been mentioned: the purchase at harvest of grains for resale later in the year when prices rise. Prior to the development of sophisticated types of credit, states that collected tithes at harvest might distribute a portion of them to the poor in the pre-harvest season. Such redistributive systems, typically, extract a portion of the harvest as hidden interest for their own maintenance and profit. Once this system becomes established at the level of a bureaucratic institution (e.g., a temple or government) it can be easily abstracted into a credit system involving loans to individuals. Bureaucratic institutions (and later private parties) with capital can purchase grains, or other storable produce such as dates, at harvest, store them in facilities designed for this purpose and systematically resell them later in the year.

We have a number of indications of how debts that explicitly bore interest may have developed in the second millennium BC. Palace industries producing woolen textiles contracted with merchants to sell these goods at given prices. They advanced the goods to the merchants, and set up a loan document to record the advance and expected payment in silver "on demand:"

> 15.435 kg of wool according to the weight of Šamaš(?), its value is 51 grams of silver, is part of the wool of the palace which Ilsumšuibni, overseer of the merchants, has received from the palace, under the responsibility of Utul-Ištar, the scribe. Warad-Ibari and Šamaš-bani, sons of Etel-pi-Šamaš, have received (the wool) from Ilšu-ibni, overseer of merchants. On the day that the palace requests the silver, they will pay it out to the messenger of the palace. 3 witnesses. Date[52]

This was an agreement to pay after the goods were sold, but there are numerous examples of correspondence indicating that merchants delayed payment even as much as two years despite multiple requests for payment from the palace.[53] Since the benefit to the palace was incorporated into the agreed upon price, there would have been no need to specify interest, but as delays in payment became common, it would make sense to add fines and eventually to make the fines accumulate on a monthly basis—in effect charging monthly interest after a specified due date in order to provide an incentive for timely payment.

While it would have been feasible to regulate rates of interest that were explicitly spelled out in a document by providing recourse in law to those who felt aggrieved by them, this would have been much more difficult when interest was replaced by labor or revenue from particular plots of land. A society in which different members were thought to be due different consideration, as was the norm in ancient Mesopotamia, would also not have wanted to be too uniform in its specification of lending norms.[54] The state, if it had a need to appear beneficent, could do better than simply regulate the terms of contracts, it could distribute food to the poor in the pre-harvest season to mitigate the tendency in the market place to gouge the poor during the lean months leading up to harvest, and it could even go so far as to issue an edict to cancel all debts of a particular type. In fact, there is strong evidence that ancient states acquired some of their legitimacy through forgiving this type of debt at regular intervals.[55]

Scholars have long debated the similarities between loans and other financially binding arrangements in Mesopotamia; and, whether this implies loans were viewed as a subcategory of commercial contracts or if, for example, the inclusion of an oath indeed meant they were not *per se* viewed as contractual obligations until the oath was dropped from the text of loan documents in Old Babylonian times. The similarities in many texts are striking. Loan documents overwhelmingly specified both quantities and type of product loaned as well as contractual or repayment obligations, and provided a typical verbal formula for a proper loan, (e.g., *šu ba-an-ti* "he took / received"). Old Babylonian contract documents similarly had two basic parts: a description of a legal act already completed; and, a promise detailing future actions agreed to by the contracting parties, also expressed in a typical formulaic verb phrase.[56]

An interesting antichretic loan (Ur, 1819 BC) including some elements quite common in the Old Babylonian period involves a slave girl rather than property as a substitute for interest:[57]

> 10 shekels of silver, a šu-lá loan, it bears no interest (máš-nu-tuku), from PN, PN2 received one slave girl PN3 by name, to bring the silver for maintenance he promised–stands as pledge. When he pays the silver he shall take his slave girl, he has sworn the oath by the king.

This antichretic loan is first defined as a šu-lá loan (a loan which typically bore interest), then this phrase is immediately followed by a phrase indicating that normal interest is not to be paid; and, finally the explanation follows: that use of a slave girl will substitute for interest until such time as the principle is repaid. At the conclusion of the loan, the loan recipient will recuperate his slave girl. Usufruct of the slave girl has the advantage from the lender's perspective that expectations of the value of the slave girl's labors most likely involve less management than a piece of agricultural property; and, might even motivate the owner to repay the loan more than would the loss of use of a small piece of land.

Once we recognize that hidden interest in the form of a variety of impositions provides significant advantages, we can sum up the Old Babylonian loan contract specifications into "Basic" objective descriptions and "Advanced" conditions intended to shape the loan in terms of advantage. "Basic" objective descriptions include, the primary parties, the commodities lent and their amounts, the dates specified and the witnesses. The typical "Advanced" inclusions reflected the relative advantages of the two parties by specifying the type of loan, explicit interest or its substitute, repayment conditions including where and when, security provided including joint responsibility mentions and penalties agreed to, and the promissory oath within loan contracts (which disappears in the course of the Old Babylonian period).[58]

While the presence of an explicit interest clause tells us something about the institutionalization of credit, it is often mistakenly used as a significant indicator of relative power between lender and borrower when the additional conditions, implicit and explicit, are at least as important, or frequently far more important. Remembering the various law cases cited earlier, explicit statement of interest may be best seen as functioning primarily to render the loan more legally defensible in case of default. While the disappearance of the oath in loan documents suggests that public opprobrium via religious beliefs is no longer necessary, it may also suggest that the ties between the state and the merchant elites (a part of the lending classes) are more developed, and that public opprobrium can now be reinforced with state and civil sanctions (as the laws cited above may indicate).

A related development that may serve to draw attention to the role of the private sector seems to have occurred in the area of land tenure. In the Old Babylonia city state of Dilbat there is some reason to believe both that land had to be sold within a kin group and that there were already well institutionalized forms of adoption to allow strangers to buy land.[59] It is probable that many earlier sales of land do not mention kinship as a prerequisite for the sale for the simple reason that it would have been an absolute given. We would argue that kinship, along with membership in an established household, were basic ways of determining whose reputation was beyond reproach and as such were merely examples of the many significant concerns addressed through attention to honor, reputation and trust.

LATER BABYLONIAN FINANCIAL PRACTICE

The region generally categorized as Babylon in the first millennium BC was, at times, conquered by various empires based outside the region, for example, the Assyrian or Persian Empires. Yet, many traditional financial practices continued little changed. The Persians tended to leave local financial instruments relatively untouched even as they instituted new tax and administrative methods or introduced additional sophistication in banking.

Some loans of the Neo Babylonian period do explicitly specify rates of interest, but it is by no means the case that they concur on the rate. In fact, records from the Nabû-ušallim archive show explicit interest rates ranging from 10 to 25 percent. Not all documents specify the time period of the interest payment, and pre-harvest to post-harvest loans do not imply a uniform rate of interest, even if both loan and repayment are in silver, without knowledge of market prices in both pre-harvest and post-harvest times. The normal way of specifying a rate in Akkadian was to specify that a shekel of silver would be added to each mina of silver (sixty shekels to the mina). This would be 20 percent per annum if the interest specified was to be paid per month (12/60). Some documents specify that interest was to be paid annually, others require monthly payment of interest, while others are unclear.[60]

The examples in table 2.3 below which illustrate a typical range in Neo-Babylonian times, have been ordered from smallest amount of capital lent to largest.[61] These examples call for a number of comments:

- There seems to be no correlation between size of loan and interest rate within the range of loan (at least fifteen fold) documented
- The interest rate varies significantly within a single period and place
- None of these loan examples are large enough to necessarily involve wealthy or influential people.

While the Neo-Babylonian period (ca. seventh to sixth century BC) is 1,400 years after Ur III, there is no reason to believe that interest rates varied or were socially negotiable only in this later period. Patronage and kinship

Table 2.3. Inconsistent Interest on Loans in the Neo-Babylonian Period.

Capital	*Interest*	*Interest per annum*
10 shekels	10 shekels per mina per year	16 2/3
11 shekels	8 shekels per mina per year	13 1/3
16 shekels	6 shekels per mina per year	10
30 shekels	1/4 shekel per shekel per year	25
48 shekels	10 shekels per mina per year	16 2/3
60 shekels	8 shekels per mina per year	13 1/3
70 shekels	1 shekel per mina per month	20
98 shekels	8 shekels per mina per year	13 1/3
150 shekels	10 shekels per mina per year	16 2/3
200 bundles of reeds	20 bundles of reeds per 100	20

Source: Jursa, "Debts and Indebtedness in the Neo-Babylonian Period."

ties may long have been far more critical in determining the rate received than the amount borrowed, even within the moderate levels of lending included in the table. To the extent that the purpose of lending at interest was in fact to secure use of an asset for the short or long term, something that must have been fairly common, we would have to assume that the rate may have been set at a level sufficient to secure that asset, given the financial circumstances of the borrower and the period intended for the loan. To the extent loans were part of a larger set of social ties, as is easily demonstrated for the Roman Republic, many factors would have determined the effective rate obtainable. That we often lack the information to document many of these factors in specific cases is unfortunate, but does not imply that they were not pertinent.

A loan from January 31, 504 BC, will serve as a point of departure for Persian practice:[62]

> *Summary*: Ten and a half minas and five shekels of silver are owed to Šaddinu, son of Madanu-aḫḫe-iddin, descendant of Šigûa, from marduk-nāṣir-apli (MNA). Interest will accrue on the ten and a half minas and five shekels of silver at the rate of one shekel per mina per month beginning in Addar. This silver plus three minas and forty-five shekels of silver are from a debt incurred for the purchase of an onion crop in King Darius' eleventh year which Šaddinu, who administers the royal lease, sold to MNA. His acreage in Bit-Ḫaḫḫuru, next to Arad-Marduk, son of Nergal-zēra-ibni is pledged to Šaddinu until the ten and a half mina and five shekels of silver plus their interest is paid. Twelve witnesses plus date and place and seal of the scribe.

The rate of 12 shekels per year per mina (of 60 shekels) is the traditional rate of 20 percent but it is purely a loan of silver to be repaid in silver. In effect, the administrator of state land sold / farmed out the right to a particular harvest to an entrepreneur, marduk-nāṣir-apli (MNA), for a particular sum which was presumably to be paid from profits on the sales of the onion harvest. The total silver originally owed in the transaction was at least 14 1/3 mina or 860 shekels (225 + 635) plus interest being charged on 635 shekels. The translator suggests that interest is not charged on the additional three minas and forty-five shekels, but we do not actually know anything other than that this text says nothing about interest on these debts. The 225 shekels could easily be what is left unpaid of a loan on which interest was charged.

We happen to have many documents referencing MNA and have in fact a document from December 30, 504 BC, involving the same parties and recording MNA's payment of the three minas and forty five shekels, again with no mention of interest.[63] It is possible that this portion was secured in some other way—perhaps one involving some form of hidden interest—such as the lender having use of some piece of land until the loan was repaid. We might expect the initial price to have been negotiated to provide risk free benefits to the state and potential, but risky, benefits to the entrepreneur. Since some of the entrepreneur's land, and its revenue, is pledged as collateral for part of the loan until such time as the loan with interest is paid, another document may record the benefits to be secured from the 225 shekels: it would be too much to expect a single piece of property always to be appropriate collateral for any particular loan. It may also be that some personal "consideration" was given to the administrator to avoid interest on part of the loan.

In this period, debts owed were often signed over to others via letters of credit. Thus in Babylon, Šaddinu is able to send another person with a letter of credit to MNA (July 22, 511 BC) and the carrier of the "letter" on receiving only five minas of the debt retains the letter until the debt is paid in full. Presumably the supplementary text recording this partial payment is all that has survived.[64]

We have mentioned that usufruct to prebendal properties could be assigned to third parties in Ancient Mesopotamia. A more sophisticated transfer of debt can be dated to Babylon in 502 BC:[65]

> *Summary*: Bēl-upaḫḫir has until 10 Šabāt of King Darius' 20th year to bring documentation of whatever he has paid of his debt to MNA's slave Madānu-bēla-uṣur. If he has not done so by the 15th of Šabāt he will have to pay to MNA the "silver" owed to Madānu-bēla-uṣur corresponding to the debts of silver, barley, dates and cattle according to the promissory notes for each. Nine witnesses, scribe, place and date.

What is most interesting about this document is that it reassigns a series of debts owed to one person, a slave, to the slave's owner within the compass of a single document by simply relying on details included only within a series of other documents. This seems to imply that all the miscellaneous debts had been assessed in silver in the original promissory notes and that payment only in silver will be accepted after the 15th of Šabāt. The debtor is allowed to provide evidence of partial payment up to the 10th of Šabāt, then is apparently allowed five days leeway; and, then from that point on becomes obligated to the slave owner for any outstanding debt. There is evidence that the slave had died already at the time of this document, so it really represents the assumption by the slave owner of credit owed to his slave.

Madānu-bēla-uṣur was one of MNA's senior slaves, and so it is probable that MNA assumed management of the debt for the benefit of the slave's estate, and is not simply taking back what was already his.[66] Credit transacted for MNA would already have had MNA's name in the documents. Exactly when the ancient prohibition on lending to slaves (*Laws of Eshnunna 16*) disappeared is not clear, but 1,270 years provides ample time for some social transformation. Despite many differences, the parallels between this transaction and transfers of credit and mortgages from one bank or person to another so common in our own time, a further 2,500 years later, are extraordinary.

Banking institutions, depending how one defines them, could be thought to date from the grain storage activities of the early Sumerian temples. We know that by Ur III many accounts both of individual merchants and of the palace were regularly glossed consistently in terms of the silver value of each commodity.[67] Although this "accounting currency" was not real market money this innovation in convertibility brings the possibility of a proper bank closer. Yet, if we focus on deposit banks in which clients voluntarily deposited funds, in expectation of a return, while allowing the bankers to invest the funds as they saw fit, other than the possibility of legal sanction, then it is clear that such deposit banks date from a much later period.

As we will see later, Greek bankers had such independent agency by the fifth century BC. There is reason to believe that this type of deposit bank saw its first development in Babylon and the earliest such bank for which we have adequate evidence is that of House Egibi whose financial affairs can be followed in some detail over four generations from 635–480 BC: exhibiting a continuity of practice from the Neo-Babylonian Period into the Persian period. Initially, House Egibi's financial activities were similar to those of many earlier wealthy businesses; varied, profitable and including loans, but using only family funds. From the late seventh century BC, extended family members, then other associates, contributed capital to investments made by House Egibi and documents suggest that deposits earned a 20 percent rate of return. Many texts also document the deposit of funds with House Egibi, by a range of individuals, male and female, in the form of securities for their own economic ventures. The depositor, unlike House Egibi, could not access the funds without the consent of the other party to such a venture—until a judge concluded no debts were still extant between the two parties.[68] The clear agency of House Egibi over deposits made by others qualifies as a new financial advance.

MESOPOTAMIAN LEGACIES

As Mesopotamians and Sir Isaac Newton discovered, a semiotic approach can motivate useful research or confuse the mind. In our era, words, too, can both convey useful information and mislead thought. The term market, like that of bank, has been used to cover an extraordinary range of different phenomena. In the Mesopotamian period, markets existed to facilitate commercial transactions but did not exist in the modern abstract sense of an efficient price structure that provided a valuation, among other commodities, of all the key factors of production at efficient levels—efficient in the sense of optimally useful for near term productive investment. Palace and temple households as well as elite private households had significant control of most labor and most land. It would be anachronistic to imagine paying, in a period without a proper currency, a "market price" for either labor or land and expecting to make a normal rate of return on the investment. This claim is quite different than recognizing that, with appropriate connections and influence, profits were regularly made from ownership or control of land and labor.

Much confusion is created by thinking in terms of the presence, absence or prominence of markets rather than looking to the characteristics of the price structure for key productive inputs. To further complicate the issue in Mesopotamia, labor costs varied from minimal for slave labor or labor tied to land already controlled, to high when labor was scarce and had to be hired in the market. In such an economy, neither potential income nor typical market prices, by themselves, predict investment value or average costs and, not insignificantly, considerable profits can often be obtained by using social ties to enhance investment opportunities. This is true even in the much later feudal period in Europe which did have a fairly developed currency.[69]

It would be more defensible to argue that social negotiation, which may have included varied considerations such as social position and family or institutional ties, would, along with risk and opportunity, have had important roles in the determination of rates of return. In the course of time, a recognition of a need for adaptability became the norm as *commenda* contracts came to dominate trade and oriented returns toward flexible rates via specified shares in whatever profits or losses were obtained. We noted that state production in Ur III appears to have been conceptualized in terms of loans to foremen with incentives for efficient levels of production built into the loan structure. It seems reasonable to assume that major state or temple or private estate participation in and support for commerce and production long predated the extant documentation, and that this represented a significant and enduring societal endorsement of lending itself, which was viewed as having instrumental agency and contributing to the general expectation of increase, within an increasingly accepted social hierarchy.

Legal compendia (cases) of Mesopotamian states consistently specified different punishments based on social status, even as they often exhibited more gender equality than class or ethnic equality. The many punishments that had to do with commercial practice seem to be imbued with concerns over social capital as manifested in social networks, class, prestige and institutional ties. While we have much better material on this for later periods such as the Early Roman Republic, we would argue that it is critical to read even the Mesopotamian record with an eye to social capital and networks of influence.

The gradual transformation through time of lending practices into better specified and more sophisticated forms, valid over a wide range of political territories, recognized the ways in which the customs and infrastructure of the financial sector provided sources of revenue. Increasing specificity addressed issues of risk, particularly in the private sector, by relying on the possibilities of legal sanctions rather than institutional sanction, writ broadly. As more and more issues were incorporated explicitly into financial documents, loan flexibility also enabled the continued recognition of social capital, even as this ended up raising broader ethical issues, revealed in law cases. Such issues, for example, were related to the antique perception that when loans were roughly between social equals, shared risk and advantage ought to be more equal.

By the Old Assyrian Period a broad social range of private merchants engaged in supra-local trade, as well as participated in the regulation of trade, and it became customary across the Mesopotamian world to include a rich set of loan conditions in explicit written form. By Old Babylonian times, the specification of an oath began to disappear from loan contracts. As it became customary for more conditions to be specified the requirement of an oath became less cogent. Perhaps, as many merchants engaged in trade in towns where they were relative strangers and, more significantly, not local residents, the polytheistic religious traditions and the prominence of different gods in particular localities made the oath a less useful part of a loan document which already included a number of clearly spelled out provisions to help the creditor collect what might be due.

The extraordinary financial record that has survived, thanks to the durability of cuneiform tablets, provides the most complete record of credit and finance for any early civilization. Still, it would be a mistake to refuse to imagine what is not explicitly documented. We know that by 1822 BC, accountants were tracking expenditures in a spreadsheet form with summation both across rows and down columns to enable accurate assessments. Palaces, temples and elite merchants were regularly tied into extensive long distance trade networks and there were elaborate social hierarchies in place. In the first millennium BC, financial practice created written documents enabling both loan transfers and the recognition of collateral in sufficiently flexible forms to accommodate a wide range of social reliability and social capital. These sophisticated forms more explicitly reveal a recognition of networks of social and cultural capital that undoubtedly existed in earlier periods but were hidden behind the sparse documentation of temple lending or perhaps were dealt with primarily through oral discussions and social custom.

In early Sumerian times, interest itself may have been seen as both natural and ethical because people and things had internalized an originally religious obligation to increase and promote the prosperity of the gods. Even inanimate things served as a locus for divine signs and living things (plants and animals) contributed to divine goals when they increased. People, institutions, and governments may have all been "on board" with this project. This attitude seems to have been anything but ephemeral. A hymn to Šamaš, recovered from the library of Assurbanipal praises lending at standard rates but disparages lending at exorbitant rates.[70] In a polytheistic world it might not seem morally problematic that the gods of different cities, though, according to myth, engaged in similar projects, would often be in conflict with each other. Nevertheless, we may imagine how fundamental lending was in early Mesopotamia by remembering that early Sumerian cities, such as Lagash and Umma, could imagine resolving a territorial dispute through a lease of land (ca. 2400 BC) packaged as an apparently standard loan at 33 percent interest.

NOTES

1. Robson, *Mesopotamian Mathematics: 2100–1600 BC*, v.
2. Gelb, Steinkeller, and Whiting, *Earliest Land Tenure Systems*, chapter 1 of the text volume provides general conclusions from which these remarks derive.
3. Gelb, Steinkeller, and Whiting, 140–51.
4. The contributors to Gibson and Biggs, *The Organization of Power* provide an overview of these reforms and of the social hierarchies, as exemplified in administrative and personal seals, in Ur III. In particular, Zeitler, chapter 6, suggests that the chief administrator of the temple of Inanna at Nippur was an inheritable position. Winter, chapter 5, establishes both the relative independence of merchants and their social position below that of high level administrators through an analysis of cylinder seals.
5. Steinkeller, "The Ur III Period," in Westbrook and Jasnow, *Security for Debt in Ancient Near Eastern Law*, 57.
6. Steinkeller, "The Ur III Period," in Westbrook and Jasnow, 57, states the scholarly consensus is that lenders were objective-oriented, to acquire use of land or goods, not profit-oriented and so rates of interest were primarily intended to be prohibitive to assure the security for the loan stayed in the hands of the lender.
7. Steinkeller, "The Ur III Period," in Westbrook and Jasnow, 49.
8. The figure of daily wage is controversial because of ambiguities both about the time period intended and the status of the recipient: a single person cannot consume 5 liters of grain in a day but a large family could well do so. Some accounting examples even seem to make more sense interpreted as 7 sila for a week.
9. Steinkeller, "The Ur III Period," in Westbrook and Jasnow, 53. Steinkeller suggests 1 *bur* = 18 *iku* (1 *iku* = 3600 m^2) of land would produce 30 *gur* of barley equal

to the weight of 30 shekels of silver. Taking the square root of (3.6 times 3600 m^2 = 12,960) we get a field of 113.84 meters on a side.

10. Steinkeller, "The Ur III period," in Westbrook and Jasnow, 57. Steinkeller suggests that it may have been the man's wife who was pledged.

11. Postgate, *Early Mesopotamia,* 187. Since prebendal land was a key payment to institutional functionaries this suggests an economic situation in which assets, comprising packages of land and labor, including usufruct rights to these packages were readily evaluated at their productive value. Such loans of prebendal land originating from state or temple institutions to third parties might have been made by those who needed to repay debts or by functionaries who had a surfeit of lands—in lieu of commercializing the production from some of those lands.

12. Early records specify interest of 20 percent, 24 percent, and 33 percent—see main text below for examples. Debt explicitly bearing interest may have first arisen in Sumer (in the third millennium BC) as temples endeavored to standardize debt payments from merchants involved in long distance trade (southern Mesopotamia needed metals, stone, and other raw materials and was dependent on long distance trade) perhaps originating as fines for late repayment of loans. More generally, early lending at interest may have been primarily linked to foreign trade. Hudson, "Reconstructing the Origins of Interest-Bearing Debt and the Logic of Clean Slates," in Hudson and Mieroop, *Debt and Economic Renewal,* 21–24, 42.

13. Hudson, Reconstructing the Origins of Interest-Bearing Debt and the Logic of Clean Slates. Hudson and Mieroop, 23–24. Hudson, "How interest rates were set," also notes that much later the initial rate of interest in Greece was 10 percent in line with their *dekate*, while in Rome it was 1/12 in line with their duodecimal system (based on twelve months in a year). That later ages generally accepted lower rates, given the choice of unit available, probably reflects some degree of progress (from the debtors point of view) and is not just a result of convenience.

14. Magid, "Sumerian Early Dynastic Royal Inscriptions," in Chavalas, *The Ancient Near East*, 7–8, 14.

15. Mieroop, "A History of Near Eastern Debt," in Hudson and Mieroop, 64–65.

16. Foster, "Ebla and the Origins of Akkadian Accountability," 298–306.

17. Nissan, Damerow and Englund, *Archaic Bookkeeping*, 88.

18. Robson, *Mathematics in Ancient Iraq*, 73.

19. This is a summary of and comment on the translation of Nissan et al.'s figure 69 (discussed in Nissan, Damerow, and Englund, 83–85). At this time the barley measures were 10 sila = 1 bán, 6 bán = 1 barig, and 5 barig = 1 gur.

20. Nissen, Damereow, and Englund, 88. While it is true that ancient states from the Indus to the Nile had numerous obligatory holidays it is more plausible that these would simply impact the annual level of productivity than the level of productivity in this ledger. Nor is it plausible that men had one in ten days off due to state holidays and women had one in six days off for the same reason. Laborers presumably had to perform some work in households even during holidays yet there is no evidence for a simple labor legislation for work by prebendal labor, or even for captives or slaves in greater Mesopotamia. Exactly why Nissen et al. interpret the tablet as indicative of holidays is unclear. It is much simpler to assume specific days of labor inputs are just

that and they are in effect part of a loan to an overseer who is expected to provide a return given an incentive to do so.

21. Similarly, Nissen, Damereow, and Englund find (p. 83) laborers missing in an account from the Fara period city of Šuruppak (figure 66a, p. 80) but of these ten are listed explicitly as not to be counted (without giving reasons but presumably there were reasons) so those missing from the summation are 73 and inputs add up to a total of 733 laborers. If we assume an overseer has a 10 percent incentive for male labor then the nominal summation is in fact his obligation (660) not an elementary arithmetic error. In general, apparent mistakes may suggest residual modern misunderstanding not archaic incompetence. Some accounts may list labor obligations and others list provisions of labor to an overseer and they may be summed differently accordingly. This interpretation may be supported by difference in two tablets (66a and 66b) such as the notation on 66b that the labor is assigned to someone ("given over to") while 66a seems self contained, and possibly a foreman / overseer's own account, that makes no reference to another individual.

22. Actually 11.09 percent. If we assume that the 620 days to be reimbursed have to be reimbursed at five-sixths the level he makes from the 1,232 days then he really would also get one-sixth of those days for a total of 1,336 days or 12 percent of the total.

23. Nissan, Damerow, and Englund, 83, note that such quotas were not established until Ur III times.

24. Johnson and Garfinkle, *Growth of the Early State*, 79–80.

25. Sharlach, *Provincial Taxation in the Ur III State*. This major study is based primarily on the archives of Umma, Lagash, and Puzriš-Dagan during the reign (forty years) of Shulgi and Ibbi-Sin using about 37,000 tablets.

26. Steinkeller, "The Administrative and Economic Organization of the Ur III State: The Core and the Periphery," in Gibson and Biggs, 22, 25, 28, 32.

27. Sharlach, 121.

28. Hickman, *Organization of Manual Labor in Ur III*.

29. Originally published in 1897 by Thureau-Dangin; I have taken this from Sharlach, 71ff.

30. Michalowski, "Charisma and Control," in Gibson and Biggs, 51.

31. Hudson, "Reconstructing the Origins of Interest-Bearing Debt and the Logic of Clean Slates," in Hudson and Mieroop, 12.

32. AUCT 3 492 (collated from photographs). Cited in Steinkeller, "Money-Lending Practices in Ur III Babylonia: The Issue of Economic Motivation," in Hudson and Mieroop, 109–137, especially pp. 130–31.

33. Since Steinkeller, Ibid. suggests that 18 *iku* produce 30 *gur* (1 *gur* = 300 liters, 1 *iku* yields 500 liters) of barley, so 1500 *iku* would yield 750,000 liters. He concludes the lender owns the land and receives the output and that interest charged constitutes the cost of the labor needed to harvest the land. Unfortunately his calculations of what that might amount to make too many unreasonable assumptions in my view. Among other assumptions he claims there must be a 33 percent rate being charged (30,000 liters) even though there is no reference to this in the document.

34. Robson, *Mathematics in Ancient Iraq*, 71, provides an account from Ur III Umma recording forty laborers for one day of harvest, fifty-two laborers for one day making sheaves and spreading them on the threshing floor and forty laborers for one day threshing.

35. See also Siegel, "Slavery during the third dynasty of Ur."

36. Steinkeller, "Money-Lending Practices in Ur III Babylonia: The Issue of Economic Motivation," in Hudson and De Mieroop, 109–137, especially 119ff. Steinkeller instead suggests a 20 liter per man-day wage equivalent in his discussion of this document based on an assumption of a 33 percent standard interest rate for the period in question yet he notes that both institutional wages and wages in private employment may have been 6–10 liters per day (p. 119 and 129). His argument also leads him to conclude some loan documents imply a prevailing thirty-two liter agricultural wage in one case. Steinkeller suggests these putative abnormally high wages simply reflect the labor shortages of the Ur III period. This insistence on standard interest rates but wildly variable wages is implausible in the extreme: everything we know from credit studies suggests different creditors can access different rates much more easily than agricultural labor can get superb wages and the presence of standard interest in this case may simply be unjustified.

37. Steinkeller, "Money-Lending Practices in Ur III Babylonia: The Issue of Economic Motivation," in Hudson and Mieroop, 109–137, especially 128.

38. See discussion of literature in Skaist, *Old Babylonian Loan Contract*, Ur III loan contracts are discussed in Chapter 6, especially pp. 224ff, the rest of the book deals with the Old Babylonian period.

39. Barjamovic, Hertal, and Larsen, *Ups and Downs at Kanesh*.

40. Veenhof and Eidem, *Mesopotamia*, 90–93.

41. Barjamovic, Hertal, and Larsen, *Ups and Downs at Kanesh,* 75.

42. Veenhof and Eidem, 92–93.

43 Larsen, "Partnerships in the Old Assyrian Trade," 119–45, especially 125. See also Robson, *Mathematics in Ancient Iraq*, 135.

44. Veenhof, "'Modern' features in Old Assyrian Trade," 336–66, especially p. 345.

45. Veenhof and Eidem, 92–96.

46. Wells and Magdalene, *Law from the Tigris to the Euphrates*, 99: The case of the elusive debtors.

47. Finley, "Debt Bondage and the Problem of Slavery," in Shaw and Saller, *Economy and Society in Ancient Greece*, 150–166. This idea is discussed at length for the Babylonian case by Steinkeller, "Money-Lending Practices in Ur III Babylonia: The Issue of Economic Motivation," in Hudson and Mieroop, 109–37.

48. The extensive number of edicts forgiving debt in the ancient world are discussed in Hudson and Mieroop, Ibid. Charpin, "Les prêteurs et la palais: les édits de mîšarum des rois de Babylone et leurs traces dans les archives privies," in Bongenaar, *Interdependency of Institutions*, 185–211 supports an alternative explanation that the surviving evidence implies the greatest number of debts were incurred in the years immediately preceding a mîšarum edict and that the edicts were themselves a response to unusually high levels of indebtedness.

49. Robson, *Mathematics in Ancient Iraq*, 166, provides this table which I have slightly modified: although the figures add up correctly they only do so on the assumption that they involve ĝeš and ĝešu (10 ĝeš) whereas Robson inadvertently puts šaru rather than ĝešu even though in her Appendix she correctly glosses šaru as 36,000 sila or 600 ĝeš. In the cuneiform, numbers are shown only in a place system; neither words (ĝeš or šaru) would be provided whereas the words from the metrological system (gur, barig, ban, sila) are represented in the cuneiform.

50. Park, *Early Trends*, 293–330.

51. We follow Michael Hudson, Reconstructing the Origins of Interest-Bearing Debt and the Logic of Clean Slates in Hudson and Mieroop, 14–15 in this reconstruction though we would emphasize the complexity of accounting and book-keeping in an era before most commodities were valued primarily in terms of a monetary price that made them easily commensurable. Kula, *An Economic Theory of the Feudal System*, has stressed that there were intractable problems associated with pretending the market priced things reasonably prior to the development of a truly capitalist system.

52. BM 80644. Charpin, "*Marchands du palais*," 32. Date is second millenium but chronology is debatable so assigning a specific year is not very useful at this point.

53. Mieroop, "Credit as a Facilitator of Exchange in Old Babylonian Mesopotamia," in Hudson and Mieroop, 166–67. This may imply that one *iku* of land can be expected to produce significantly more than 60 liters of grain but exactly how much more is unclear—presumably the number reflects both normal interest given expected yields. Missing text has been interpolated [] or () by the translator. For an overview of land ownership see, Renger, "Institutional, Communal and Individual Ownership," 269–319.

54. Article 8 of the Code of Hammurabi, for example, states that theft from a "god" or "palace" must be restored 30-fold while theft from the lower classes, *mushkinu*, requires 10-fold repayment. Edgerton, "Amêlu and Mushkênu in the Code of Hammurabi," 62, pointed out that in general the elites, *amêlu*, were compensated for offenses against them more highly than commoners.

55. Hudson and Mieroop provide numerous examples of states periodically forgiving agricultural debt and even argue that this was a norm.

56. Skaist, *Old Babylonian Loan Contract*, 23–25). Scholars have suggested that the need for the oath implied that borrowers could not be held legally responsible for at least some conditions of the loan so they took an oath to use religious belief and public regard to shore up their credibility in the eyes of the lender. Given the importance of public regard even in the Roman era this is a strong argument. "He borrowed" is Kohler's translation of šu ba-an-ti, see discussion in Skaist, 22–26. Norman Yoffee (personal communication) suggests "took / received" is a better translation. Skaist, 207, notes that the use of the oath in loan contracts during the Old Babylonian period was almost entirely limited to loan contracts from Ur and even there it was not universal.

57. UET 5 323 translation by Kienast, cited and reinterpreted in Skaist, 206–7.

58. This is a brief reclassification of the list provided by Skaist, 26, 207.

59. Yoffee, "Aspects of Mesopotamian Land Sales," 127.

60. Jursa, "Debts and Indebtedness in the Neo-Babylonian Period: Evidence from the Institutional Archives," in Hudson and Mieroop, 197–220.

61. Jursa. Ibid., 199. NB: 60 shekels = 1 mina. Interest rate calculation example (Capital = 70 shekels): 70/60 = 1 1/6 mina, 12 shekels per mina per year = 14 shekels, divide by 70 shekels = 20 percent.

62. Dar 453 / BM 31423 dated to Babylon in 31 January 504 BC. Abraham, *Business and Politics under the Persian Empire*, 433–35. My summary of Abraham's translation.

63. Document Dar 472 (duplicate of BM 31977, dated December 30, 504 BC. Abraham, 438–39.

64. Abraham, 264–65.

65. Abraham, 441. My summary of Abraham's translation.

66. Abraham, 442.

67. Ouyang, *Monetary Role of Silver*, uses the somewhat misleading term "balanced" for such accounts meaning not that the inputs and outputs are balanced but that the balance is calculated in silver.

68. Bogaert, *Les origines antiques*, 105–18.

69. Kula, *Economic Theory of the Feudal System*, has long since made this point in the context of Poland between 1500 and 1780.

70. The hymn includes the lines, "The honest merchant who pays loans by the—standard, thereby to make extra virtue, is pleasing to Šamaš, he will grant him extra life, he will make (his) family numerous, he will acquire wealth." Translation by Foster in 1993, cited in Monroe, "Money and Trade," in Snell, *A Companion to the Ancient Near East*, 176–77. It is unclear to scholars when the original of this hymn was composed.

Chapter Three

Financing Ancient Egypt's Organizational Economy

In this chapter, though we talk about justice, we cannot even begin to do justice to the astonishing richness and artistic creativity that contributed to the resilience of ancient Egyptian society for nearly three thousand years. The work of many brilliant Egyptologists goes some way to doing that, but even a visit to Egypt or to a museum can only provide a glimpse of its aesthetic splendor. We will draw attention to the Egyptian genius for soliciting long term financial projects using recurring surpluses to motivate long-term endowments designed to generate income and employment. By focusing on what we believe to be the key aspects motivating ancient Egypt's financial and economic prosperity, we hope to shed light on the interconnections between chaos, cultural creativity, and the resilience that enabled its long-term productivity. We will argue that in the context of a chaotic riverine flood system that produced frequent surpluses, cultural and religious factors created a milieu that motivated the development of a system of credit and investment allowing Egypt's organizational economy to continuously transform and to remain prosperous for millennia. It may be useful to consider Simon's depiction of our modern organizational economy:

> Suppose that [a mythical visitor from Mars] approaches the Earth from space, equipped with a telescope that reveals social structures. The firms reveal themselves, say, as solid green areas . . . Market transactions show as red lines connecting firms . . . the greater part of the space below it would be within the green areas, for almost all of the inhabitants would be employees . . . Organizations would be the dominant feature of the landscape . . . [the visitor] would be surprised to hear the structure called a market economy . . . Wouldn't "organizational economy" be the more appropriate term . . . The choice of name may matter . . . it may strongly affect our choice of the variables that are important

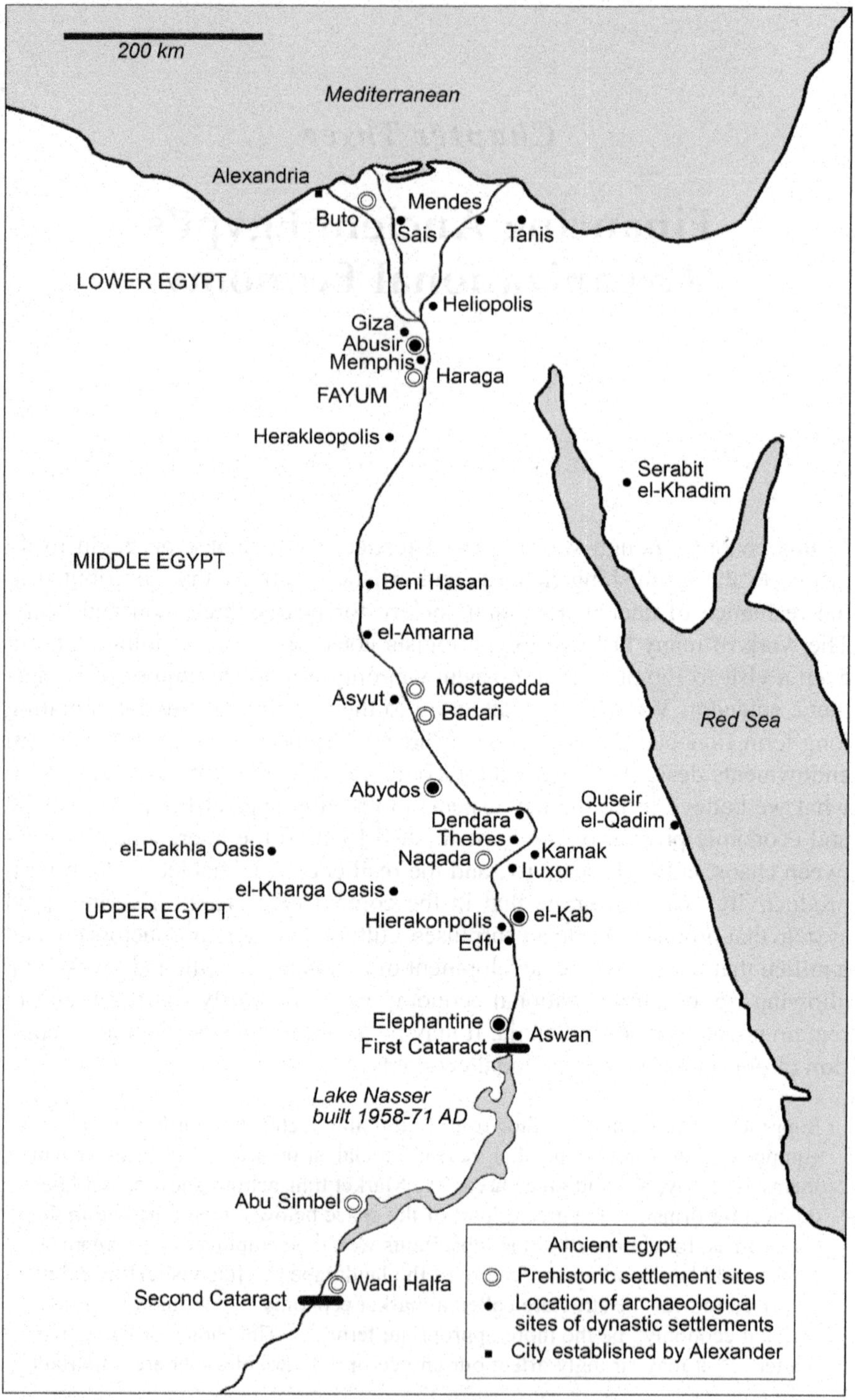

Map 3.1. Ancient Egypt Predynastic to Alexander.

enough to be included in a first-order theory of the phenomena.[1] —Herbert A. Simon

PREHISTORY

What came to be known as ancient Egyptian culture first developed in Upper Egypt, more or less in the center of modern Egypt, along the Naqada bend of the Nile between modern Asyut and Elkab, near modern Luxor. This area of the Nile Valley had proximity to the Eastern and Western deserts and Lower Nubia as well as a relatively short route to the Red Sea. Influence from the Western deserts, Nubia to the south, contact through the Red Sea with Mesopotamia and interaction with cultures in Lower (northern) Egypt combined into a creative "conjuncture" that produced something original and vital. The northern part of this middle stretch of the Nile is associated with the prehistoric Badarian heartland around Qena (especially the sites of Matmar, Mostagedda, and el-Badari) while the southern portion was the center of the Amration prehistoric culture at the Naqada bend of the Nile and south to the first cataract at Elephantine (especially Mahasna, Abydos, Naqada, el-Amra, Elkab).[2] Inhabitants of the region had long engaged in mobile livestock herding, foraging, fishing and, to a lesser extent, hunting. Sometime in the fourth millennium BC they began to engage in flood recession agriculture and to establish sedentary communities in which a significant part of the population did agriculture on the receding edge of the Nile inundation (in the late summer). By about 3100 BC, the basic lineaments of the Old Kingdom, including significant reliance on agriculture, were already in place.

While a cultural mix helped give rise to ancient Egypt's civilization, environmental factors were also at play.[3] These environmental factors are of fundamental importance to understanding the rise of Egyptian civilization and the role that credit played in it from the beginning.

The Nile, north of the first cataract, with the river flowing south to north, and the wind generally coming from the north, is eminently navigable. While the flood plain in Nubia is narrow, once north of Elephantine (the first cataract), the flood plain is much more generous. As the Sahara began to dry up in the late Holocene (5800–4500 BC), the eastern bank of the Nile had flood plains that became increasingly suitable for cultivation as well as ample areas suitable for foraging for wild birds and game. Fekri Hassan argues that major fluctuations in flood levels can be documented from 8000 BC onward, and that severe droughts occurred regularly during this period.[4]

Only near the end of the predynastic period did the core cultural area in Upper Egypt became significantly dependent on agriculture; and, it is worth emphasizing that the much narrower flood plain in lower Nubia, just to the south had dramatically less agricultural potential.[5] This suggests we would be unwise to disregard Nubian cultural or demographic influences in the early formation of Egyptian civilization, just because its earliest efflorescence was north of the first cataract, and not south of it. Prior to this period, there would have been major commonalities in livelihood strategies and significant cultural mixing.

While early scholars were at great pains to insist influences on early Egyptian civilization came from peoples of the Fertile Crescent, more recent scholarship has been decidedly happier to recognize the originality of Egyptian civilization; and, what it owed to the great cultural diversity of the upper (southern) Egyptian region. While in time, Egyptian civilization used an extensive collection of canals and dykes to optimize use of the annual flood, this level of infrastructure investment would not initially have been needed. Flood recession agriculture around natural depressions has the highest returns to labor of any agricultural system. In such systems, the annual flood renews the soil and provides sufficiently long periods of inundation to make agriculture possible on appropriate soils (*ceteris paribus* those with adequate clay content) without subsequent rainfall.[6] Flood recession technology involving small dykes to retain or release or connect water in natural depressions, is not only adequate in areas of relatively low population levels, but also much more practical than building extensive infrastructure.

This low level technology takes full advantage of the contributions of nature: it maximizes annual returns to labor while minimizing the losses to infrastructure in years of high flood. In the course of time, the variability in the flood and concentration of populations in particular areas, probably encouraged the development of social hierarchy to deal with flood variability, enabling *de facto* the harnessing of those lower in the hierarchy as a labor force to build increasingly extensive infrastructure that provided both somewhat greater stability to societal production levels; and, helped to facilitate the support of the expertise that is the hallmark of civilization.[7]

We may infer from recent work that the annual variability in the Nile flood made adequate inter-annual water storage quite impossible, even when Egyptian civilization was at its height, even though it was heavily invested in grain storage. Thus, when hydrologist Hurst was asked to calculate the optimal size of a dam on the Nile, he concluded that no such optimum could be calculated.[8] This early recognition that the flood pattern did not have a simple mean useful for calculating an optimum led the first mathematician interested in chaos theory, Benoit Mandelbrot, and James Wallis to write an article confirming through mathematical analysis the chaotic nature of the Nile flood.[9] Their cogent points are first, that a chaotic flood has no optimal estimator; in other words, the mean of any particular sequence of years is not an unbiased estimator of any following period. This means that a sequence of low levels has no implication that it will imminently be followed by more of the same or by higher levels. The second implication is that, though the flood is a deterministic system, its unpredictable levels result from nature adding up unpredictable rainfall from a variety of upstream watersheds whose subsequent riverine surges can end up additive or sequential in time to unforeseen degrees. Both factors lead to increase unpredictability of the height of the flood or the duration of the high level mark, even as the total volume of the flood is directly dependent on total precipitation within the collective watersheds.

Each of these factors has relevance for which areas and which parts of the Nile are flooded and for how long the waters are high enough to create the soil moisture levels needed to sustain subsequent agriculture. The topography of a flood plain varies significantly, and because annual floods bring topsoil with them, the topography is rearranged each year. A small difference in annual flood height, therefore can have unpredictable impacts on the surface area inundated. Given that downstream areas are affected by how much water is retained upstream, because they are flooded later, it is not surprising that ancient Egypt had nilometers up and down the Nile and decentralized the decision making for opening and closing canals and dykes to the level of the nome: effectively providing at least forty-two different decision making regions.

The few high level mark measurements available for the first five dynasties indicate a ninefold range (from about 20 inches to about 180 inches) in the annual flood and these fluctuate dramatically—though many years nevertheless are missing in this sequence, a mere fifteen of the sequential readings have a range that is within fifteen inches.[10] Subsequent periods, however, are better documented, (e.g., 650–1550 AD). While these show similar ranges of fluctuation, they also demonstrate the complete inutility for prediction of even decadal averages.[11]

This unpredictability effectively weakens any hypothesis that the recourse to grain storage dramatically facilitated the development of civilization. It is likely that such variability, once settlements began to rely on the potentially high returns from flood recession agriculture, would have posed a political problem. In years of low flood levels, quarreling over access to relatively scarce land obviously is a less desirable solution to this problem than is establishing a social hierarchy that lets people with lower status know what to expect; and, hence, encourages them to be prepared to focus on livestock raising or other livelihood strategies when necessary. This system is known from other flood recession regimes such as that of the Senegal River where the status hierarchy among a single ethnic group maintains dual livelihood strategies—agricultural vs. pastoral. There, agriculturalists are allocated land first and pastoralists engage in agriculture only as a secondary activity when floods are excellent and land is available.

Thus we can imagine flood variability first promoting hierarchy as a way to deal with riverine fluctuations and consequent food shortages. Subsequently, it is probable that this hierarchy took on other social functions, such as promoting a long-term religious perspective to better justify social inequality. In other flood recession regimes, hierarchies are often based on a "founders first" principle, and late-comers have only secondary rights.[12] Given the range of livelihood options in the early Nile (including foraging, livestock raising and fishing), the existence of a social hierarchy might have simply meant that many people had to resort to something other than agriculture to a greater or lesser extent in particular years. One might imagine that given initially low population levels, people might simply move away from existing settlements to cultivate somewhere else on the floodplain. For security reasons, however, it is likely that in order to be less susceptible to raiding or depredations of livestock, agriculture would have been concentrated in areas where there were both optimal soils and sufficient population to make it secure.[13] Likewise, the alternative livelihood strategies would have been preferable to risking labor investment on agriculture lands where returns were unreliable.

Perhaps the most important ecological observation we can make here is that significant variability in the level of the Nile's flood is not only well-documented, but has critical implications for grain surpluses in the dynastic period.[14] A grain surplus may be minimally defined as production above the basic requirements of the population. The critical point is that as Malthus much later pointed out, population has the potential to absorb surplus.

Repeated surpluses should thus be seen as a potential oddity calling for an explanation. We would argue that the variability of the Nile flood kept population at far lower levels than could be supported in good years. If inter-annual storage, (that in the Biblical Joseph story[15] is presented as an exceptional grace), was regularly sufficient, then population levels could have been maintained near the long-term mean of production. (LTMP)

In figure 3.1, we can see that given the chaotic nature of the flood with its consequent unpredictably long runs of low flood; and, a complete inability to predict near-term flood levels, population in Dynastic Egypt would have to have been kept at significantly lower levels than the long-term mean production (LTMP). We might define "necessary mean production" (NMP) as the level of production at which a population could be consistently supported and sustained without major social unrest *in poor years,* given the available population, technology, storage capacity, and trade. Actual production (AP)

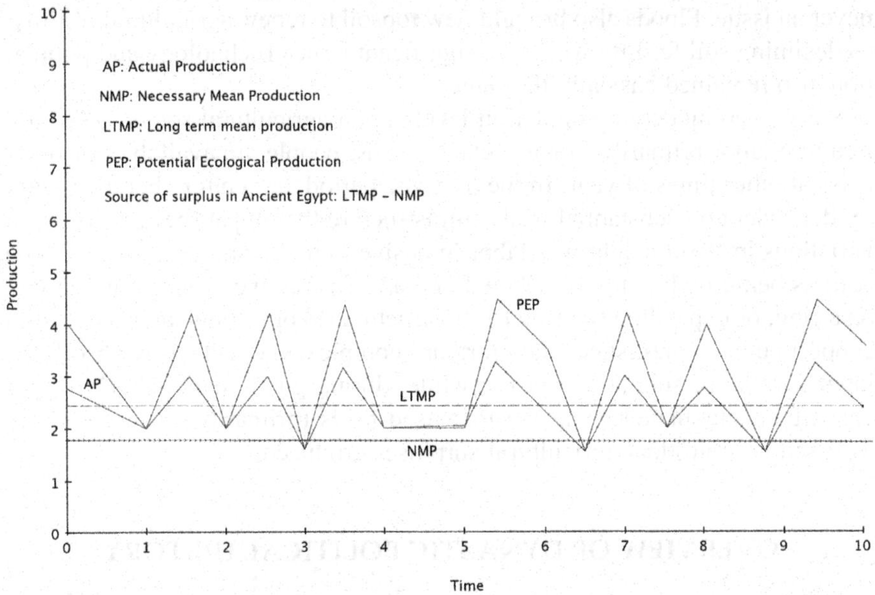

Figure 3.1. Source of Surplus in Ancient Egypt.
Original Plot by Thomas K. Park.

would vary, by definition, around LTMP, and frequently exceed NMP, providing the operative national surplus. The only back up for production below NMP would be storage, and a major trade in staples. Were NMP to approach LTMP, for example, due to population growth, the incidence of social unrest would soar *in poor years,* and society would founder. Limitations in labor supply, technology for production, and storage would have also prevented ancient Egyptians from taking full advantage of potential ecological production (PEP) in good years, though in poor years they might have had the labor and infrastructural resources to extract the full ecological potential.

This implies that the subtraction of societal needs (NMP) from the actual long-term mean production (LTMP) levels would represent an aggregate potential, and actual source of realizable surplus that would be available for sociocultural projects including monumental construction, armies and foreign trade. Egypt's reputation for endless grain surpluses, itself an exaggeration, would have been due not just to the fertility of the soil, and its endless renewal through flooding, but just as importantly to the relatively low population levels that for ecological reasons were the norm. Egypt was special in a number of additional ways. Due to the substantial difference between the water level at flood, and the water table the rest of the year, salinization was never an issue. Floods also brought new topsoil to renew agricultural fertility, so declining soil fertility was not a significant issue. Technology and population also remained basically the same.

Since even moderate population levels in an agricultural society need agriculture labor primarily in particular seasons, people are available for other tasks at other times of year. In the dynastic period, agriculture became heavily dependent on substantial water infrastructure that in part because of large variations in flood height was labor intensive to maintain. Floods have to be seen as being both potentially beneficial and destructive. Thus, maintaining, restoring, or expanding the water infrastructure (to open new lands needed to support new temples, state, and mortuary complexes) could easily absorb the labor surplus of suboptimal years; while, during good years, labor's wages could be accumulated using the increased taxes (primarily but not entirely assessed in grain) that agricultural surpluses produced.

OVERVIEW OF DYNASTIC POLITICAL HISTORY

Modern social science is interested both in the links between investment and productivity; and, in what enhances creativity, including political creativity. Ancient Egypt, despite its unification in most periods, was based on a decentralized system of administration that recognized twenty southern nomes and twenty-two northern nomes, each of which had a sufficiently distinct ecology that they were differentially impacted by floods. This decentralized system encouraged both the diversity of temples devoted to specific gods, and the continual efforts of kings during different reigns to refurbish or enhance the temples to them; and, to spread that investment out among the various nomes—with particular emphasis on key areas in Upper and Lower Egypt. For nearly three thousand years, unification was an ongoing political, cultural, and economic project funded by investments of the surplus and motivated by Egyptian cultural and religious conceptions.

Egyptian conceptions pinned hopes of the afterlife on dying in Egypt, while Egyptian cultural understandings held that Egyptians were intrinsically superior to other ancient societies. These basic perspectives precluded incentives to live elsewhere. The main long-term settlements outside the Nile valley proper were in the oases to the West. Ancient Egypt had an almost complete lack of interest in foreign colonies, and maintained strong preferences for self-sufficiency in culture, religion and economy. Control of a wider area less susceptible to chaotic fluctuations in production could have sustained a population sufficient to put pressure on long-term productive capacities but, that this did not happen cannot be inconsequential to the long-term flourishing of ancient Egypt.

The basic political structure of dynastic Egypt symbolized Upper Egypt by a white crown and Lower Egypt by the red crown. This duality meant that a proper king had to be king of a unified Egypt; and, such a king was properly represented wearing a double crown. Egyptians brought symbolic representation to the art form of the double crown. They often depicted it with a ureus (raised cobra: the goddess Wadjet) on the front or added horns of various types to a depiction of a king to symbolize his support of a particular god recognizable in its animal incarnation. The king was regularly represented as having the protection of two titulary goddesses, Wadjet of Lower Egypt, and the vulture goddess of Upper Egypt, Nekhbet.[16]

Similarly, the "sedge" came to symbolize Upper Egypt, while the "bee" came to stand for Lower Egypt. The elaboration of symbolism in political representation was fundamental to the drive to bring imagery up to date with current religious beliefs, and currently popular deities. For almost three thousand years, this enhanced the continual tension that motivated kings to make sure they expended funds on temple building, mortuary cult construction, and symbolic representation in both parts of Egypt. Some kings even had two tombs, one in Upper Egypt (e.g., in the Valley of the Kings) and one in Lower Egypt (e.g., in Giza or Saqqara). Temples in Egypt often followed what is thought to be predynastic styles: a curved roof sloping to the back in Upper Egypt, a flat roof in Lower Egypt. Each style even had a hieroglyphic mini representation. Hieroglyphs at the fourth dynasty step pyramid of Djoser, for example, depicted multiple representations of each type, presumably to emphasize the unity of Egypt.[17]

Egyptologists have divided the dynastic period into an Old Kingdom, a Middle Kingdom, a New Kingdom; and, a Late Dynastic Period separated by first, second, and third intermediate periods. No such periodization, of course, exists in the ancient records. The main criteria Egyptologists use to define such periods has been the apparent disappearance of a unified Upper and Lower Egyptian polity, during epochs when contenders from various parts controlled less than the whole area between the first cataract and the delta. Initially, prejudices for political greatness led scholars to assume anything less than political unification must have automatically involved decline in other areas such as security, welfare, culture and morals. With the development of alternative approaches to history, such as the Annales school (spearheaded by Braudel for European and Mediterranean history), it gradually became apparent to archaeologists and historians, that such a simplistic dependence on political dynamics was less than persuasive.

Administrative and economic systems of dynastic Egypt developed first in upper / southern Egypt around Naqada, Hierakonpolis, and Abydos. The most distinctive features of ancient Egyptian culture including monumental burials, hieroglyphic inscriptions, institutions served by vast numbers of highly skilled craftsmen, and a focus on elaborate material support structures for the afterlife all first appeared between Abydos and Luxor (before 3000 BC); and, are now thought to have developed independently from administrative and economic advances in Mesopotamia.[18]

While this chapter is not the place to provide even a cursory overview of Dynastic Egypt's politics, domestic or foreign, our analysis of the financial structure necessarily involves some basic historical contextualization. Many erudite historical studies are available but the reader of this chapter may want to consult table 3.1, showing dynastic periodization and a few brief remarks.

Unfortunately, while the archaeological record can shed some light on aesthetic standards, and reveal moments of social turmoil, we are still far from a full understanding of what happened to welfare and cultural life during the intermediate periods and few scholars would suggest we are in great shape for Old, Middle, New, or Late periods either—though great monarchs tend to engender more textual evidence that survives than others. There is still a lively debate about most aspects of dynastic Egypt including "classical" views that the intermediate periods represented general decline not just political disunity. However, it is surely more likely that some general decline might have precipitated disunity than that there is a simple one-to-one correspondence between prosperity and unity between 3100 BC and 332 BC. Indeed, if Ptolemaic or Roman history are any guide, unified control did not simply imply economic or cultural prosperity. The nome structure might, in fact, suggest that prosperity throughout dynastic history could be more locally established, and need not have required a unified state.

While many aspects of religious and administrative culture had enormous continuity in Mesopotamia, political control changed repeatedly between 4000 BC and the end of the Neo-Babylonian empire (539 BC). The much greater political continuity in Egypt, despite dynastic changes and intermediate periods, correlates with a much greater institutional stability and development. From our perspective, the real genius of dynastic Egypt was its development of institutions intended to endure the ages. While no temple or mortuary complexes were capable of enduring significant portions of dynastic history, ancient Egyptians aimed at building institutions with long-term financing, and consequently developed the most sophisticated systems of long-term institutional financing in the ancient world. This institutional financing is perhaps one of Egypt's greatest contributions to economic prosperity. We will argue that this sophistication involved a careful imbrication of

Table 3.1. Overview of Egyptian Chronology

Period	*Dates*	*Dynasty*	*Remarks*
Predynastic	c.5300–3000 BC	Naqada I, II, III	Badarian, Amratian, Gerzean (upper Egypt)
Early Dynastic	3000–2686	1st & 2nd	Abydos first capital
Old Kingdom	2686–2160	3rd–6th	Memphis becomes capital, pyramids of Giza, Saqqara
First Intermediate	2160–2055	9th–11th	Multiple records of famine due to low flood levels. Some evidence that this period saw a widening of literary attention and a democratization of the afterlife. 9th and 10th at Herakleopolis. (B.G.T 116)
Middle Kingdom	2055–1650	11th–14th	11th at Thebes, with unified Egypt, 14th and 15th at Avaris in Delta
Second Intermediate	1650–1550	15th–17th	A proliferation of recorded kings with probability high that many reigned simultaneously. 15th = Hyksos dynasty, 16th and 17th at Thebes
New Kingdom	1550–1069	18th	Thebes, Amenhotep IV at Amarna, by end Libyan mercenaries dominate army
Ramesside	1295–1069	19th–20th	Great building projects, military campaigns, and economic upheavals
Third Intermediate	1069–664	21st–25th	Great army comanders control upper Egypt. 22nd dynasty at Tanis. 23rd at Leontopolis. Nubian conquest by Piy established the 25th dynasty (747-c.664). Recentralization by 26th dynasty
Late Dynastic	664–332	26th–30th	1st Persian Period 27th (525–404), 2nd Persian period late 30th (343–332)
Ptolemaic	332–30	Macedonian then Ptolemaic	After Alexander's conquest, the Ptolemaic dynasty was established by Soter I in 305
Roman	30 BC–AD 395	NA	Egypt became a province of Rome under Augustus on August 31, 30 BC
Byzantine / Coptic	395–641 AD	NA	Byzantine power in Egypt ended with the Muslim conquest of Alexandria by 'Amr ibn al-As from 641–3 AD

Source: Dates and details from: Ian Shaw, ed. *The Oxford History of Ancient Egypt*. Oxford University Press, 2000 and B. G. Trigger, B. J. Kemp, D. O'Connor, and A. B. Lloyd. *Ancient Egypt: A Social History*. Cambridge: Cambridge University Press, 2008.

religious and cultural beliefs with institutional forms of behavior; and, one of the most rigorous, even daunting, ethical systems of all time.

LANGUAGE, WRITING, AND MATH

Writing is one of the keys to developing more sophisticated forms of credit. Egyptians developed writing in the fourth millennium BC, and had writing capable of representing full syntax by the late Early dynastic period. Throughout the Old Kingdom, writing was limited to what could be fitted into a strictly defined space, and used non-script forms, tables, layout, and pictorial elements to convey more complex issues.[19] The large corpus of extant Pyramid Texts from the third millennium were inscribed from 2300 BC onward in mortuary contexts, and so remained invisible to all but a few specialists. Personal letters, medical treatises, and magical spells intended for broader use first began to appear around 2400 BC.[20] Almost simultaneously, a cursive form of hieroglyphic writing was developed that used ink to write on papyrus and perishable surfaces.

From the late Early Dynastic period the use of this cursive writing expanded. Although by the time the Greeks gave this Hieratic script its name, it was used primarily for religious purposes. Originally it was used for administration; black ink for the body of a text and red ink for headings and special topics or to distinguish assets/receipts from obligations to the institution. Instructional texts for clerks focused first on the Hieratic, and then secondarily on hieroglyphic forms perhaps because the former had far and away the greatest demand in administration.[21] The native terminology referred to both scripts as *mdw-nṯr*, or "god's words." A third script, Demotic, that came into use in the seventh century BC, derived its name from the Greek word for "popular." Demotic script differed significantly in its use of ligatures to create logograms, which facilitated the speed with which concepts could be written. [22]

The three Egyptian scripts were used almost exclusively for Egyptian, an Afro-Asiatic language, and were rarely used to represent foreign languages.[23] These scripts were thus culturally hegemonic, and extremely stable for several millennia, reflecting almost no dialectal or language shifts.[24] The Pyramid Texts were followed by the Coffin Texts which, though similar, adorned coffins themselves. In time, texts on papyrus, collectively referred to as the Book of the Dead, came to accompany mummies in their tombs and included a wide range of topics and spells to provide the traveler all the instruction necessary for a successful transition to the afterlife.[25] While Egypt's hieroglyphic notation stayed in use from 3250 BC until 400 AD, it was relegated to notations on monuments and walls by 2600 BC. Egyptian hieratic including a base ten ciphered-additive system replaced it on papyri for most records and texts; and, by the seventh century BC a Demotic notation,[26] also using a base 10 ciphered-additive system, joined the Hieratic system, and both continued in use for the next millennium.[27]

POLYTHEISM AND THE GODS OF ANCIENT EGYPT

The Judaic, Christian, and Islamic monotheistic traditions posit an omniscient and omnipotent God. For believers this poses two key logical issues: how is there free will if the future is known; and, why is there evil in the world if God made the world just as it is. These issues have proven quite stimulating to theologians. Polytheistic religions posit gods who though more powerful and more knowledgable than human beings have similar personalities, and so themselves engage in evil or counterproductive activities.[28] From this standpoint, free will is not in jeopardy; and, the existence of evil is merely a given, not a logical paradox. As religious ideas create truth and support the social order, they often play a fundamental role defining codes of conduct and justice. Because such beliefs surround ideas about fairness, they invariably are important to credit, and so need to be looked at carefully.

Ancient Egyptians believed in many gods and goddesses. Some 1,500 are known by name, though we have detailed knowledge for fewer than five hundred of them.[29] As well, each god could have many aspects. These divinities were part of a complex theogony (stories of the origin of the gods) that was connected to a number of cosmogonies (stories of the origin of the universe). Ancient Egyptians also believed both in an afterlife and that there would be an end to the world. The afterlife itself was viewed as being an abode for human beings who were good in this life; and as the dwelling place for the divinities until the end of the world. No set of myths is ever entirely consistent, but Egyptian religion clearly endured for three thousand years in part because it was continuously renewed, reinvented, and reinvigorated; and this involved the waxing and waning of the importance of particular divinities.

Early beliefs included a group of eight or nine initial divinities, while later elaborations frequently focused on triads of gods (e.g., nuclear families—father, mother, and child) or other combinations. Egyptians later elaborated the idea of the potential immanence of one divinity within another. Over time, as particular gods became more or less popular, the less popular ones would be regularly assimilated as a facet of a more currently significant god, thus a single god might bear the name Amun-Re or Ptah-Nun or even Ptah-Sokar-Osiris.

Ancient Egyptians believed both in a basic inescapable order to the world: no one was immune to judgement after death and that even the gods had limitations on their power; so gods too were subject to the laws of the world and in the end would perish with it. Yet, they also believed that human action could be aided or thwarted by the gods; and that both gods and humans could acquire skills in magic (*heka*), dream interpretation, and (within limits) even prophecy. Human dreams were often viewed as one of the ways for gods and humans to communicate. Similarly, magic via oral recitation, recitation plus ritual action, or even the power of declarative statements by powerful people, such as kings or great sorcerers, were seen as efficacious ways to accomplish a wide range of effects, including persuading or even coercing the gods to cooperate or provide help.[30]

The normal practice to write the names of dynastic kings within a cartouche[31] reflects both the magical power of both a king and his name, and the need to protect that name within a magical circle (or oblong in this case). The use of encirclement for protection guided ritual processions to encircle temple precincts. In Egyptian the word for "to go around" was *pekhert*, which is the root of the English word prescription.[32]

The efficacy of human magic was impressive but nevertheless limited. Texts show magicians reviving a drowned person to talk with, but do not show them being able to stop death, or thwart that person's progress after death toward judgment. Importantly, it is as if neither recourse by humans to prayer, ritual, or magic could affect the "balance" of good and evil that individuals commit in this life; and it was this "balance" alone that counted in the end. Divinities could do somewhat more. So while Isis could revive Osiris after his dismemberment by Seth, even briefly restore his member and virility, even her magic had its limitations.[33]

Most of what we know about Egyptian divinities comes from later texts. Even so, they give us clues about earlier periods that are relatively convincing. The Egyptian name for the town of Hermopolis in Middle Egypt was Khemnu, a name that was used at least as early as the fifth dynasty, and meant eight-town, referred to the place where the Sun god came into being. One of the myths, written down much later, was that Hermopolis was the town where the original group of eight deities that represented elements of the original cosmos (which the Greeks referred to as the Ogdoad) were first worshipped. It is certainly plausible that Khemnu got its name from this same myth long before the surviving version was written. Mythology suggests that these eight gods existed as four male-female pairs: Nun and Naunet (water), Heh and Hauhet (infinity), Kek and Kauket (darkness), Amun and Amaunet (hiddenness). Each male and female pair were in a position to create other deities and the world.[34] At the moment of the world's creation, Atun, the sun god was said to have been born out of the primordial flood. Next created were Shu (air) and Tefnut (moisture), then Geb (earth) and Nut (sky), who in turn created Osiris (who became the underworld deity), Ist / Isis (who was greatest of the goddesses and possessed powerful magic), Seth (who was the problem child, the deity of chaos), and finally Nephthys (who was similar to her sister Isis, but primarily viewed as a funerary goddess).

The earliest deities in Egypt for which there is archaeological documentation were zoomorphic, with the earliest perhaps being the cow and the falcon. These two were followed by the jackal, gazelle, ram, and baboon. Eventually as the divinities proliferated even reptile and insect divinities became common. Some early representations show mythical zoomorphic creatures. When anthropomorphic figures appear they often are represented as having an animal aspect or an additional zoomorphic incarnation. The Narmer Pallette (ca. 3000 BC) thus has two long necked mythical creatures: two bovine / human heads and a falcon in prominent positions adorning its two sides along with a king wearing the double crown of unified Egypt and depictions of those conquered / slaughtered.

Other genealogies show deities genealogically related in numerous ways that we need not detail here. Early on sun gods were elevated to responsibility for life itself, for example, Re or Osiris who, fittingly, becomes the judge in the underworld (a transition zone to the afterlife, itself also imagined as in the sky). In time, a number of key divine occupations emerged: attention to prosperity in this world, and an orderly procession to the afterlife; support and provision of aid for the forces available in this world, including military might and the magic needed to maintain order, as well as the sowing of chaos, death, and disorder; and, most fundamentally, insurers of justice as an essential element of both an ordered universe, prosperity in this life, and access to the afterlife. We have space to illustrate these concerns with only a few of the many deities.

While devotion to different divinities over time was the norm, a few early deities—primarily those that helped the king and his government to maintain order—became increasingly important. The god Ptah, the god of craftsmen, is attested in Memphis as early as the first dynasty. In time, he became increasingly important as aesthetic production becomes essential both to temples and to mortuary construction. The Ibis god, Thoth (Djehuty), viewed as the god of scribes and scholars, was represented on predynastic slate palettes. He is mentioned frequently in the Old Kingdom pyramid texts.

Prosperity also requires reproduction as any Marxist would attest. Khnum, a ram god connected with fertility, was thought to control the inundation of the Nile from a base around the first cataract. Because of his association with fertility, Khnum also came to be seen as the god of pottery who shaped all living things on his wheel. The goddess Hathor, the mother of Horus, a cow goddess, represented female sexuality and fertility, and also came to be seen as the goddess who watched over foreign lands and trade. Min, the god associated with male fertility, was depicted in ithyphalic form with his left hand holding his erect penis. The Apis and Mnevis bulls, only one of each existed at a time, were viewed as incarnations of the divine, and so were lavishly cared for during their lives, and after death were embalmed as symbols of strength and of male procreative powers.

Kings were expected to use force to maintain order and to conquer foreign lands; neither, however, was thought to be possible without divine support. Isis who was pre-eminently capable in magic, provided support in war, and conveniently had paramount healing abilities. The goddess Neith, one of the most ancient deities attested in prehistoric and early dynastic times, had multiple manifestations as warrior, creator, mother and funerary goddess. She also had an association with Lower Egypt, and so was often shown wearing the red crown of Lower Egypt. Nekhbet, the vulture goddess, who is often depicted wearing the white crown of Upper Egypt, was associated with El Kab (south of Luxor), and served as a tutelary goddess. The sky god, Horus, the falcon was depicted as a tutelary deity for kingship itself, such that all kings had a Horus name (among their five names). Horus had an early cult center in Hieronkonpolis (south of Thebes). Eventually, Horus, under the name Re-Horakhty, became assimilated to the sun god. Order after death was also critical. The scorpion goddess, Serket, provided protection for the coffins of the dead so that progress to the afterlife could proceed unimpeded. Anubis, the jackal god, was called the lord of the West, and was often depicted as sitting as a guide in the boats that the dead used to cross the underworld into the afterlife.

In addition to Seth, the brother of Isis and Osiris, the crocodile god, Sobek, is mentioned in the pyramid texts as the "raging one," and as the son of Neith. Another god particularly associated with primeval and continuing chaos was Apophis, the huge serpent god. Apophis was associated with dissolution, darkness and non-being; and, was thought nightly to try to hinder the sun god Re as he crossed through the underworld from rising again in the East. Apophis, also, devoured the unjust, and any who ventured to cross into the afterlife without proper instruction. At the end of time, the world was expected to dissolve back into primordial chaos, despite all the efforts of deities and others. The distinction between constructive and destructive deities was not always clear. The lioness goddess, Sekhmet, known as the mistress of red linen, was both depicted as a stupendous aid in war, and as an enormously destructive goddess associated with plagues and slaughter. A formal rite developed to appease Sekhmet and ward off her seven arrows of misfortune. Khonsu, the moon god, was a bloodthirsty deity in the Pyramid texts, but later came to have healing powers, and morphed into Khonsu "the decider of the lifespan."

The goddess Maat whose name came to mean truth, justice, and cosmic order was associated with Osiris (as the very judgment imposed by Osiris in the underworld), but was usually viewed in mythology as the wife of Thoth. She was also in a sense the order imposed on the cosmos; one that had to be continually maintained to be preserved. Her association with Thoth suggests the significance of the ritual and symbolic work done by scribes and scholars in the maintenance of order and justice. While she had a small temple in Karnak, Egyptian kings were regularly depicted as presenting offerings in temples throughout Egypt that included a small figurine of Maat. Ritually seen, kingly obligations to temples may be seen as including regular maintenance of truth and justice in the world. Egyptian states had limited control of religious institutions but recognized and worked with their enormous social and economic importance.[35] We will discuss Maat at greater length in the context of justice and law in subsequent sections.

RELIGION AS ECONOMIC IMPETUS

While true mortuary cults, dedicated to this developed cosmogony were only for elites, over the centuries, the belief grew that the afterlife was something any human could access if their behavior in this world was just. Their behavior was depicted as being judged by particular gods, for example, Osiris or Thoth, who placed the person's heart on scales to be balanced against a feather. If the burden of guilt on their heart in this life weighed more than the feather, then they would be denied access to the afterlife, and would be devoured by Apophis. By predynastic times, the Eastern bank of the Nile became a symbol of this world; and the Western bank stood for the afterlife. The dead were mummified and buried on the West side of the Nile. Elaborate rituals of mummification and burial prepared a deceased with all that they needed, including written instructions needed to make it successfully through judgment, and to make the lengthy traverse, through the many gates of the underworld (Duat), required to reach the celestial afterlife.

Religious festivals in ancient Egypt appear to have been celebrated throughout the year divided according to the seasons. The calendar had three seasons (Akhet-Indundation, Peret-Growth, Shemu-Harvest). Each season lasted four months of thirty days, plus five special epagomenal days, for a total of 365 days. In these special five days, the festivals of Osiris, Horus, Seth, Isis and Nephthys were apparently celebrated sequentially.

Inferring the normal from incomplete records is impossible, but an extant list of festivals suggests that during Akhet, important festivals for Osiris, Thoth, Ptah took place (in Memphis and Thebes); Opet (the benign hippopotamus deity of Thebes), Hathor (in Edfu and Dendera), Sekhmet and Sokar (the falcon god of Memphis) were also celebrated. In Peret, key festivals for Nehebkau (a serpent god), Horus, Min, Mut (Theban mother of the gods known only by the end of the Middle Kingdom), Renenutet (a serpent god known from Old Kingdom texts), and "victory in battle" were held. During Shemu, festivals to Khonsu, Min and Re-Horakhty and "The Beautiful Feast of the Valley," "The Beautiful Meeting (of Hathor and Horus)" and "The Opening of the Year" were standard. Many of these were national celebrations, and were held throughout Egypt. There were, however, a few that focused on specific places in Upper or Lower Egypt.[36] Many, but not all, deities had one or more specific cult centers; and, these were distributed up and down the Nile from Elephantine to the delta.

Just as the fluctuations in attentions paid to different divinities were a continuing feature of Egyptian religion, so too were the corresponding fluctuations in temple building up and down the Nile, which were essential to changing patterns of worship. There is some evidence to suggest that recent interests dominated the extant set of temple interests.[37] While many temples and mortuary complexes have survived the ravages of history, well quarried stone was long a valuable commodity, and abandoned or ruined edifices were very tempting places to find stone for a new construction. For example, many structures incorporating stones from a previous building have those inscriptions turned face down so as not to be readable. Since temples fundamentally required estates, laborers, and religious officials of various types, temple management was extremely complex. Not only were their many calendrical obligations, a need to rework theogonic and political statements, but in particular, the daily financial management both of production and of nourishment of the gods and goddesses, were tasks that necessarily entailed both short-term and long-term planning. Many who worked in temples had what have been called prebends: workers that provided services in return for revenue derived from lands to which they had legal claim for support, even as those very lands were legally obliged, first and foremost, to provide the essentials for particular religious rituals.

From an investment perspective, estates inevitably decline over time: even buildings need repair, but the construction of new temples, or refurbishment of older ones corresponds to a continuous reworking of religious ideas. The construction of elaborate mortuary complexes for funerary rites, including, most spectacularly pyramids, on the West bank of the Nile also required massive investments. National surpluses provided the means for both on a major scale. Even though surpluses derived from agriculture would have varied from year to year, military conquest also brought in revenues. Of course, the military had to be fed; and, so were themselves in part tied to the availability of agricultural surplus. However, while they had to be fed when at home, they could and did forage (pillage) when abroad. The main significance of military conquests would have been that they brought in a variety of goods otherwise not available in Egypt, for example, gold from Nubia, cedar from Lebanon or turquoise, copper, and malachite from the Sinai. As store houses of value, these products would have also had significant financial benefits to the economy.

The text on the statue of Peftuaneith of Abydos discusses eloquently and at length the temple constructions and improvements Peftuaneith carried out for King Apries (589–570 BC) and Amasis (570–526 BC) during the Saite period (twenty-sixth dynasty). It includes the following discussion of work in Abydos:

> I reported the condition of Abydos,
> To the palace, to his majesty's ear.
> His majesty ordered me to do work in Abydos,
> In order to rebuild Abydos;
> I labored greatly in restoring Abydos,
> I put everything belonging to Abydos in its place. . . .
> I built the temple of Khentamenti,
> As a solid work of eternity,
> At his majesty's command,
> That he might see prosperity in the affairs of Tawer.
> I surrounded it with walls of brick,
> The shrine 'rk-hh was of one block of granite,
> The august chapel of electrum,
> Ornaments, divine amulets, all sacred objects
> Were of gold, silver, and all precious stones.
> I built the wpg-sanctuary. [set up] its braziers,
> Dug its pond, planted with trees.
> I provisioned the temple of Khentamenti,
> Enlarged its income,
> Established with daily supplies,
> Its storehouse furnished with male and female slaves.
> I gave it a donation of a thousand aruras,
> In the countryside of Tawer,
> Provided with people and herds of all kinds,
> Its name being made "Osiris-town."
> So as to make a divine endowment of it for all time.
> I renewed its divine endowment of bread, beer, oxen, and fowl,
> Exceeding what it had been before.
> I made for it an orchard.

Planted with all fruit trees.
Its gardeners being foreigners,
Brought in as prisoners.
Thirty pints of wine were given from it daily
To the altar of Khentamenti,
As an offering from it for all time.
I renewed the House of Life after its ruin,
I established the sustenance of Osiris,
I put all its procedures in order.
I built the god's boat of pine wood,
Having found (it) made of acacia wood.
I suppressed crime in Tawer,
I guarded Tawer for its lord,
I protected all its people.
I gave income from Tawer's desert to the temple.
Having found it in the hands of the count,
So that Abydenes would have burials.
I gave the ferryboat of Tawer to the temple,
Having taken it away from the count, . . .
His majesty praised me for what I had done.[38]

These constructions were in Abydos in Nome Eight, the Great Land, of Upper Egypt while the kings during the Saite dynasty lived in Sais in the delta. Khentamenti was a name for Anubis the Jackal god, whose center of worship under this name was in Abydos. The name is a minor variation of *khenty-imentiu,* meaning "foremost of the westerners," representing his importance in the transition to the afterlife, and his association with Osiris.[39] Though the account is from the late period it is likely to be reasonably representative of the obligations that kings claiming the double crown felt to fund temple construction throughout Upper and Lower Egypt. Temples and mortuary cult centers received revenues from their own assets, but if they were really to prosper, they required major inputs from the state or even from the private sector.

In some periods, commerce in religious objects, such as mummified kittens, destined as mortuary or temple gifts reached extravagant levels. Religious observances, more generally, were probably a significant stimulator of production and construction throughout Egyptian history, but the major role the state played in directing and supporting religious rituals would be hard to exaggerate. Writing in the sixth century BC, Herodotus recounted that Naucratis, on the Canopic branch of the Nile fifty kilometers from the sea, was the first Egyptian city and trading emporia established to house foreigners and that it had altars/temples dedicated by residents from twelve Greek cities.[40] While support given to temples traditionally took the form of an endowment bearing long-term benefits, as trade in the Mediterranean flourished another option became possible. The Stela of Naucratis was erected by King Nectanebo I (380–362 BC), the founder of the thirtieth dynasty, to record a grant, in perpetuity, to the temple of Neith of one tenth of the tax revenue from local manufactures, and one tenth of the local customs revenue on sea-born imports.[41]

The importance of keeping temples up to date included other measures that went beyond refocusing them on sustaining the currently appropriate divinities. Kings not only used these structures to record their conquests (portraying their success as in part due to the support of one or more gods or goddesses), but also were assiduous in putting their name into significant portrayals of mythic events. This frequently involved chiseling out a previous monarch's name, and replacing it with their own. Egyptologists, for example, somewhat jokingly refer to Ramses the Great (1279–1213 BC) as "The Great Chiseler."[42] Nevertheless, the most prominent examples of such rewriting of history exemplify political or religious correctness. Thus, following the reign of Queen Hatshepsut (1473–1458 BC), her name was erased even from her own constructions as if such a successful female ruler could not be acknowledged. Similarly, after the reign of Amenhotep IV (1352–1336 BC), also known as Akhen-aten, a methodical effort was made to erase this "heretic" king from history. Chiseling ones name into a pre-existing relief could not have brought the general approbation that erecting and endowing a new temple, such as that to Khentamenti, might produce. Although new temple construction probably involved greater investments than refurbishing temple estates, these relative differences are hidden to us by the limitations of the archaeological record.

JUSTICE (MA'AT) AND THE LAW

There is much about everyday practice in ancient Egypt that is still unknown because the main material used to record literature, personal records, and more generally financial records, was papyrus that is far less durable than Mesopotamian clay tablets. Even so, many texts on stone or papyrus survive, and fair numbers of ostraca (potsherds) that non-elites often used to write upon provide us many details about everyday life. Such texts tell us about political conquest, monument building, the gods and their ties to humanity, and religious beliefs concerning cosmology and the afterlife. We know that many people worked as bureaucrats or dependents/employees of state or religious institutions, that large numbers made their living in the private sector, and that though there were significant numbers of slaves in many periods, they comprised a relatively small fraction of the total population.

From the earliest times, ancient Egypt appears to have engaged in extensive long distance trade up and down the Nile, into Palestine, with the Eastern Mediterranean, and to a lesser degree with Mesopotamia through the Red Sea. As an increasingly wealthy civilization, this encouraged the extensive development of commercial law that made basic distinctions between private property and goods associated with government office, even as both could be involved in trade. A Middle Kingdom text, the Instruction of Ptahhotep, advises men, in the interest of marital peace not to contend with women in court,[43] confirming many other indications that gender equality before the law was the expected norm. In time, legal development gave rise to organization and procedures premised on key notions about justice and jurisprudence were applied to inheritance, marriage, property, commerce, and torts. The expectations of divine judgment in the afterlife (thought to apply to king, commoner, and slave alike) profoundly influenced both ancient ethical perceptions and jurisprudence.

A section of Papyrus Ani, a version of the Egyptian Book of the Dead (ca. 1500 BC) entitled *The Book of Going Forth by Day*, provides spells, instruction, appeals to a multitude of gods, and abundant similes to help spirits traverse the underworld's gates, avoid dangers, and make their way safely to the afterlife. A famous passage, the declaration of innocence before the gods of the tribunal, illustrates the key need to behave in this world with justice (*ma'at*). The many declarations include: "I have . . . done no wrong, . . . not stolen, . . . not slain people, not destroyed the food offerings, not reduced measures, not told lies, not done grain profiteering, not robbed a parcel of land, not discussed secrets, not disputed about property, not struck terror, not disputed the King, not been impatient, not harmed the bread-ration of the Gods, not stolen the Khenef cakes from the Blessed, not stolen Hefnu-cakes of a youth, not slain sacred cattle."[44] These assertions of innocence clearly reflect a list of possible or even common crimes in ancient Egypt. The assertions also reflect a deep concern to show behavior exemplifying both docility toward authorities and respect for the proper financing of religious institutions. As well, some of the assertions explicitly focus on honesty in interpersonal relations: no lies, no short changing of grain measures, no theft of land, and no use of threats (presumably to gain advantage). In short, justice applied to all, and any illegitimate use of force, in any guise, could only threaten one's prospects in the afterlife.

Eighteenth dynasty papyri provide us a more or less full text of the Instruction of King Merkare from his father (whose name is not preserved) of the ninth or ten dynasty (ca. 2160–2025 BC). This instruction covers many themes similar to the ones in the Attestations of Innocence in the Book of the Dead, but "ethical" behavior is also praised for its utility in the here and now:

Do justice, then you endure on earth;
Calm the weeper, don't oppress the widow,
Don't expel a man from his father's property,
Don't reduce the nobles in their possessions,
Beware of punishing wrongfully,
Do not kill, it does not serve you . . .
Do not prefer the wellborn to the commoner,
Choose a man on account of his skills,
Then all crafts are done.[45]

The Middle Kingdom (ca. 2055–1650 BC) tale of the Eloquent Peasant makes similar points from the perspective of a commoner. The peasant's tale is told as a sequence of nine petitions before the court over the theft by a rich man of a rural peasant's goods en route to market. The petitions are considered so eloquent that they were approved, or so the tale tells us; resulting not only in the restitution of all stolen property, but in the transfer of all the rich man's wealth to the peasant. The petitions consist of contrasting injustice with true justice in the form of instructions provided gratuitously as clarifications and admonitions to the judges:

The magistrates do wrong,
Right-dealing is bent sideways,
The judges snatch what has been stolen.
He who trims a matter's rightness makes it swing awry:
The breath-giver chokes him who is down, . . .
"The measurer of grain-heaps trims for himself,
He who fills for another shaves the other's share;
He who should rule by law commands theft,
Who then will punish crime? . . .
None light of heart is weighty in conduct.
Be patient so as to learn justice,
Restrain your [anger] for the good of the humble seeker.
No hasty man attains excellence,[46]

The New Kingdom (eighteenth dynasty: ca. 1550–1069 BC) *Instruction of Any* provides the perspective of a middle class, minor official, but adds the notion of human epistemological inadequacy as part of the reason for ethical behavior:

A man may be ruined by his tongue,
Beware and you will do well.
A man's belly is wider than a granary,
And full of all kinds of answers,;
Choose the good one and say it,

while the bad is shut in your belly . . .
One man is rich, another is poor,
But food remains for him [who shares it.]
As to him who was rich last year,
He is a vagabond this year;
Don't be greedy to fill your belly,
You don't know your end at all . . .
When last year's watercourse is gone,
Another river is here today;
Great lakes become dry places,
Sandbanks turn into depths.
Man does not have a single way,
The lord of life confounds him.
Attend to your position,
Be it low or high;[47]

The vizier Rekhmire (ca. 1479–1425 BC) puts the focus on general principles required by those in authority, who by this time all imagine making their way to the afterlife. He had written on his tomb both the Pharoah's speech installing him as vizier (A) and his autobiography (B). The following excerpts illustrate the key themes of justice for those in authority:

(A) Do not judge unfairly, God abhors partiality; this is an instruction, plan to act accordingly . . . A magistrate who lies comes out as he deserves. Lo, you succeed in doing this office by doing justice . . . He who does justice before all people, he is the vizier. Lo, a man remains in his office, if he acts as he is charged . . . Do not act willfully in a case where the law is known; for as regards the headstrong man, the Lord prefers the timid to the headstrong man.[48]

(B) I judged both [the insignificant] and the influential; I rescued the weak man from the strong man; I deflected the fury of the evil man and subdued the greedy man in his hour . . . I succored the widow who has no husband; I established the son and heir on the seat of his father. I gave [bread to the hungry], water to the thirsty, and meat, oil and clothes to him who had nothing . . . I was not at all deaf to the indigent. Indeed I never took a bribe from anyone.[49]

The Ramesside *Instruction of Amenemope* (ca. 1295–1069 BC) clearly focuses on the afterlife, through avoiding greed in this life, and emphasizes the ephemerality of wealth, and so the value of focusing on one's long-term outcome:[50]

Do not falsify the temple rations,
Do not grasp and you'll find profit,
Do not remove a servant of the god . . .

Do not move the markers on the borders of fields,
Nor shift the position of the measuring-cord.
Do not be greedy for a cubit of land.
Nor encroach on the boundaries of a widow.
The trodden furrow worn down by time,
He who disguises it in the fields,
When he has snared(it) by false oaths,
He will be caught by the might of the Moon. . . .
Do not set your heart on wealth,
There is no ignoring Fate and Destiny;
Do not let your heart go straying,
Every man comes to his hour. . . .
Do not assess a man who has nothing.
And thus falsify your pen.
If you find a large debt against a poor man,
Make it into three parts;
Forgive two, let one stand. . . .
Beware of disguising the measure,
So as to falsify its fractions;
Do not force it to overflow,
Nor let its belly be empty.
Measure according to its true size,
Your hand clearing exactly.
Do not make a bushel of twice its size,
For then you are headed for the abyss.
The bushel is the Eye of Re,
It abhors him who trims;
A measurer who indulges in cheating,
His Eye seals (the verdict) against him.

Justice under the Nubian kings was viewed as similarly motivated by a search for religious merit. Thus, Harwa, the High Steward of the "divine Consort of Amun," Amenirdis, daughter of King Kashta (twenty-fifth dynasty ca. 747–656 BC) had written onto his memorial stela:[51]

I have done what people love and gods praise,
(As) one truly revered who had no fault,
Who gave bread to the hungry, clothes to the naked,
Removed pain, suppressed wrongdoing;
Who buried the revered ones, supported the old,
Removed the want of the have-not.
A shade for the child,
A helper for the widow,
One who gave rank to an infant.
I did these things knowing their weight,

And their reward from the Lord of Things . . .

The Egyptian term for truth and justice, *ma'at* began with a clear focus on elite obligations to maintain order and then, perhaps during the first intermediate period, gradually acquired connotations of justice for all, including the poor.[52] The Egyptian worldview also linked society, nature, and the afterlife in a grand scheme where justice and honor in this world was tied inexorably to justice and honor in the afterlife. This was a hierarchy of honor in which the goal was to be honorable, not presumptuous or arrogant.[53] Whether accounts of gifts of people (of "head") refers to slaves, assignments of people to a status something like European serfdom, or merely transfer of captives newly defined as employees whose freedoms were constrained in some other way, is unclear to the experts.[54] Nevertheless, all experts agree that social hierarchy became important early on, and that justice expressed as equality before the law was quite a distinct issue from any questioning of the fairness of income or wealth distribution in this life.

These excerpts minimally illustrate an ideal, that may have been irregularly or incompletely attained, yet they contrast favorably from a modern perspective with Mesopotamian legal codes that failed to suggest ever that different social strata should be treated absolutely equally. Thus, as we have seen, in

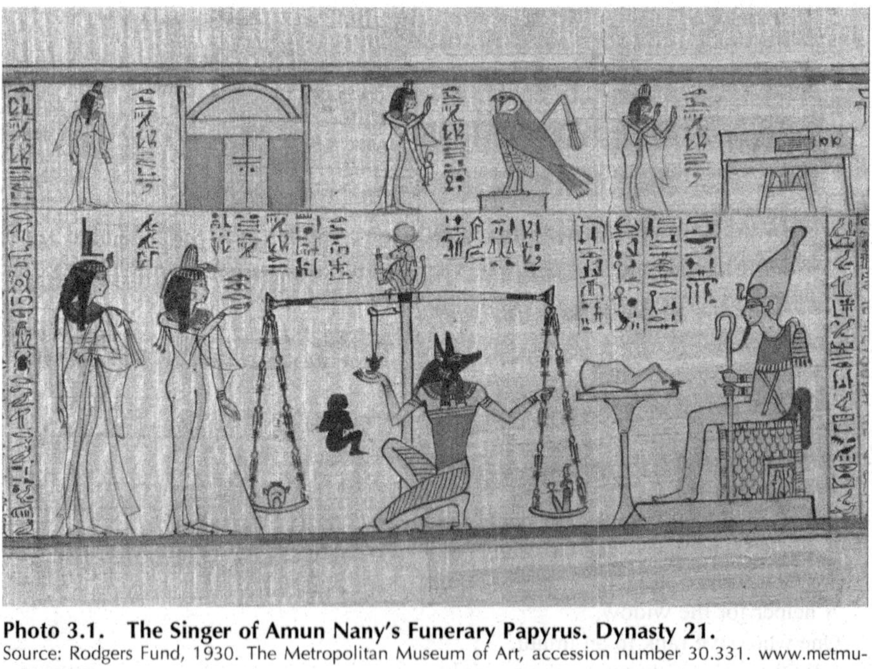

Photo 3.1. The Singer of Amun Nany's Funerary Papyrus. Dynasty 21.
Source: Rodgers Fund, 1930. The Metropolitan Museum of Art, accession number 30.331. www.metmuseum.org

the fourth through the first millennia, Mesopotamian rulers continued to prescribe differential punishment and rights to different social strata. Although Egyptian civilization might be said to have introduced the world to an ethics applied to all citizens, it is not clear that ethical norms were applied equally to people who were not yet incorporated properly into Egyptian society.

FINANCING ANCIENT EGYPT

Dynastic Egypt flourished without money for several millennia as a vast bureaucratic state comprising countless institutions, inter-related through religious and political ideologies, whose basic finances relied on keeping track of a network of obligatory flows. Egyptian materials available provide a fair picture how of how temple finances were administered. One function of private traders was to exchange excess estate goods for commodities the estate needed. Some private trade networks were used to sell goods pilfered from tombs. More generally, private trade complemented the major institution based economy from predynastic times onward.[55]

The Egyptian state's original approach involved a proliferation of institutions devoted to a pantheon of gods based on the belief that life-after-death required a long-term investment in funerary cults. It was not enough to have a tomb provisioned with materials needed in the initial period after death, it was also important to care for the tomb *in perpetuo* (in principle—though Egyptians knew this was likely to be impossible). So just as it was thought useful to bring along both supplies for nourishment and livelihood in the afterlife, along with elaborate instructions for how to overcome the many obstacles to accession to the afterlife, part of the proper preparation for kings was to provide long-term funding for living employees so they would continue to maintain funerary structures.[56] In principle, this involved envisaging long-term investment as producing a return on investment, reaped at least in part in the afterlife. In the world of the living, institutions had endowments comprised of payments owed, personnel obligated, and productive lands from which revenues could be gleaned. In the course of time, as aspirations to the afterlife became more and more widespread, individuals tried within their own means to emulate the nobility. Because significant preparations for the afterlife brought persons renown and respect both before and after death, the incentive structures for investment in the here and now were intertwined with religious beliefs.

State and temple administrations were run in comparable ways, except that at one level they were in competition. Initially, the state might have been able to claim that all institutional lands belonged to it, and assess taxes accordingly even if in the short-term some lands given to important officials were temporarily off the tax ledgers.[57] In time, however, once the principle was established that such endowments belonged permanently to a temple, and so were no longer taxable, increasing amounts of land that otherwise might produce taxes for the state, produced few state revenues unless exceptional measures were enacted.[58] It is probable that as increasing numbers of Egyptians became workers of temple lands, the proportion of taxable income from non-institutional related commerce (at ports, gates, and markets) may also have diminished as the ratio of bureaucrats to producers increased (although population growth might have counteracted this to some degree). Over time, revenue streams became increasingly specific to institutions. Consequently, a tradition evolved going back to the Old Kingdom of issuing decrees to explicitly protect particular institutions from the exactions of others.[59] Nevertheless, the state occasionally did assess taxes on temples, and on some temple lands.[60] These fairly general constraints may have provided state incentives for both external conquests, and for expansion of agriculture within the Nile valley.

Although the terminology used in administration is still debated, there is a recent emerging consensus about a number of terms. Egyptians made no effort to define the administrative terms they used, and wrote no treatises on economics or finance, at least that have survived.[61] A term that does appear frequently, *ẖrt*, in public documents is translated by scholars as "obligations" or "requirements," but other modifying terms are less clearly understood.[62] The best evidence comes from the New Kingdom period, but it should be remembered that this is midway, 1550–1069 BC, through dynastic history. Simple deliveries (inputs) were referred to as *inyt*, while the concept of obligation was captured in the more ideological term *inw,* which has been translated as "what should be brought." A review of all known uses of the term notes that *inw* includes both "gifts" and "tribute," and so included both payments made under duress as well as those given freely. If we recognize that symbolic violence often disguises socially or culturally inescapable obligations as gifts, we can conclude that the recipient, the state or occasionally temples, classified what we see as two categories under the same term for ideological reasons.

A term shedding light on how the ancient Egyptian economy worked at the level of labor is a term, *b:kw*, that references, fee, corvée labor, fines, contractual labor or even wages. Its primary meaning was that of obligatory payment related to labor. This term may have been ubiquitous. A scribe notes that everyone (scribes, craftsmen, traders, serfs and the workers of Deir el-Medina in the valley of the kings) had *b:kw*.[63] A related term, *b:kw-rmṯ*, referred to obligations to temples.

Obligations sometimes require careful assessment, and Egyptians used the term *htri* for them. This was an abstract obligation to render material goods to an authority, government or temple, and referred to a particular proportion of the available total.[64] As this term was combined with many others, it would appear that it was common practice for authorities to tithe at particular levels.

The role of destiny itself shows up in a fiscal term, *š:y(t)*, which has been translated as "what is destined" or "what has been decided." It could embrace cattle, geese, precious metals or stones, and other products.[65] As an abstract obligation used to cover different quantities and types of products without an implication of a particular proportion, the concept would have great utility when specific quantities were needed for ceremonial or state occasions.

A specific term used for grain, *šmw*, that literally meant summer or harvest, was a proportional levy. There is some evidence that particular types of land were also assigned to the palace for harvest. A harvest levy might depend for its percentage on the types of lands in question. At the same time, the officials who delegated this responsibility sometimes boast how they, in a given year, collected many times the amount their predecessor had collected in previous years. For example, during the reign of Ramesses IX, a High Priest of Amun at the Mortuary Temple of Siptah claimed to have doubled the *šmw*.[66] This suggests either that the previous year's levy was for a less productive year, or that the proportion in the previous year was quite small, and the rate was doubled without serious objection—perhaps because there was a better harvest.

There also was some form of a tax, paid in kind, by high officials. The term, *tp-ḏrt*, usually referred to valuable cloth, metals or minerals, but not to grain, and was received by the state from temple officials. However, it is unclear if this was a personal obligation, or more likely, an obligation of office funded by institutional assets.[67]

If the surviving data are representative, it would be reasonable to conclude that temple personnel routinely kept detailed accounts of revenues owed temples, revenues received, outlays made, and obligated, and regularly calculated the difference or net outstanding credits and obligations. The records of a temple dedicated to a particular god were both submitted to the central administration of the god or gods in question; and, periodically scrutinized by its visiting inspectors.

Personnel, typically, were paid partly with advances of bread and beer, as well as in a few other key commodities, and partly through loans of land which brought with them both usufruct rights and obligatory payments of portions of the harvest. Individuals who worked temple lands would have owed some of their harvest to the temple, but may also have used some of their production for their personal expenses, including payments to a variety of other institutions, even to temples of other gods or to their own or ancestral mortuary cults, as well as for business expenses including state taxes on commerce. Those who could, such as elites, endowed their own mortuary cults with ample lands to maintain a long-term revenue stream. Although such cults did not last forever,[68] it is probable that the amount of non-obligated lands varied significantly both in area and productivity but may never have been high, so that royal cults frequently may have had to transfer lands from older obligations to newer ones.

A fifth dynasty document (mid-second millennium BC) preserved on a stela records a purchase that illustrates well the sophistication of the ancient credit system. A governor, Meten, who is given a royal grant of four aroures (or one setat = 0.275 ha) of cultivated land (including the peasants and other things on it), buys an additional 200 aroures that come with peasants and various benefices as well as obligatory offerings of one hundred loaves of bread per day from the temple of the *ka* of the royal mother Ni-maat-hap.[69] This purchase, in effect, transfers the long-term rent payments (100 loaves a day) from a temple to the buyer, which itself presumes that a long-term obligation or debt has a price and can be purchased. While it is unlikely that we are dealing with a sophisticated futures market, the peasants on the land had obligations to the temple, the temple bakery had obligations of bread to the official owning and administering the land, and such intertwined credit arrangements could be sold as a package.

A ledger in the Abusir archives (ca. 2350 BC) which records the offerings made to a temple has columns for the amounts registered or expected, the amounts received, and the remainder outstanding: with the second written in black and the first and last (debit) columns in red ink. This temple ledger, also, suggests that, one hundred years after being endowed, its revenues had fallen to about half of its original endowment. Working accounts such as from the Abusir archive also suggest that standardized duty registers with rows and columns were made up for recurring events such as festivals, and that individuals holding usufruct on institutional land would be assigned particular tasks each day on a thirty day (month) chart, though they might be assigned different tasks on different days.[70]

It is not usually clear from such records what proportion of an individual's total obligations were being fulfilled, or what proportions of individual income such payments in bread and beer represented. However, more elaborate records, such as those of the Wilbour Papyrus (ca. 1147–1143 BC) which took the form of a cadastre of 2,800 plots of land along a ninety-mile section of Middle Egypt, allow a number of additional conclusions to be drawn:[71]

- data from working records were occasionally summarized in lengthier reports

- even such syntheses (as the Wilbour Papyrus) were emended and reworked by multiple scribes
- officials unconnected to the institutions owning the land were called in to supervise or manage properties; and, there may have been a long tradition that they be paid 7.5 percent of the crop as a management fee
- there is reason to believe that for the people working institutional land, the share of the harvest they received or paid out, and the obligations tied to the land changed over time.

Despite the fragmentary nature of such records, ancient Egypt much of the time had a well-functioning economy in which institutional credit established current and long-term obligations for a substantial proportion of the population. A major sector of the economy worked on institutional credit and obligation (debt), supplemented by barter, and payments in standardized commodities, such as grain and beer by volume or gold and silver by weight. The economy was ideologically buttressed, and motivated by faith in the importance of an elaborate material preparation for the afterlife. Yet, its success depended as well on international trade and conquest, as well as on a highly productive agricultural system, that often produced a surplus, and was endowed with continuing infrastructural investment, a developed credit system, the means for storage, and the ability to make short-term payments for most transactions via grain products.

John Maynard Keynes introduced a model to explain economic stagnation / dynamism. His model suggested psychological variables (such as propensity to save versus liquidity preferences) had, in the statistical aggregate, impacts on real value but it also posited a claim for systematic relationships between national income, employment, and the rate of interest. Keynes imagined authorities controlling the quantity of money and viewed aggregate investment or consumption by individuals, governments and corporations as dividing up the surpluses. Most memorably, he proposed government should play an active role to stimulate the economy when the market remained depressed.

What may also be relevant to understanding the ancient Egyptian case is his general claim that market decisions were based on estimations of "real value" (i.e., relative value of various commodities) not nominal monetary value (except for money of course).[72] More recent economists such as Milton Friedman have argued that price inflation is always produced by a more rapid increase in money supply than in production.[73] Although Friedman's argument may well be correct in a monetized economy this would generally not have been the case for ancient Egypt, since if it could have been said to have all purpose currency, it would have been grain, itself the key unit of production. Keynes's focus on "real value" may be a better guide, even if it is a more difficult unit to assess.

While we might imagine a liquidity preference in ancient Egypt, it could not have had more than a minor significance for most people in the early period. Even in an economy without long-term inflation, the lack of a real currency would be problematic, as it inhibited a clear perspective on savings: grain itself deteriorates, so if its value is to be even maintained, it must be regularly replaced. As we saw for Mesopotamia, this in itself justified social investment in credit instruments. Unfortunately, surviving records do not allow us to estimate commensurable levels of real investment by individuals, and as this was likely true for Egyptians in this period, invoking psychological variables, (such as desire for the afterlife), would be difficult to quantify as a basis for institutional decision making in ancient Egypt.

A long history of criticism in the social sciences problematizes the purported source of any psychological impetus. Simon characterized modern economies as primarily organizational economies and suggested that organizations elicit both docility to organizational norms of behavior and receptivity to knowledge and altruistic behaviors benefitting the organization.[74] In the case of ancient Egypt, we have ample documentation that the belief system bolstered the position of elites first; and, only gradually expanded its reach to suggest the middle class or even the poor might profitably aspire to the afterlife. Given this historical trajectory, it does not makes sense to pretend the psychological motivations were innate or were not inculcated by institutions, for example, temples and the state. Even so, there is some merit to imagining ancient Egypt as having an economic system that could stall out or be dynamic over the long term, and we might benefit from imagining what the key variables involved might be. If we accept that institutions and ideology had enormous influence on the financial and economic structure we will have a good start.

We have discussed at length the frequent agricultural surplus: the result of a well-managed agricultural system within a chaotic flood regime that kept long-term population levels significantly under the levels that could be supported in good years. The benefits from the peaceful disposition of that surplus legitimized elites. Dramatic rituals and artistic portrayals made the promise of an afterlife, in return for orderly behavior in this life, a reasonably persuasive proposition. It cannot be irrelevant that dynastic Egypt lasted for millennia with one of the most-strict interpretations of justice in the ancient world: that your heart be so light, unburdened by guilt, that it will not outweigh a feather. The strictness of this standard may have allowed ancient Egypt to be less exploitative than other ancient societies, and this may have contributed to its long-term resilience, but this is something we probably will never know.

Modern economic models presuppose a world where people might behave irrationally on occasion, but which, otherwise, is a world that is statistically understandable arguing that, in their aggregate, preferences and calculations quite properly shape collective behavior. This would be a reasonable approach if its methodological individualistic approach did not so divert attention from the much more regular and predictable behavior of institutions.[75] In the Egyptian context where the most important things, flood levels, flood duration, water velocity, crop damage from animals, raiding, warfare, the actions of the gods, etc not only could not be estimated, it would be unproductive to explain behavior primarily as the sum of individual rational calculations based on subjective preferences.[76]

A number of additional remarks are warranted. With only grain serving as a money (of account), inflation, even in the real / Keynesian sense, would be strictly limited. To begin with, most salaries and incomes in ancient Egypt were in grain and the value of grain itself is tied to metabolic needs so the value of labor is likely to be relatively stable. Further, in an economy characterized by a web of interlocking obligations tying labor, land and grain production into complex obligations, the notion of separate independent markets for the factors of production is less than persuasive. Without true factor markets a modern capitalist model is inappropriate. The extraordinary importance of institutions, and the complexities of their motivations and financing, also argues against any comparable role for markets or individuals. Although government actions might have depended on levels of national prosperity, exactly where and when the government invested in religious infrastructure, (and this was a major economic stimulus during the whole dynastic period), would have depended not on the market, but on specific geopolitical decisions, influenced by cultural and social forces whose complex conjuncture combined in specific situations. In brief, institutional decisions would primarily have been made both for short-term benefit, and as part of long-term strategies to optimize economic, social and cultural capital.

The individual aspirations that in time motivated Egyptians to aspire to the afterlife may not have had any decisive role in the economy but they undoubtedly drove the market price of many objects used in ritual activities. The relationships between key variables would still not have resembled those of any standard modern development models. There are also a variety of other reasons related to the current state of the art in the social sciences for suspecting the economy worked differently.

Although it is highly implausible that the origins of Egyptian religious ideas (which arguably have a logic of their own) can be explained by any simple functionalism, it is reasonable to assume that beliefs played a central role in the propagation and maintenance of state and religious institutions, as these institutions stood most to gain from having the population in their thrall. Further, Egyptians believed not only in order, but also in chaos; and given their ample historical experience with flood and drought, they linked institutions to the role of coping with individual and collective responses to potential chaos. For individuals, if acting justly came to be highly valued as one road to advancement, in this life or the next, then docile behavior that neither challenges the basic justification for social hierarchy nor jeopardizes its legitimation might not require additional incentives. Accordingly, many people might become productive citizens without major rewards in this life. The pursuit of social and cultural capital by itself could be a key motivation for such behavior, and not something secondary desired because of its potential for conversion to material gain in this life.

The involvement of the government, temples and private sector in commerce, (and in some cases in long distant trade), certainly implied prices, commercial costs, and a market for many things. In ancient Egypt, non-agricultural prices (if assessed in grain: or Keynesian "real value") might have responded upwardly to national prosperity, viewed as correlated with abundant harvests, and not downward as in a capitalist economy. Even with high yields, grain values would not have declined as much as the increase in harvest, since most grain would have been consumed by individual or institutional producers and not put on the market. It is also highly likely that prices for most things varied by nome, and did not display a simple production cost + transport cost correlation at the national level. Large amounts of grain were also shipped to temples at government expense, the costs of which, given the utility of the Nile as a transportation route, would have been low. Major buyers of grain would regularly buy new grain for old based on a credit arrangement that gave them an advantage and many consumers would have their own in-house supply either from their own farm or from an institutional prebend, so they too would have limited their involvement with the market.

In ancient Egypt, the myriad credit conditions and obligations involving institutions and private parties, given the fluctuating supply driven by a chaotic flood pattern, imply that realistic expectations for relative future valuations of grain could not be calculated. Likewise, the mix of captive, slave and free (obligated) labor would have made any notion of a reliable labor market just as problematic. Although obligated labor provided some with major advantages over any competitor seeking to produce simply with hired labor, it is more likely that what labor market there was, fulfilled a demand primarily for unusual cases: situations when much higher than normal amounts of land needed to be cultivated or harvested; cases when new captive labor motivated additional construction or cultivation; or situations when mortality, drought or flood forced rearrangements of social relations of production. To imagine clear headed consumer preferences as major determinants of such an economy would be unthinkable until Egypt became more oriented toward the Mediterranean, and demand for grain in the Roman Empire began to play a significant role. Even then, we know geopolitical considerations initially dominated consumer preferences.

Given these issues, what sort of model would be more realistic. We can accept Keynes's suggestion of a major role for institutions, for example, state and religious, in stimulating and influencing the economy. We see this as motivated both by unpredictable levels of surplus, quantitatively tied to the difference between necessary mean production (NMP) and long-term mean production (LTMP), and the development of social and cultural/religious capital exemplified in networks of obligations.

Thus the main effect of investment was to extend the period of benefit that surpluses enabled rather than to create a surplus in the first place. Sraffa[77] suggested that a given investment might be viewed as enhancing output in a gradually decreasing amount over time. In this productive sense, investments are used up over a finite period. Sraffa further suggested that the current and future value of investments depended on past patterns of investment. We might thus say new infrastructure re-optimized the relationship between infrastructure, flood levels, and production that otherwise would decline to sub-optimal levels but infrastructural contribution depended on the state of current investments.

Due to the fluctuations of the flood, LTMP continued to exceed NMP on a frequent, if irregular, basis. It was such intermittent surplus (created by excess of LTMP over NMP) that enabled reinvestment; but clearly where such investment would generate the greatest returns was an empirical issue that required both knowledge of the state of other infrastructure and the politics of the moment. Throughout the dynastic period, NMP remained at a fairly static level, due to similar technologies being applied to similar land surfaces with similar numbers of people. For the dynastic period, we should also set aside the possibility that significant growth or dynamism from the consumer side influenced the price of grain; and, we should recognize that this has implications for production levels of most other products.

Markets are much misunderstood. The existence of a price does not imply that the best investment strategy is to buy all inputs at prevailing prices.[78] If "real values" in the market were unreliable/inefficient, the best option would have been to try to produce as much as possible for oneself. People, in the agricultural sector, would be happier to use the market for selling than for buying. Similarly, scribes and officials of the state or of temples, would have preferred a prebend to cover their needs, so as not to be forced to depend on the market. Traditional advice proffered in the Ptolemaic Period (ca. 108 BC) about credit suggests we might be wise to expand this conjecture somewhat to include, for those with funds, the value of investing in social or cultural capital, while otherwise avoiding over consumption.

It is quite likely that investments in the commodities market brought in less reliable returns than using wealth to build one's networks of social and cultural capital, particularly given that such networks of obligations brought both admiration as well as potential material benefits in this life and merit in the afterlife. These networks of obligation might absorb excess labor, and regularly provide greater access to agricultural property via the actions of government or religious institutions than would be possible for the great majority from any savings-financed investments in the market. Prices in the market would have been either too high to be tempting, or too low for any profit making. For the wealthy, the most desirable land purchases came as part of a package tied to religious or state institutions. The key advantage to the buyer was that such land purchases entailed labor services and benefits, including sufficient bread to pay for their servants' livelihoods, and so obviated any need for long-term reliance on the market.

For private individuals their goal was to emulate the economic behavior of institutions, and derive similar benefits through influence, allowing them to orient their economic activity both toward this world and toward the afterlife. The ideological work of the state and the religious institutions might in this way be harnessed to individual advantage.

PERSIAN, PTOLEMAIC AND ROMAN EGYPT

While the transition from Dynastic Egypt to Persian (524–404 and 343–332) and then to Ptolemaic Egypt involved significant political and economic change, there is increasing evidence that cultural change was initially much less sudden; and, that in most regards Egyptian culture changed radically only with Roman Egypt, and then much more so with the Islamic conquest in 641 AD.[79] How much economic practice changed is often unclear, nonetheless some of the material from the more abundant later literature may illuminate earlier periods as well. We examine loan documents from Elephantine during the Persian period in the Judeo-Christian chapter, and so will skip over that period in this chapter other than to note the obvious Mesopotamian influences on credit conditionalities found in loans made in Elephantine. Some proverbs dealing with lending and borrowing from the late Ptolemaic period (ca. 108 BC but thought to originate much earlier) speak to what must be seen as common knowledge:

> Borrow money at interest and invest it in farmland
> Borrow money at interest and take a wife
> Borrow money at interest and celebrate your birthday

Do not borrow money at interest in order to live high on it
Do not lend money at interest without a pledge in hand.[80]

Such implicit advice, to be willing to pay interest on socially *or* economically significant investments but not on the high life, *per se*, and to insist on security when lending at interest makes sense even today, just as it would have made sense for more than a millennia earlier in many parts of the Near East. Before this time, loan documents between private parties had reached significant levels of sophistication across the Near East. A document recording a debt from the same period (108 BC) as the proverbs has a sufficient number of relevant features that it is worth summarizing:

> The lender loans silver worth 3 1/2 *artabs* of wheat. One half of this sum is specified as 1 3/4 *artabs,* and this is also to be part of the debt. The debtor promises to pay the debt in wheat that is clean and devoid of foreign substances, that is measured in proper measures of the temple of Anoubis, and that are properly stricken (leveled off with a straight stick). The debtor also promises to cover costs of transport and all other costs and deliver this by a particular date. The debtor promises to deliver the 3 1/2 *artabs* plus the additional half or 1 1/2 times the 3 /12 *artabs* in clean wheat. Everything the debtor owns or acquires serves as security for the loan.[81]

The document makes it clear that a number of metrological issues potentially providing hidden advantages are clearly specified and unambiguously benefit the lender. The translators imagine that the 50 percent addition must be a fine, but admit in their discussion of the text that there is no indication that this is the case. Given the explicit terms of the loan which force the borrower to cover all the costs, thereby providing the lender with multiple sources of hidden interest, it is more reasonable to assume that, in a pattern derived from dynastic times, the extra 50 percent represents a traditional proportion. In the case of a private party making a loan, this could have been interest charged to compensate for potential changes in the amount of grain that the silver would buy in different seasons, or as recompense for forgone profits.

Nevertheless, the actual figure of 50 percent did not drop out of the sky. We suggest that this figure is conceptually linked to the difference between compressed and uncompressed grain: the compressed, having 50 percent more grain per given volume, would exist at the level of the granary; (i.e., as the actual amount of grain in the granaries) and remain compressed when loaned out (generally taken from the bottom of the granary. For this purpose, Egyptian scribes even created an accounting cubic cubit (the khar) with the convenient volume of two thirds a normal cubic cubit. [82]

At a macro level, surpluses appear to have been invested and, over time, this would have significantly increased the ratio of national "capital" to national "income." This in turn would lead to increasing economic roles for returns on capital and increasing levels of economic hierarchy as those with capital became disproportionately wealthy. For recent centuries, where we do have adequate if still imperfect data, changes in this ratio have been well studied by Piketty[83] who has made a strong case for the structural influence of such change on the development of high levels of social inequality. The historical data suggest that returns on capital decrease as capital becomes abundant relative to its uses so that inequality reaches high levels but never approaches total inequality (one person has everything).

We do not have adequate national data for ancient Egypt but we might imagine similar periods of increase in the ratio of aggregate capital to aggregate income (only part of the latter is itself due to wages on labor). Such periods were followed by "creative destruction" due to chaotic flood lows or highs. The environmentally derived sudden decrease in aggregate productive capital would set the stage for new capital needs with high returns on investment. This would lead to new periods of increased investment and subsequent growth in capital and its importance as a revenue stream and foundation for economic and social hierarchy. We might imagine that many such sequences maintained the long term prosperity and creative innovation of ancient Egyptian society. It should be noted that Piketty's argument differs substantially from what has been called panarchy[84] because he suggests there is no internal need for inequality or return on capital to increase or decrease in some continuous cycle because a steady state, for example, any rate of return on capital and inequality, is perfectly possible long term.

In Roman Egypt the urban population grew dramatically. With Rome supporting the notion both that the state should provide a viable currency, and that it should facilitate commerce and private production through the provision of infrastructure and security, it could be said for the first time that the Egyptian economy was significantly monetized. The evidence suggests that Roman taxation in Egypt was reasonable, and not counterproductive. Although estimates of the population in Roman Egypt differ, a reputable estimate is that it had a rural population of three million, and another million and a half in urban areas.[85] This was probably also the first period in Egyptian history when the contribution of urban industry and trade may have been comparable to or even exceeded that of agriculture. The opening of Egypt to the Mediterranean (with Alexander of Macedon's construction of the port of Alexandria, and its subsequent expansion under the Ptolemies) created a new basis for investment in Egypt, which coincided with a decline in the importance of traditional religion and the preponderant focus on grain. The subsequent Islamic conquest placed Egypt in the core of a major commercial empire, and irrevocably changed the ideological justification and pattern of investment.

UNIVERSAL JUSTICE EMBODIED IN LAW

Property Law

Scholars have suggested that some form of small scale common property may have been the norm in predynastic Egypt. This would fit well with flood recession agriculture. The extrapolation that early Kings may have been viewed as owning all property may be unjustifiable. Social institutions, whether initially kin or community based, are more plausible land holders. We know that, in the course of time, institutions from temples, to mortuary cult centers, to governments at multiple levels used agricultural properties to fund salaries, and so created an extensive system of prebends to fund those who provided institutional services including both ritual services and agricultural labor. Despite the social significance of institutional portfolios of properties, and those associated more directly with kingship, there is clear evidence of wider social participation in property ownership.

As early as the second dynasty, it is clear that Egyptians treated property as private. By the New Kingdom, there is abundant evidence of land being held by the state, by religious and private institutions, and by private individuals.[86] Land tenure traditionally involves a set of rights that may be, but generally are not, all owned by a single individual or institution. Taxes and labor obligations represent liens on the property; and, legal institutions may also prohibit specific usages for the property or dictate how the property may be inherited, sold, or otherwise conveyed over time. As land typically endures longer than individuals, families or even most institutions, whatever laws or customs prevail in a given period, are all subject to transformation over time. Private holdings in ancient Egypt often had liens in the form of obligatory rent or taxation or labor obligations. In many parts of the world, including the Nile, property value has often been inseparable from rights to water. This would be the case especially when water reached the fields via canals or other channels that were controlled by others. Given the variability in the Nile flood, and the consequent annual variability in *de facto* property values, obligations born by agricultural producers had the potential to damage production, unless calculations of the amounts due took these *de facto* fluctuations of property values into consideration.

This basic supposition of variability must be seen as critical to understanding property law in ancient Egypt. At one level, such fluctuations provided institutions and the wealthy a motivation to have a large portfolio of lands situated in a variety of ecological contexts. It also gave rise to legal appeals to justice by those whose obligations were not adjusted to the real conditions of production. This ecological context may also be relevant to understanding why ancient Egyptians failed to develop compendia of law cases like those in Mesopotamia as such fixed examples may have been unsuited to the regularly changing circumstances that were in fact the norm in Egypt. At another level, ancient Egyptian concern with the long-term maintenance of a deceased's prospects in the afterlife, through the endowment of tombs with estates generating revenue for religious services, mandated a legal structure that could operate reliably long after an individual's death. Modern trusts do something similar, but most Egyptians with resources, truly thought long-term and hoped to establish an endowment that would operate effectively for eternity. Even if no endowments endured for eternity as their establishers hoped, the pyramids are ample testimony to such hopes.

The Harris papyrus (Ramses III: 1186–1154 BC) suggests that 20 percent of the population was employed by temples holding a total of 750,000 acres (estimated at 33 percent of the arable land in Egypt).[87] Private property could be held individually or jointly and by men or women though the small holder properties listed in the Wilbour Papyrus (Ramesside Period: Year 4 of reign of Ramses V, ca. 1142 BC) suggest that far more men (89.2 percent) than women (10.8 percent) held property.[88] Fifty-four occupations are listed for smallholders, including people in animal husbandry (32.7 percent), military (21.4 percent), religious (16.4 percent), agriculturalists (9.7 percent), scribes and administrators (5.8 percent) as well as domestic servants, artisans, sailors, slaves, foreigners and others. Religious institutions held more than 91.8 percent of the land listed in the Wilbour Papyrus, confirming what surviving ancient structures also suggest, that next to the state the greatest landholders were temples and mortuary cults.[89] A considerable portion of the remaining arable land may have been in the hands of lesser endowments set up by prosperous individuals or deceased officials such as Vizier Rekhmire. All endowments oriented toward eternity provided long-term revenues for their employees in the present.

In subsequent Roman terms, property law in Dynastic Egypt accepted *accessio,* (the establishment of possession via labor as in the acquisition of ownership rights by someone who rebuilt an abandoned house), and bailment contracts such as *usus*, (the continued ownership of property such as a donkey by someone who contracts the use of a donkey to another). However, in Egypt this did not automatically imply *usus fructus*, (i.e., that ownership of the donkey's foal went along with *usus*). Not surprisingly, ancient Egypt also recognized life estates, that is the transfer of property rights to a person for their lifespan. They also recognized more complex trusts used to establish endowments dedicated to maintaining a person's welfare in the afterlife.[90] Not unrelated to these provisions, high positions such as vizier or nomarch were generally hereditary and became the means to perpetuate the support of mortuary cults and rituals for family members. At one level, this treated the nonmaterial asset of high office on a par with private material wealth such as property, even if we would have to view it as an indivisible property. As such, Egyptian law recognized at several levels the value of nonmaterial assets, such as services, and treated them in law much as it did real property.

In time, the Old Kingdom term for a specific deed of conveyance, *imyt-pr*, evolved into a more general term for that which was conveyed, and was used to transfer land irrevocably. Rather than having wills executed post-mortem, if an Egyptian wanted to transfer land to someone not in a customary position to inherit, the conveyance was done before death by filing a *imyt-pr* with the municipality.[91] Scholars have reconstructed inheritance customs as including in descending order the rights of children, grandchildren, brothers and sisters, and parents. There was also preference for a child taking care of parents in old age, and a premium put on keeping land within the family even to the point of appointing a single executor-manager of the estate.[92]

Conveyance of property either via will or sale typically involved the *imyt-pr*, that had to be registered with the state before witnesses, and was then retained in the archives, for example, of the vizier.[93] This meant that contestations or corruption often involved the vizier's office. The honesty of that office, thus became especially critical to social justice. The Pharaoh also assessed property owners a tax based on both real estate and personal property, that was initially assessed twice a year, and then later assessed annually.[94] This tax was levied on both private and crown property in the hands of individuals. In some periods at least, even slaves were treated as property owners, and taxed accordingly. Typically, nomarchs, judges, and temples paid no taxes.[95] Some scholars believe the exemption for temples primarily involved corvée labor.

Most taxes were paid either in grain or in labor services. While ancient Egypt never developed a true currency, accounts and obligations were primarily kept in grain though tribute and obligations to institutions might include a variety of other material contributions. Large payments were often made either in precious metals: first in copper (Old Kingdom), then in silver (Middle Kingdom), and even gold (New Kingdom) or in fine textiles. Both precious metals and grains would have greatly facilitated international trade.[96] Normal salaries were generally paid in grain, grain products or other rations though the state often awarded great service with silver or real estate or slaves.

Commercial Law

Early on, dynastic Egypt developed a coherent legal identity for organizations, including temples and government offices, and private syndicates. There was little difference in the day to day financial management of temples and government properties, other than that the latter had potential revenues above and beyond those directly derived from their own productive or commercial activities. The government received taxes from a wide base and could invest those revenues in any of its enterprises, gifting them to particular temples or constructing new temples, or even endowing recipients with its munificence, including providing individuals with long-term revenue sources of their own. A trustee, *rw'dw*, of a private trust/syndicate could administer its joint concerns within limitations, just as an individual might arrange their own affairs. For instance, during the 4th dynasty a man named Heti set up a family trust, with his son as the initial trustee, from which his heirs could draw income, though its assets remained indivisible for perpetuity.[97] In principle, this allowed the trustee to act as an economic agent transacting business as long as this did not involve selling off assets.

Although adequate details are lacking, if a trust could make profits, necessarily it could also incur debts; and, it is not immediately obvious how such legitimate debts might impact revenue, and not assets. Until more evidence appears, we are left with the weak hypothesis that a range of institutions (under the constraints that institutions, individuals or other parties of influence imposed) resolved obligations of many kinds incurred in ways that best suited their own disposition of material, cultural or social assets, labor, and revenue. The extreme social, personal, and religious significance of the long-term prosperity of institutions must have motivated those responsible to have recourse to all resources possible to maintain their institution's prosperity and welfare.

Under the Middle Kingdom, there appears to have been a noteworthy increase in merchant activity, and trade expanded much further than during the Old Kingdom. Under Amenhotep III (ca. 1390–1352 BC) in the New Kingdom, merchant based foreign trade became so important that a coast guard was established to patrol the delta, and turn away unauthorized boats.[98] More generally, because the private sector had its own resources: largely agricultural land but also recourse to trade, while the state and temples were the center of a massive network of obligations, neither were normally involved in large scale redistribution. Even in the New Kingdom, workers such as those of Deir el-Medina engaged primarily in barter to obtain goods from the private sector.

These constraints did not preclude the use of longer term contracts in the private sector. The term for legal obligation, *sn.h*, in the 20th dynasty had originally meant to tie or bind.[99] Lease agreements specified a continuing agreement for the lessee to pay a rent to the lessor in exchange for occupation of the premises. Contracts were equally accessible to men and women, with each having the ability to enter into binding agreements.[100] While many contracts involved an immediate exchange, they also testified to a long-term acceptance of that exchange.

Unfortunately, the paucity of data for much of the dynastic period, makes certainty about specific aspects of ancient tenure elusive. Nevertheless, a number of famous legal cases establish the long genealogy of private property ownership in ancient Egypt. The most famous involved a dispossessed heir, Moses, who produced in mid-thirteenth century BC some three hundred years of documentation to establish, successfully, his right to a piece of property stolen from his father.[101] Documentation for the establishment of mortuary cults from private property goes back at least as far as King Menkaure in the fourth dynasty (2500 BC) who established an endowment of two *aroures* of land (5,479 m^2) to provide for the local temple to Hathor, and for the mortuary cult of a deceased noble named Khenuka.[102]

The most elaborate mortuary cult for which a record survives, that of Hepadjefi, Governor of Asyut whose cult was established in 1950 BC, used a set of ten separate contracts to obligate a series of people and entail three plots of land. The governor only used his personal property for the land contracts. He specified that the recipients of all contracts did so in their official capacity, and that their personal heirs could not inherit their contracts; rather, the subsequent occupant of their office would inherit the lands, the revenues, and the obligations that went with the endowments.[103] Members of the military were often simply given grants of land by the state for services rendered. Though we cannot presume the Wilbour papyrus is representative of Egypt, as a whole, by the Ramesside period such grants in some areas may have risen to approximately 20 percent of the land.[104]

Just as in Mesopotamia, contracts could involve major enterprises. In the reign of Amenhotep III (ca. 1390–1352 BC), a certain Messuia had a weaving enterprise, and agricultural estates for which he hired slaves on a per-day "hire for services." His contracts were "sale of labor" arrangements that relied on the oath of the provider of the slaves, perhaps because it involved a continuing obligation for future provision of services.[105] A standard procedure in ancient Egypt in the case of breach of a loan contract was for the creditor to take the debtor to court. The debtor would be forced to take an oath to promise full payment by a fixed date or to endure "100 blows," and repay double the debt if again in default.[106] Apparently, the surviving record of such cases suggests that multiple defaults were frequently incurred before actual punishment was imposed.[107] We might remind the reader that in Mesopotamia, reliance on the oath as integral part of contracts disappeared in the Old Babylonian period (1894–1595), that is, at least two centuries before Messuia's enterprises.

THE EGYPTIAN LEGACY

Ancient Egypt exhibited an extraordinary cultural and economic resilience for nearly three thousand years in large part because Egyptians had access to a frequent surplus, and created cultural and religious organizations that adequately motivated members of their society to use that surplus to optimize society's productive capacities. Egyptians set almost inspirationally high expectations for just behavior that must have protected the legitimacy of both the government and the religious infrastructure, except in periods of extreme crisis.

Although initially access to the afterlife was presented as something for the gods and those closest to them, access became, in time, so democratized that even normal Egyptians did not want to live abroad for fear of losing access to the rituals, including embalming and burial on the west bank of the Nile, that gave them a claim to the afterlife.

While passage to the afterlife was difficult and required both a just life and adequate instruction, in later periods the latter could be had in the form of a nicely illustrated "book of the dead" to accompany the spirit in its journey. In time, it even became more important to retain illustrations of the key points than to have a complete text. Thus with time, access, however difficult, must have increasingly been presented as within the reach of many, and the focus of the elite on the first article of faith, living a just life, might have provided a real basis for social and organizational solidarity.

Dynastic Egypt's financial innovations focused attention on investments that held long-term promise, and were structured to endure through the elaboration of networks of social and political capital. The legal code enabled investments that created obligations and institutional solutions that could long outlast the individual. Positions could be inherited with the perquisites and obligations ensured by long enduring religious or state institutions. By making entree to the afterlife entail both justice in this life and access to complex instructions for the trip through the underworld, Egyptians heightened the prestige of literacy, and legitimized the elite status of scribes, the staff of religious institutions and high government officials. This, as well as the putative kinship of kings with deities, must have helped put the general authority structure of society largely beyond criticism.

We have suggested that it was largely the state and religious institutions that acquired the great bulk of capital and accordingly became increasingly influential and prosperous during those periods without capital destruction. They engaged in significant ideological / religious management and careful economic policies designed to maintain political and economic influence. When elite actors derive most of their income from investments, labor has little bargaining power and can, accordingly, be paid modestly. That such major institutions co-opted significant portions of the population, in the form of prebends, would also have disarmed criticism of the *de facto* social inequalities. We might imagine as well that repeated destruction of the bases for elite superiority might facilitate the development of an egalitarian ideology that we have seen gradually became embedded in this radically unequal society.

The extraordinarily rich textual evidence for concern with justice, and the development of the first conception of justice which applied the same rules to people of all walks of life, as well as to women and men equally, amply demonstrate the extraordinary cultural accomplishments of ancient Egypt.

Egyptian accounting techniques were both sophisticated in terms of measures, and extraordinary in terms of routinizing institutional work flows. This bureaucratic accomplishment, undoubtably, was linked to the need to tie most work to organizational offices or roles which new individuals might in due course occupy. Egyptian investment in institutions oriented toward a long-term future must be seen as innovative financing on a massive scale that like loans in other societies was expected to produce a significant annual return.

While Mesopotamia had state and temple institutions, they were generally not as routinized nor as fixed on the long term as those of Egypt. Mesopotamian gods were also less concerned with universal norms of justice; like humans they were fickle, and similarly in need of constant attention. Their almost arbitrary communications had to be read and interpreted before their will could be implemented. In Egypt, by contrast, it would not have been reasonable for humans to trick the gods with a fake king, nor would Egyptian deities be expected to demand injustices from their servants. There was a tight tie between Egyptian ethical and religious systems and Egyptian financial accomplishments that finds echoes down the ages in related ideologies linking justice and finance in increasingly explicit ways.

NOTES

1. Simon, "Organizations and Markets," 275–76. Simon's description of the modern capitalist economy may be taken to imply we should take especial care that our

current misapprehensions about the importance of the market not persuade us to over emphasize the role of the market in ancient Egypt.

2. Midant-Reynes, *The Prehistory of Egypt*.

3. Trigger, "The Rise of Egyptian Civilization," in Trigger et al., *Ancient Egypt*, 21, has suggested that while flood recession agriculture, as in Mesopotamia, clearly preceded the development of the Nile civilization its large scale implementation required developed systems of control and hierarchy: With all due respect to one of Park's former teachers, the order should be reversed: these initial responses to risk led to the development of systems of social hierarchy and control which later facilitated the rise of bureaucratic civilizations.

4. Hassan, "Dynamics of a riverine Civilization," 51–74. Hassan (53) attributes the development of a hierarchical civilization to the role of easy transport in facilitating inter-regional cooperation and to psychological factors related to the uncertainties of the Nile floods and consequent agricultural problems. This is not that far from the position we are taking though Hassan seems unaware of our earlier and much more detailed explanation attributing the development of hierarchy in early Nilotic societies to the political need to cope with uncertainty: Park, "Early Trends toward Class Stratification."

5. Trigger, "The rise of Egyptian Civilization," in Trigger et al., *Ancient Egypt*, 68. Even today and during the medieval period tiny plots of agricultural land in lower Nubia have had extraordinarily high value.

6. High returns to flood recession agriculture are well documented both for the Nile and elsewhere. Hassan, Environment and Subsistence in Predynastic Egypt, Clark and Brandt *From Hunters to Farmers*, 62 suggests that energetic returns to wheat cultivation in flood recession agriculture could have been as high as 113:1. Park, "Early Trends toward Class Stratification," 92–3 and Note 2 provides an extensive discussion of the returns to labor and production per hectare for various grains. Chibnik, "Double-Edged Risks and Uncertainties," Cashdan, *Risk and Uncertainty*, 279–302 provides similar arguments for returns to flood recession rice cultivation.

7. Park, Ibid.

8. Hurst, "Long-Term Storage Capacity," 116, 770, and "Methods of Using Long-Term Storage," 319.

9. Mandelbrot and Wallis, "Noah, Joseph, and operational Hydrology," 909–18 and "Some Long-Run Properties," 321–40.

10. Park, "Early Trends," figure 3, p. 103. The data plotted can be found plotted in Bell "Oldest Records of the Nile Floods,"—figures plotted were furnished to Park by Bell.

11. Figures 4 and 5 in Park, "Early Trends" for the 650–1550 CE period incorporate adjustments for Nile siltation rates from Popper, *The Cairo Nilometer*. Not surprisingly, this period also shows wild fluctuations of similar magnitude (approximately 100 inches between the lowest reading and the highest). Significantly, even decadal averages in this period (Park 1992, figure 4) show a large range (approximately forty inches) looking as chaotic as the annual distribution with only a few sequences of two to three decades showing small fluctuations (e.g., five inches).

12. Kopytoff, *The African Frontier*.

13. This argument has been made at length in Park, "Early Trends" through a comparison between the Nile regime and that of the Senegal River where early civilizations and later caste systems proliferated amidst a flood recession regime not too different than that of the Nile.

14. These points are discussed at length with graphics of flood levels in Park, Ibid., 90–117.

15. Genesis 37–50. It is thought by Egyptologists that there is some historical value to this passage and some feel that it may correspond to fifteenth dynasty or Hyksos period (1650–1550 BC).

16. The twelfth dynasty chapel of Senwosret I, in Karnak, depicts Wadjet behind Nekhbet in profile with each "standing" on a basket: perhaps representing the containers in which grain was measured.

17. Wilkinson, *Complete Temples of Ancient Egypt*, 18.

18. Bard, "The Emergence of the Egyptian State" in Shaw, *The Oxford History of Ancient Egypt*, 65, 78.

19. Egypt's decimal, cumulative-additive hieroglyphic numerical notation was used in Egypt from 3250 BC to 400 AD. Although both Egyptian and Mesopotamian lunar calendars intercalated an additional month on occasion to get back in step with the solar year, throughout this time, unlike in Mesopotamia, the number six never assumed any fundamental importance in the Egyptian numerical system. This argues, despite evidence of contact even in predynastic times, for only a modest Mesopotamian cultural influence on Egypt.

20. Baines, "Scripts, High Culture, and Administration in Middle Kingdom Egypt," 26 in Houston, *Shape of Script*. As Baines notes the earliest forms of writing clearly began as hieroglyphs designed for high cultural or sacred use on temple walls, monuments, tomb walls and coffins, scarabs, and seals. The elegance and partially pictographic character of hieroglyphs has been a focal point of later fascination with ancient Egyptian society. In time, dynastic writing evolved to represent consonants as well as pictographic symbols. In no case did it represent syllables such as was the norm in Sumerian. This fact, and the reliance of cuneiform on the construction of words and sentences out of rearrangements of a simple wedge shape, suggests at most minimal influence on the development of Egyptian writing from the slightly earlier Sumerian logo-syllabic script.

21. Baines, Ibid., 28.

22. Hieroglyphs could be written left to right or right to left to suit artistic needs, but they were always oriented to have faces looking toward the direction in which the text began. Nevertheless, most hieroglyphs texts were written from right to left, and both Hieratic and Demotic scripts were written exclusively from right to left. Archaeological preservations suggests that extensive texts appear first chiseled on monumental constructions or painted on walls; and then appeared on papyrus. In the process, they spread from exclusive use by elites to regular use by a much broader, if imprecisely known, segment of the population.

23. Nevertheless, as Baines, "Scripts, High Culture" notes two clear transition periods should be noted: (a) between the Early and Old Dynastic periods; and (b) in the First Intermediate period perhaps beginning in upper Egypt when a shift toward what

is now called classic Egyptian can be seen, probably under the influence of a broader use of writing by a wider variety of individuals in a less unequal society. (30–3). This version of Egyptian, referred to as classic, developed new forms of text and endured for 1,300 years from the Middle Kingdom until in the seventh century BC when the Demotic script was developed. (62). Aramaic texts become common in the sixth to fifth centuries BC, while under the Ptolemies 332–30 BC, Greek came into fairly widespread use, as did Latin in the Roman Period (30 BC–395 AD). Coptic was developed as a script written left to right that borrowed from both Greek and Demotic (which was pretty much abandoned by the fifth century AD) and is the only Egyptian script to have vowels on a parity with consonants.

24. Baines, Ibid., 25–63. Daniels and Bright, *World's Writing Systems*, 73–83, 287ff.).

25. Comment by Oden Goelet in Faulkner, *Egyptian Book of the Dead*, 137–70.

26. Richards, *Mapping Time*, 147–52. Englund, "Administrative Timekeeping in Ancient Mesopotamia," 121–22.

27. Chrisomalis, *Numerical Notation*, 44–56.

28. In the context of a study of Greek and Hindu polytheism, Napier, *Masks, Transformation, and Paradox*, makes this point eloquently.

29. Wilkinson, *The Complete Gods and Goddesses of Ancient Egypt*, especially pp. 6 and 70–71). Most details of the following general discussion of Egyptian deities also come from Wilkinson.

30. Lloyd, "Heka, Dreams and prophecy in Ancient Egyptian stories." Szpakowska, *Through a Glass Darkly*.

31. Cartouche is the French word for cartridge, and was used by Napoleon's expedition to describe these inscriptions.

32. See the commentary by Oden Goelet, Jr. in Faulkner, *The Egyptian Book of the Dead*, 146–47.

33. The myth of Seth and Osiris's quarrels and Osiris's final legal success before the tribunal of the Ennead is well known as is the role of Isis in reviving him from the dead after Seth cut him to pieces and scattered the fragments up the Nile where they were eaten by fishes. In the myth, Isis through her powers recovered everything except the penis but was able to fashion a new one for Osiris.

34. Wilkinson, *Complete Gods*, 16.

35. Baines, *High Culture and Experience in Ancient Egypt*, 184.

36. Wilkinson, *The Complete Temples of Ancient Egypt*, 98.

37. Analysis of the Ramesside period Wilbour Papyrus suggests that 58 percent of the temples listed were constructed in the nineteenth and twentieth dynasties, a few (2.1 percent) in the previous dynasty and the foundation date of the remaining 39.8 percent could not be definitively ascertained. Katary, *Land Tenure in the Ramesside Period*, Appendix F, Table V39, p. 308.

38. Lichtheim, *Ancient Egyptian Literature* Vol III, 34–35.

39. Wilkinson, *Complete Gods,* 187.

40. Herodotus, *The History*, Book 2: #178 lists these cities as Chios, Teos, Phocaea, Clazomenae, Rhodes, Cnidus, Halicarnassus, Phaselis, Mytilene, Aegina, Samos, and Miletos.

41. Lichtheim, Vol III, 86–89.

42. It is known for example that he usurped (placed his name on) hundreds of pre-existing statues and deities cf Dijk, "The Amarna Period and the later New Kingdom," in Shaw, *The Oxford History of Ancient Egypt*, 299.

43. Lichtheim, *Ancient Egyptian Literature* Vol I, p. 69 lines 21–27. While the text is from the Middle Kingdom the practice presumably antedates the text considerably.

44. Faulkner, *Egyptian Book of the Dead* Chapter 125, Plate 31. While the earliest examples of the B of D began to appear in the thirteenth dynasty (1773 BC), the earliest more or less complete example dates to the sixteenth dynasty, found on the coffin of Queen Mentuhotep, wife of King Djehuty. Papyrus Ani which is a composite of ready-made illustrations and text with Ani's name inserted after the fact here and there was beautifully illustrated, but textually incomplete, and the Faulkner translation has filled in the missing parts from other sources.

45. Lichtheim, Vol I, 100–1.

46. Lichtheim, Vol I, 173–74, 178.

47. Lichtheim, Vol II, 140, 142.

48. Lichtheim, Vol II, 23–24.

49. Versteeg, Law in Ancient Egypt, 23.

50. Lichtheim, Vol II, 151–52, 155, 157.

51. Lichtheim, Vol III, 27.

52. The three famous texts, *The Instruction of Ptahhotep*, *The Lament of the Eloquent Peasant*, and *The Admonition of Ipuwer* among others trace the development of a concept of social justice as social upheavals of the Intermediate periods force elites to rethink the social order. Baeck, *Mediterranean Tradition in Economic Thought*, 28.

53. Assmann, *Ma'at: Gerechtigkeit und Unsterblichkeit im Alten Ägypten*, has suggested that *ma'at* might be termed "vertical solidarity."

54. Private servants in the Middle Kingdom were called *bak* and could be inherited while servants of an institution, referred to as *hem-nisut* (male) and *hemet* (female) or collectively as *meryt* people, remained servants of new appointees in the institution. Both types of servants were referred to collectively by the term *djet* which comprised all the working servants of an individual. How their freedoms and rights compared with those of the working classes in better known times is not clear. Grajetzki, *Middle Kingdom*, 148.

55. Kemp, *Ancient Egypt*, 232ff, 244.

56. Goelet, "Accounting Practices and Economic Planning in Ancient Egypt before the Hellenistic Period," in Hudson and Wunsch, *Creating Economic Order*, 236 suggests that the royal funerary arrangements in upper Egypt mentioned in the Abusir archives were active from seventy to 250 years though Pepi I made exemption decrees in favor of two pyramid cities built by Snofru three hundred years earlier. Pirenne, *Histoire des institutions et du droit privé de l'ancienne Egypte*, 186 noted that inscriptions, of the Royal Chanceller under Pepi I to Pepi II boasting of the charitable things they have done, refer to the funds given from their perpetual foundations.

57. Malek, "Old Kingdom," in Shaw, 105.

58. Gae Callender, "Middle Kingdom," in Shaw, 172ff suggests that by the Middle Kingdom, lands belonging to temples or pious foundations had become tax exempt in

part or in full, but that otherwise the state collected taxes and imposed corvée labor. Dijk, "Amarna Period and the Later New Kingdom," in Shaw, Ibid., 292 also notes that in the time of Tutankhamun a treasury official was sent to the temples from the Delta all the way to Elephantine (south of the Nile bend) to levy taxes on temple revenues.

59. Kemp, 238 makes this point and provides detail on one such decree, the Nauri Decree of Seti I, dating to the New Kingdom.

60. Kemp, 193 notes that in the twentieth dynasty, during a period of economic crisis, the state taxed temples and even taxed a particular category of state land (*khato*) that was administered by temples.

61. Warburton, *State and Economy in Ancient Egypt*, 26.

62. Warburton, 28. The following discussion of terminology relies on Warburton (1997: 219–91).

63. Warburton, 28. The following discussion of terminology relies on Warburton (1997: 256–57, 260; footnote 929) who also concludes that the term translated as serf, *smdt*, must have been a tenant obliged to pay only a part of his harvest.

64. Warburton, 28, 276–77.

65. Warburton 28, 278–80.

66. Warburton, 285 wrongly, we think, concludes that the implication that he only doubled the levy implies that it was already at a high level.

67. Warburton, 28, 290–91.

68. Currently, we do not really have any way of estimating an average duration of these cults.

69. Pirenne, *Histoire des institutions,* 356ff.

70. Goelet, "Accounting Practices and Economic Planning in Ancient Egypt before the Hellenistic Era," in Hudson and Wunsche, *Creating Economic Order*, (245, 255).

71. Goelet Ibid., 237ff and 256ff. Eyre, "Feudal Tenure and Absentee Landlords" IN Allam, *Grund und Boden in Altägypten*, 119ff.

72. Schumpeter, *History of Economic Analysis*, 1174–179.

73. Friedman, *Money and Economic Development*, 28.

74. In a pair of articles, Herbert Simon argued that the modern capitalist economy is best described as an organizational economy rather than a market economy and that organizations inculcate altruism; docile employees are open to advice do better themselves and promote the organization's welfare even more than their own; Simon, "Organization and Markets," and "Altruism and Economics."

75. Keynes, *Treatise on Probability*, makes a detailed critique of what is called the frequentist model of statistics and then elaborates the rules of a subjective theory of probability. This approach was later developed in a more succinct form, for example, by Jeffrey, *Subjective Probability*, and these days is a well-known approach to statistics.

76. Warburton provides such an argument. Though we find his scholarship and discussion of Egyptian terminology most enlightening we are not persuaded by his overly Keynesian model.

77. Sraffa, *Production of Commodities*.

78. Kula, *Economic Theory of Feudal System*,141 suggests that during the feudal period in Poland it was in fact most rational to avoid reliance on purchasing from the market to the degree possible by producing as much as possible for one self.

79. Shaw, 14. Goelet, in Hudson and Wunsch, 216 suggests that the traditional economy was not transformed, even though money appeared for the first time, and certain "home truths" of the traditional dynastic economy were carried on through the Persian and Ptolemaic periods.

80. Lichtheim, Vol. III, 172.) These proverbs come from the Instructions of Ankhsheshonqy papyrus which can be dated to circa 108–30 BC but as proverbs presumably date from an earlier time.

81. Pestman, *Recueil de textes démotiques et bilingues*, 42ff.

82. For a detailed discussion on ancient recognition of grain compressions see the Appendix on grain compression which considers this issue in both Mesopotamia and Egypt.

83. Piketty, *Capital in the Twenty-First Century*.

84. Gunderson and Holling, *Panarchy*.

85. Rathbone, "Roman Egypt," chapter 26, in Scheidel, Morris and Saller, *The Cambridge Economic History of the Greco-Roman World*. Most notably, Rathbone discusses demography (p. 699) and monetization (p. 712ff) as well as changes in taxation (p. 716ff).

86. Versteeg, *Law in Ancient Egypt*, 101–3.

87. Lloyd, "The Late Period, 664–323 BC," in Trigger et al., 302.

88. Katary, *Land Tenure in the Ramesside Period*, Appendix F, 307. Katary provides a careful analysis of the Wilbour Papyrus providing useful statistics on the data. The Wilbour Papyrus provides accounting for approximately 5 percent of the agricultural land in the regions it covers (23), but it shows the institutional land owners having portfolios of land widely scattered with taxes based on land quality (yield) not area and that everything depended on location with some lands sown in grain and others, such as river bank, sown in vegetables and flax (245–47, 257–58).

89. Katary, Appendix F, 292, 301–2.

90. Versteeg, 109ff.

91. Versteeg, 19.

92. Ward, "Land Ownership in Ancient Egypt" IN Khalidi, *Land tenure and social transformation*, 68.

93. Versteeg, 113.

94. Versteeg, 117.

95. Versteeg, 121.

96. Versteeg, 206.

97. Versteeg, 144–47, 191.

98. Versteeg, 190.

99. Aristide Théodorides, The Concept of Law in Ancient Egypt, IN Harris, *Legacy of Egypt*, 315.

100. Versteeg, 193.

101. See discussion and references by Ward, in Khalidi, 64.

102. Ward, Ibid., 65.

103. Ward, Ibid., 66. Note that in the Egyptian tradition such a successor might well be a son but that inheritance was to the occupant of an office indicated that other genealogical heirs to someone's personal fortune had no rights to the assets that went with the office.
104. Katary, *Land Tenure in the Ramesside Period,* Appendix F, Table V16, 301.
105. Théodorides, "Concept of Law in Ancient Egypt" in Harris, *The Legacy of Egypt,* 291, 313.
106. Lorton, "Treatment of Criminals."
107. Versteeg, 199–200.

Chapter Four

Finance and Social Capital in Classical Greece and Rome

Recognizing that finance is intrinsically tied to ethical milieu as well as social capital, and regularly motivated and rendered possible in cultural forms by hidden interests, we have chosen Attic Athens and Rome during the period of the Roman Republic (509 BC–27 BC) because they provide the best-attested early discussions of the ethics of lending, the importance of honor, status, and social capital to credit, and the dual importance of the public and private spheres to finance and status. The Agora of Athens and the Piraeus also embody the two main financial approaches that went on to influence global finance: the first set the path followed largely in Europe and the second led the Islamic world in another fruitful direction. The role of ethics in the classical world was inextricably tied to honor as the following attest:

> *Amicitia* can be seen as a system of social exchange generating various resources. If we try to assess the global importance of this exchange to the Roman economy we find a number of significant contributions. On the micro-level, *amicitia* strongly influenced the position and success of individuals. On the macro-level, it generated conditions that contributed to the relative success or failure of economic sectors (an effect most clearly visible in the sector of finance).[1]

> They found Lucretia weeping in her room. "Are you all right?" asked her husband. "No," she replied, "how can anything be all right if a woman has lost her honour? In your bed, Collatinus, you'll find the sign of another man. But only my body was violated, my mind is innocent, as my death shall attest. Promise me that the adulterer will be punished. He is Sextus Tarquinius. . . . As for me, although I absolve myself of guilt, I do not release myself from paying the penalty. From now on, no woman can use the example of Lucretia to live unchaste"

> with that she took the dagger she had hidden in her clothes, plunged it into her heart, and fell forward dead. Her husband and father cried out.[2]

In 509 BC, both Rome and Athens were city-states. Athens probably had a resident population of around 40,000,[3] and dominated a large hinterland of 2,600 square km[4] with a population on the order of 200,000.[5] Rome was of a comparable size, with a resident population of between 25,000 and 40,000, and had a hinterland of 775 square km. [6] The political landscape both in Greece and the Italian Peninsula consisted of an amalgam of sundry peoples, organized into tribes and small city-states.

These cities were also alike in that they had recently overthrown tyrant kings—moving Athens to set up a democracy, and Rome, a Republic. They both attempted to build empires through military conquest. Athens attempted this first against Persia, then against Sparta, but was defeated in the Second Peloponnesian War (413–404 BC), and soon lost her empire.[7] While Athens was not to become a superpower, Macedonia, under Philip II (382–336 BC) and his son Alexander the Great (356–323 BC) built and ruled a short-lived empire that at its greatest extent included Egypt and spread across the Persian Empire into parts of India. After Alexander's death, the empire was divided among its royal families who then proceeded to fight each other for the original kingdom. Rome, too, was bent on conquests, and early on began fighting with neighboring tribes and city-states. By the time of the first Punic War in 265 BC, Rome had extended its control over most of the Italian boot. Following the destruction of Carthage during the third Punic War (149–146 BC), Rome became the dominant power in the Mediterranean, conquered Macedonia, and soon reduced Greece to a Roman province.[8]

Two features stand out in both societies. First, the logic and principles of hierarchy permeated their institutions and colored most social interactions—aristocrats and commoners, masters and slaves, husbands and wives, household heads and dependents, young and old, and so on. Second, kinship ordered many aspects of society, and shaped social relations. Individuals were members of families, patrilineages, clans, phratries, and tribes as well as members of larger groups such as commoners or aristocrats first, then Romans or Athenians. This meant that people were viewed and treated not simply as individuals, but always as members of particular corporate groups.[9] As each of these groups had economic, political, and religious dimensions their structure, constraints, and dynamics influenced their economic actions.

Roman households were often large and complex units, and were organized around descent from a senior male, the *paterfamilias*. Beyond a husband, his wife, and their offspring, households could include extended kin—both blood relatives (*cognati*), and relatives by marriage (affines), as well as freeborn clients, *liberti* (free slaves), and slaves.[10] The Roman household was itself a corporate group that controlled property: land, crops, animals, houses, storage bins, and sheds, among other forms of wealth. It functioned like a miniature state, as an economic unit, a system of defense, and the implementor of law and government.[11] Under Roman law, the *paterfamilias* held absolute authority and power over his family. He was the legal owner of all its property. He alone had the power to sell, mortgage, or borrow against its property. He was judge and jury for its members, and could kill them or sell them into slavery—and state authorities under normal circumstances would not intervene.[12]

The corporate character of the Roman family was explicitly expressed in matters of inheritance. Under Roman law when the *paterfamilias* died, though his physical person perished, his legal personality survived, and his successor inherited his "entire legal position" including all of his rights, debts, and property. For the *paterfamilias* to die without a will in Roman eyes was seen as a particular horror, as it left the family without protector and threatened the household's very existence. If this happened, his "estate" was divided among his direct descendants.[13] If there were none, it went to the nearest paternal agnate (such as uncle, brother, or cousin)—and should these not exist, his clan decided how his estate was to be divided. Since succession was of paramount importance,[14] it was customary for the *paterfamilias* to name a successor in his will. While often his successor was a son or a brother, should a *paterfamilias* not have these, or not believe them competent to head the family, he might adopt a son (commonly from within his patrilineage) and declare him to be his successor in his will.

By the Late Republic, women also had gained the right to make a will;[15] and, commonly, all but the poorest Roman citizens made wills.[16] A person's will was not merely a means of passing on property to one's heirs, but was also a way to honor friends and family.[17] The public nature of wills meant not just that the property inherited was public knowledge, but that one's social ties were made public as well. Arguably, wills were also a means of passing on one's network, primarily including close friends and relatives, and thereby one's social capital to one's primary heirs.[18] To ensure such social capital and insure that the principal heirs would receive their inheritance, the deceased would often include politically influential persons among the heirs.

Ancient Greek households *(oikoi*), like Roman ones, were economic and social units that were based on patrilineal relations, with women marrying into them. The *kyrios,* or lord of the household, was usually its oldest male and the household, beyond the wife and children, often included extended family and slaves.[19] As its master, the *kyrios* not only was its protector and owner of its property, but was also the members' legal representative before the wider community (*polis*). However, unlike the Roman *paterfamilias*, the authority of the Greek *kyrios* was not absolute, and the state did intervene in matters of abuse or mistreatment.[20]

The institutional foundations for economic and social capital suggest finance in Attic Greece or the Republic of Rome cannot be reduced to individual strategy. Although the main material we examine in the following sections on finance focuses on individual concerns and efforts to construct social capital we do not pretend to provide an adequate economic model for either the Early Republic or for Attic Greece. We deliberately narrow our scope to consider, within the given social structures, the social and cultural reasons individuals went about building their own significance and wealth. The material available makes it possible to illustrate in some detail key strategies and attitudes that probably predate the period and that have continued in altered forms down the ages.

In early Rome, without the protection of a powerful patron, a man was at the mercy of those who stood over him in the social hierarchy. While instrumental friendships are widespread and common phenomena, Roman patron-client relations were formal and all-inclusive. The closest analogies might be Godfather relations in the Sicilian Mafia, or *cacicazgo* relationships in Mesoamerica or Latin America. At the top levels of Roman society stood its elites (aristocrats, patricians, large landowners, senators, equestrians (knights), nobles, and rich would-be-nobles) whose power, wealth, positions, and social networks enabled them to dispense patronage to clients (protégés, plebeians, freedmen, and even slaves).[21] Usually, this relationship was initiated with a gift or favor that a person could not fully reciprocate, placing the client morally in the patron's debt.[22]

Powerful patrons offered political protection, economic help, and access to people within a network[23] that included not just the patron's clients, but also those who moved in his circles as equals. Such networks could be very large. It is said that "when the Claudii *gen* left its Sabine territories to settle in Rome it came with some 5,000 clients."[24] While patrons provided protection for clients, the size of a patron's entourage also enhanced his status and power—especially if it were greater than those of his peers.[25]

Public display was a key aspect of patronage. Each morning a patron's clients, gathered in front of his residence for the *salutario* (a ritual greeting) to pay him homage and to express their gratitude; and, not to appear was tantamount to repudiating their loyalty.[26] In return as a gesture of friendship, clients received a gift (*sportula*) of food or money so that even the poorest of them would have something to eat that day. Some clients then would be invited to dinner, or to accompany a patron to the forum.

In stark contrast to Roman power where wealth and patronage were on display, in Athens patron-client relationships were much more private than public in nature. Where Roman law defined the obligations between patrons and clients, Athenian law did not provide patronage legal footing.[27] Indeed, since the use of personal connections to gain favors went against democratic ideals, Athenians were suspicious of patron-client relations generally, and particularly concerned about their influence in the public sphere.[28] To lessen the sway of clientship, the Athenian state instituted measures such as paying jurors, and providing public welfare measures to aid the poor.[29] A strongly Greek ideology of *eleutheria* (freedom) with its great emphasis on independence and self-sufficiency also tempered patron-clients relations since such dependence was seen as akin to slavery, so much so that no respectable Athenian would willingly admit to having a patron.[30]

ECONOMY OF ATHENS AND ROME: TRADE AND THE STATE

In 509 BC, food production in Athens and Rome was still rooted in smallholder agriculture and herding. Both territories were hardscrabble lands with poor soils,[31] so both cities had chronic problems feeding their growing urban populations.[32] Fourth century figures for yields suggest that Attica could only produce 20 to 50 percent of the grain needed to feed Athens.[33] Rome's situation was no better. Both cities depended on combinations of trade and warfare to deal with shortfalls. Led by trade, Greeks, like the Cretans and Phoenicians before them, began to colonize the Mediterranean as early as the eighth century BC.[34] By the fifth century, there were some 1,500 Greek colonies,[35] spread across the Mediterranean, like so many frogs around a pond.[36] Athens as a sea going power imported grain and traded with the Greek colonies that dotted the coasts of the Mediterranean, the southern Adriatic, the Aegean, the Mermara Sea, the Bosporus, and the Black Sea. Additional colonies were located in Syria, Egypt, and Libya.[37]

Rome in the fifth century was not yet a sea power, and would not become one until the outbreak of the first Punic war in 264 BC,[38] and so it depended largely upon trade, particularly for grain with neighboring peoples. Trade, however, was complicated—requiring trusted partners and treaties—costs already made it impractical to cart foodstuffs long distances overland, and if one had to cross through foreign territories it would have been prohibitive. With a growing population to feed, the logic of military expansion and trade became increasingly interlocked leading Rome to conquer first neighboring peoples, then peoples all across the Italian peninsula, then eventually moving overseas, including Alexandria in Ptolemaic Egypt with its grain surpluses. Conquered territories provided Rome not just booty, tribute, and slaves, but also markets and increasing trade, generating the wealth needed to field troops and to engage in warfare.

Rome and Athens had significant markets if not ones where all key inputs to productive processes were efficiently priced (labor and land being obvious exceptions). Due to the presence of slaves as well as hired labor, labor prices would not consistently reflect their value in subsequent productive processes. The price of land was similarly distorted by the legal role land played in establishing citizenship. In case of disputes, participants had quick and easy access to courts, where even foreigners might get fair treatment.[39] In Rome, *Curule aediles*, the magistrates in charge of the slave, livestock, and grain markets had similar duties.[40] Given the large population of poor, jobless, and slaves, the average consumer had limited buying power; cumulatively, however, they represented substantial demand. Where the real money lay was in trade at grand scales. Transportation by sea and navigable rivers permitted trade of staples (e.g., grain, wine, oil), metals, stone, and timber in prodigious quantities.[41]

Where modern markets tend to be impersonal, in these ancient markets, while legal regulations played a role, everything was more personal, and heavily reliant on social capital. Many prices depended on social relations, not just a person's own standing and reputation, but also those of kin and friends. Such relations opened and closed doors, so being an insider or outsider affected access to credit, financial deals of all sorts, and other opportunities. In Athens and Rome, state officials also supervised markets, enforced rules, guaranteeing the quality of goods, overseeing weights and measures, and may have fixed a maximum price for some goods.[42]

Outside the market, many commodities circulated based on reciprocity among social equals.[43] Social relations between friends and kinsmen were knit together based on exchange of gifts and services. Such relations of reciprocity were often key elements in business transactions; and the gifts and favors exchanged implied fiduciary responsibilities to act (without thought of self-interest) on each other's behalf.

In Rome and Athens state and religious bodies organized systems of redistribution in which a portion of tribute or tithes and offerings was reallocated and directed toward segments of the population. Tribute and taxes supported military expenditures, public building projects, and the support of orphans. Because state expenditures tended to be made in cash, they pumped cash into the market as recipients spent these funds to meet their needs. Similarly, feasts organized by religious cults amassed and redistributed food in enormous quantities.[44] Just how important such redistributions were depended on their frequency and the ratio of distribution amounts to population.[45] In classical Athens as many as 2,000 head of cattle would be sacrificed for state festivals, but as the state had a population of 120,000 to 250,000 adult males, this probably meant that each would receive a kilo or less of meat.[46] Doubt-

Photo 4.1. Terracotta Amphora (Jar). Herekles and Apollo vying for possession of the Delphic tripod—seat of oracular pronouncements. Ca. 530 BC.

Source: Purchase, Joseph Pulitzer Bequest, 1963. The Metropolitan Museum of Art, accession number 63.11.6. www.metmuseum.org

less, religious expenditures on buildings and other material requirements as well as loans by temples, such as the temple of Apollo at Delphi which lent at 10 percent, also pumped monies into the market.

Military conquests, at least initially, proved a cash machine for both states, tribute providing massive infusions of copper, silver, and gold, grains and other commodities, as well as large numbers of slaves.[47] This influx of slave labor changed the logic of production, particularly in mining and agriculture. In mining, slave labor vastly increased the quantity of copper, silver, and gold used in coinage, but also the supply of iron and lead, for weapons and other uses. Agricultural based on peasant production was limited both by poor lands and soils, but more fundamentally by access to labor. As long as production depended on household labor, the land that could be worked was limited. The conquests of new territories and peoples, besides creating vast numbers of slaves taken as prisoners of war, also expanded tribute and grain imports.

Slavery made cultivating larger areas and growing more lucrative crops possible. As large *latifundias* growing commercial crops displaced small-holder subsistence agriculture, peasants flooded into cities and swelled the numbers of the urban poor. In time, as the number of slaves expanded,[48] even households of modest means might aspire to a slave or two, and soon slaves could be found in almost every corner of the economy. Aside from laboring in the fields and working in households as domestics, slaves could be found working for butchers and bakers, and sundry shops. They formed part of the work force that made pottery, armor, swords, and other crafts. They helped run businesses, serving as secretaries, clerks, and accountants. Educated slaves provided services of scribes, teachers, librarians, artists, musicians, entertainers, and even doctors. Slaves even formed part of the state's labor force used to build and maintain public works. As well, they formed part of the apparatus that supplied government services and kept the state's administrative machinery functioning. In Rome, slaves staffed the mint and the state's granaries.[49]

The impacts of slavery on labor markets would have been felt by workers, craftsmen, shopkeepers, day laborers, and the jobless who had to compete with them. In Athens, one consequence of slavery was that Athenians despised wage labor, and would not work for others on a permanent basis except under extraordinary circumstances, since doing so would put them in the position of a slave.[50] This individualistic attitude seems to have been inherited by the Islamic world. In Rome, the growing mass of poor, jobless, underemployed, and hungry plebeians was a potent recipe for civil unrest. Grain shortages or price hikes often led to political unrest.[51] Since local production was never sufficient, much of Rome's grain supply had to be imported. This allowed Rome's wealthy to speculate in essential commodities, to fill storehouses with grain and wait for a bad harvest to reap enormous profits.[52]

In the face of shortages, Roman magistrates seeking to curry public favor and curb unrest often used their power and personal influence to secure grains from allied or subject states. In 121 BC, for example, the tribune Gaius Gracchus established a system that provided adult Roman men a monthly grain ration at a set price. In 58 BC, this became a free monthly ration to those entitled.[53] Public and private rituals, festivals, and feasts also redistributed large quantities of food, as did the *sportula* that Roman patrons gave daily to their clients. By contrast, although Athens also had chronic problems securing enough grain to feed its population, its grain trade was strictly regulated, and while merchants were permitted to import grain, they were forbidden to export or stockpile it.[54] When food shortages occurred, although one state-sponsored grain distribution is attested, in Athens the usual practice was to offer traders incentives to encourage imports and seek donations from the rich to subsidize grain sales. The profits made by traders at such times were deeply resented.

Tribute and taxes provided the backbone of state finances in both economies. Yet, exacting tribute and taxes was problematic. Neither Rome nor Athens did so directly, but instead used tax farmers. While the bidding for these contracts guaranteed the state upfront revenues, it also resulted in abusive collection practices that were deeply and universally resented.[55] A similar system of bids applied to leasing state owned mines, and to contracts for public building projects.

Though merchants might act alone, often they formed companies and partnerships. As trust was essential, merchants looked to their kin and friends. This system guaranteed that government contracts, leases, and other concessions went to those with money. It also lent itself to abuse and corruption: defined largely as extortionate profits not as favoritism, which was more likely to be viewed as honorable behavior. With empire the scale of trade increased, bringing with it even greater temptations. In Rome, where the wealth of patricians came from their land, rents, and investments, trade was considered déclassé. It was good to be seen spending money lavishly, but bad to be seen grubbing for it. As early as 218 BC, a law was passed "to prohibit senators from engaging in any lucrative activity based on trade."[56] All this did was to encourage doing business through friends, particularly in the equestrian class who were often principles in such trade, or alternately business was done through clients or freedmen.[57]

ACADEMIC PERSPECTIVES ON GRECO-ROMAN FINANCE

Scholars of the classic period in Europe until not too long ago, divided rather unambiguously into two groups about the nature of ancient economies. Following Polanyi,[58] some claimed the ancient world had an institutional structure that made it intrinsically non-capitalist (the unfortunately named primitivist position); while others, traditionally referred to as modernists in classics (and formalists in anthropology), argued that commerce and the economy in the ancient world had fundamental similarities to the situation in recent centuries.[59] Another position among scholars of the ancient Near East as well as of Greece that resembles the Polanyi position argues that ancient polities were significantly different than modern ones in that they regularly used debt forgiveness as a means to stabilize political crises. Some scholars also have pointed to the numerous edicts along these lines as an explanation for the low volatility of interest rates and prices.[60]

Moses Finley, a classicist, advocated a position along Polanyi's lines and argued for a primitivist theory making a series of strong claims: classical Greece and Rome shared a common economic system characterized by the lack of a true market principle, the economy was fundamentally embedded in the political system (predominance of the political over the economic), there was a lack of properly rational economic decision making, and there was a concomitant over-riding importance of status (hierarchy) in economic decision making.[61] Although there is little reason to doubt both the importance of elite positive sanctions for gift giving or performance of civic duties and elite disdain for money grubbing, commerce and "inn-keeping,"[62] most recent scholars do not endorse Finley's full theory.

As soon as Finley's book was published, critiques of his model began to be made, though it is fair to say that as a scientific hypothesis his model was extremely stimulating, his model now is generally viewed as deficient in any number of ways. In particular, the claim that the classic world had a common unitary economic system no longer stands up to modern scrutiny. Similarly, his notion that for a lengthy period of time there were no substantive or significant transformations in the way this economy worked defies current historical and anthropological common sense.

R. Descat, for example, notes that between the fifth and the fourth centuries BC the relationship between the market and agriculture transformed markedly, commercial and artisanal wealth (derived from buying and selling) developed significantly, and there were important developments in a market for land as well.[63] Perhaps, the most famous alternative was proposed by K. Hopkins, a tax and trade model, in which in the Roman period especially, taxation forced peripheral areas (in which the taxes were collected but rarely spent) to develop export trade to sustain the taxation.[64] P. Leveau similarly proposed that we recognize a lack of regional homogeneity based on a model he referred to as the "organizing state," with the obvious implications that not all states organized the economy similarly.[65]

These criticisms, and many others, seem to fit at least one current economic theory, the theory of transformational growth developed by E. Nell, as well as what we have learned from the Annales school of history. Building on such positions, we endorse a more Hereclitan position than Finley: one in which economic and other institutions are viewed as in continual transformation. In this view, there is no significant role for long-term static economic structure nor even for positing price optima, however defined (including for the cost of credit), or other reasons to suppose there might be no motivation for change. In this view, technologies in use (social, financial, and economic) are continually transformed and evolve subject to intellectual, demographic, social, economic, and environmental forces.[66]

There are persuasive reasons to think that in classical Greece and Rome the distribution of power, and social networks of friendship played a greater role in decisions about credit than did a "rational" search for efficiency. In this limited sense, Finley and Polanyi seem fully vindicated. As Sraffa pointed out in 1960, economic efficiency is poorly defined even within a fully capitalist economy because no one in an economy using compound interest can actually calculate the most efficient pattern of investment without the ability to predict future interest rates and prices.[67] Given our focus on continuous transformations in the broad social aspects of credit as well as our concern with the development of new financial technologies over time, we see no place for simple theoretical dichotomies such as "modernist" or "primitivist" approaches.[68] From this perspective shifts in political alliances go hand in hand with shifts in economic potential and financial motivations. As Foucault remarked in the 1980s, the idea of post-modernism makes no more sense than modernism (modernity), because similar types of transformations (of rationalities) occur throughout history.[69]

ATHENIAN PERSPECTIVES ON FINANCE IN THE CLASSIC PERIOD

While modern Greece may appear to many as either a poor country or a failed state, the more profound view recognizes that from the eighth to fourth centuries BC[70] Greek innovations in democracy and political science, literature, drama, philosophy, logic, and science were critical to the development of modern Western civilization.[71]

Yet, insightful as this view may be, many Greek ideas built on preexisting ideas developed in surrounding and preceding societies. In the area of financial thought, like many other domains, Greek ideas did not arise *ex nihilo*, but were derived from a variety of Near Eastern ideas that Greeks proceeded to refine, develop, systematize, and theorize in an unprecedented way. Greek mathematics and banking owed much to Babylon, Greek sculpture borrowed from Egypt, the Greek alphabet came from Phoenicia and the names of most Greek musical terms and instruments came from non Indo-European languages. Yet, the character of the *polis* and ideas about citizenship in Greek city states were dramatically different from those of ancient Mesopotamia as was much of Greek thought, particularly in philosophy and the social sciences. The simplicity of Athenian social structure and the small size of Greek city states kept the financial system less elaborate than that of the Roman Republic and subsequent Empire.

Although a wide range of institutions such as banks, brokers, companies, and partnerships, provided a core infrastructure for the economy it would be a mistake to read these in terms of modern equivalents. We have discussed the origin of deposit banking (ca. 635 BC) in the chapter on Mesopotamia. By the fourth century BC,[72] Greek and Roman banks although they offered a range of services including deposits, loans, and payments to others in distant places,[73] were private, being owned in most cases by a single principal with limited capital. Being private, they were unregulated, and their books were not open to scrutiny by the state or other individuals. In contrast to modern banks, access to these services, as might be expected, depended on personal ties and relationships which in turn were tied to one's position in the social structure.[74]

Before examining financial practice in classical Greece in more detail, some appreciation of classic economic thought beginning with Plato (427–348 BC) may be helpful. In the *Laws,* where lending at interest is forbidden on the grounds that it is deleterious to the state, Plato states:

> Money must not be deposited with anybody whom one does not trust. There must be no lending at interest, because it will be quite in order for the borrower to refuse absolutely to return both interest and principal. . . . I will never concede. . . . that the rich man can become really happy without being virtuous as well: to be extremely virtuous and exceptionally rich at the same time is absolutely out of the question. "Why?" it might be asked. "Because," we shall reply, "the profit from using just *and* unjust methods is more than twice as much as that from just methods alone, and a man who refuses to spend his money either worthily or shamefully spends only half the sum laid out by worthwhile people who are prepared to spend on worthy purposes too. [i.e., as well as on 'neutral' objects]. So anyone who follows the opposite policy will never become richer

than the man who gets twice as much profit and makes half the expenditures. The former is a good man" the latter is not actually a rogue so long as he uses his money sparingly, but on some occasions [i.e., when he makes money (by dishonest means)] he is an absolute villain; thus, as we have said, he is *never* good.[75]

There is a lot in this passage, some of which we will unpack later, but it is important first to note the focus on civic virtue and the distinctions made within the ranks of the less than virtuous. It also should be noted that Plato makes a fine distinction between usury and simply charging interest in small amounts; it is important to note that in Europe this distinction dates back to the Greeks. Plato's hostility to lending at interest is rooted in the notion that loans should be components of relations of reciprocity based on trust. Because unjust loans automatically reap more profit than just ones (those without interest), they accord an indefensible advantage to the unjust. This sets the stage for suggesting there may be unjust conditions on a loan; but it also implies some conditions may be justifiable, even if not indicative of virtue. Plato makes an exception to this rule forbidding interest that portends later concerns. He writes:

Law 74. (a) If a man takes delivery of a piece of work and fails to pay for it within the agreed time, he must be charged double; (b) if a whole year elapses, then notwithstanding the rule that loans in general do not bear interest, he must pay an obol per drachma [i.e., 200 per cent in interest per annum (6 obols = 1 drachma)] for every month in arrear.[76]

This example seems to take into account the losses incurred to the lender based on a delay in payment or, as we would now say, the opportunity cost of money. The subtlety of the argument goes far beyond the notion that interest is always bad or, as in the Hebrew case, always bad if charged to one's own co-religionists, but otherwise alright. In ancient Greece, charging interest was common, and Plato seems to want to discriminate between acceptable and unacceptable practices on the basis of general principles. The temple of Apollo on Delos, for example, regularly charged 10 percent on loans from the fifth to the second century BC.[77] Another of Plato's references to lending at interest occurs in the Republic. There, Plato not only critiques lending at interest, but suggests lenders should do so at their own risk:

The money-makers, on the other hand, with their eyes on the ground, pretend not to see these people, and by lending money they disable any of the remainder who resist, exact as interest many times the principal sum, and so create a considerable number of drones and beggars in the city.

A considerable number indeed.

> In any case, they are unwilling to quench this kind of evil as it flares up in the city, either in the way we mentioned, by preventing people from doing whatever they like with their own property or by another law which would also solve the problem.
>
> What law?
>
> The second-best one, which compels the citizens to care about virtue by prescribing that the majority of voluntary contracts be entered into at the lender's own risk, for lenders would be less shameless then in their pursuit of money in the city and fewer of those evils we were mentioning just now would develop.
>
> Far fewer.[78]

This passage presages one of the Islamic solutions to the perceived injustice of lending at interest that we will examine later, though whether it had a direct influence, or if this reflects simply thought of the time, is still unclear. The later *commenda* contract which became common in Judaic and Islamic commerce as well as other common loans (such as the *qard*) had to specify that both the lender and recipient of a loan shared risk and profit in appropriate amounts. Plato's argument, which is proposed as a purely rational one rather than as a deontological ethical position, argued for a symbolic theory of money,[79] according to which money should represent wealth symbolically, and so have no value or substance in and of itself. This is the form of money that Plato felt an ideal state should enforce.

Aristotle (384–322 BC) espoused a different monetary theory; that money's principle function was to serve as a medium of exchange as well as a measure and a store of value.[80] It was in effect a particular type of commodity. Aristotle's theory dominated most thought on the subject until the nineteenth century. Yet, Aristotle maintained a carefully argued disregard for lending at interest. His argument in his *Politics,* that while household production was natural, trade was unnatural, and most unnatural of all was usury, influenced people for more than 2,000 years:

> There are two sorts of wealth getting . . . one is a part of household management, the other is retail trade: the former is necessary and honourable, while that which consists in exchange is justly censured; for it is unnatural, and a mode by which men gain from one another. The most hated sort, and with the greatest reason, is usury, which makes a gain out of money itself, and not from the natural object of it. For money was intended to be used in exchange, but not to increase at interest. And this term interest (*tokos*: offspring), which means the birth of money from money, is applied to the breeding of money because the offspring resembles the parent. Wherefore of all modes of getting wealth this is the most unnatural.[81]

Aristotle views usury as unnatural because he defines natural things as having a source of movement or growth inherent in them that he refers to as their nature:

> From what has been said, then, it is plain that nature in the primary and strict sense is the substance of things which have in themselves, as such, a source of movement: for the matter is called the nature because it is qualified to receive this, and processes of becoming and growing are called nature because they are movements proceeding from this. And nature in this sense is the source of the movement of natural objects, being present in them somehow, either potentially or actually.[82]

In hindsight, Aristotle's attribution of a theoretical construct about natural fertility and infertility to loans of money is clearly an early case of the fallacy of misplaced concreteness. Yet after several millennia in which the idea that money grows has been conflated with growth in real world goods or services, it should be possible to understand the degree to which, in ancient Greece, Aristotle's view was not seen as obviously fallacious.

Credit in classical Greece came from a wide range of sources: disreputable lenders of small sums in the market, lenders specializing in maritime trade, bankers specializing in "landed"—for example, non-maritime investments, explicit elite loans to polities, the implicit loans to cities of anyone performing a civic service (liturgies) and, undoubtedly the most common, loans among friends (*philoi*: friends, acquaintances, and those befriended up to and sometimes including fellow citizens) for either particular joint ventures or to help out someone in need. As we have seen, Plato found the last two categories to be the most likely to qualify as virtuous credit.

While surviving documents suggest loans between friends comprised by far the largest group, there are good reasons to believe that those for other kinds have not survived in similar proportions, so the frequency of each type of credit even in classical Athens cannot accurately be estimated. Referred to as *eranos* loans, loans between friends were intended to be reciprocated. Elites who sought public approbation might extend them to a much wider circle than that embracing their friends. Work on *amicitia* in the Republic of Rome,[83] on banking in the Athenian economy, and on lending and borrowing in Attic Greece all show that the technologies of credit were intimately intertwined with networks of friendship and patronage across the classical world, and it is only much later that such interconnections came to be associated unambiguously with corruption.[84]

The Greeks seem to have defined *eranos* as the underwriting of a venture by a group of friends with agreements of a schedule of repayments. This involved specific provision of funds by each friend, but also specification of the schedule of return each expected. To a considerable degree their structure may have resembled *nautika* loans with the addition of a schedule of expected repayments. Just as bankers could use various funds at their disposal to lend, so friends could assemble funds for a venture expected to yield sufficient financial or social benefits. These arrangements were sometimes combined with bank loans to finance projects, and did not necessarily have to involve only friends. In the past, scholars assumed *eranoi* among friends were interest free, but apparently there is no example of even a single such arrangement that was clearly interest free, while there are known interest free loans by bankers to individual clients.[85] Though this point is disputed, it may be a less important issue to resolve than is often assumed.

All the conditions put on a loan are important, and it may simply be that loans from friends had decidedly more friendly conditions than those from strangers. We know that Apollodorus commuted an *eranos* loan of 1,000 drachmas to a gift, and that Plato was ransomed by a stranger who preferred the honor of freeing him over a reimbursement of the ransom.[86] While this does suggest that the line between gift and loan was one that could always be crossed, it may be simply that the latter example was much less common than the former; and hence *eranos* loans may regularly have had decidedly more friendly provisions and consequences than most loans between strangers.

Aristotle's take on the difference between *eranos* loans by friends (*philos*) and loans involving explicit *tokos* seems to have been that the former were based on character (*ēthikē*), while the latter were based on rules (*nomikē*) or explicit conditions (*epi rhētois*); and, that the two categories had to be kept separate.[87] Aristotle added an interesting observation to this discussion: noting that in some places there was a law prohibiting the use of written documentation (e.g., of the conditions) of a loan—thereby forcing loans to be based on character. A clever variation on this idea was the apparent insistence in Cnossos that loans should be viewed as "snatched"—thereby making it possible when necessary, given a lack of documented conditions, to charge the borrower with theft, and so recuperate the funds.[88]

If surviving records in Athens are representative of actual practice, the vast majority of loans to individuals were for nonproductive purposes.[89] Of these, most were clearly *eranos* loans by/to friends or fellow citizens (*philoi*) in immediate need; for example, to help pay a ransom, a fine, an obligatory major liturgy (civil service) or even to finance the repayment of another loan. Loans by individuals or bankers were less usual, but nevertheless common.

One little-appreciated characteristic of credit is that the prevailing rate of interest (even where there is one) rarely can be usefully extrapolated to an annual rate. In most times and places, loans with onerous conditions are taken to meet urgent financial needs—as when food stores run out and a peasant seeks a short-term loan until the harvest. This explains the paradox that on average the poor pay higher rates than the rich. Their need is more urgent, the amount small, and their finances often adequate as long as the period of the loan is brief. This brevity also explains the historical rarity of compound interest.[90]

In classical Greece, most loans would also have been short-term, and would have addressed a short-term problem or opportunity. Using a variety of subsequent loans, and especially relying on subsequent *eranos* loans with conditions that were not onerous, would have had enormous benefits in terms of spreading out the period of repayment. Subsequent *eranos* loans could pay off preceding ones; and, as long as the borrower had an adequate source of income, this procedure would allow them to recover gracefully from a potentially catastrophic event. From a financial perspective, the importance of low cost (friendly) loans can be seen as a form of social insurance rather than, as has been customary, as an indication of a prioritization of friendship over hard-nosed commerce. The high esteem in which such loans were held surely helped to reinforce this essential social institution.

Greeks had a lot to say about *philia* (friendship) and *charis* (service to others) as exemplary virtues that defined honorable conduct:

> When it comes to acting for others, we [Athenians] are different from most people, for we acquire *philoi* not in consequence of what others do for us, but by doing it for them. He who confers the benefit (*charin*) is in a stronger position . . . whereas he who owes it is slower to act, since he knows he returns the kindness not as a favour (*es charin*) but as a debt (*hos opheilēma*).[91]

> . . . it is by exchange that they hold together. This is why they give a prominent place to the temple of the Graces [*Charitōn*]—to promote the requital of services; for this is characteristic of grace [*charis*]—we should serve in return one who has shown grace [*charis*] to us, and should another time take the initiative in showing it [*charis*].[92]

A traditional meaning of *charis,* found in Homer and subsequent works, is "gratitude" for a service rendered as well as "attractiveness" and kindness.[93] The idiom of *philia* (friendship) and *charis* (which carried meanings of charitable giving and grace or gratitude)[94] were crucial to honorable conduct even in patron-client relations.[95] The second passage above, by Aristotle, basically suggests that it is behavior of this type which holds society together; and, that the recognition of mutual obligations is unending.[96] The first of the two passages from Aristotle, expresses the same idea, but adds the notion that the return of such a benefit requires more careful consideration. Recognizing that the first service rendered would most likely be in response to a significant need, no return that did not provide a comparably apposite benefit would be adequate.

In the fifth and fourth centuries BC, these ideal perspectives had some real world counterparts in the Greek concept of *tokos* or yield and the Greek propensity for dichotomizing all things, and in particular all lending, into either maritime loans (*daneismata nautica*) or landed loans (*daneismata eggeia* or *eggeios ousia*), for example, loans secured by land, not real estate loans *per se*.[97] The term for yield, *tokos*, is too narrowly translated as "interest." In the case of maritime loans, yield was based on acknowledgment of risk and ones share of investment; while, when associated with landed loans, it derived from a fixed time-referenced rate (e.g., interest of 12 percent per annum).

"Landed" loans did not necessarily involve real estate. They merely did not fit into the category of maritime loans where yields were justified on the basis of entrepreneurial factors contributing to the enterprise—much as later came to be the norm in the Islamic world. The distinction is thus not whether yield could be expressed as a monthly rate, in both cases they could after the fact, but whether the duration of the loan was used to calculate the total *tokos*. In maritime loans, the duration had no direct bearing on the *tokos*—a voyage that visited many ports and sold different goods in different ports, and so took considerable time, might yield less per month than a quick voyage that made a "killing" on one particular commodity's price differential in two places but it might at the same time yield more total profit. Only when time is truly money would this be even possibly contradictory.

Attic Greece had two commercial areas; one in the Piraeus (Athens' port) called the *emporion* where maritime loans were made, and one in the city, called the *agora,* where landed loans were made. The clear division of the two financial districts captured the conceptual imagination, and all lending was thought to fit intrinsically into one of these two categories—even if we today would not so divide them based on the features of the loans we might choose to emphasize, for example, the collateral, liability, the period of the loan, or the interest rate. Extravagant yields were associated with maritime lending—as were high risks—so an investor might borrow money at high rates to participate in a ship's voyage.

By comparison, high rates for "landed" loans were regularly viewed as seriously immoral. Financial assets in legal discussions were explicitly categorized as cash, maritime loans, and landed loans; and, the latter two spheres were regarded as completely distinct: it was thought improbable that someone in the *agora* would lend at landed rates for an enterprise in the maritime realm; and, no one in their right senses would borrow at maritime rates for an enterprise normally financed in the *agora.*[98]

A classical European definition of the maritime loan includes the provision that the ship and/or its contents alone are the collateral. There is ample evidence that this definition had no correlate in classical Greece, yet much of the argument over the role of credit in maritime trade (referenced in the texts as *nautika*) has relied on this anachronistic formulation. The practice in Athens was flexible, and as far as scholars can tell, without any universal legal constraints: that is to say the only legal strictures were defined in the contracts (*syngraphai)*. Contracts could use collateral other than the boat or its contents, they could also define the obligatory rate of return (*tokos*), and any other conditions: where the ship should go, what commodities to buy for what leg of the voyage, prices allowable for sales of the commodities, and the time frame after return within which the principle and *tokos* had to be returned, etc.[99]

An example of a *nautika* loan for which full details are known is a loan of 3,000 drachma to finance merchants who were to buy wine in the northern Aegean, sell it (perhaps as far north as a Dnieper river port on the Black Sea), and return to Athens. The lenders were to get 625 drachma in yield, plus their principle back within twenty days of the merchants' return to Athens. The loan stated clearly that the yield was unrelated to the date of return, and would not go up if the return were the following calendar year.[100] Constraints were specified to prevent abuse: the legal itinerary could be specified; and, as this case also illustrates, the delay after arrival in Athens within which principle and yield had to be paid could be written into the loan contract.

By contrast, a possibly typical landed loan, executed by Demosthenes' father involved the loan of a talent of silver at the fixed interest of one drachma per mina per month, that is one percent per month (both Greeks and Romans usually calculated interest in percent per month, so this can be assumed unless otherwise specified).[101] For landed loans, yield increases over time, but loans could be called or cited as an asset, as in this case, at any subsequent time. Cohen suggests that an Athenian audience would be aware of the going rate for landed loans; and, consequently, many were simply referred to as "at interest" while yields for maritime loans had to be specified because of their inherent variability.[102]

Both the actors and the social scene in the Piraeus may have been distinct from that of the Agora and Athens proper. There were many more foreigners in the *emporion* than in the *agora*, and a general opprobrium inhibited Athenian elites from directly participating much in maritime trade. Some scholars have even suggested that nontraditional attitudes (less disdain) toward work and non-estate sources of wealth were common in the Piraeus.[103]

Athenian society, like that of Rome, placed a premium on traditional landed income, and the ability of a leisured and landed nobility (citizens) not to have to work, while it simultaneously cast aspersions on commerce and people in commerce—particularly the unscrupulous sort, but possibly also exemplified by maritime commerce. The Romans, who emulated much from classic Athens, felt that merchants could only gain respect if they took their wealth and invested it in land.[104] In more parochial Athens, access to land ownership by non-members of the citizenry was more restricted. On occasion, even in Athens, prominent foreign merchants who made substantial contributions to civic affairs could be rewarded by citizenship, but this social mobility became much easier later during the Roman empire.

A culture of elite superiority, brought with it a practice of assigning costly civic functions (liturgies) to elite citizenry, with the most burdensome liturgies assigned to the wealthiest—those who could afford should expend and gained honor by so doing. There were other levies on Athenian citizens; most importantly, *eisphora*, such as the levy for the Peloponnesian war which raised 200 talents or individual *eisphora* of three to four thousand drachmas, and levies to maintain the fleet; a trireme might run 3,000 drachmas (half a talent). Athens at its height had 120 ships at sea (representing 60 talents of capital). While accurate estimates of basic taxes are not available, one estimate is that Athens collected 2 percent on imports and exports, annually producing 30 and 36 talents, respectively. Estimates of the typical citizen expenditures on liturgies are 100 talents a year, split among 1,000 people, with the top 100 perhaps paying 1,000 drachmas on average. Wealthy citizens (the top 300) might be expected to have annual cash incomes from their rural estates of two to five talents, or more, depending on variations in climate and market conditions. Social obligations were merely a part of a citizen's most important expenditures, rural income only part of elite income, and state income a fraction of elite income.[105]

While financing a festival, a trireme, or other civic needs, brought prestige, the typical Greek citizen, not avidly aspiring to fame or upward mobility, first thought of finding a way to escape his duties, and often only performed them as a last resort. To this end, a legal suit (an *antidosis*) could be brought by one citizen against a second citizen in order to have the opportunity to prove publicly that the first was actually poorer than the second; and, therefore, the latter should in fact be assigned the civic duty in question.[106] In this regard, it turned out to be critical to have as much of one's wealth out of the public eye as possible; and, this proved to be a fundamental service provided by bankers (*trapeza*). Greek love for dichotomies expressed this concealment in terms of wealth being in the visible (*phanera*) or invisible (*aphanēs*) part of the economy.[107]

Because bankers ran their business as part of their household economy, which in Greece meant out of public view, discovering the full portfolio of loans and debts a person might have developed would among other things require examining the full set of records of all bankers; and, this was not legally possible for the state or for individuals. Thus, a citizen could produce witnesses to debts to counteract assets in the public sphere, while not acknowledging credits in the invisible sphere, and so present a picture of poverty that, though inaccurate, allowed one to beg off of more expensive civic duties. Elites were able to continue to claim innate superiority due to inherited landed wealth while feigning, through the help of a banker, financial difficulties to avoid civic responsibilities. This basically meant that the system had the flexibility to be manipulated by the elite who could, to a significant degree, choose whether prestige and honor were needed at a particular time or whether financial slight of hand was more advantageous. This flexibility may be something that is very much the norm historically though the details and our knowledge of them differ across societies.

Just as the fixed interest on landed loans was probably compatible with maintaining the prestige of citizens; the appeal of better returns (12.5 percent to 30 percent) in maritime investments (*nautika*) had to be balanced by their high risks, and the awful prospect of poverty and social disgrace in the event of loss. Many Greeks, however, concluded that while an individual venture might have a significant risk of failure, on average the returns were excellent. The large volume of maritime shipping, its importance to Athens, and the statistical predictability of maritime risk might have led to the development of maritime insurance, but this does not seem to have occurred, *per se*. Instead, the record suggests that lenders and investors spread their own risks.

All ventures had multiple investors, and bankers raised their rates on loans to clients investing in *nautika* to compensate for variation in risk. Many smaller, usually also younger, investors went along on the voyages to safeguard investments. One incentive of *nautika* was that in classical Greece the norm was to absolve the borrower of his debt if there was a shipwreck or piracy (but see Demosthenes 56 discussed below). Lenders, obtaining high enough rates on average, could afford to let the borrower off the hook if the cargo serving as collateral was lost; in some cases, lenders specified additional collateral or had recourse to debt collection.[108] Given that typical yields were 20 to 30 percent (over an unspecified time period), the statistical risks incurred by lenders in the *emporion* who adopted a risk management approach and spread their risks, must have been low enough to be appealing.

There are good reasons to believe that bankers, in and outside the Piraeus, participated in financing maritime trade: directly or indirectly. An interesting example among the surviving cases of bank financing of maritime loans (i.e., *nautika*, not the modern formal and anachronistic definition of maritime trade) comes from Demosthenes 56, where a vessel carrying cargo for multiple investors was damaged and had to be left in Rhodes rather than returning to Athens.

The evidence suggests that each cargo shipment had its own contractual arrangements. These *syngraphai* (written contracts) specified what would happen in the event of a loss. For example, in the case of a ship damaged in a storm that still made it to a port, its captain was absolved from liability for the ship itself, and one of its passengers—Dionysodōros— who in Egypt had borrowed 3,000 drachma also secured by the ship was also absolved of his debts. However, as all the cargo itself was transported by other means to their destinations, the obligations related to each part of the cargo shipped were honored.[109] This example argues strongly against the existence of any formal over-riding rules in maritime financing; and, again suggests that each contract was free to define the terms according to the estimates of risk.

While we have few details of the ventures funded by the *aphanēs* or invisible economy, once we make our definition of *nautika* less anachronistic, and allow indirect financing through bank clients, we have no reason to believe banks did not participate heavily in maritime trade. One of the key issues for bankers would have been liability for debt. To avoid the bank being called as a debtor by other creditors, thereby further jeopardizing all client deposits, a bank client could get a loan from his own bank, and participate in the maritime venture as his own agent, essentially leaving the bank itself out of any general liability for maritime investment.[110] While classical Athens had no arrangements for some investors to be "passive, investors" or "*supracorpo,*" as the Italians later defined it, something similar is accomplished by this example of the intransitivity of lending itself: your borrower owes you, but you are not liable for his debts. The actual investors in a maritime venture would not only share benefits but might have to share responsibility: all the more so if one of their agents were on board and directing activities.

Land was so frequently used as collateral for a loan in money that the landscape (especially from 500–200 BC) generated inscribed stones (*horoi*) which recorded key components of the loan intended to prevent the landowner from concealing the preexisting liens on the property when seeking further loans. The Greek terms *hypotheke*, *prasis epi lysei*, and *apotimema* distinguished the key purpose of the *horoi*. It has been argued persuasively that none of these corresponds closely to modern equivalents; and, that in particular the *hypotheke,* despite its etymological association was not really a mortgage. Still, as long as these simple glosses are not seen as real equivalents, we can summarize the three terms as recording security in various forms.

Hypotheke, the most simple and common, represents an encumbrance of the land in return for a loan, providing some measure of security for the lender but without the same recourse to law as modern mortgages do. The term *prasis epi lysei* (sale on condition of release) provides a revokable sale analogous to a *rahn* in Islamic law in which the buyer gains right to use of the land in return for an annual payment for a specified number of years. The "sale" can be revoked if the sum loaned is returned at the end of an agreed period. The "hidden interest" on the loan is gained by interim use of the land. The final term, *apotimema,* represented either recognition of receipt of a dowry and the encumbrance of the land to guarantee its return, if necessary; or the use of land as security for the estate of an orphan to be returned to the orphan at their majority.[111] The *horoi* served to record security for value received, including simple monetary loans but also embracing institutionalized arrangements for marriage, inheritance, and managing the estates of minors. In all cases, they do not have precise modern equivalents, because the general financial institutions underlying them differ substantially.

An apposite example of this institutional difference can be seen by comparing a modern pawn shop and the *prasis epi lysei*. In the modern pawn system, people in need of funds agree to a temporary sale but the value of the object pawned to the money lender is primarily based on its potential future sale price; on the assumption it is not redeemed (at loan plus interest). In the case of *prasis epi lysei,* the interim annual usufruct value of the land is the basis for the amount lent, and the (hidden) interest is already received before the loan is paid off, so all that is left to pay is the "principle." By contrast in the pawn system, while the collateral guarantees the principle—there is no usufruct, so set interest rates and time limits are enforced. If permitted, renewal is only possible if the interest due is paid within a specified time frame. Thus, though both are revocable sales the conditions are extremely different.

Many of the attitudes underlying financial arrangements in classic Greece have their correlates in the Roman world. Both share a certain disdain for profit maximizing, and place emphasis on *charin* or its Roman equivalent *liberalitas* (behaving altruistically to enhance honor). Both manage reputation with explicit awareness of obligations to both civic institutions and personal networks through careful manipulation of financial options and long-term investment.

We should note that some of these commonalities are intrinsically tied to a distinctively different conception of time than that behind the modern algorithm that time is money. The focus in the *emporion* was on a gamble over risk and benefit without regard to time absorbed by the voyage, but paying attention to it once the voyage was over. In the *agora,* by contrast, bankers were expected to actively produce income on a well-defined periodicity. Intermediary lending, from the bankers to clients in the Piraeus, could partake of both systems: involve a well-defined periodicity with the client and charge an interest rate commensurate with profits on maritime trade; for example, a significant portion of the expected 30 percent on the investment rather than the simple 10 percent per annum due the bank's depositors.

Building networks of mutual obligation, a key in both Attic Greece and the Republic of Rome, was accomplished only over a lifetime and so could not allow for any simple valuation of time. This heterogeneity of attitudes toward time carries forward through the Roman era into the later Islamic era. As we will see, Islam goes even further along the lines of the Piraeus model to formally disregard the time is money equation, and substitute for it an algorithm calculating inputs, risks, and liabilities to justify benefits, and becomes almost as dependent as classic Athens or Rome on building reputation for long term profitability.

SOCIAL CONSTRUCTION OF FINANCE IN THE REPUBLIC OF ROME

During Rome's lengthy history, both society and economy evolved and transformed; changing even such foundational issues as the legal status of women or the political system itself. Basic transformations in social institutions affected legal instruments as well as customary financial behavior. Later changes during the Empire were due in part to the development of a less parochial society that incorporated a much greater variety of people; and, in part to a transition to a heterogenous economy stretching over vast geographic areas. We focus our discussion on the narrower world of the Republic, both to make the discussion of social networks and social capital more manageable, and because the Republic was much more comparable to Attic Greece.

Classicists wish they had more detailed records of the life of normal people during the Roman Republic and Empire,[112] and concur that the vast bulk of records focus on a small fraction of the population (variously said to be 5 to 25 percent), yet we still have a much richer understanding of finances, and the social role of credit in the Roman period than of any other ancient Mediterranean or Near Eastern society. While there were some technical/financial elaborations of credit during the period of the Roman Republic that are not yet known from earlier times, we will first focus on ties to the sociocultural aspects discussed in earlier sections of this chapter.

We need to emphasize that the Roman situation cannot be simply mapped onto other ancient cultures for which we do not have comparable data nor can we say, because we cannot illustrate earlier parallels, that the Roman use of credit is likely to have been without precedent. It may be that Roman civilization built a particularly elaborate version of a system of social honor that relied on multiple ways of implementing networks of credit and reciprocal obligation among the elites.

At their most fundamental level, networks of reciprocal obligation provide timely access to credit or investment opportunities that serve to accelerate capital turnover and increase its annual return. The idea of multiplier effects or of externalities implies that within a given time period, networks of balanced reciprocity can accelerate the economy. Such multiplier effects increase the total potential for economic benefits through involving greater numbers of people with varied expertise, insights, social capital and energy in the increased use of an initial capital endowment. This is the fundamental advantage that a network of people has over an individual. The more disparate and complex the economy the more this is likely to be the case.[113]

The pithy claim that "time is money" embodies an insight that was first seriously examined in the nineteenth century when economists such as Jevons initially, and naively, ventured the notion that the amount of capital invested needed to be distinguished from the amount of investment of capital (this latter term incorporated the time each piece of capital was invested and summed over all years). This formulation was an improvement over ignoring the length of time capital was invested, but it was still misleading because it simplistically tried, by defining time as a concrete variable, to derive the going rate of interest directly from the advantages due to extending the period of production in a single production process.

Economists suggest that prevailing interest rates are linked to prevailing profit rates and need to be incorporated into any measure of the real value of profit: as an investment netting less than the prevailing rate of interest would be unattractive, since leaving it in a bank would be preferable. Sraffa's sophisticated twentieth century analysis of profit showed that the real value of invested capital depends on, rather than causes, the going rate of interest over the period of investment; and, that as interest compounds over time, it is vain to pretend to know in advance what the relative value of invested capital will be over a future period without the, improbable, full knowledge of future rates of interest.[114] This insight embodies a switch to social or system causality to replace Jevons' simplistic causality of time and money.

Even if thinkers did not fully understand the reasons; and, even if twentieth century reasons were only beginning to be relevant in Roman times, Roman elites undoubtedly saw that there were benefits to be had by all in using their networks to mobilize people with a range of skills, information, and social capital as this would increase the turnover of capital. Some of these advantages were primarily social, but others might be best characterized as economic. Veyne characterizes Romans as torn between two versions of social obligation: civic duties and duties that are incurred through friendship.[115] Networks of friendship provided the lanes in which individuals sought both a start in life, and a way to enhance reputation even in later years. Gifts, favors, and presents were the coin of the realm. They could lead to significant returns in time and establish a core support group in the meantime. Solidarity was expected among friends, and Roman society looked very harshly on those who exhibited less than the expected levels of *gratia*.

In Rome, the authority to make financial or economic decisions was rooted in the *paterfamilias*; even sons had no financial independence until their father died, and so relied on his permission even to engage in a career in politics (significantly this is due to the costs involved). Early on, daughters once married (at age twelve or later) were largely dependent on their husbands, in theory and in practice even if they had inherited wealth. Later, if they were of age and no longer had a guardian, or if they were divorced, they were able to manage their own funds. Though usurers often tried to lend to youth, for collection, if necessary, when their fathers died, laws were enacted repeatedly to make it illegal for them to lend to youth, or to collect such loans when the father died. While youth could act with their father's permission, and funds (a *peculum*), a more general law forbade lending to someone under the age of twenty-five, though individuals without a *paterfamilias* were deemed independent once considered adult (usually at fourteen).[116]

Women had guardians (*tutores*) in the Republic when no *paterfamilias* survived; either their husbands when married or those appointed by law (the institution of *tutela legitima*) or through a will. The latter institution (*tutela testamentaria*) provided an appointed role for guardians to manage an inheritance but *tutores* sacrificed their own reputation if they were shown to mismanage or rob the estate. The role of guardian was generally assigned to a family member or close friend because these very people might be motivated to impugn the motives of anyone else. By the Late Republic, many adult women, including but not limited to widows, had the right to take their own financial affairs much more completely into their own hands. Under Claudius (41–54 AD), even the *tutela legitima* was abolished.[117] Roman women had the right to divorce on their own decision; even a Jewish woman who was a Roman citizen, could chose to use Roman law rather than Jewish law, for this purpose, and divorce her husband without his permission.[118]

Greece and Rome had copious slaves and some scholars suggest that slave production was the basis of wealth in both societies.[119] The deficiencies in the historical record rule out any convincing quantification or persuasive assessment of the relative economic roles of various social strata in classical Greece or Rome, though slaves undoubtedly had a smaller productive role in Greece. However, since our focus is on financing the economy rather than production itself, we can safely leave this question about their quantitative productive contribution open.

Roman elites viewed themselves, definitionally, as people of leisure whose adult activities were most properly aimed first at glory and renown (making their way up the *cursus honorum*); though they recognized that substantial assets and activities producing financial profit, along with skills in rhetoric from a classical education, or social capital more generally, could facilitate this. Thus, Roman obsession over the public reading of significant wills, which combined their hopes of adding substantively to their economic assets with their pleasure in being mentioned (itself adding to the luster of their own reputation), was even for elites more a matter of how such mentions might advance their own name and reputation than wealth *per se*. The *ordines* were regularly mentioned in wills, even in the testaments of those who had not been *ordines,* because leaving something to an important person was the best way to assure that the will was properly executed, and because elite reputation benefited from all honorable actions and inclusion in a will was an indication of a life of *liberalitas* (or *benignitas* analogous to the Greek *charin*).

We need not assume a simple profit maximizing ethic, as a conscious primary goal among Roman elites, to recognize that Roman elites were far from immune to financial considerations in their social networking or their aspirations. Roman society was cruel to insolvent debtors, even after the *lex Poetelia Papiria de nexis* abolished debt bondage in 326 BC.[120] Many of the most prominent elites began life with vast assets, or acquired them as part and parcel of their political careers, and so had less need to use social networks to profit maximize than might otherwise have been the case. Although this may have been true for senators, knights, municipal nobles, or rich families (hopefully) en route to becoming nobles (who constituted perhaps 10 to 15 percent of the population in position to act as patrons), this might not have been true for the other 25 percent of the population that participated significantly in their social networks as their clients.[121]

At the core of Roman "society" were networks of friendship (*amicitia*) that provided a matrix both for patron-client relationships and a range of more formal types of credit. This social matrix was founded on a complex of core values: *liberalitas* (generosity: originally expressed in terms of efforts on others' behalf, a disposition toward providing *beneficia*), *gratia* (the disposition toward ensuring a response to *beneficia*), *fides* (loyalty or obligation to behave honorably: the bedrock on which society was built), *beneficia* or *officia* (acts of generosity viewed as duties), *beneuolentia*/*amor* (an impulse toward generosity outside of duty) as well as the goals of constructing *existimatio* (reputation or *fama*) and *dignitas* (honor seen as including *honestas*, integrity and virtue, and more generally as a socially conferred valuation of one's person).

For Romans, *amicitia* (friendship) was a quasi-kin like relationship based on relations of reciprocity, affection, and trust.[122] Friends were treated like beloved kin, and *officia* (favors) were done for them without thought of profit, a fact that became part of Roman law governing the *mandatum*, an informal contract between friends based on a handshake. Roman jurists interpreted the *mandatum* so strictly that one was not allowed to benefit from the services provided, even indirectly.[123] Despite their hierarchical nature patron-client relations were also cast in an idiom of friendship. However, rather than expecting a comparable exchange of gifts and favors—which almost by definition was impossible—*amicitia* permitted clients greater flexibility in reciprocal exchange as long as appropriate expressions of gratitude were made. Patrons did favors for their clients out of *benignitas* (kindness) and *beneuolentia* (good will), for which the proper payments expected were viewed as expressions of *gratia* (gratefulness).

While patron-client relationships assumed a hierarchical relationship the broader category of *amicitia* involved interdependencies of every sort. Rather than requiring a simple equal relationship in terms of comparable interchange of gifts, *amicitia* allowed and even mandated delay in return and flexibility in the currency in which *beneficia* and *officia* returned benefits when expressions of *gratia* were made. Thus, *beneficia* in the form of services rendered or material gifts bestowed could honorably be returned even in the form of a legacy in a will that would only produce value (wealth and honor) when one party was deceased.

While individuals sought to build *existimatio* and *dignitas,* society relied on *fides* because it was so extensively committed to networks of credit. Default on debt not only destroyed an individual's *dignitas,* it threatened the entire credit structure. Society immediately isolated the defaulting or insolvent debtor (who was now characterized by *infamia* rather than *dignitas*) who became as well subject to extreme legal punishments.[124] This threat of social isolation itself pushed individuals to use friendly networks of credit whenever possible. Romans distinguished *mutuum* from *faenus* as opposites: the former were felt obligations which gave rise to *beneficia* that themselves motivated abiding *gratia,* while the latter were loans that were motivated only by self-interest and extinguished all obligations once repaid. Indeed, *faeneratio* had such a bad reputation by the Late Republic that Cato put it on a par with murder, pointing out that traditionally (in earlier times) a *faenerator* would be fined quadruple the amount in question while a thief would only be assessed double.[125] By relying on networks of *mutuum*, Romans were both to some extent insured by societal reliance on *fides* and driven to participate in ever wider networks—in effect striving not to put all their eggs in one basket, and instead trying to tie as many people as possible to their future prosperity. This increased the probability of avoiding default to one or more lenders by appeals to incurred obligations from others.

A member of the Roman elite was expected to exhibit civic virtues especially *liberalitas,* which was a positive virtue that ranked next only to the passive virtue of *iustitia* (abstention from evil).[126] Recipients of *liberalitas* had a moral obligation to express *gratia* for what they received. Friendships also were viewed as involving more specific virtues such as *beneuolentia/amor* between individuals, but an over-riding concern was to use respect for norms to attain and maintain *existimatio* and *dignitas,* which were viewed as the key social goals that justified an individual's lifelong efforts and established his own and his family's identity. Cicero famously noted, *ubi autem est dignitas, nisi ubi honestas* (where is there *dignitas* where there is not honesty: Att. VII, 11, 1) as well as *cura nihil aliud nisi ut valeas* (care for nothing else except that which you can do well). His advice may be purely pragmatic; that is, to focus on behavior that is compatible with core values such as *dignitas* and which therefor is viable long term. Cicero would even use his estimations of others' *dignitas* (*dilectus dignitatis:* choice of worthiness) to decide where to bestow *beneficia*. People's opinion of you (your *existimatio*) was in large part based on how one maintained one's *dignitas*. This in turn depended on respecting the key societal values in public and private including giving honor where honor was due.

That prestige was a principle value may be seen in other Roman practices such as rationalizing infanticide; at least until the second century AD, this was viewed as a way to focus one's patrimony on a few excellent candidates for high status. This was linked to a utilitarian conception of a basic parity between the status of an adopted and a natural son; it was the preparation of a son for success, and his subsequent success that brought benefits, not the actual blood relationship. While preoccupation with status and obligation is undeniable, in practice its importance in the Roman Empire rivaled the link between citizenship and civic obligation in Classic Athens.

Veyne devotes two chapters to a critique of the anachronistic misunderstanding that, under the Roman Empire, a regular intermingling of public office with private status was a sign of corruption.[127] He suggests, on the contrary, that Romans viewed networking and use of influence to attain or maintain public office as normal and legitimate behavior. He suggests in addition that laws, though framed in universal terms, were regularly superceded in their application by rhetoric about reputation and honor furthering claims to nobility, and that this too was not found morally objectionable. On these assumptions, influence may have been even more critical to personal success than in modern times (though this may be disputed in quite a few modern states). Similarly, the importance of extensive networks of reciprocal (and publicly admired) obligation would have been critical to economic prosperity.[128]

It would probably be wrong to imagine that elites felt no obligation to those outside their status. Rather, it is more likely that, just as prestige and honor were top values, these were viewed as entailing behavior that in our more individualistic age might be seen as altruistic. Emperors provided bread for the public in Rome not just because it lessened the probability of a riot, but also because that was what Emperors did. Nobles frequently spent funds in ways that were of broad benefit to communities (and not just in the form of bread and circuses) because that was what notables did—it serves little purpose to try to explain all such behavior in self-centered individualistic ways for a period in which the notion of the modern self had yet to be conceived.[129] Nor does it follow, because notables frequently benefited in social or economic ways from their other than self-centered behavior, that such benefits were the paramount motives for their behavior rather than auxiliary considerations. We need to avoid both anachronistic and ethnocentric explanation even in an area as central to modern society's genesis as the Republic of Rome.[130]

Among the more formal credit arrangements were partnerships of a particular and flexible Roman variety (*societas*). These involved cooperation between partners (*socii*) for any designated common purpose, although the contribution by each member need not be the same (e.g., money, in kind, labor, etc.). Roman *societas* had a very different legal status than modern corporations or later trading companies; they could make contracts, purchases, sales, and own property.

Because it lacked corporate status, outsiders doing business with it, had no legal recourse against it, since from a legal perspective, it had no corporate existence; their only recourse was against the individuals directly involved in a transaction.[131] Since the *societas* had no formal separate corporate existence, they existed only as the designated interdependencies among members, and the agreement (unless otherwise specified) to share profits and losses equally. Each partner advanced the other something, and shared in the return produced by the joint effort.

In exceptional circumstances a *societas* could be transmuted into a legal entity, but the principal known example is the *societates uectigalium* which was formed to collect taxes on behalf of the Republic.[132] The obvious need to hold all members collectively responsible motivated the creation of this exception to the rule. Since the goal of a *societas* was to make a profit, no *beneficia* were expected between *socii,* but the *societas* was viewed as an activity ruled by *fides* and having implications for *dignitas* just as any network relying on ties of *amicitia*.

The variety of forms of agency (*procuratio*, *mandatum*, and *negotiorum gestio*) similarly relied on *fides* and contributed significantly to the *dignitas* of the agent. To be asked to carry out a complex financial management for an absent owner represented primarily a symbolic compliment that heightened ones reputation, providing that the management tasks were well executed.

Because a *mandatum* was an informal consensual contract that was carried out without remuneration, failure or fraud brought *infamia*. Thus, direct payment or making off with some of the proceeds was strictly forbidden and a death knell to *dignitas*: the hidden benefits came in the form of social capital not economic capital.[133]

The *negotiorum gestio* was a less specific (less defined) action on behalf of the principal which also required that it be exclusively in the principal's interest, and that no economic benefit accrue to the *negotiorum gestio* but since it involved no specific mandate failure did not bring *infamia*.[134] By contrast, a *procuratio* usually had broader powers[135] than a simple *mandatum* and, due to the complex decision making required for such an appointment, might receive remuneration either in the form of direct salary (referred to as *procuratores salariarii*) or in the form of *gratia* - directly from the person for whom they acted, or from those obliged to that person. Thus, for example, L. Egnatius Rufus sent a *procurator* (L. Oppius M. f.) to Cilicia to manage his affairs. Since the details could not be known in advance, the procurator had to have a flexible and unspecified appointment. In this case, we know that Cicero wrote letters on behalf of L. Oppius to obtain advantages for him from the legate Q. Galius and the governor Q. Marcius Philippus—thus invoking their *gratia* to Cicero on behalf of L. Oppius—an expression of Cicero's own *gratia* or *beneficia* extended to L. Egnatius Rufus who used it to benefit his own *procurator*.[136]

In the material, as in the moral sphere, practical realities affected opportunities for credit. The presence of maritime grain transport and grain markets did not imply a uniform price for grain, or subsequent lack of opportunities for arbitrage. Indeed, local shortfalls did result in significant general price fluctuations. Areas at some distance from a port benefited little from marine transportation of grain, since land transport was prohibitively expensive; and, the largely self-sufficient character of most rural areas kept them out of significant trade relationships with urban areas. Thus, the maritime grain trade lessened price fluctuations in only a small subset of Roman territory: primarily urban areas with or near ports. Aside from maritime trade in grain, the primary opportunity for credit based on grain was local speculation within the year, based on the predictable fluctuation of prices upward in the months leading up to harvest and downward after the harvest.[137]

Undoubtedly, the deterioration of grain in storage over the course of the year lent an additional incentive to this speculation. In this sense, the Roman Empire resembled ancient Mesopotamia or Egypt, from which it received a substantial part of its grain. Generally, low levels of urbanization meant that rural areas absorbed much of the excess population, leading to low rural per capita productivity, though high mortality levels kept population growth fairly insignificant over the long term so underemployment not unemployment would have been the norm in rural areas.[138]

This overall picture needs to be complemented by noting the role of some cities, and citizens, in providing a significant and economically stimulating level of employment and loans in time of need. The development of large rural estates increased labor productivity, and the consequent production of a surplus. Romans over time increasingly sought efficient tenants who would be driven by the rent they paid to invest more capital per unit area in order to produce at higher levels. The investment based system that developed often involved capital as well as security of tenure provided by the landlord, to encourage production. The alternative was to have tenants who would cannibalize capital assets, knowing they had no security of tenure, and so produce at progressively lower levels.[139]

ORIGINALITY OF GRECO-ROMAN FINANCE

Among the most basic arguments we can derive from the Greco-Roman case is that credit is first and foremost a social relationship, and that cultural logics play through such relations, giving them a distinctive vector and content that shapes forms of credit and their terms. A modern social scientist or historian will be tempted to advocate network analysis to discover the "true" workings of ancient economies but as a superb scholar[140] has already noted the available data, though intriguing, is not adequate to reconstructing most of the network variables one might desire; for example, network densities, development over time of networks or a firm relationship between networks and the economy. Our own view is that the clear importance in Greece and Rome of reputation, friendship, and honor represent evidence that trust needed to balance risk if the economy were to flourish.[141] Risks could be high and poverty was a social catastrophe for elites. Even major non remunerative expenditures might be required, but the role of friendship ties was critical to moderating the risks associated with investment in any economic activity.

Whether credit was directly used in productive investments or to develop social capital is quite inconsequential. One might imagine networks of friends and social capital, more generally, as a basic social insurance package without which the economy could never have prospered. It may be possible to link risk, social capital, and economic prosperity in the ancient world in more detail, but this is a task for future scholars. The elaborate societal concerns and social practices of the Early Republic provide a particularly charming, if naively self-serving, example of the imbrication of the social and the economic. We may expect earlier as well as later societies to be no less dependent on forms of social insurance for their prosperity; even if in some cases their greater proximity in time renders them less charming or their vast distance in time obscures details.

Although the Early Republic of Rome and Attic Greece have a great deal in common, as this overview has attempted to show, there were important differences between their underlying building blocks, cultural values, and logics that gave their economies a distinctive cultural character. This was expressed not only in the obvious contrasts between a Greek democracy and a Roman republic, but also seen in basic disparities in attitudes; for example, toward patronage—with Roman society celebrating it and Athenians viewing it as suspect if not shameful. The differences in Roman and Athenian social, political, economic, and cultural systems as previous sections have shown fundamentally shaped their use of credit, its forms, and how its technical aspects such as terms of payment, security requirements, collection practices, and interest rates diverged.

At a general socio-economic level, we can imagine the past populated by institutions which helped optimized the use of social, cultural, and economic capital by addressing risk and liability. Yet, even in the ancient world, we would need to define what we mean by optimal, and recognize that there is a distinction between arrangements that lead to massive environmental damage, the eastern Mediterranean was almost completely deforested in ancient times, and arrangements that actually had greater net social or economic benefit over the long term.

There are financial structures which are more or less capable of facilitating economic activities and of adapting to demographic, economic, and social change. Greek institutions embodied key financial ideologies, but they were heavily focused on facilitating the activities of a small elite in a small rather parochial, if brilliant and original, town. Clearly, the Roman system falls into the more capable category. Properly developing these distinctions, in even a remotely persuasive way, would unfortunately require a major book of its own and is beyond the scope of this chapter. Our concern in this chapter has been to detail the ways in which Roman forms build and develop in parallel to Greek institutions and set the stage for their continued development as the Roman Republic transformed into the Roman Empire.

Athenian credit institutions included the key architectures that dominated Europe and the Islamic world in later centuries and focused them in two distinct areas: the Agora and the Piraeus. The maritime risk assessment based trade of the Piraeus became the model for the Islamic world while the Agora's time based fixed interest rate system developed in manifold ways in Europe. Both systems were represented in the Ancient Near East and Mediterranean—especially if we recognize the importance of hidden forms of interest, but they were elegantly elaborated and thought through in classical Athens.

Verboven's study of *amicitia* in Rome details the ways hidden interest embodied in social ties as well as institutionalized forms of credit were ineluctably interdependent. It makes little sense to imagine the specific forms of loans, banking, and partnerships as somehow each operating independently of social norms and values or following quite different logics. Rather, we should recognize that in the Early Republic, as in Attic Greece, an ethical system rooted in the honor, generosity and social obligation of elites prevailed in the banking sector with specified rates of return and in the risk based financial ventures typical for maritime trade precisely as it dictated more general considerations of social behavior.

The details of the Roman example can help us envisage a similarly unified socio-economic set of values and networks of obligations elsewhere in the ancient world even where the data available is less rich or the networks less elaborate. Such interrelated values and their implementation in practice were dynamic and transformed, if not easily at least readily, as classical Athens gave way to imperial Rome. As we have seen, elaborate credit documents existed in the Near East since the Sumerian period but it is highly probable that they, too, would be better understood as tied into something comparable to the network of friendships, credit and hidden interest so thoroughly elaborated in the early Republic.

It may be as serious an anachronism to imagine elites in the ancient world viewing lending at explicit interest as the primary way to get ahead, without regard for social insurance, social approbation or risk, as it is to pretend market activity was either negligible or that, even from the perspective of societies' elites, it even approximately optimized supply and demand by setting efficient prices for all factors of production. Formalist analyses of the classical world tended to ignore the importance of risk and liability while those inspired by Polanyi have had a tendency to imagine qualitative or epochal changes on the way to the present where there have been great continuities.

We would suggest that there are so many financial continuities between the classical period and the present that it makes little sense to imagine the two financial systems as fundamentally different. To some degree, the modern economy provides a more efficient set of prices and a greater focus on investing according to those prices. It still may be best, imitating the Foucault of 1983, to suggest that modern finance is like earlier finance or, rather, never quite the same: any claims to a great rupture with the past are less than persuasive. We might add that where social networks and finance are intertwined, and different classes participate to such radically different degrees in the economy, the assumption of "social optimization" adds little to the analysis.

NOTES

1. Verboven, *The Economy of Friends*, 341.

2. Lefkowitz and Fant, *Women's Life in Greece and Rome*, 133. The rape of Lucretia was recounted by Livy, *History of Rome* 1.57.6-58. Sextus Tarquinius was assassinated shortly later.

3. Morris, *Burial and Ancient Society*, 5.

4. Ibid.

5. Schwartz and Nicols, *After Collapse*, 80.

6. Ward, Heichelheim, and Yeo, *A History of the Roman People*, 61.

7. Boardman, Griffin, and Murray, *Oxford Illustrated History of Greece and the Hellenistic World*, 418.

8. Hornblower and Spawforth. *Oxford Companion to Classical Civilization*, 438.

9. Maine, *Ancient Law*, 173.

10. Ward, Heichelheim and Yeo, *History of the Roman People*, 43–46. Women usually would return to their natal households after a divorce, or if death of their husband occurred before children were born.

11. Ward, Heichelheim and Yeo, 42–43.

12. Ibid., 43.

13. Maine, *Ancient Law,* 177.

14. Maine, 176.

15. Veyne, *The Roman Empire*, 75.

16. Verboven, 183–84.

17. Verboven, 183–84, 194: "It was customary to appoint heirs in the second and even third degree in the case the heir[s] in the first degree would not or could not accept their shares. The institution of heirs in the second and third degree offered the maker of the testament the possibility of honoring a virtually unlimited number of 'friends' without unduly fragmenting the inheritance."

18. Verboven, 216–19.

19. Cox, *Household Interests*, 190.

20. Parker, *Polytheism and Society at Athens*.

21. Verboven, 11.

22. Verboven, 54.

23. Verboven, 90.

24. Le Glay, Voisin, and Bohec, *A History of Rome*, 31.

25. Verboven, 105.

26. Verboven, 86–91.

27. Zelnick-Abramovitz, "Did Patronage Exist in classical Athens," 79.

28. Aristotle in his *Ethica Nicomachea*, divided philia into three types based on what motivates them: (1) true friends who wish only good for one another; (2) friendships based on seeking pleasure; and (3) friendship based on what is useful. Patron-client relationships would fall into his third category. While he notes that all three kinds are based on reciprocity, only the first is enduring, the others are by their nature short-lived.

29. Zelnick-Abramovitz, "Did Patronage Exist," 76–77.

30. Zelnick-Abramovitz, 79.

31. For Greece: see Davies, "Classical Greece: Production," in Scheidel, Morris, and Saller, *The Cambridge Economic History of the Greco-Roman World*, 342–352; for Rome: see Verboven, 154–55.

32. Boardman, Griffin and Murray, 211–13; Le Glay, Voisin, and Bohec, 45, 108.

33. Boardman, Griffin and Murray, 213.

34. Boardman, Griffin and Murray, 18–19.

35. Waterfield, *Xenophon's Retreat*, 126.

36. In the *Phaedo*, Plato has Socrates suggest that the earth is a large sphere suspended in some homogeneous material and that "we live around the sea in a small portion of it between Phasis and the Pillars of Heracles, like ants or frogs around a swamp." Cooper, *Plato Complete Works*, 93.

37. Boardman, Griffin and Murray, 18–19.

38. It was not until the last decade of the fourth century BC that harbor facilities were built along the bend of the Tiber to facilitate maritime commerce. It became clear that by that time, food had to be shipped from sources along the western Mediterranean easily reached by sea. In 348 BC, Rome signed a trade-treaty with Carthage, agreeing to not establish colonies in Sardinia or North Africa in return rights to trade with Carthage and her colonies in Sicily. Archeological evidence also indicates that harbor facilities only began to be built around 390 BC, and that Ostia was founded in 335 BC to protect the mouth of the Tiber. See Le Glay, Voisin, and Bohec, 52.

39. Boardman, Griffin and Murray, 213.

40. Frier and Kehoe, "Law and Economic Institutions," in Scheidel, Morris, and Saller, 120–21.

41. Morris, Saller and Scheidel, "Introduction," in Scheidel, Morris, and Saller, 10.

42. Möller, "Classical Greece: Distribution," in Scheidel, Morris, and Saller, 371–74.

43. Möller in Scheidel, Morris, and Saller, 370.

44. Sitta Von Riden, "Classical Greece: Consumption," in Scheidel, Morris, and Saller, 405–6.

45. Greenberg, *Santiago's Sword*, 148–82.

46. Sitta Von Riden in Scheidel, Morris, and Saller, 395–96.

47. David, *Roman conquest of Italy*, 82–83, 89.

48. For Rome: see Morel, "Early Rome and Italy." For Athens: see John Davies, "Classical Greece: Production," in Scheidel, Morris, and Saller, 504–10, 352–55.

49. Kamm, *Romans*, 114.

50. Boardman, Griffin and Murray, 216. The most comprehensive discussion of slavery in classical Greece is, Ste. Croix, *Class Struggle in the Ancient Greek World*.

51. Hornblower, and Spawforth, 285.

52. Hornblower, and Spawforth, 285; Veyne, 155.

53. Hornblower and Spawforth, 285.

54. Boardman, Griffin and Murray, 213.

55. Smith, *Dictionary of Greek and Roman Antiquities*.

56. The Lex Claudia, see Le Glay, Voisin, and Bohec, 108.

57. Le Glay, Voisin, and Bohec, 108.
58. Polanyi, *The Great Transformation*.
59. The classic work in anthropology addressing this controversy is Le Claire and Schneider, *Economic Anthropology*.
60. See in particular Hudson and Mieroop, *Debt and Economic Renewal* and Hudson and Wunsch, *Creating Economic Order*. For Greece, D. Asheri, Leggi greche sul problema dei debiti, *Studi classici e orientali* 18: 5–122, cited in Millett, *Lending and Borrowing in Ancient Athens*, 21, 49, listed forty examples of debt forgiveness between the sixth and first centuries BC. In a related vein, precautions against forgiving debt which abound in the record also support the importance of the topic. In Greece this ranged from forcing a return of interest (*palintokia*) to full cancellation of debt (*seisachtheia*) such as that associated with Solon in the sixth century.
61. Finley, *The Ancient Economy*, and *Ancient History*. Andreau, "Twenty Years after Moses I." Finley's "The Ancient Economy," chapter 2 in Scheidel and von Reden.
62. Leslie Kurke, "Money and Mythic History: The Contestation of Transactional Orders in the Fifth Century B.C.," chapter 5 in Scheidel and von Reden. The term used for innkeeping (*pandokeue*) had the rich connotation of hospitality of gods and aristocratic heroes as well as a degraded sense, defined by accompanying details, of gross exploitation of travelers who had nowhere else to stay (p. 160). This lent a special flavor of betrayal of all that is right and good to the charge.
63. Descat, "L'économie antique."
64. Hopkins, "Rome, Taxes, Rents and Trade," chapter 10, in Scheidel and von Reden.
65. Leveau, "La ville antique."
66. In this position we follow both Kula, *An Economic Theory of the Feudal System* and Nell, *General Theory of Transformational Growth*.
67. Sraffa, *Production of Commodities*, argued for an almost Gramscian model of the capitalist economy which took the power of major corporations as its starting point.
68. Classicists such as M. I. Finley, referred to as Primitivists, and their opponents, the "modernists," have argued at enormous length over whether the classic economy was intrinsically non-capitalist or not. For a recent overview see Andreau, *Banking and Business in the Roman World*, 6–7. The controversy is also referred to in the literature as the "Bucher-Meyer controversy." Our view is that this very antinomy is based on a conceptualization of the economy that is too narrow, on the one hand and too asocial on the other.
69. Structuralisme et poststructuralisme, in Foucault (*Dits & Ecrits* II, 1266–267). Interview with G. Raulet from Telos, vol. XVI, no. 55, spring 1983. Foucault here argues against his own claims early in his career that modernity was a rupture with the past and suggests both that it wasn't and that consequently post-modernity also makes no sense. He makes a much more modest claim about the present: "Non, c'est un jour comes les autres, ou plutôt c'est un jour qui n'est jamais tout à fait comme les autres."
70. While specialists refer to classical Greece as the period from 479 to 338 BC—ending with the abolition of democracy, in this chapter for simplicity sake we will use

classical more loosely to cover the eighth to fourth centuries BC in their entirety—bearing in mind that most sources do deal with the 479–338 period.

71. John Stuart Mill for example suggested that the defeat of King Xerxes at the battle of Salamis (479 BC) was a more important fact of English history than the Norman Conquest (1066 AD). Boardman, Griffin and Murray, 7.

72. Bogaert, *Banques et banquiers dans les cités Grecques*, provides a detailed discussion of data available on banks and bankers in the various Greek cities of antiquity including those of Attica (61–94). Aeschylus' Agamemnon (457 BC) compares the god Ares to a money (gold) changer and early bankers such as Archestratos worked in Athens in the late fifth century and even had citizenship by 394 BC. The earliest deposit banker we know much about was Pasion who had been a slave of Archestratos but was freed sometime before 395 BC.

73. Termin, *Roman Market Economy*, 204. Andreau, *La vie financière dans le monde Romain*, provides a broad picture of bankers and money men from the Republic to the early Empire.

74. Harris, "The Late Republic," in Scheidel, Morris, and Saller, 521.

75. *Plato, Laws*, Book V: 742–43. Brackets incorporate translators footnotes. Note that the Laws reflects Plato's ideal state not the current practice in Greece. Cooper, *Plato Complete Works*.

76. *Plato, Laws*, Cooper, Book XI: 921 c, d.

77. Hornblower and Spawforth, 760.

78. Plato. Cooper, Republic. VIII: 555–56.

79. Schumpeter, *History of Economic Analysis*, 56.

80. Schumpeter, 62.

81. Aristotle. McKeon, *Basic Works of Aristotle* Politics book I, ch.10. Bekker: 1258a39–1258b7.

82. Aristotle. Barnes, *Complete Works of Aristotle*, Metaphysics, Book V: Bekker: 1015a13–19.

83. Verboven.

84. Millett. It is worth noting that Millet takes the position that *eranoi* were always interest free while Cohen, *Athenian Economy and Society*, insists there is not a single example where this is clear.

85. Cohen, Ibid., 210.

86. Millett, 55, 60. Apollodorus was a former slave who became wealthy and the son of Pasion, the banker, who left his affairs in the hands of a neighbor, Nicostratus, while he took a voyage around the Peleponnese as a trierarch. His oration in his suit of Nicostratus which has survived includes many details about credit arrangements.

87. Millett, 41. The point is made in the Nicomachean Ethics, Bekker:1162b21–63a6.

88. Millett, 42.

89. The modern economic definition of productive and nonproductive loan may be just as anachronistic as that of maritime loan. The distinction focuses on loans for direct material production and seems a bit stilted in the age of information. The distinction may also be largely irrelevant in ancient Greece, an age of *philia*.

90. *tokoi tokon* = compound interest was known in classical Greece but references to it seem to be invariably derogatory such as in Theophrastus' depiction of the Penurious Man (*mikrologos*) who is merciless in collecting debts and charges compound interest. For a discussion of compound interest in Greece with key references see Millett, 185.

91. Funeral speech of Thucydides (II.40.4) Millett, 123.

92. Aristotle. Barnes, Nichomachean Ethics, Bekker: 1133a2–5.

93. Millett, 123.

94. Davidson, *Greeks and Greek Love*, 39–43.

95. Millet, 121–22; 112–13.

96. Aristotle's theory of ethics in the Nicomachean ethics is based on the principle that ideal values depend on the relevant sphere of human activity; for example, moderation in eating or sex but generosity with regard to the management of property. The Aristotelean position on the distinct ethics of lending to friends clearly is part of this larger perspective.

97. The immediate following discussion is based on Cohen, *Athenian Economy and Society,* 45ff and 132. Landed impersonal loans in the fifth to third centuries BC are thought to have averaged 1 percent per month or 12 percent per annum—Millett, 105.

98. Cohen, Ibid., 49–51.

99. For a lengthy discussion of this point see Cohen, Ibid., 163ff.

100. The passage detailing this loan (from Demosthenes 35) is cited in Cohen, Ibid., 54–55.

101. The passage detailing the loan from Demosthenes 27.9–11 is cited in Cohen, Ibid., 52. One talent had approximately half a hundredweight of silver and at this time represented about 6,000 drachma; there were 25 drachma to a stater, 100 drachma to the mina and 60 mina to the talent. The loan at this rate would generate 720 drachma a year. A free workman's income in this period would most likely have been about 240 drachma a year (Cohen, Ibid., 22–23) so a loan of a talent would correspond in the early twenty-first-century United States to one half of a million dollars on which 12 percent was made annually (assuming a worker salary of $20,000 a year). Demosthenes considered himself well-born and better than those who were not—as did Greek society.

102. Cohen, Ibid., 60.

103. Von Reden. *Der Pirāus*, 66–72. Cited in Millett, 191.

104. Veyne, 123.

105. Osborne, "Pride and Prejudice, Sense and Subsistence: Exchange and Society in the Greek City," in Scheidel and Von Reden, *The Ancient Economy*, 120–28. Osborne's figures come largely from the Phainippos case in the Demosthenes corpus, Davies, *Athenian Propertied Families*, and Davies, *Wealth and the Power of Wealth*. Classical Athens at this time would have had about 25,000 residents.

106. Cohen, *Athenian Economy and Society,* 198ff.

107. Ibid., 190ff.

108. Ibid., 142.

109. Ibid., 165.

110. Millett, 189.

111. Finley, *Ancient History*, especially chapters III and IV.

112. Veyne provides an accessible discussion of Roman life and culture almost devoid of source references. The fraction of people involved in patronage networks at least included elite classes, as well as the poorer people on the fringes of such networks who were not elites but, unlike others outside of such circles, they did have access to patrons who could protect them from the rapaciousness and corruption so endemic to Roman society. Verboven, 108 suggests that about 25 percent of the Roman population might have been tied into the patronage networks maintained by elites who formed roughly 5 percent of the population. Veyne (134) puts 80 percent outside of the elite group and defines them as those who really had to work for a living.

113. We can measure complexity in basic information theoretic terms such that an elegant centralized administration would be less complex than a more chaotic economy with many individual and group actors pursuing different strategies. A textbook equilibrium based market economy of small competitive firms might also be fairly simple but a real world with significant roles for the market, government administration, and corporate players would have enough increased complexity that networks might provide significant advantages.

114. Dobb, *Theories of Value and Distribution*, Sraffa, *Production of Commodities*, Chapters 7 and 8.

115. Veyne, 88.

116. Veyne, 23ff.

117. Verboven, 201ff.

118. Hecht, et al., *Introduction to the History and Sources of Jewish Law*.

119. Ste. Croix, *Class Struggle in the Ancient Greek World*, provides the most extensive argument along these lines.

120. Verboven, 86.

121. Verboven, 11; 46–7. This book focuses primarily on this top 10 to 15 percent of Roman society during the Late Republic.

122. Verboven, 228–29.

123. Ibid.

124. Ibid., 335.

125. Ibid., 171.

126. Ibid., 35–40. It is worth noting that civic virtues such as *liberalitas* were ineluctably part of private social networks at the same time since how one maintained ones social networks fundamentally represented how one fulfilled ones civic duties—in the eyes of all.

127. Veyne, 95–138.

128. While we are far from imagining that Weber's bureaucratic rationality is fully implemented in any modern country, we do think Weber's idea of bureaucratic rationality is more relevant to understanding modern bureaucracies than ancient ones.

129. For Rome see Erdkamp, *Grain Market in the Roman Empire*, 306–16. Charles Taylor, *Sources of the Self*, provides ample evidence that a modern self-centered interpretation for Roman behavior is virtually certain to be anachronistic.

130. While we find ethnocentric bias deplorable, since different cultures can be presumed to generate a different set of motivations, we accept no mandate to refrain from moral evaluation of institutions on relativistic grounds: to the contrary, we would, for example, on moral grounds prefer a Weberian bureaucracy to a patrimonial one in twenty-first century North America even while we recognize that it might have been well near impossible to implement such a bureaucracy in second century Rome. This near impossibility, in our view, is also no reason to consider the normal discriminatory character of Roman justice laudable though it provides reasons for not impugning individuals for failing to prevent what we (anachronistically) see as corruption.

131. Verboven, 277–84.

132. Ibid., 278.

133. Ibid., 265–74 describes the uses to which the *mandatum* could be put as including recovery of debt and searching for sources of credit as well as most other productive activities needing an honest representative.

134. Verboven, 230.

135. At the limit an appointment as *procurator omnium rerum* reflected very high levels of trust and decision making. Verboven, 254.

136. Verboven, 232, 235–49.

137. Erdkamp, 317–25.

138. Population growth rates for the ancient world are mere guesses but there is no reason to think, in the absence of modern medicine, that they would have have exceeded, in any but exceptional cases, the 0.3 percent per year of pre-modern (1650) Europe. Meadows et al., *Limits to Growth*, 41. Estimates of 100 million people on planet earth in 500 BC and 200 million in 200 AD by Pontin, *Green History of the World*, 91 imply an annual rate of only 0.1 percent The best estimates suggest not only that populations in the ancient world were neither static nor uniform geographically but that, outside the zones of empire where immigration and wealth generation added to populations, growth rates were probably as low as 0.05 percent annually. Cohen, *How Many People Can the Earth Support?* 28.

139. Erdkamp, 328–29.

140. Verboven, 346 ff.

141. Verboven, 180 notes that the Roman financial system depended largely on "respect for the moral matrix of *amicitia*."

Chapter Five

Justice to Altruism

Early Judaeo-Christian Finance

The ethical milieu introduced by the Judeo-Christian tradition transmuted the honor based concerns of Rome and Athens into a more general set of ethical considerations applicable to commerce. When poverty is an omnipresent threat and social inequality is great, wealth and honor can easily appear as divine dispensations. Justice then can readily be seen as imposing both respect for that dispensation, and a return obligation. The Judaeo-Christian tradition slowly moved beyond this Babylonian legacy toward a version of universal justice that recommended honoring the poor, and devaluing wealth in this world. Egyptians and even Romans had preceded them on this road. Yet, this was a troubled trajectory that raised, in the course of time, many ethical, economic, and social issues that impacted the practicality of earning income, and the need to address the inequalities that went hand in hand with prosperity. The Bible provides an initial source of material for consideration:

> 1 Chronicles 29:12. Both riches and honor come from You, and You rule over all, and in your hand is power and might.
>
> Job 30:15. Terrors are turned against me; they pursue my honor as the wind, And my prosperity has passed away like a cloud.
>
> Proverbs 15:33. The fear of the Lord is the instruction for wisdom, And before honor comes humility.
>
> Isaiah 10:1. Woe to those who enact unjust statutes and who write oppressive decrees.
>
> Matthew 6:19. Do not store up for yourselves treasures on earth . . . But store up treasures in Heaven.

> Matthew 6:24. No one can serve two masters . . . You cannot serve God and mammon.
>
> Matthew 5:3. Blessed are the poor in spirit, for theirs is the kingdom of heaven.
>
> Matthew 7:2. for as you judge so will you be judged, and the measure with which you measure will be measured out to you.
>
> Matthew 7:12. Do to others whatever you would have them do to you. This is the law and the prophets.[1]

The Old Testament is riddled with references to economic transactions of many sorts: buying, selling, trading, and lending. As its chapters and verses have been viewed as sacred, such references have prescriptive qualities that became the foundation for Jewish and then Christian law. Although we begin this chapter with a rather narrow focus on Jewish law relevant to investment, the broader argument we make is that Jewish law and commercial practices cannot be understood without reference to a broader historical and social context, or the moral discourse in which it is embedded. Because the development of the fundamentals of Jewish commercial law is complex and covers a history that reaches across at least two millennia, from the exodus (before the twelfth century BC to the eleventh century BC), we shall begin by providing some landmarks to help the reader across this vast and complex terrain.

The Bible not only contains materials from much older oral traditions, but was itself written over a period of a millennium—during a time of profound social and economic change that saw among other things the rise of the Jewish state, exile in Egypt and Babylon, the introduction of coinage, and later conquests by Macedonians and Romans. Not surprisingly, it contains many statements that seem to contradict one another. While for academics interpretation requires putting such passages into their proper historical context, for the Jewish rabbis, judges, and sages who first interpreted these sacred texts as law, the problem was how to reconcile such contradictory materials; and, how to justify their decisions and apply these laws in very different countries and contexts. Historically, the evolution of Jewish law involved the compilation of cases that began in the Biblical period, and the subsequent elaboration of their interpretations by Jewish sages (see table 5.1). Central to the argument we make is that while Jewish law has its roots in the scriptures, during its evolution it moved from a system of case law—consisting of how judges ruled on the particular facts of problem cases—such as Solomon's settlement of the dispute between two women over who was the mother of a baby—toward a system of universal principles that should be applied to all cases.

One of the central issues in the development of Jewish law about lending was to whom the law applied. Some passages, we argue, clearly set a brother standard, and universally condemn any lending that was conditional, or that could be seen as exploitative. Other passages, suggest that the brother standard only applied to other Jews; and, that separate standards applied to strangers. In either case, a brother standard recognizes that in a close knit community applying the sorts of tactics found outside the community would be an explosive recipe that could set brother against brother. Historically, we argue that one of the central events in the development of Jewish commercial law was the Babylonian captivity (597 BC to 538 BC). In Babylonia, Jews were thoroughly exposed to Mesopotamian commercial practices; and, when they were allowed to return, brought these back to Israel where they continued to be a major influence on Jewish scholars for the next fifteen hundred years.

Evidence suggests that early Jewish trade was primarily with other Jews. Long distance trade was dominated by other peoples such as the Phoenicians, Babylonians, etc. As the Bronze Age transitioned into the Iron Age, Jews began to connect with the merchants of Biblos and then Tyre and slowly moved toward participation in long distance trade. Following their Babylonian captivity, and certainly with the rise of Greek and Roman empires, an emerging Jewish diaspora brought Jews into close contact with other peoples who had very different commercial practices and moral standards. Faced with this, Jewish sages began to distinguish brother and stranger standards, first applying the stranger standard to "foreigners," basically non-Jews; but as Jews also resided in lands ruled by others, they went so far as to suggest that Jews abroad needed to conform to the laws of the land, in effect this was a principle of "when in Rome do as the Romans do" that allowed Jews in other places to act like other foreigners even toward their own people.

There were established institutions already in place, for example in Ptolemaic Egypt and subsequently in Roman Egypt, which provided separate legal courts for "strangers," but not for each type of stranger. Jewish law, we argue, not only links these traditions to Babylonian codes and financial practices, but as Jewish merchants participated in both Christian and Muslim societies, their commercial practices have been uniquely influential in helping to shape commerce both in the Christian and Muslim worlds. We will look briefly at the thinking of the early Christian church in this chapter, and more extensively at Muslim financial thought in the next. Table 5.1. briefly summarizes the history of Jewish jurisprudence.

BROTHER VS. STRANGER STANDARDS

Although Biblical texts on lending had enormous influence on Christian and Jewish practice in most periods, their implementation in Biblical times is a

Table 5.1. Thumbnail Periodization of Jewish Law.

Dates	*Period*	*Comments*
1st C. AD	Biblical	Case law exemplified in the older and newer books of the Old Testament. The older books include those of the Pentateuch and others dating to before the destruction of the First Temple by the Nebuchadnezar in 586 BC when most Jewish elites were taken captive to Babylonia. Many returned after 538 BC. In 70 AD a Jewish revolt against the Romans led to the destruction of the Second Temple.
1st–3rd C. AD	Tannaitic period	First development of "Halakhah" influenced by Roman conquest and dual legal system (Jewish and Roman courts).
3 C. AD	Mishnah	A codex of laws originally developed at the end of the Tannaitic period by Rabbi Judah Ha-Nasi which came to be seen as an authoritative summary of the Oral Law.
5th-6th C. AD	Talmudim	Completion of the Palestinian Talmud in 5th c. AD and of the Babylonian Talmud in 6th c. AD.
6th-11th C. AD	Geonim	Term is derived from the title, ga'on, given to the sages heading the Academies of Sura and Pembedita in Babylonia. In time, sages were recognized from many lands and their writings acknowledged as critical guides to law. It is important to remember that this body of law developed in Islamic societies and was clearly influenced by Islamic law and the situation of Jews as subject peoples.
11 C. AD on	Ashkenazim and Sephardim	These two bodies of law developed by scholars (rishonim) and became somewhat distinct: Ashkenazim (originally meaning German scholars) and Sephardim (referring to Spanish scholars) both rapidly spread (e.g., Europe and Russia vs. Spain and the rest of the Islamic world). They greatly expanded the role of interpretation, the subject matter of Jewish law and brought it up to date with world events in more innovative ways than that of the Geonim sages.

Source: This table is derived from N. S. Hecht, B. S. Jackson, S. M. Passamaneck, D. Piattelli, and A. M. Rabello, eds. *An Introduction to the History and Sources of Jewish Law*. Oxford: Clarendon Press, 1996. This table is constructed from material in Hecht et al., *An Introduction to the History and Sources of Jewish Law*.

matter of some controversy. It may be best to begin with an examination of the key passages and their most obvious implications. The Bible[2] contains many negative comments on lending at interest and usury, but even in the Old Testament, they are not all homogeneously negative. Some passages seem to make a blanket condemnation of usury,[3] and promise a decidedly bleak future for anyone engaging in it:[4]

> Ezekiel 18:8–9. if he does not lend at interest nor exact usury, if he holds off from evildoing, judges fairly between a man and his opponent; if he lives by statutes and is careful to observe my ordinances, that man is virtuous—he shall surely live, says the Lord God.

> Ezekiel 18:10–13. But if he . . . lends at interest and exacts usury—this son certainly shall not live. Because he practiced all these abominations, he shall surely die; his death shall be his own fault.

> Ezekiel 18:16. He has kept his hand back (from taking from) the poor man and has not taken, advanced or accrued interest: he has followed my rules and obeyed my laws.

> Proverbs 22:26–7. Don't be one who "strikes the palm," who stands surety for debt; if you do not have the wherewithal to pay, he (the creditor) will take your bed from under you.

The book of Ezekiel it should be noted was written while the prophet was in exile in Babylon between 593 and 571 BC,[5] and no doubt reflects his personal encounter with Mesopotamian lending and personal practices, and leaves us with little doubt that he found it appalling and morally wanting. Stylistically, Ezekiel basically follows Greek models of rhetoric, indicating that the book probably underwent redaction in the Greco-Roman period.[6] Greek rhetoric advocated using explicit comparison (e.g., between the character of two contrasting people) in making moral arguments. The parable of Lazarus and the rich man, exemplifies this long tradition of concern with justice in the Eastern Mediterranean.[7] In a typical Greco-Roman example the two contrasting people die, and are judged in the underworld. The rich man is found guilty of numerous crimes of greed and sexual excess, and is condemned to Hades; while the poor man is found to have an unblemished soul, and is conveyed to the isle of the blessed. The Egyptians also envisaged similar pairs facing judgments in the afterlife; and, indeed, the Greeks explicitly imagined getting their mythology from Egypt. The comparisons in the Bible of rich and poor that surround discussions of the morality of lending are thus part of a much richer regional traditional moral literature and rhetoric.

While Ezekiel clearly condemns usury, other passages are not universal condemnations. Deuteronomy, for instance, allows usury between strangers but not between brothers:[8]

> Deuteronomy 23:20–21. You shall not demand interest (*neshek*) from your countrymen on a loan of money or of food or of anything else on which interest is usually demanded. You may demand interest from a foreigner (*nokri*: a non-resident alien), but not from your countryman, so that the LORD, your God, may bless you in all your undertakings on the land you are to enter and occupy.

The earliest passages which expressly forbid usury focus on loans to the poor (where presumably usury is less forgivable than in loans to others) and seem to assume some lending with interest among Jews. The following two passages are the oldest mentions of usury (scholars believe they both date no later than to the eighth century BC):[9]

> Exodus:22:24. If you lend money to one of your poor neighbors among my people, you shall not act like an extortioner toward him by demanding interest from him.

> Leviticus: 25: 35–8. When one of your countrymen is reduced to poverty. . . . Do not exact interest (neither *neshek* nor *tarbîth*) from your countryman either in money or in kind. . . . You are to lend him neither money at interest or food at a profit.

If this passage from Exodus, in fact, dates to the eighth century BC, which was before the invention of coinage, the translation "money" is somewhat suspect. In Hebrew "אִם־כֶּסֶף" or silver is used, and at that time would have referred to bits of silver or non-standardized ingots of varying purity, rather than state-issued coin.[10] Nevertheless the principle is clear, demands over and above what was lent are condemned. We might speculate that in particular among kin ordered tribes, and given Jewish preferences for endogamy, "acting like an extortioner" or making profits in economic transactions that reduced kinsmen to poverty, would have caused social havoc among kinsmen and neighbors, and so might be morally sanctioned.

THE INFLUENCE OF BABYLON'S COMMERCIAL PRACTICES ON JEWISH LAW

While the distinction between lending to fellow Jews and lending to non-Jews (where interest is allowed) has often been taken by Jews as a general ethical principle, it is likely that it originated around the time that Jewish exiles in

Mesopotamia returned to Israel. Recent biblical criticism tries to understand these passages in their historical context. These arguments focus on the political and historical intent behind passages—suggesting that interpretations that fail to take this historical context into account are likely to be mistaken. Mary Douglas[11] suggests, for example, that passages in Leviticus, Numbers, and elsewhere that speak of a recurring obligation to forgive debt (variously discussed as on the sabbatical / seventh year or the Jubilee year—every fiftieth year) deal with the conflicts between Jews returning from exile in Babylon and those who had remained behind in Israel. The former might have frequently leased lands on their return; and, might have become indebted to land owners who had remained behind.

Hence, discussions of the iniquity of lending at interest to one's countrymen, while recognizing the normalcy of other lending at interest, would represent the increasing political influence of the returnees, and as their numbers increased, they may have attempted to negotiate a more favorable financial position than the norm for themselves. We should hasten to add that interpretation at this level of sophistication has been confined to recent Christian and Judaic scholars, and has never had any historical influence we know of on financial practice. The biblical passages on the forgiveness of debt obviously have parallels in the earlier common Babylonian practice of official proclamations forgiving debt, and may have resonated with the returnees for this reason.

Roger S. Nam's study, based on the Book of Kings (roughly tenth century BC, pre-exilic Israel), notes that, in addition to market and livelihood related lending (that was initially ancillary to long distance trade by non-Jews), there is good evidence for asymmetrical redistribution (by the government) as well as evidence for symmetrical reciprocity. With respect to reciprocity, a clear distinction was made between non-elite reciprocity of the sort that involved investment in social bonds and maintained the critical voice of prophets (by provision of alms of bread and water by the populace in return for prophecy); and, the numerous cases where kings tried to bribe prophets to take their side, only to find their gifts refused by prophets who preferred to maintain their integrity (in the eyes of God and the people).[12] Thus, honor, at least that of prophets, frequently took precedence over material gain even in the presence of significant political pressure. Overall, we should not be surprised if social opprobrium often weighed more in decisions than short-term gain.

Despite these admonitions against lending at interest, it was a practice common in the region; and presumably was not uncommon in ancient Israel or there would have been no need for strictures against usury. The two Hebrew terms for interest were *neshek* (literally "a bite") and *tarbîth* ("an increase"). The former at first referred to any type of loan (cf. Dt 23:20) which seems to have been restricted to loans of money / silver, while *tarbîth* came to be used for loans in kind (cf. Lv 25:17 which also uses the cognate "*marbîth*"). The term *neshek*, bite, seems to apply to a specific rate more than the vague *marbîth*. Thus, it came to be used for loans in silver—following Mesopotamian practice. There is reason to believe the Jerusalem temple itself lent at interest.[13] Nehemia 5:11 is the only passage that seems to refer to interest as a rate in quantitative terms:

> Return to them this very day their fields, their vineyards, their olive groves, and their houses, together with the interest [one hundredth] on the money, the grain, the wine and the oil that you lent them.[14]

JEWISH LENDING, TERMS, AND CONDITIONS

Biblical law had two terms for "pledges," and lists of what could and could not be pledged. The first term, *'abot*, is etymologically linked to a verb that simply means lending, while the second, *habol*, is similarly linked to a verb that means to seize. Thus while people were enjoined to lend to the poor, they were unambiguously cautioned against loans that resulted in seizing other Jews' property, and especially that of the poor.[15] As a precaution against default, a lender could insist on security in the form of a pledge (*habol*) handed over to the lender, or in the form of the borrower's own person or that of someone who stood as surety (the *nôshe*). In the case of persons pledged as surety, they would have to surrender themselves to the lender (and could be seized) if the loan became due and was not paid, and they would then work to pay off the interest and, if necessary, the principal as well.[16] 2 Kings 4:1–7 tells how the prophet Elisha saved a woman from having her two children taken as debt-slaves for a debt she could not repay, by increasing her supply of oil, so she could sell it to save her children. Amos (5:11) even suggests that collection of debt with interest or without is completely unjustified if the debtor does not have the means to repay it out of surpluses. This would imply that paying overtime should not be expected.

Various types of partnerships, implicitly involving credit, are described in the Talmud which was compiled between 200 and 500 AD. Jewish law blended the concept of joint ownership and partnership (*shûthafût*), so that partnerships involved an advance from each partner which became their joint property. The partners shared in the profits or losses from this joint capital; and, at later date, if profits outweighed losses, they could pull out their part of the capital. *Shûthafût* partnerships, thus, in our terminology, count as advancing credit with an expectation of gain— though without a contractual promise of a specific level of gain. This perspective assumed that profit without risk (usury) was qualitatively different than profit derived as a non-guaranteed return in which risk was shared.[17]

The Hebrew *shûthafût* or partnership could refer to two basic types. In the first, the partners provide the various components of the enterprise (labor, capital) in particular proportions and reap profits in those same proportions. The second type, one partner provided the capital, and the other provided the labor, (later referred to preferentially by the Arabic terms *qirād* or loan or *mudāraba* "mutual participation in an enterprise."[18] In the first case, each partner was fully liable for his (occasionally her) proportion of any losses. This form of partnership, however, was not as well suited to long distance trade as the second, which was in fact the basis for the Islamic *commenda*. Maimonides's code, for example, states that as far as partnerships are concerned, the customs current in a country "are binding, so long as no stipulations are made to the contrary."[19]

Another type of loan for business ventures found in the Talmud is the *'isqā* in which an investor (lender: *malveh*) provides capital to an agent (borrower: *loveh*) for trade. Although the liability and profit were negotiated between lender and borrower, generally, the lender/investor was supposed to accept higher liability than the borrower/agent to avoid any semblance of usury. Thus two variants are mentioned: either the investor assumes two-thirds liability for the principal and shares equally in any profits; or both accept equal liability for the principal, but the agent receives two-thirds of profits.[20]

While later Talmudic interpretations of partnerships, clearly made such distinctions, the evidence suggests a latish development, as individual Israelite merchants were engaged primarily in local trade, and initially seem not to have participated in long distance trade where reliable partnerships are most critical. With the collapse of the Bronze Age kingdoms, Phoenician merchants came to dominate the long distance trade networks in the eastern Mediterranean, and Jewish merchants seem almost exclusively to have done local trade, and relied on Phoenicians and others for long distance trade. Various passages in the Bible, for example, Ezekiel 27:8 and Isaiah 23 criticize foreign control of long distance trade such as the following critique of the Phoenicians (Isaiah 23:8–9, 18):[21]

> Who has planned such a thing against Tyre . . . whose merchants are princes, whose traders are the earth's honored men? The Lord of hosts has planned it . . . her merchandise and her hire shall be sacred to the LORD. It shall not be stored up or laid away (וְסחי אלו רצאי אל), but from her merchandise those who dwell before the LORD shall eat their fill and clothe themselves in choice attire.

The assumption behind this passage (as well as others) is that the reason for Yahweh's anger was that supply would be plentiful were it not for Phoenician hoarding and monopolistic behavior in long distance trade that directly caused harm to Israel.[22] Lexicographic analysis of commercial terminology also shows Semitic roots gradually change their meaning; during the transition from Bronze Age to the Iron Age words changed from less to more commercially focused:

> The Bronze Age binomial root *motar/mahsor* means "excess/deficit," but during the first millennium, this same term now means "profit/loss." The Late Bronze Age semitic word *kly* means "consume," but in the Iron Age also takes on the definition of "to spend." the term *mhr* "equivalence" later functions as "price" and *mkr* "exchange" later means "sell." The market terminology . . . of *rkl* and *shr* did not appear in the entire Ugaritic corpus, striking considering that Ugarit was the port city par excellence during the flourishing Late Bronze Age.[23]

SHR (סחר), which in the Book of Kings means to trade, is usually translated into the Greek term for trading emporium (ἐμπορος) that derives from a semitic root meaning to travel, while one of the new terms for "merchants" *raklim* (רכלים) is primarily found in the post-exilic (after 659 BC) passages such as the diatribe against Tyre in Ezekiel 27:8.[24]

These passages are important in establishing the chronology of Jewish subsequent participation in long distance trade where the use of sophisticated financial instruments became particularly important. De Vaux notes that:

> The Israelites did not take to commerce until late in their history. Foreign trade or big business, was a royal monopoly . . . Private citizens in Israel did business only in their own locality. . . . Real commerce was in the hands of foreigners, especially the Phoenicians . . . Even after the Exile the Jews brought agricultural products to Jerusalem, but the Tyrians sold imported goods there (Ne 13:15–16) . . . It was in the Diaspora and by force of necessity that the Jews became merchants. In Babylonia the descendants of those exiles who did not take part in the Return are found as clients or agents of big commercial firms. In Egypt, in the Hellenistic period, we know from the papyri that some were traders, bankers or brokers. The Palestinian Jews gradually followed suit, but the wise men, and later the Rabbis, were far from approving of it. Though Ben Sirach says that the profits of commerce are legitimate (Si 42; 5), he also observes that a merchant cannot live without sin (Si 26; 29; 27:2).[25]

In the early period, Jews participated in the Near Eastern tradition of written contracts for sale and made loans as discussed above. The Book of Sirach (written in Hebrew c. 200–175 BC) already is concerned about the particular ethical issues arising from long distance trade (Si 42: 1, 3–7):

> But of these things be not ashamed, lest you sin. . . . Of sharing the expenses of a business or a journey or of dividing an inheritance or property; Of accuracy of scales and balances, or of tested measures and weights; Of acquiring much

or little, or of bargaining in dealing with a merchant . . . Of numbering every deposit, or of recording all that is given or received.[26]

JEWISH LEGAL CODES

The Old Testament contains several sets of legal codes, in the sense of compendia of rulings called *ma'aseh* by Tannaitic scholars (first to third century AD) who introduced the *Halakhah*— a collection of 613 rules and practices based on biblical commandments and rabbinic decisions. The *Halakhah* is composed of several sets of codes. The first set, known as the Covenant code, (Exodus 21:1–24) has perhaps the closest parallels with Babylonian codes, which modern scholars view as compendia of exemplary legal cases rather than as laws formulated to be general rules.[27] The second is a set of non-sacral laws (Deuteronomy 15, 19, and 21) that covers topics such as murders, captives and polygamy. Scholars also refer to a set of codes found in Leviticus and Numbers, as the Holiness Code (Leviticus 17–26) or the Priestly code.

By the Tannaitic period Jewish law began to develop *Halakhah* or general law whose logic stood in explicit contrast to law based on specific case rulings. Case law, *ma'aseh*, (literally "action," i.e., judgment) had given rise to innumerable debates over the applicability of a specific ruling to other cases.[28] This distinction is perhaps best seen as a text analysis issue, in that the rise of *Halakhah* provided the more general logic necessary for the extension of legal examples to other cases and other lands. What is important to note is that prior to the Tannaitic period, Jewish law formally resembled Babylonian law much more than it did subsequently. The basic idea of *midrash* (to search) came to be applied to both legal texts (*Halakhah*) and religious narrative (*Haggadah*).

THE EARLY JEWISH DIASPORA— EVIDENCE OF TRADE AND LENDING

The most detailed early diaspora evidence for more sophisticated trade comes from papyri written in Aramaic in Egypt especially in Amarna (Elephantine). These Aramaic texts belong to a community of Jews and Arameans who traveled back and forth between Elaphantine, Abydos, Thebes and Memphis, Migdol and Syene and were written during the first Persian occupation of Egypt (ca. 525–405 BC). This was a period of heightened cosmopolitanism in Egypt, during which both officials and merchants regularly participated in long distance trade. The following elaborately conditioned loan of silver is an early loan document found from the Jewish community in Elephantine:[29]

Date	487 BC
Parties	Gemariah son of Ahio said to PN son of Jathma, saying
Loan	You gave me silver, 3 1/2 shekels
Interest	and it will increase upon me (at the rate of) 2 hallurs of silver per silver shekel per month [amounting to 5 percent per month]
Repayment I	until the day that I pay it to (you)
Interest II	and the interest on your silver will be 7 hallurs per month and the month in which I shall not give you interest it will be capital and shall increase
Repayment II	And I shall pay it to you month by month from my allotment which they will give me from the treasury
Receipt	and you shall write me a receipt for all the silver and interest which I shall be paying you
Penalty	and if I do not pay you all your silver and its interest by the month of Thoth year 36, your silver and its interest which remains upon me will double and will be increasing upon me month to month until the day that I pay it to you.
Witnesses	Akban son of Shamashuri, Kozri son of Jehoram, Maahseiah son of Jedaniah, Malchia son of Zechariah.
Scribe	Gemariah son of Ahio wrote the document upon the instruction of the witnesses who are on this document.

The significance of this loan lies in that it specifies the source of revenue available to the recipient of the loan (a scribe with a salary from the treasury), and carefully specifies a monthly interest rate that gets added to the principle if not paid. Its repayment structure involves a deadline for payment, as well as a serious penalty clause for late payment (doubling of the remaining debt all to be paid on the same monthly terms until the debt is paid in full). It also names witnesses who can pressure the scribe to repay. Although lenders have in the intervening 2,500 years thought up a few more clauses that might be added to such a loan, its explicit consideration of so many issues argues for a significantly monetized and commercial environment (even if money was primarily envisioned in terms of weight of silver rather than specific coins).

A comparable loan in the Ananiah archive (456–402 BC) made thirty one years later provides for some recourse in case of additional contingencies:[30]

Date	456 BC: 7th Kislev that is 4th Thoth, year 9 of Artaxerxes the King

Parties	said Jehohen daughter of Meshullach, a lady of Elephantine the fortress, to Meshullam son of Zaccur, a Jew of Elephantine
Loan	you gave me a loan of silver, 4 that is 4 shekels at its interest
Interest	it will increase upon me (at the rate of) silver, 2 hallurs per shekel per month, that is 8 hallurs per month, if the interest become the capital the interest shall increase like the capital, one like one
Security I	and if a second year come and I have not paid you your silver and its interest which is written in this document you Meshullan or your children have right to take for yourself any security which you will find (belonging) to me—house of bricks, silver or gold, bronze or iron, slave or handmaiden, barley, emmer or any food which you will find (belonging to me until you have full (payment) of your silver and its interest.
Validity I	and I shall not be able to say to you, "I paid you your silver and its interest" while this document is in your hand and I shall not be able to complain against you before prefect or judge, saying "You took from me a security" while this document is in your hand
Inheritance	and if I die and have not paid you this silver and its interest it will be my children (who) shall pay this silver and its interest
Security II	And if they not pay this silver and its interest, you Meshullam, have right to take for yourself any food or security which you will find (belonging) to them until you have full (payment) of your silver and its interest.
Validity II	And they shall not be able to complain against you before prefect or judge while this document is in your hand. Moreover, should they go into a suit, they shall not prevail while this document is in your hand.
Scribe	wrote Nathan son of Anani this document at the instruction of Jehohen
Witnesses	And the witnesses herein: Osea son of Galgull, Hodaviah son of Gedaliah, Ahio son of Pelatiah, Agur son of Ahio
Endorsement	Document (sealing) of silver of the debt which Jehohen daughter of Meshullach wrote for Meshullam son of Zaccur
Note	The endorsement suggests that security was indeed seized and the document then served to legitimate title to the seized property.

While these two loans are about equal in size, the contrasts in their terms and conditions could not be greater. In the first, the salaried scribe is clearly considered a good risk and the conditions placed on the loan do not include rights to seize property. The woman, Jehohen, by contrast has no salary to guarantee the loan and waives her rights to any and all property (up to the value of the loan) should she default on the loan, and further entails her children and their property. Apparently, her potential income is less than that of the scribe; and, as it would serve no purpose to double the debt if she defaults, security is instead sought among her possessions. These two loans suggest that conditions on loans were tailored to fit the circumstances rather than standardized (there were many options for security among which the lender might choose). While one option was recourse to an accepted interest rate, this clearly was little more than a part of the conditions imposed on a loan in Elephantine.

The material from Elephantine papyri suggests that, by the fifth century BC in Persian-controlled Egypt, Jewish communities regularly made loans at interest between Jews and ignored Old Testament strictures against such practices. The community in the fortress of Elephantine at this time engaged in trade up and down the Nile, and had a large temple for the substantial Jewish community that corresponded regularly, during the Persian period in Egypt, with Jewish authorities in Judah. Hence we might suppose that their practices were not deviant for the times.

Before the Tannaitic period (first to third century AD), it is clear at least in Egypt under Ptolemaic rule that Jews still lent at interest to other Jews. Two papyri, available in online collections, from the Faiyum provide documentation that suggests the practice was normal and diverged little from common practice among other Egyptians (see chapter on Egypt). The first (P. Tebt. 3.1 817) is a mortgage (November 4, 182 BC) in which Appolonius, a Jew of Epigone, lent two talents and three thousand drachmas of copper money without interest for one year to Sostratos, also a Jew of Epigone. Though the initial loan had no interest and was secured by a house and appurtenances, the papyrus further specifies that if the loan is not repaid and the security is not delivered unencumbered, then Sostratos will forfeit (owe) the original loan plus an additional half of the principal and will pay overtime interest at the rate of two drachmas per mina per month.[31] The contract is also specified as valid everywhere.

The second papyrus (P. Tebt. 3.1 818) involves the renewal of a loan (174 BC) between "Ioudas, son of Iosephos and Agothokles, son of Ptolemaios, Jew, taktomisthos of the infantry of Molossos stationed in the Herkelopolite nome." The sum lent is two talents five hundred drachmas of bronze money for twelve months with interest at two drachmas per mina per month. The loan is said to be the "amount Agothokles still owed to Ioudas out of five talents which he had received from Ioudas as an advance toward a money-changing [ἐργασίας μεταβολικῆς] business in partnership." The contract further specifies that if he does not repay the loan when it is due, it shall be increased by half (ἐὰν δὲ μὴ ἀποδῶι καθὰ γέγραπται, ἀποτει σάτω ἡμιόλιον). Both contracts have a classic increase by half clause so common in Egypt; and, despite the Ptolemies, like the Romans to follow, both permit charging interest;[32] essentially allowing minorities to largely follow their own religious rules. In the Ptolemaic period, Jews not only spoke Greek but were, like ethnic Greeks and Macedonians, legally classified together as ethnically not-Egyptian.

Rabbi Hillel, the Elder,[33] one of the sages during the Tannaitic period associated with the development of the Mishnah and the Talmud, was asked to address the issue of cancellation of debt in the sabbatical year. In response, he issued a *prozbul* (from Greek *pros boulé*, i.e., before the council) or formula that could be used by the lender. This involved signing a declaration before the court affirming that "as regards any debt owing to me that I may collect it at any time that I wish," and having the judges and witnesses also sign it.[34] This procedure headed off recourse by debtors to the Greek courts for debt forgiveness.

The Mishnah[35] goes so far as to broaden who is tainted by usury:[36]

> These transgress a negative command: the lender, the borrower, the guarantor, and the witnesses. And the Sages say: The scrive also. They transgress the command "Thou shalt not give him thy money upon usury," and "Take thou no usury of him," and "Thou shalt not be to him as a creditor," and "Neither shall ye lay upon him usury," and "Thou shalt not put a stumbling-block before the blind, but thou shalt fear thy God. I am the Lord."

This broad condemnation clearly includes all those who might be seen as party to the crime, and goes well beyond anything in the early Christian tradition. Perhaps this is due to the impact of an increasing legalism in Greek and Roman law that early on replaced more communal moral arguments with rules empowering universal application of the same standards of guilt and punishment to people in a disputatious society whose roles were as different as scribe and lender, especially where the existence of usury itself could be less than self-evident.

The broadening of the prohibition on interest from interest itself (*ribit*) to include the "dust of interest" (*avaq deribbit*) was a Talmudic innovation that presages several later Islamic concerns. The Talmudic literature (5th–6th C AD) advocated even more strongly than the Old Testament that usury between Jews was prohibited; and, included in its purview anything that looked like usury even as it continued to rationalize the permission to loan at interest to gentiles. The Baba Bathra (Gemara) provided a particularly broad description of usury:[37]

> The creditor may not dwell without charge in the debtor's courtyard or hire it from him at a reduced rate, since this counts as usury. If a man sold his field and was given a part of the price and said to the buyer, "Pay me (the rest of) the price when you will, and then take what is yours," this is forbidden. None may set up a shopkeeper on the condition of receiving half the profit, or give him money to buy produce with on the condition of receiving half the profit, unless he is paid his wage as a laborer.

The first clause covers what became a common practice throughout the Middle East, and was the norm in Morocco even in the twentieth century. The second clause qualifies as usury an advance of part of the price without the "buyer" taking possession until later after the complete purchase price is handed over. In effect, the seller would get a loan of funds that can be invested without handing over his property. This means that in the end when he gets the full price and turns over the property he has received more than the full price in two forms: that of revenue for a time from use of the property as well as returns from his investment of the advance. The third clause is clearly the most problematic in as much as it prohibits loans from taking the place of remuneration for labor and perhaps recognizes the fungibility of "profit" when labor and capital are unequally balanced.

A case in the Gemara of the *Jerusalem Talmud* illustrates the difficulty of refusing to generalize:[38]

> You meet the case of a house situated in a fortified city. A person can rent it and then buy it the following year. The rent received is a type of interest permitted by the Torah. R. Meir says that it is not true interest, while R. Judah says that it is interest, but is permitted by the Torah. R. Hezekiah makes this remark: they say that this is interest permitted by the Torah. If it permits interest here, what about elsewhere?

The general Talmudic explanation for Jewish prohibitions on usury between Jews (e.g., *The Siphra on Leviticus*) was the claim that the exodus itself was provided by God to the Jews conditional on accepting the commandments on usury (among others); and, that the breaking of God's commandments is what brought the Jews to be subjugated to their enemies. The specific laws demanding charity to brethren over-rides any economic benefits usury might provide to the lender, since of course, he was able to make those loans to gentiles. In short, an obligation of charity to one's Jewish brethren should override any right to extract benefits from loans.

NEW TESTAMENT AND CHRISTIAN ATTITUDES TOWARD LENDING

Early Christianity's moral critique of money, trading practices, taxes and inequalities in the Roman world that surrounded them—spills out in the New Testament in passage after passage, for example: "Greed is the root of all evil" [1 Timothy 6:10]; or "It would be easier for a camel to pass through the eye of a needle than for a rich man to enter the kingdom of heaven" [Matthew 19:24].[39] Yet, there is only one reference to usury, and this appears in the parable that compares the kingdom of heaven with the man who in preparation for travel to a far country puts his wealth in the hands of his servant; and on return is pleased with those who invested it well, and displeased with those who simply hide their share and returned it him without any increase.[40] The latter servant is in fact rebuked for not at least lending it out to the money changers (who obviously also lent money); and, consequently not having principle plus interest to repay the master:

> Matthew 25:24 Then he which had received the one talent came forward and said, Master, I knew you were a demanding person, harvesting where you did not plant and gathering where you did not scatter; so out of fear I went off and buried your talent in the ground. Here it is back. His master said to him in reply, "You wicked, lazy servant! So you knew that I harvest where I did not plant and gather where I did not scatter? Should you not then have put my money in the bank so that I could have got it back with interest on my return? Now then! take the talent from him and give it to the one with ten. For to everyone who has, more will be given and he will grow rich; but from the one who has not, even what he has will be taken away. And throw this useless servant into the darkness outside, where there will be wailing and grinding of teeth."

The traditional (Catholic) metaphorical interpretation of this passage is that God's investment in us is not to be left mouldering, but should instead be fruitful and multiply, for example, faith, hope, and charity should not be hidden, but be put to work. In this context, the possibility of exploitation is obviously irrelevant—if the Master in question is the Lord, the loan is seen as a gift that brings an obligation (of increase) with it. However metaphorically intended, the comprehensibility of this parable relies on a similar practice in the commercial world.[41] Nevertheless, what that condoned practice was is unspecified in the New Testament, and it might include not only loans of the sort found in Elephantine, but the practice of banks investing funds in partnerships or other ventures in which risk was shared as well as loans contracted at fixed interest rates. In brief, the New Testament while it does not provide any condemnations of usury, does not clearly approve it, for the passage is understood as an allegory, and the Old Testament is itself ambiguous. This may explain the complexity of church doctrine concerning usury over the subsequent centuries.

Early Christian theologians followed Rabbinic example in their development of biblical exegesis. Origin (185–251 AD), for example, suggested three ways to read scripture: first, a literal or historical approach which uses linguistic and literary tools; second, a reading which searches for the allegorical meaning; and third, searching for the moral message behind the text. Obviously the last two options focus attention away from the literal meaning. Later Christian thinkers,[42] such as John Chrysostom (347–407 AD) and Ambrose (339–397 AD), were happy to criticize the rich and emphasize the value of charity to the poor; and, like virtually all early Christian leaders, they denounced usury as counter to God's message of charity, but they also slowly contributed new ideas.

Underlying their view of the economy was a profound moral framework in which a person's every action was the subject of divine judgment. This frame set a standard of brotherly love entailing fairness and charity, which not only flatly condemned all forms of usury, but called upon Christians to lend to the poor in need, *gratis*. The poor stood in parallel to "bretheren" in Jewish law. To charge anything for the use of money, was not only a usurious deed, but a sin. Early Church thinkers made three types of arguments against usury: that it was against divine law set forth in the scriptures; that it was against human law (defined by legal codes); and, ultimately that it was against natural law. Following Aristotle's logic, they argued that, since money is in itself a sterile element, the idea that money should produce interest is unnatural because inanimate objects cannot reproduce.

New Christian ideas about usury began with ideas of just prices and economic fairness—both of which required that the parties freely agree without any coercion to the transaction. A just price, for instance, would compensate a farmer for his labor and other costs, but if he were to extort a higher price from a buyer because of a food shortage, even if the buyer out of desperation were willing to pay it, such profits would be akin to usury. John Chrysostom argues explicitly that even though a debtor may agree to pay interest on a loan, he does so only because he is coerced by urgent needs. Saint Augustine's (354–430 AD) argument against usury is not simply that it is forbidden by scripture, but that moneylenders prey upon the misfortunes of others. Augustine's view, rather than Aristotle's, had the greatest durability, and is still at the root of Western ambiguous attitudes toward lending; those of Karl Marx as much as those of the Catholic Church.

The broad demographic base of the Roman Empire also proved to be corrosive to narrowly ethnic perspectives, and it is likely that the Roman focus on legislation and citizenship helped broaden Christian outlooks both before and after Christianity became a state religion (post 323 AD). Christian theologians followed Rabbinic example in their development of biblical exegesis even as they began to extend its implications to all people. With the conversion of the Roman Emperor Constantine the Great (reigned 306–336 AD) to Christianity in 312 AD, the qualms Christians theologians had about usury could become the basis for laws prohibiting usury. This was somewhat more problematic in the East where credit was an essential part of long established trading practices than in the West where credit was primarily used to finance consumption.[43] As a result, a split arose between the Greek church in Constantinople, and the Latin church in Rome over usury. While both churches shared the same low opinion of usury, the Greek church instead of issuing a blanket condemnation of usury as had the church in Rome, only prohibited its clergy from engaging in usury, and merely constrained engagement in this practice by decreeing acceptable rates of interest.[44]

In the East, the Byzantine Emperor, Justinian 1 (reigned 527–565 AD) made the move toward regulating usury by creating a sliding scale that preserved the 12 percent rate established under Roman law in 88 BC only for nautical loans (*foenus nauticum*). Eight percent could be charged for business loans. For ordinarily people not borrowing for business purposes, the permitted rate was 6 percent. Whereas, distinguished people (read wealthy and powerful) and farmers (read landowners) paid only 4 percent.[45] Already the special nature of the poor might seem to have been replaced by the special merits of the rich, though the scale is more likely to reflect an assessment of differential risk in lending.

Although most early church authorities took the position that loans at fixed rates of interest were immoral, given the importance of commerce in the Mediterranean world, loans at interest were certainly common, just as were countless sources of hidden interests. It may have been normal for members of the clergy to shun loans at interest,[46] but this is unlikely to have been the norm for ordinary Christians in the early centuries, especially in the East.

In the chapter on Mesopotamia we noted MNA's receipt of a letter of credit dated to 511 BC. Only one of the key activities of bankers by this time was to change currency but their activities always involved both complex estimations of value and a search for a opportunity to exact a premium. At a most basic level a bill of exchange is merely a letter of credit that can be couched as an exchange between two currencies. Bills of exchange can thus be viewed either as a loan (e.g., the holder of the bill purchased the bill in one place and later received the bill's monetary value in the local currency of another country at a rate that conceals the interest accruing to the bill provider) or it can be viewed as a simple currency conversion involving no interest and at most a fee for the convenience of processing. Given the time it took to travel, delays in communication, the reality of commodity price fluctuations between markets that impacted purchasing power and the general uncertainty of relative monetary values in the past and future, it would be hard to demonstrate that a bill of exchange actually qualified as a loan at a particular rate of interest. Long before medieval times, even the church itself began to appreciate the potential value of complex financial transactions, and so the problem of usury became one of how to define it in such a way that it only applied to a loan, and would not preclude other useful financial arrangements such as bills of exchange.[47]

Although Christians initially lived as a minority in the Roman Empire, they inhabited a society in which loans at interest were common place and their society, as we have seen, did not view loans as the be all end all of commercial wisdom: focusing instead on honor and social networks. In the course of time, the Christian interpretation of what is wrong with usury expanded but Christians seem to have long relied on a resemblance of usury to theft and general notions of justice—both Greek in origin but modified by Augustine—rather than a negative comparison with an ethical obligation of charity to one's brethren being preferable to pursuit of profit. Until the Reformation, there was a distrust of wealth as well as profit at the core of Christian moralizing—even if many Christians pursued both wealth and profit. While the Judaic tradition abhorred greed and exploitation it was more prone to honor its Babylonian roots in seeing nothing essentially wrong with lending at interest or with making money The position in Western Christendom continued to be that there is something intrinsically wrong with lending money at interest until Aquinas and his followers introduced the idea of opportunity cost (realistically foregone opportunities available to the lender) and argued that a rate of interest on loans at or below the opportunity cost of money was moral.

Both Judaic and Christian traditions found generosity and altruism honorable, and found problematic those who could not honor God above wealth. Both also held that the only legitimate way to wealth, seen as a mere dispensation from God, involved following the law and the prophets. Yet they, like the Muslims we discuss in the next chapter, each put their own unique spin on the ethics of credit. It was left to Muslims, however, to devote financial brilliance to the issue of banishing, to the degree possible, opportunities for hidden interest. In this, they built on Jewish ideas in a most original way and institutionalized Jewish and Christian ideas about altruism in innovative ways.

NOTES

1. *The New American Bible*, 1991.
2. Ibid.
3. A computer search of the Bible for usury yielded the following mentions of lending: Old Testament: Exodus 2:25, Leviticus: 25:36–7, Deuteronomy 23:20–1, Nehemiah 5:6–11, Psalms 15 15:5, Proverbs 28:8, Isaiah 24: 2, Jeremiah 15:10, Ezekiel 18:8, 13, 17, Ezekiel 22:12, New Testament Matthew 25:27, Luke 19:23.
4. Psalms 15 15:5 also makes a general claim that the righteous do not lend at interest and Proverbs 28:8 suggests that those who charge interest will themselves get no benefit from the practice—their increase will accrue to God alone: "He who increases his wealth by interest and overcharge gathers it for him who is kind to the poor."
5. Petersen, *Prophetic Literature*, 139.
6. Petersen, Ibid., 166; Verboven, Ibid.
7. Hock (1987: 447–63).
8. Leviticus: 25:36-7 also proscribes lending at interest between countrymen but see below.
9. Meislin and Cohen, "Backgrounds of the Biblical Law against Usury," 250–67.
10. Davies, *A History of Money,* 60–64.
11. Douglas, *In the Wilderness*, cites an enormous scholarly literature and is much influenced by rabbinic thought. Key Biblical passages include: Numbers 36, Nehemia 5:1–13, Leviticus 24–6, Jeremiah 29 and 34, 2 Chronicles 36:21.
12. Nam, *Portrayals of Economic Exchange in the Book of Kings*, 99. See also chapter 5 for an extensive but cautious discussion of the role of markets in pre-exilic Israel.
13. de Vaux, *Ancient Israel*, 170.
14. The Hebrew word is *mê'at* and the Latin Vulgate translates this as *centisiman* while the typical English translation merely says "interest." Neufeld, "The Rate of Interest and the Text of Nehemia 5:11," 198. In Latin *centesima* are the hundredth part of something. The interpretation of "1 percent" would mean 1 percent per month or 12 percent per annum which was a common rate in those times but as the Hebrew has only an abbreviation (the "m") a simple translation as "interest" may be safer.
15. Tykva Frymer-Kensky, "Israel," in Westbrook and Jasnow, *Security for Debt in Ancient Near Eastern Law*, 252–53.
16. de Vaux, 172.
17. Our best information on Jewish contracts comes from the Geniza documents but since most Jewish merchants adopted Muslim contractual forms we will discuss Jewish contracts more fully in the chapter on Islamic credit.
18. Goitein, *A Mediterranean Society*, Vol. I, 170–71.
19. Ibid., 171.
20. Udovitch, *Partnership and Profit in Medieval Islam*, 199.
21. Translations from *The New American Bible*, 1991. My insert of Hebrew text, cf. Nam, 159.

22. Translations from *The New American Bible*, 1991. Nam, 159 discusses the implications of this passage and other similar ones.

23. This passage is a synthesis of some of Liverani's points, "Political Lexicon and Political Ideologies in the Amarna Letters," 41–56 many of which are also discussed in Nam, 159–60.

24. Nam, 157–59. Although Nam does not provide the origin of the term raklim (םילכר) in Hebrew, Lane (Arabic-English Lexicon Vol. 1: 1148 suggests the classical root in Arabic [rkl]) referred to kicking as in getting a horse or donkey to ride and so the term might have come to characterize merchants who did not travel on foot and used pack animals. It would then have been an appropriate term to describe a new form of merchant who had to cover greater distances.

25. de Vaux, 78–79.

26. Translations from *The New American Bible*, 1991. The Hebrew text was translated into Greek around 132 BC by Sirach's grandson and from there into Latin.

27. It is not clear that modern scholars have a similar consensus that the Halakhah was formulated as a set of exemplary cases and not as a set of general prescriptions.

28. Peretz Segal, "Jewish Law during the Tannaitic Period," in Hecht et al., *An Introduction to the History and Sources of Jewish Law*, 106.

29. A full exegesis and notes are given in Porten et al., *The Elephantine Papyri in English*, 256–57. Our summary has left out some details used to calculate the loan amount of 3 1/2 shekels since the actual money was a mixture of Ptah (1 deben = 10 kite) and Persian coins (1 karsh = 10 shekels) where the Persian karsh was lighter than the Ptah deben. In Elephantine, the total was assessed by weight measured on a scale with locally defined stone weights.

30. Porten et al., 203–5.

31. A talent of silver was equal to 60 minae; and one mina was equal to 100 drachmas.

32. Alfredo Mordechai Rabello, "Jewish and Roman Jurisdiction," in Hecht et al., 145.

33. The traditional dates given for Rabbi Hillel, the Elder are that he was born in Babylon 110 BC and died in Jerusalem in 10 CE.

34. Segal, in Hecht et al., 79–109, 131.

35. The Mishnah is a collection of opinions by rabbinic sages during the Tannain period from the first century and second century BC that presents the actual cases along with the debate on the matter, and the judgment given by notable rabbi.

36. Maloney, "Usury in Greek, Roman and Rabbinic Thought," 101.

37. Maloney, 99–100.

38. Maloney, 103.

39. *The New American Bible*, 1991.

40. This parable appears in similar detail and import in Matthew 25:14–30 and Luke 19:10–28.

41. Proponents of "Christian atheism" interpret this passage from Matthew as an indication that the bad servant has committed the crime of opting out of normative behavior and as such has challenged social expectations—in short the bad servant is a good revolutionary (albeit one not willing to commit a crime). Žižek, *Less than*

Nothing. Hegel and the Shadow of Dialectical Materialism, 114. This interpretation, understood however as an allegory, would imply that just as the servant opted out of the commercial spirit expected of him so in the allegorical world he opted out of the Christian spirit of love expected of him and so was cast out and there was "wailing and grinding of teeth."

42. Ferguson, *Encyclopedia of Early Christianity.* See articles on usury, John Chrysostom, "Ambrose, Origen, and Social Thought."

43. Kuznets, "The Doctrine of Usury in the Middle Ages," 14.

44. Kuznets, 12.

45. This case is discussed at greater length in our second volume, Greenberg and Park, *Hidden Interests in Credit and Finance: Power, Ethics, and Social Capital across the Last Millennium*, forthcoming.

46. Vööbus, "The institution of the Benai Awiama and Benat Qeiama in the Ancient Syrian Church," 19–27 notes that the rules of this fifth century AD order of monks and nuns among other things specifically forbade usury. That clergy in the fifth century had to be admonished about it suggests that in society at large loans at interest were at least not uncommon.

47. Roover, "The Scholastics, Usury, and Foreign Exchange," 257–71.

Chapter Six

Islamic Finances and the Eastern Mediterranean

By the fourth century AD, Byzantium had begun to dominate the eastern Mediterranean while Christians of various sorts were common on both sides of the Mediterranean and even into the Sasanian empire where both Persian and Aramaic were common languages. Early in the seventh century, in western Arabia, the prophet Muhammed (d. 632 AD) received a series of revelations that gave rise to the spread of Islam, one of the world's great religions, and precipitated conquests that created an Islamic world, rewarding literacy in Arabic, that spanned from Spain and the Maghrib to Indonesia in the east.

Initially, this world displaced the Sasanian Empire in the core areas of the Near East and spread west and east. Eventually, much of the Mediterranean area, and under the Ottomans even the Byzantine Empire, was conquered. In the dark ages Muslim commerce dominated, by the eleventh century the revival of European power and the better ports on the northern coasts favored European commerce. Islamic accounts reflect both Arab distrust of the sea and their domination of it for a period:

When God created the Mediterranean he addressed it, saying,

> "I have created thee and shall send thee my servants. When these will ask for some favour of me, they will say 'Glory to God!' and 'God is Holy!' and 'God is Great!' and 'There is no God but God!' How wilt thou then treat these?"
>
> "Well, Lord," replied the Mediterranean—"I shall drown them."
>
> "Away with thee—I curse thee—I shall impoverish thy appearance and render thee less fishy!"[1]
>
> The Christians could no longer float a plank on the sea.[2]

Centuries of warfare between Byzantium and the Sasanian Empire, following on millennia of changes in rulers, may have oriented the inhabitants of the Near East to some degree of indifference to whether they were ruled by Sumerian, Akkadian, Egyptian, Assyrian, Latin, Greek, Persian, or Arabic-speaking rulers. Like the Persians before them, the Arabs initially did not insist on major ground level changes in customary practice. Accommodation to local custom became as standard in the Islamic world as it was in the Catholic world and probably contributed similarly to its earthly success.

The original center of Islamic power in the Hijaz of Arabia soon shifted to more populated and central areas: Damascus in Syria under the Umayyads and then, under the Abbasids, Baghdad in Iraq. By the tenth century, the Islamic world was politically fragmented but still, to a considerable degree, culturally unified at least around a consensus that Muhammed was the last and most important prophet and that the revelations he received, embodied in the text of the Quran, were to be seen as the core basis of a religious and ethical system relevant both to political, social and financial practice.

Major ruptures had by this time appeared both in the legitimacy of other sources of religious and legal doctrine and in political practice, but few Muslims insisted that these ruptures represented the same level of ethical or religious differences as those between Jews, Christians and Muslims for neither Jews nor Christians recognized the divine origin of the revelations conveyed by Muhammed.

Finance in the Islamic world was influenced by commercial practices developed in Mesopotamia, conditioned by the ethical traditions associated with Israel and Egypt, in particular, and in large part came to be shaped by the philosophical and social ideas developed in Greece and the Early Republic of Rome. A major additional input came from the Islamic world with its own meticulous transformations of both religious and commercial traditions. The excruciatingly meticulous rules from the Qur'an and Abu Hanifa cited later in this chapter, provided a starting point for a financial system that grew to be exceedingly sophisticated yet still focused intently on justice and transparency: two hallmarks of Islamic finance. After its development in the Arabian Peninsula, Islam spread through the Fertile Crescent and across North Africa into Spain, before expanding into sub-Saharan Africa, India, Indonesia, and much of southwest Asia, Anatolia, and parts of southeastern Europe.

We will focus in this chapter on an intellectual milieu and financial practice that became standard across the medieval Mediterranean but are well documented in the Islamic world from the Maghrib to southwestern Asia. In so doing, we look at the developments in credit and commerce within the Islamic world before modern financial practices were implemented in Europe or the Mediterranean. Our geographical center of focus will be Egypt whose long distance trade during the early Islamic period thoroughly transformed the Mediterranean.

Any simple summary of commercial conditions in another era cannot begin to detail all the significant peculiarities of the time but a simple comparison of the view of the Mediterranean exemplified in the opening citation from Muqaddasi (945/6–991) and the Roman view of the Mediterranean as "*mare nostrum*" suggests that even at the end of the first millennium Muslim geographers were less at ease with maritime travel than Romans in the early Roman Empire. Muqaddasi's perspective implicitly recognizes the risks associated with trade and may owe something to the legacy of ancient Egypt, which, despite vast familiarity with riverine travel never produced a significant fleet that was at home on the high seas.

In the early centuries of the Christian Era (CE), trade goods tended to move at somewhere between 25 and 50 km a day, boats tended to port or shore every 50–70 km while couriers could travel most rapidly by taking the earliest boat at each port. A shipment from Baghdad to Qayrawan (roughly Tunis) might take six months; and, one from Alexandria to Fustat (Cairo) might arrive in four to five days. Conditions varied enormously and even travel between Alexandria and Fustat could, at times, be hazardous in the extreme. In good times, a shipment directly between two ports could be both the most rapid and the most secure, but, as Muqaddasi's apocryphal story suggests, Muslims initially found shipping in the Mediterranean more hazardous than they would have preferred.

Governments had their own postal service for government matters, but merchants could generally rely for correspondence (letters and very small packets) on commercial couriers who plied particular routes on regular schedules. Jews were not to travel on the Sabbath, and this regularly posed problems for those who wished to travel with a Muslim caravan over land. This may indeed have been one of the overriding motivations for partnerships, as well as more informal commercial ties, between Muslim and Jewish merchants. On ship, a Jew could without onus be carried forward by the boat even on the Sabbath, so Jewish merchants had uninterrupted mobility once embarked on the sea.[3]

EARLY ISLAMIC DYNASTIC CHRONOLOGY AROUND THE MEDITERRANEAN

We cannot fit a discussion of Islamic political evolution across what became the Islamic world from Spain to Indonesia in this chapter. Our focus on financial developments fortunately does not depend crucially on the reader's broad grasp of Islamic history.[4] Nevertheless, a few remarks are in order. As the Islamic world expanded outward from Arabia, a concept of an Islamic community, the *umma*, began to take hold: it was conceived of as a world without frontiers, in the modern nationalistic sense of citizenship, in which any Muslim was welcome anywhere.

Travel over long distances did not begin with Islam nor did an associated travel literature. One of the earliest accounts in the Roman period is the first century AD account of a traveler from Gades (Cádiz) to Rome who left four silver goblets embellished with the story of his travails at a sanctuary at some hot springs at Lake Bracciano north of Rome.[5] In the Islamic period a merchant in the west could travel east and establish themselves where they chose, and, similarly, those at the eastern end of the Islamic world could expect the same welcome traveling to the west. Scholars not only traveled to study with the learned but constructed their own reputations, formulated as an *ijaza*, through study of particular texts with a sequence of great scholars.

Great scholarship went into verifying the biographical details of other scholars so that chains of transmission *isnad* (اصناد) for authoritative texts, especially *hadith* (حديث), could be evaluated. Travel that was advantageous for Muslims was so as well for Jews—though on occasion local Jews were subjected to impositions that foreign Jews, though they might be residents, were not. That citizenship did not have a legal significance meant that taxes were primarily assessed on trade (e.g., the movement of goods including their entry into towns). Certain merchants were allocated state monopolies over particular trades. In addition, tax farming was contracted out, as it often had been in the past, and was generally imposed at the community level based on the number of resident households rather than a simple capitation rate.

Islamic conquests outside of Arabia led to a fiscal distinction between *kharaj* lands, long deemed taxable because of the way rights were negotiated by an original non-Muslim population; and those lands not subject to the *kharaj* tax, which were either lands directly conquered or occupied by Muslims. Another tax, not levied on all, was the per capita *dhimmi* tax. It was paid only by resident non-Muslim people "of the book" (e.g., Jews and Christians). Jews, who were more common than Christians in the Islamic world, usually had their own community spokespersons (the Nagid); and decided most financial disputes between Jews within their own communities. Other larger non-Muslim communities, such as those of Copts in Egypt, had similar arrangements.

Until the more recent era of capitulations initially negotiated by Europeans with the Ottomans, all cases involving one or more Muslims were dealt with by Islamic authorities or Islamic courts on the basis of Islamic law. Many non-Muslim merchants would regularly back up agreements made with their co-religionists using Islamic rulings just in case their own community had difficulty enforcing payments. Non-Muslims and Muslims regularly engaged in joint ventures and enterprises: with the main exception being things explicitly prohibited by one or the other religion: for example, Jews drank and traded in alcoholic beverages while Muslims should not. This meant that a Muslim trader could get into trouble having a Christian or Jewish agent for they might not avoid prohibited types of trade but a Muslim could be the agent of a Christian or Jew as long as he, himself, abided by Islamic law and traded only those things allowable.[6]

Islamic dynastic history, properly speaking, began with the third Caliph Umar who ended up establishing a basis for institutionalizing an Islamic polity with a capital in Mecca. His success was bitterly opposed by the followers of Ali, Muhammed's son-in-law, and this led to the first schism in Islamic religion between what came to be referred to as the *sunni* and *shi'a* branches of Islam. The huge area that came to be included in the Islamic world had an enormous range of customs, referred to in Islamic law as *'urf*, that to significant degrees, along with dynastic ideologies, shaped the implementation of financial law and practice. Early Islamic society included a notion of gratitude (*ni'ma*) on which patron-protegé commercial ties were based.[7] Later Islamic legal scholars did their utmost, presumably for practical reasons, to accommodate the law to local custom—primarily overruling custom when it contradicted clear Islamic principles.

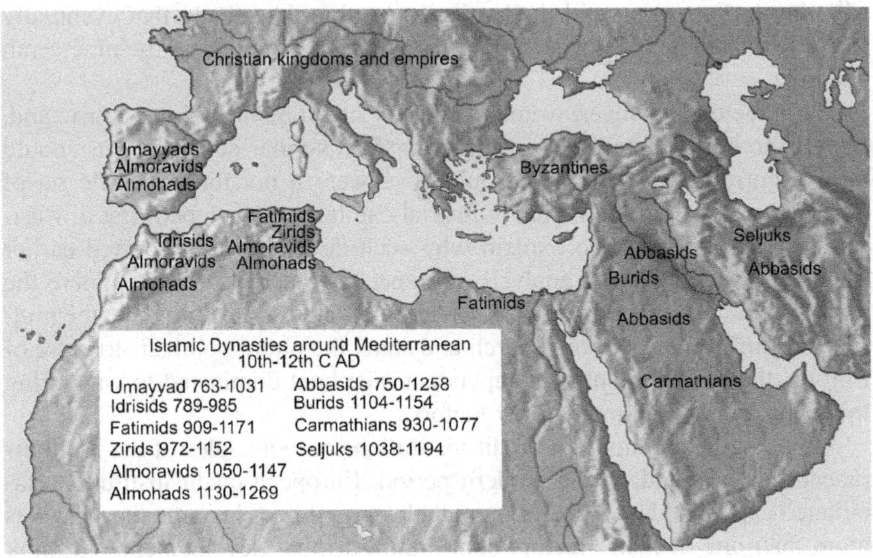

Map 6.1. Islamic Empires to Twelfth Century AD.

Our chronological focus in this chapter will be from the beginning of the Islamic period to the twelfth century, but of necessity we will examine most closely commerce and finance in Egypt and reference other areas and times to clarify critical issues. To economize space, table 6.1 (p. 193) egregiously simplifies Islamic history, providing only the most basic political chronology for the periods and dynasties in the Islamic world that need to be referenced in this chapter. Most aspects of the early development of Islamic financial change and practice can be fruitfully examined within this geographical and chronological framework. While our focus will be on Islamic finance and credit, we should emphasize that in this period all Muslims, Jews, and Christians relied regularly on Islamic financial instruments for dealings in the Islamic world.

A NECESSARY ASIDE: THE ISSUE OF PRODUCTIVITY IN THE ISLAMIC WORLD

While in this chapter we have little interest in studying regional productivity *per se*, we should say up front that we find completely unconvincing the notion several scholars, most prominently Rodinson and recently Kuran (see note 9), have put forward that there were simple and fundamental obstacles to development built into Islamic commercial law. On the contrary, we subscribe to the position that there were a host of specific historical factors contributing to Europe's rapid modernization and rapid growth, that eventually led to its economic precedence over the Islamic world during the nineteenth century.

These factors, however, were not socially or economically necessary; and, there is no basis, therefore, for suggesting that similar developments should have occurred elsewhere, and would have were it not for a specific set of obstacles. Our key point is that industrial capitalism developed first in western Europe, and trying to explain why such developments occurred earlier nowhere else, through an analysis of a specific other place, is to ignore the many institutions of Europe that together facilitated something new; the multifarious influences between church and state, the plural political structure of Europe, the development of independent merchant dominated towns during the feudal period and many other factors.

Although the evolution of credit institutions on both sides of the Mediterranean differed, and, in the modern period, European credit institutions facilitated capitalist development, nonetheless we do not imagine that this was more than one of many factors contributing to that development. To think otherwise is to commit either a basic logical fallacy that economic causes

Table 6.1. Islamic Chronology around the Mediterranean to Mid-Thirteenth Century AD.

Date AD	*Period*	*Discussion*
c. 610	Revelations	At about 40, Muhammed began to have visions and hear what was to become written down as the Qur'an.
622–628	Medina	Islam develops politically.
629–632	Mecca	Muhammed conquers Mecca in 629 and establishes it as the capital and dies in 632.
632–634	abu bakr	Muhammed's adjutant and first successor
634–644	umar b. al-khattab	2nd Caliph generally accepted except for the faction supporting 'alī. Murdered in 644.
640	Egypt conquered	General 'amr b. alī 'as occupied Egypt for the Umayyads.
644–656	uthman b. 'affan	3rd Caliph from the Banu Umayya, "executed" in 656, 'alī made caliph but challenged by Mu'awiya the governor of Syria. Beginning of schism between sunni and shi'ī.
661–750	Umayyads	With defeat of 'alī the Umayyad dynasty forced the partisans of 'alī from power and *shi'a* moved primarily into the then periphery: Iran and some oases in the Sahara.
711	Spain and North Africa	Andalusia begins its development as a series of Islamic caliphates and states as Islam arrives in Maghrib. Cordoba became capital of al-andalus in 787 and soared to great heights of culture until conquered in 1236 by Ferdinand of Castile. Last Andalusian dynasty, the Nasrids, fell to Christians in 1492.
749–1258	Abbasid: Iraq and Baghdad	Capital in Baghdad ruled much of the Islamic world
788–959	Idrisids: Fes	First dynasty in Fes
909–973	Fatimids in Tunis	A *shi'ī* dynasty claiming descent from 'alī, a Mediterranean power
973–1171	Fatimids in Cairo	Move to Cairo represented growing strength
1038–1194	Saljuqs of Iraq and Persia	Turkish dynasty that ruled much of Central Asia and Near East
1073–1147	Almoravid	Nomadic conquest of Maghrib from Atlantic to Libya
1130–1269	Almohad	Nomadic conquest of Maghrib from Atlantic to Libya
1169–1252	Ayyubid: Egypt	Saladin founded dynasty after defeating the crusaders
1261–1517	Abbasid: Cairo	Ruled by the Mamlukes—former military slaves of the Ayyubids

operate independently of a social matrix, or to seriously underplay the role of many significant social, political and economic factors. Oversimplification is no virtue, or as a paraphrase of Einstein puts it, "Everything should be made as simple as possible, but no simpler."[8]

Our position may be most easily understood through a brief examination of the contrary position.[9] Kuran, who is writing in the twenty-first century, and so has the benefit of more recent scholarship than Rodinson, suggests that the absence of merchant associations and corporations was in part due to the promotion of well-defined partnerships under Islamic commercial law, in which each partner shared both benefits and risks based on their proportion of the investments. His list of negatives includes prohibitions against apostasy and other significant constraints on foreigners, that forced foreigners to conform to Islamic legal norms prior to capitulations to European powers. He further suggests that several key legal elements holding back the Islamic world included inheritance laws that mitigated against trans-generational accumulation of wealth, political needs that both prevented guilds from evolving into corporations and tax farming that prevented the rise of centralized economic power. Kuran also points to polygyny with its tendency to amplify the dispersive character of Islamic inheritance.

Inconsistently, Kuran also considers the *waqf* system (religious endowment) rules: including that there be a single administrator and a charitable purpose, at least in the long term, as obstacles to capital accumulation and the formation of corporations.[10] His key argument hinges on the inflexibility of the *waqf* rule that the administrator was always held accountable for proper management, arguing that this inhibited him from making economically advantageous decisions.

This critique of the economic value of the *waqf* system has been suggested by many before, but involves a number of significant misunderstandings. *Waqf* (pl. *awqāf*, also called *habous* in the Maghrib), the legal act, establishes a legal manner of voluntarily relinquishing the right of disposal of property by its owner in order to endow an institution or person with the legal usufruct of that property. The term is regularly used to refer to the property endowed (technically, *al-mawqūf*) as well as to the legal act itself (*al-waqf*).

Just about anything owned (including land and water rights) could be endowed to another in this way. Agricultural or urban real estate were by far the most common forms of property, and the most common recipients were either institutions such as mosques, shrines or schools, or relatives.[11] The most repeated misunderstanding of the *waqf* is tied to the claim that when large numbers of urban or rural properties are endowed to an institution neither their rents, fixed by the articles of endowment, nor the overall valuation of the *waqf* itself keep up with market value, and so, supposedly, this leads to a less than optimal use of real estate.[12]

This claim is naive on several counts. It fails to recognize that while annual rents are often fixed by the legal arrangements and change slowly, the market sets the much more significant key right (*haqq as-serrut* or *haqq al-miftāh*) which gives the occupant the right to occupy the property and use it. This right is auctioned off by the institution to a private user, and the winner of the auction pays a hefty sum for a life's usufruct. Young men rarely can afford the better properties; so, at the occupant's death, when the property is re-auctioned, the previous owner has held the property only for a limited number of years. Given traditional life expectancies and the slow change in property values, such auctions have undoubtedly been more than sufficient to impose an efficient use of capital.

The ancillary notion that because significant changes to endowments (such as exchanging one parcel of land for another or acquiring new parcels) required approval of a *qadi* (a judge), this requirement was a major obstacle to maintaining or improving the capital valuation of the *waqf* is just as naive. It flies in the face of the many examples of *waqf* that remained prosperous, and indeed grew in prosperity over the course of several centuries. It ignores as well that this proviso served as a check on risky decisions, and undoubtedly saved many *awqāf* from an early demise.

The social and economic advantages of this institution were many: and included keeping productive property from being subdivided through inheritance; providing long term funding for valuable social institutions both religious and educational; financing private commerce;[13] providing a significant revenue stream in the form of taxes from properties that regularly produce a surplus; providing a productive and lasting source of prestige and upward mobility for those with funds;[14] and, last but not least, ensuring that significant institutions have sufficient wealth to provide a countervailing force to despotism in its local and regional forms. Some of these very arguments have been used to make the case for the positive role of the Catholic church and its many monasteries in the economic growth of western Europe, as we will see next.

A number of *waqf* characteristics varied across time and place, as endowments in Ancient Egypt[15] had done. Even so, typically the endowment was regarded as irrevocable; the administrator was considered bound first and foremost to promote the economic sustainability and prosperity of the endowment and, secondarily, was constrained to follow the specifics of the endowment contract unless the first requirement imposed some change and a *qadi* approved that change. Taxable land remained taxable, tax exempt land remained tax exempt.

Nevertheless, some possibility existed to transform taxable land, via substantial payment to the authorities, into tax exempt land. The two main types of *waqf*, familial (*ahlī*), and institutional (*khayrī*: philanthropic), were legally the same (though mitigating circumstances and the obligations of the *waqf* administrator might be different). Many institutional *waqf* endured for several centuries or more, and dealt successfully with their changing circumstances by finding new revenue sources as needed via new endowments and new negotiations with authorities. In the eighth century, when Abu Hanifa were still debating the form and legality of the *waqf* institution, its legality for a time was justified as a form of interest free loan that thus might be revocable, but this view did not long survive.[16] In the long run, the *waqf* proliferated precisely because of its economic advantages in preserving wealth.

The *waqf* belonged to a group of practices which recognized the financial potential of real estate not just its value as a commodity.[17] An innovative way of blending capital and real estate was the common practice of exchanging use of a house (rent free) for the usufruct of a sum of capital. This was a transaction in which no interest was charged or owed, no real sale effectuated, nor any permanent endowment made, so it was ethically as suspect as it was common; perhaps in part because the parity of the advantages to each party could not be adequately assessed, and perhaps in part because in practice it was often a way for smooth operators to take advantage of widows.

The *rahn*,[18] which has been compared to a hypotheque or mortgage, was another common credit instrument. In the typical case, the usufruct of real estate was exchanged for a defined period of time for a sum of money usually amounting to somewhat less than the annual productive value of the land. At the end of a year, the contract could be renewed or the capital that had been exchanged for the usufruct could be returned in its entirety. Most *rahn* examined in rural Morocco in the twentieth century[19] involved multiple transactions of increasing disadvantage to the property owner; and, clearly represented a practice pursued primarily when a land owner was in financial difficulties. Both these forms of transaction as well as others,[20] historically served to integrate real estate and the market without direct recourse to real estate sales, though how just or effective their results were in practice is as difficult to estimate as the impact of the institution of foreclosure is today.

The vast wealth of Rome at its height, of Mughal India, or of many Chinese dynasties without the development of industrial capitalism should suggest that capital accumulation and the existence of options for capital investment have never been the critical issue. The great similarity of commercial institutions on both sides of the Mediterranean for many hundreds of years, and the greater wealth for many centuries on the southern shore is indicative of this as well. Restrictions on lending at interest applied to most people on both sides of the Mediterranean, but the high number of sales on credit, at higher fixed prices than cash sales, functioned on the northern and southern shores in a similar economic fashion: the delay in payment compensated for price differentials.[21] It is unlikely that a simple failure to lend at interest had much economic significance.

The simple differences of the sort described by Kuran must be seen as almost insignificant More significant is the particular ethical and technical path followed by Islamic countries for it was both fruitful and admirable as well as different than the path followed in Europe.

THE DEVELOPMENT OF ISLAMIC COMMERCIAL LAW

In their search for justice in commerce, early Islamic jurists sought to eliminate chance, forbid usury and make commercial rules clear and unambiguous. Islamic scholars were very much in favor of commerce and almost all would have themselves been involved in minor or even major commerce. Rather than a hostility to commerce, the rules were intended to promote commerce and production by making expectations explicit and rewards directly tied to investments of labor or funds while fairly allocating risk and liability. Taxes, such as zakat, were not levied on working animals nor on loans—the lender was to pay the zakat when repaid.[22] The following examples were both formative and illustrative of Islamic concerns:

> Forbidden to you are . . . partition by the divining arrows; that is ungodliness.[23]
> Every loan which secures advantage to the lender has no good in it.[24]
> Shurayb said, "Pre-emption [belongs to those dwelling] in front of the doors." We do not adhere to this, Pre-emption belongs to adjoining neighbours, and that is the verdict of Abu Hanifa.[25]

Even though the initial direction taken by the Islamic world's commercial law seems to have been settled between the eighth and tenth centuries (the *sunna* was established and the *shi'a* traditions well distinguished from *sunnism*),[26] there were many refinements over the following centuries. The reasons for the choices made seem to be tied to the gradual predominance of juridical thinking over theological or philosophical approaches.[27]

This led to a reliance on casuistic reasoning: economic argumentation from cases that fit well with Hadith[28] based religious forms of argumentation. Early theological disputes in the Islamic world concerned, most prominently, the anthropomorphism of God, and arguments for atomism versus dualism. The former was eventually evaluated as a threat to the inscrutability of God; and the latter, in some formulations, as a threat to free will. Theological arguments led to a number of major quarrels involving the anathematization (تكفير) by one party of the other, some of which involved serious persecution, and even killing of opponents. In the reasoning of these centuries, a divergence of theological opinion was easily assimilated with the idea of heresy (ارتداد from ردة or rebellion) which became inextricably linked to apostasy (كفر), which was normally punishable by death.[29]

One theologian, muhammad b. sa'īd al-urdunnī, was executed for adding the phrase "God willing" (ان شاء الل) to the statement "there is no prophet after him" (لا نبية بعده) , that is, after Muhammad.[30] More relevant to the general opinion were the religious persecutions under the Abbasid caliph Ma'mūn (1229–1232), referred to later as the "*mihna*" (tribulation), and the fondness of early kharijites (in the eighth century) for anathematizing their religious opponents (تكفير—declaring them apostates). Not everyone was cowed by dogmatism. One of the most intriguing reactions to such narrowness was the Kufan scholar Ubaydallāh b. al-Hasan al-'anbarī's statement that—every reasonable interpreter is correct (كل مجتحد مسي[31]). Less we imagine this is a precocious "postmodern" view we should remember that Herodotus similarly thought all "histories" needed to be accepted as significant viewpoints.

With the tragic death (661) of Muhammad's son-in-law 'alī b. abī tālib, a schism between the followers of 'alī (who went on to develop the various shi'a traditions) and the sunni world occurred well before the full differentiation of the orthodox sunni schools. Extremist practices left such a general distaste for theological argument (علم الكلام) among the sunni that a limited diversity of opinion, in the form of various schools (مذاهب) of legal thought, (فقه) came to take precedence over theological argument or philosophy (فلسفة). Four principle sunni schools (relying heavily on the sunna or tradition about Muhammad) were founded by Abu Hanifa al-Nu'man (699–767), Malik b. Anās (710–796), Abu 'abd Allah Muhammad al-Shafī'ī (767–820), and Ahmad b. Hanbal (780–855).

In time, the sunni Islamic world, on which we focus, moved toward a greater emphasis on practice than on belief, which within the constraint of subscribing to a small set of fundamental beliefs and practices allowed for diversity of belief and practice in less fundamental areas. The *shahada* (شهادة) which took its first half from Sura 37:35 (there is no God but Allah), and its second half from Sura 48:29 (and Muhammad is his prophet) formed the core undeniable belief (to which were usually added belief in the final judgement). The core practices, referred to as the pillars of Islam were derived from a tradition of the Prophet Muhammad formulated in a Hadith (حديث) which reported that Muhammad, the messenger of God had said that Islam is built on five things: namely the *shahada* (1. a belief in God and his prophet and 2. denial of any other god, 3. praying five times a day, 4. giving mandatory alms (زكات), and 5. fasting during Ramada)n.[32] Making the Hajj, if possible, and providing other charity (صداق) were also important. From this perspective, anathematizing other Muslims for differences of opinion that did not differ on these basics came to be viewed as unacceptable extremism.

The Qur'an provided ample support for an even less rigid approach including Sura 2:256 "there is no compulsion in religion" (لا إكراه في الدين) and what has been called the *Ayat al-bīrr* (Sura 2:177) which clearly admonishes the believer that mere practice of the pillars is not itself good (البرر), and that this requires generosity not just to those close to us but also to orphans, the poor, travelers and beggars as well as efforts to free slaves—all in addition to giving charity, saying prayers and believing in the last judgment.[33]

In the course of time, the founders of the four major sunni schools provided compendia of interpretations of real or imagined situations that soon developed into a tradition of casuistic economic reasoning that paralleled and almost indistinguishably blended in with similar thinking on strictly religious matters. Many of the examples in this chapter come from these and later compendia. The Islamic world consolidated in subsequent centuries into areas that had significant legal consensus regionally, but equally significant legal diversity between regions. At the risk of being overly superficial, we can say that the four sunni schools might be ranged from conservative to liberal in terms of legal interpretation as follows: Hanbali, Maliki, Shafi'i, and Hanafi. In populous places, such as Cairo, several schools coexisted and Muslims could pick and choose between them to some degree.

Casuistic economic argumentation from known cases involved an explicit attempt to evaluate each new case by extending ethical concepts present in earlier cases through the use of analogous reasoning (*qiyās*). This involved both analysis of the elements in earlier cases, and the development of synthetic concepts to focus attention on what was important in them; and, in consequence, to exclude extraneous detail.

The Islamic world inherited many ideas from the classical world but three of the most relevant to understanding financial practice were the notions that money did not itself generate wealth (a belief accepted in the form Aristotle presented it); that returns should be in proportion to investment (of time or money borrowing from Plato's critique); and, that risk and liability should be shared.

This last inheritance really was the part the model from the Piraeus in which investors spread their risks between various ships and shared in profits and risks according to their participation levels (necessitating the evaluation of the relative value of labor and material goods). Both Plato and Aristotle, though for different reasons, dislike money being lent at interest. Yet, the the full practices of the Agora, which were often financed by bank loans at fixed interest rates, and hid all such transactions from public scrutiny, clearly were incompatible with principles of fairly sharing risk and profit. When expectations for loss or profit are highly unpredictable, as in the medieval period, fixed rates may seem particularly arbitrary; and, the greater unpredictability related to long distance trade would have amplified the apparent unfairness of fixed rates of interest, especially when combined with the lack of any liability on the part of a lender as was the case in early contracts in Mesopotamia.

CREDIT, PROFIT, AND REPUTATION: THE LINKAGE BETWEEN HONOR AND PROFIT

Credit in one form or another was fundamental to commerce in the Islamic world and it took many forms including both explicit partnerships and informal obligations. The Geniza records suggest that medieval merchants in the Islamic world took on an extended number of mutual obligations involving no formal contractual specifications; and, indeed, spent much of their time engaging in trade for distant colleagues simply on the basis of mutual trust and the exchange of letters or funds.[34] Time spent doing a colleague's business was reciprocal and repaid by that colleague doing one's own business in another market. Rather than viewing such favors as an intolerable burden, merchants seem to have viewed them as part and parcel of the successful construction of commercial networks. Common terms for this relationship included *suhba* (companions) and *saddaqa* (friends) while the explicit term for cooperation, *mu'amala* (having dealings), was most frequently used.[35]

Such requests could be specific as to commodity and the acceptable price to be paid or they could provide complete leeway using the phrase "with guidance and blessing (بقسم ولرزق) which was short for "with the guidance of God and his blessing" (بقسم الله ولرزقه*),* that is, let God guide you how to invest the money and how to make a profit. An example from March 5, 1026 written in Arabic, with some Hebrew, by a Persian in southern Iran to a merchant in Fustat reads in part:

> My impositions on you are manifold, but I am no stranger to you. I have sent . . . robes . . . mantles . . . silk . . . I hope that, with God's support and gracious help, everything will reach you in good condition and that after arrival you will handle its sale at your discretion and then purchase with its proceeds whatever you deem fit...Please handle this matter as you deem fit, for your money and mine are one and all profit I make comes from your pocket.[36]

The two merchants were not partners in any formal sense and the letter specifies no division of the profits rather it assumes that, as a reputable merchant, the recipient will keep exact accounts of the revenues earned, and retain nothing for himself. Presumably, there was a *quid quo pro* but not in the sense of a subsequent opportunity for profits from goods purchased with the Fustat sales sent in return to Iran later accruing to the Fustat merchant, all such specific profits accrued to the Persian merchan. Rather, if the Fustat recipient expended his own funds to purchase goods in Fustat and shipped them to Iran, the Persian merchant would sell those goods in southern Iran on a similar no profit to himself arrangement. Even partners, between whom accounts to the penny were standard, could provide free benefits to each other. Thus a merchant in Alexandria writes (ca. 1060 AD) to his brother, who is his partner in the Maghrib, with whom after making a tidy profit on pepper, he has had many issues:

> "But, brother, I would not like to take the profit for myself. Therefore I transferred the entire sale to our partnership. May God reward me for what I do for other people. I do not expect gratitude from men."[37]

Udovitch[38] notes that such transactions were referred to in Arabic as *ibdā'a* (إبضاعة); he resorts to calling them quasi-agencies for lack of a better English term, (citing Bergsträsser's lugubrious Geschäftsführungsauftrag—approximately: business-direction-assignment as more accurate). Udovich defines *ibdā'a* as tasks done for others without any commission, compensation, or profit. There are two parties in an *ibdā'a*: the first provides resources to the second who provides the service (buying, selling) free of charge, and returns principle and profit to the first party. Since there is no partnership all normal commercial risk falls on the first party, unless the second party engages in illegal behavior, in which case recourse to the law is possible. The second party does risk harm to his social capital, but has no financial liability. It is quite clear that this is closer to the Roman *mandatum* than the *negotiorum gestio* that we have met earlier; and so *ibdā'a* might be better referred to as mandates than quasi-agencies. If indeed it was the norm for much of commercial activity in the Islamic medieval period to be done in the form of mutual *ibdā'a*, we should not be surprised to find other correspondences with Roman commercial practices and customs as well.

Most discussions of medieval Islamic commerce, following indigenous scholars' perspectives, are centered on the juridical components of commercial law, with its focus on profit, along with some emphasis on the adaptation of that law to the realities of trade in different times and places. While early scholars, such as Schacht, argue that the role of custom and the adaptation of contract law to custom was significant,[39] Udovitch goes further to suggest that custom had a major influence on the differential implementation of commercial law; and, that this was explicitly acknowledged by Muslim jurists.[40]

Judicial extrapolation from analogy has significant difficulty dealing with differences in custom or situation, consequently Muslim jurists regularly allowed, in the formulation of contracts, for expertise, reputation, and local practice or custom so long as, given these considerations, basic principles were respected. The general idea of supplementing strict analogy with other juristic considerations was referred to as *istihsān* (إستحسان), and seems to have been begun by Abu Hanifa (d. 767 AD). Concern for the public good (إستصلاح) was also explicitly addressed. Nevertheless, this approach can hardly be said to be sociologically aware: it still does not explicitly recognize the response of commercial law to societal configuration. It provides no obvious answer to any sociological questions about why society is the way it is or even, for example, a persuasive explanation for the proliferation of *ibdā'a* relationships. This is not to say Islamic commercial law failed to change with the times. On the contrary, Islamic jurists and legal scholars devoted enormous effort to reconciling the law with the current needs of commerce.

An anthropological explanation, focusing on the establishment of honor and reputation in society (e.g., the Roman example) via intensive networking, may make sense of *ibdā'a,* even if, on average, monetary and labor benefits or costs to individuals balanced out, so that there were no net profits. It is also not impossible that most *ibdā'a* might, when reciprocated, provide a small net profit due to increasing each merchant's opportunities for trade. If a significant proportion of a merchant's time was devoted to *ibdā'a*, however, the difficulty in evaluating them from a utilitarian perspective lies elsewhere.

To explain *ibdā'a* as implicit profit making arrangements, we need to compare those arrangements with the alternative uses of funds; and, it staggers belief that all the special measures taken in more formal contracts add neither a significant measure of security nor of profit. If we take social networking and social capital into consideration, the participation in *ibdā'a* may have facilitated commercial and social efforts in a world where mutual trust and social honor were extremely important. The free services established reputation and honor in ways paid services could not. We, therefore, should probably view *ibdā'a* as not driven by near term profit and, unless we subscribe to anachronistic notions of man the maximizer in its narrowest sense, we should rather view *ibdā'a* as a window into social networking in a society where honor and reputation were as desirable as wealth, even if neither was entirely disconnected from the world of contracts.

An instructive example, having nothing to do with *ibdā'a,* that sheds some light on the inadequacy of an anachronistic narrow focus on profit, is the distinction between loans for use, the *'ariyya* (عرية) that are quite similar to the Roman *commodatum* and loans for consumption the *qard* (قرض) that are similar to the Roman *mutuum*. Shaybāni gives an example: Two men are partners in a *mufāwada* (مفاوضة) or unlimited partnership (discussed later in this chapter). One of them loans out a donkey belonging to the partnership free of charge (a loan for use), and the donkey dies from overloading (an early free rider problem). According to the rules of partnership, one could conclude that the lender of the donkey owed his partner half the value of the donkey. Yet,

Shaybani concludes that the lender owes nothing, because custom requires people to make loans for use all the time, of little things and big things, and if someone did not do so no one would loan things to them.[41]

We should note that it is not just custom *per se*, but honor and reputation that is at once involved. Here, the case is phrased in terms of utility,[42] because Muslim jurists focused on profit and utility not on societal organization, but the argument from utility is not convincing. People would be unlikely to behave in dishonorable ways toward a specific individual who was stingy about making loans for use to them since their own reputation depends on consistent normative behavior. The real reason, we would suggest, is that there was a normative expectation for people to behave honorably. Medieval Muslim jurists were as biased toward finding a profit motive to justify behavior as early-twentieth-century neoclassical economists, with similar drawbacks to the understanding of human nature or the organization of society.

Explicit partnerships, with the exception of family partnerships, were normally established for specific purposes and were usually of quite finite duration (a few months to several years), after which accounts were to be settled in front of witnesses and then could be renewed or not.[43] Most partnership accounts were evaluated annually by the partners. The Geniza documents suggest that disputes were common; and sometimes not easily resolved because busy merchants might forget the particulars of an arrangement, even including whether the trade had been on the basis of a true partnership or a less formal arrangement.

In one case, a merchant (‘ulla) in Cairo gave another merchant (Yahyā) funds to trade in the Maghrib (the west). At the time the account was to be settled (mid-eleventh century), ‘ulla claimed the funds were a *commenda* in which the agent (Yahyā) was to receive one third of the profits. The latter merchant (Yahyā) claimed it was a partnership to which he had contributed 50 dinars plus his labor, and he was due 50 percent of the profits. He supported this position by arguing that the other arrangement had indeed been agreed to but only for trade in nearby Damietta.[44] This disagreement relied on the more flexible norms for a *commenda,* that both parties do not share equally in liability and divide the profits as agreed (with much leeway in how they decide to do this). While in a standard partnership (see "limited partnership, *'inān,* and unlimited partnership, *mufāwada*, below) the norm was to share both liability and profit equally.

In the Islamic world, as in ancient Rome, it would be hard to exaggerate the importance of reputation. The *iqrār* (إقرار literally a settlement) was a document which both acknowledged debt and promised a mode and period for its repayment.[45] Notably, it did not specify terms of interest, but it often specified the installment amount and frequency of each installment. It also acknowledged both the debtor's debt to the creditor, and pledged the full assets of the debtor as security (including the shirt on his back) as well as the assets (and shirts) of his heirs. Logically, this is a bit problematic because in the normal case, by the time people became heirs, they might well have creditors and debtors of their own, so the pledge is, formally, somewhat stronger than the reality could be. In so far as the heirs are concerned, the creditor would stand in line with other creditors; and, as is the case these days, would be paid on the debt only what a judge deemed was appropriate. The existence of the *iqrār* suggests that in a world based on trust and credit, it was useful to have a way for individuals to enhance their honor and shore up their credit worthiness by pledging as surety their net worth and that of their heirs.

Paper

There is reason to believe that even by the tenth century, the Islamic medieval world had a largely paper economy.[46] While gold and silver coins often served as currency, because their heterogeneity varied widely across the wide Islamic world, they were usually valued by weight and purity, as in the ancient world, and were often treated as commodities in their own right. Various forms of paper instruments also served as money; and several of these had distinct advantages over coin, which was far more hazardous to transport, and required that stocks of other commodities be immediately liquidated. The simplest procedure was to write up a document transferring credit or assigning debt (*hawāla*). This term means to change or transform, and the French word "*aval*" for endorsement of a bill of exchange derives from it.

An example found in the Geniza documents involved a Maghribi merchant who sold flax in several places and had to pay the merchant whose flax he had sold. He effected payment through a major trading house (Nahray b. Nissīm) in Fustat by means of a *hawāla*.[47] This would have involved the trading house having a branch near the flax merchant's area of activity that facilitated their payment to the flax owner of what the Maghribi merchant owed. The Maghribi trader, would initiate this transaction, through the more convenient branch near him (presumably where he regularly did business) by paying in the amount owed.

Within a city like Fustat, simple checks were much in use; and, involved the writer asking a banking firm that held some of his funds to pay the bearer a given sum in a particular currency. Larger businesses kept a reasonable amount of funds with reputable bankers for just this purpose. There is no indication that bankers were paid to keep the funds nor that they charged for the service.[48] It would seem that the primary benefit for providing this service was that it enhanced their reputation, and having such deposits meant they had cash on hand for their own (profitable) local commerce.

A more complicated arrangement for paper payment was the "note" (رقع). The note basically was an order for payment, and was often treated as cash if it were issued by a reputable banker or businessman. Heirs often found several such notes among the things that they had inherited. Such notes could also be sent as payment out of town, and were even negotiable (could be sold). Negotiability of notes probably implied one of the following: that there was a range of reliability among the notes; that there were potential delays in obtaining the conversion of notes to cash; or that some people were in a better position to get them paid up with alacrity. Each of these situations would provide a basis for buying / selling notes at a discount.

A Persian term, *suftaja*, was used in much of the Middle East during the medieval period to represent a more specific and regulated paper transfer of funds. In this case, a merchant would pay a sum plus a premium to a local branch of a banking firm that had a branch or affiliate in some other town. In return, the merchant would receive a *suftaja* for the sum in question on the other branch or affiliate. The latter would then have to pay the *suftaja* immediately on its presentation or be assessed a daily fine for any delay. Obviously, this required the presence of liquidity or easy conversion to liquidity. Given such requirements, even banking firms might decline to write a *suftaja*, despite the premium, because they were not sure their affiliate could produce the sum in question without delay.

The Geniza documents suggest that a typical fine would be 1 dirham per 20 dinars—approximately three eighths of 1 percent per day.[49] While it is unclear what premium a firm might have been able to obtain, it stands to reason that it would be constrained by any merchant's alternative: the transport costs of goods of comparable value which was usually less than 4 percent in transport and another 4 percent in fees.[50] Although the implication requires a little arithmetic, these figures might justify the bankers' agreement to pay out from another branch via *suftaja*, assuming as a maximum an 8 percent premium paid to them, as long as their branch office could pay out the sum in significantly less than twenty-one days from the date on which the suftaja was likely to be presented for payment.[51]

Government offices also used paper to transact their business as much as possible. Thus, to buy flax from a government estate in Egypt, the normal procedure was to pay cash to an accountant who would then issue government chits for the amount paid in; and, subsequently, these chits would be taken to the estate and used to pay for the flax there.[52] The chits could then be entered into the accounts of the estate, but the estate managers would not themselves have to handle cash.

Credit

From the eleventh century on, aside from commercial loans, credit was often provided for consumption to Jews in need or to passing Christian pilgrims. In such cases, Muslim money lenders regularly loaned sums at interest (*riba*), which, because the recipient was not a Muslim, was considered legal. One such loan in 1239 AD in the Geniza collection was at an annual rate of 16 2/3 percent (a sixth).[53] Recourse to loans at explicit interest for commerce or between Muslims seems always to have been considered illegal.

Strictures against usury, such as those noted earlier in this chapter, were often based on worries about unlike exchanges. Thus Ibn Malik, for example forbade selling silver in return for a later amount of gold because the exchange was likely to conceal an increase (*ar-ramā'*), which was the same as usury (*ar-rabā'*).[54] All authorities said silver had to be sold for silver, gold for gold, and each had to be equivalent. That this admonishment against currency speculation was so common, may imply that it was a common practice. Nevertheless, sales on credit were normal, and loans were often viewed as being comparable to deferred payments. Abu Hanifa and Ibn al-Malik made an exception for the selling of debts themselves:[55]

> A man ought not to sell a debt he is owed by a person unless it is to that [same] person, because sale of a debt is an uncertain transaction about which it is not sure whether it will be paid or not.

Clearly, the outcome of many loans was uncertain, so it is likely the concern over selling debt had more to do with the third-hand nature of the transaction. The problem was that without a face to face relationship, trust was difficult to establish, and so seriously amplified uncertainty. These worries also underline how critical honor and trust were to Islamic commerce even in the earliest period. Granting substantial loans to young untested individuals to finance a small business (earning the lender a share of profits) was routine, and was viewed as meritorious and a form of charity. The issue of deferred payments for sales, that is buying on credit (see discussion of '*īna*), was problematic for many reasons; and often had to be shored up with ancillary conditions. When a request to alter a deferred payment agreement was brought before Ibn Malik, the judge refused to approve the early payment of the loan, in return for lowering the total owed, on the grounds that to do so would put the clear specifications of the original sale (on credit) in jeopardy.[56]

The common practice of depositing funds or commodities with bankers also raised judicial concerns.[57] Although such deposits specified no earnings for the bankers, in return for a mere written guarantee to a depositor of timely access to the funds or commodities, having the funds enabled bankers to lend money out and make profits. Although such deposits remained common, for strict interpreters of the law they were a cause of concern precisely because the banker's benefits were not specified in the deposit contract and their use and benefits were deliberately concealed by omission.

For depositors such agreements offered security. Because the banker had ample funds, the depositor's future access to his capital would be more or less immediate. The alternative of depositing money or goods in the hands of a smaller merchant, brought a higher risk that his capital might be lent out and the funds tied up in a loan that could not be readily called in. Islamic law developed no way to clearly put a value on security, perhaps because it could not think in statistical terms about returns on investment, and insisted instead on an individualistic perspective. Insurance involves spreading risk and averaging costs, an insight Islamic banking today is still reluctant to acknowledge.

JUSTICE AND CLASS BIAS

Commercial law in the Islamic world differed somewhat from region to region, but there were considerable similarities as well. We will begin by noting some of the key features of the law in its *maliki* version as they pertain to commercial activity. Goitein notes that for the most part, even in the Middle Ages, Jewish traders used Islamic-like partnerships as well as the Islamic *commenda* because traditional Jewish versions of these were less flexible. It is important to note that employment was generally considered less honorable than being in business for oneself; so the vast majority of commerce in the Islamic world was carried out by people with partnership-like contractual relationships rather than employer-employee relationships. Even today, those employed, by the government, would rarely view simultaneous engagement in trade as ethically dubious, it is clear that in earlier periods this was absolutely the norm in the Islamic world.

In the past, just as today, there were those who pretended that legal contracts were fair, since each party could choose to enter into them or not, and presumably would not do so if they believed they were unfair. This naive position is really little more than a hidden bias for the social status quo. Many agreements are severely constrained both by law and social position. Even medieval Islamic judges differed on what was thought to be fair.

An example from 11th century Valencia (in Islamic Spain) provided by al-Wanšarīsī illustrates the case of two judges differing on what class of society to support, with each supporting their position on the base of legal principles.[58] This case involved a renter who contracted to pay a specified rent in dirhams (*darāhim al-sikka* struck by *al-qaysī*) each of which at that time was equivalent to one sixth of an ounce of gold. Before the rent was paid, the Sultan declared the former currency invalid and issued another dirham, each dirham worth one third of an ounce. The owner of the property promptly asked to be paid the agreed number of dirham but in the new double weight currency. A first judge ruled that this was correct because the Sultan had ruled use of the former dirham invalid. A second judge ruled in favor of the renter saying that the contract's dirham had to be viewed as those specified and current at the time the contract was issued, and this determined the gold value owed as rent. The class bias of the first judge is patent as is the greater justice of the second.

Another case discussed by al-Wanšarīsī from ninth-century Cordova dealt with sharecropping (مناصفة), and similarly shows blatant class bias.[59] The case concerned a dispute between a sharecropper and the owner of the property; the former was to provide half the seed plus the labor. The latter insisted that the "labor" included planting, weeding, harvesting and all the processing including threshing, winnowing, and transporting to the owner. A first judge sided entirely with the owner, while a second judge sided entirely with the sharecropper who claimed his obligation stopped with harvesting because additional obligations were not explicitly specified. Thus, the second judge opposed a broader than customary interpretation of "labor," and required further specification if a non-customary interpretation were to be allowed.

This explicit and populist reliance on custom for legal interpretation of specific clauses has been the norm rather than the exception throughout the Islamic world. Yet, another judgment that al-Wanšarīsī cites, also from nineth century Cordova,[60] indicates that clarity of specification is really the key. When asked whether it was licit to hire a worker to cultivate a garden in return for half, a third, or some other portion of the harvest, the ruling was that all of the above are legal. This suggests that custom was relied on not *per se* but because, in default of other specification, the customary interpretation had to be assumed to be that implied in a contract.

All societies implement law based on interpretation. Because such interpretations cannot be expected to exclude all forms of social bias, the hidden interests of social classes regularly shape the implementation of commercial law. A rather unusual case which explicitly tries to eliminate bias due to male chauvinism has also survived from eleventh to twelfth-century Cordova.[61] A woman made a gift (وهبة) of half her dowry (صداق) to her husband, and the husband accepted the gift in front of witnesses. The judge is asked if such a gift is legal. We should note that such a gift was highly unusual, given that if a woman was divorced her dowry normally had to be returned and it often constituted the greater part of the woman's assets. The judge ruled that the gift was legal if it was witnessed by a man and at least two women; in doing so the judge precluded the normal option of simply having two male witnesses.[62]

Occasionally, an Islamic judge's decision makes the significance of social class explicit, but more often this can be read between the lines. An example from fifteenth century Granada that makes explicit reference to class involves a female slave whose master went off on a trip to Tunis without providing for her welfare.[63] A notable of the court who discovered that she had been left without any support took it upon himself to provide for her; and, when his total expenses reached the normal price for a female slave, he persuaded the qadi to transfer the slave to him. When this had been done, he freed her, and then married her. When the former owner returned, he argued before the qadi that he had left some provisions for her; and, as she was able bodied, she had the means to obtain further support for herself. In his decision, the judge explicitly acknowledged that both parties held equally high status at court, but refused to alter his judgement, and allowed the marriage to stand.

The explicit specification of the relative status of the parties reflects the importance of reputation in the evaluation of oral testimony. Presumably, the judgment included their respective status in order to define the case as a precedent that could be referenced in cases primarily where both oral arguments have the same putative value. Islamic law thus allowed, via reputation, an entrée for differential treatment under the law.

The basic principle that terms of a contract need to be clear can be illustrated with an example from fourteenth century Bougie (Algeria) also included in al-Wanšarīsī's compendium.[64] The question raised is whether it is legitimate for someone buying a measure of grain to shake and stir it to settle the grain. It is also implied that the buyer wants the measure to be topped off after such treatment. The response noted that this was completely forbidden; and, that the correct procedure was simply to take the measure as presented (presumably grain has simply been poured into the measure), and with the hand strike off any amount above the rim. Thus, the legitimate measure is one that has been stricken and not settled or compacted. It is interesting that, even in such a simple case, it was understood that the meaning of a measure could be used to promote the interest of one party over the other, and that the remedy was to have an unambiguous definition that precludes such hidden interest.

A second example illustrates the problem of what might be called mixed or confused relationships. This example from tenth-century Cordova,[65] involves an investor who wishes both to sell merchandise to someone for six dinars; and, also to have an agreement that if the merchandize is resold for more he will share in the profit.

The problem this poses is that one party, the originator, has a guaranteed return of six dinars, while the other's revenue from the merchandize is entirely at risk. The jurist finds this unacceptable and insists that the proper arrangement is for the originator to receive his base price up front, and to put the second party on salary for the sale, and, further, to specify that anything above six dinars is shared, and anything less than six dirhams would be a loss to the employee. In effect, the correct arrangement envisages a guaranteed salary earned to recover the six dirhams paid out to initialize the transaction, and a potential shared benefit from selling the goods for more than six dinars. The employee has a potential benefit from more such opportunities if he does well, that is, finds a good price, and little opportunity for collusion against the originator given the nature of the market where such behavior would soon be discovered.

The original, unacceptable, design involved a single transaction with an unbalanced mixture of a secure investment for one party, and unequally shared risk for both parties which was deemed illegitimate. In the approved practice there are two separate transactions. The first is a contribution of capital and a salary. The second is a partnership involving a share (as partner) in profits from any sale above the minimum valuation of six dinars.

More generally, it is fair to say that Islamic commercial law recognized that hidden interests may often be concealed within commercial contracts, and tried hard to eliminate such potential biases by making all clauses as explicit and clear as possible; as well as by making an effort to declare ambiguities in expressions to be illegal. The contract from Valencia that we previously examined involving obvious class bias clearly stated the type of dirham to be paid, yet this specification was ignored by the first judge who approved a doubling in rent, valued in gold. That example, thus, illustrates both the effort to be explicit and the reality that sometimes the interests of the powerful may still prevail, even though in this case a more honest judge happened to overrule the earlier injustice.

Despite its imperfections, a core agenda of Islamic commercial law was to expose potential interests that might lay hidden, and to ensure that contracting parties not only knew what they were contracting, but had made agreements that were fair at least in the sense of clearly linking the amount of returns and risks to the amount of investment (material or human). These preoccupations obviously benefited commerce, and thereby economic growth. They illustrate that concerns with justice and honor, as well as profit or utility, were regularly at play.

FORMAL COMMERCIAL RELATIONSHIPS: THE PARTNERSHIP

The explicit declaration of contracts had a long history in Mesopotamia that set the stage for Islamic contractual law. Though a partnership might endure in the sense of being renewed for a long time, formal partnerships were usually defined for specific periods of time, at which point a full accounting would be made, and the partnership could be closed out or renewed. Early on the subtlety of Islamic commercial law shows in its fine distinction between such contractual partnerships and other ethically binding partnerships, that came to be known as proprietary partnerships (*sharikat al-milk*), involving no explicit contract.

A case[66] discussed by the Hanafi jurist Shaybani in his *kitāb al-amālī*, centuries before this distinction was fully developed, is illustrative. A man "buys" twenty dirhams for one dinar from a seller. Subsequently, he finds that a few of the dirhams are underweight, and so returns those to the "seller." Shaybani argues that this gives him a partnership, *sharika*, in the seller's dinar proportional to the number of returned dirhams, for example, if he returned five, he would have a 25 percent interest in the dinar, or in benefits accrued to its expenditure.

Such non-explicitly contracted partnerships came to be formulated, by the tenth and eleventh century AD, as a particular category distinct from those in which responsibility, profit, liability, and risk are explicitly detailed. It would appear that one of the most common examples of such partnerships involved domestic slaves who were often shared in this way, and came to the attention of the law when one "owner" tried to unilaterally manumit them, something that brought religious merit to the owner. Ibn Malik allowed only one form of "credit" partnership: when two or more people jointly bought a slave on credit, they became partners in the slave.[67]

Another common use of the proprietary partnership was for housing. The majority of houses mentioned in the Geniza documents, whether owned by Muslims or Jews, were described as being held in joint undivided ownership, and had multiple families in residence.[68] These implicit partnerships were of minor significance to commerce in Hanafi or Maliki law, perhaps because turnover for housing or slaves was slow in comparison to the dynamism of regular commerce.

The legal concerns of Shafi'i about contractual partnership are quite different: for him the basic prerequisite for any such partnership is the intermingling (*ikhtilāt* اختلاط) of assets. Shafi'i taught that any other form of partnership was tantamount to gambling, and was null and void.[69] His reasoning seems to have been that labor, risk, and profit could not be separately reckoned, so although partners could have unequal shares, those shares applied to everything if it was to be deemed a partnership. The key to this advocation of intermingling was that it should be impossible for one partner to argue that a particular transaction was done either with their own or the other partner's funds, labor or commodities. To further ensure the intermingling of assets,

Shafi'i insisted that entry into a partnership had to be on the basis of currency, and that this had to be currency of the same denomination to eliminate hidden advantages. Although, this would have been impractical for partners living in widely separate places, Shafi'i did allow the *commenda*, as a contractual arrangement not to be viewed as a partnership *per se*.

The Roman *societas* was a partnership from the inside. Partners could have claims on each other and agree to share resources or labor for a common purpose. Outsiders, however, could only have claims against the partner with whom they had dealt, and their claims could not spill over to other partners.[70]

In Islamic law, unlike Jewish law, partnership liability (*maḍmūnan* مضمون) was always unlimited,[71] but this should not be misunderstood. Clearly, a merchant might have a single partner, or multiple and distinct partnerships with multiple people, and it would be unethical to claim that a debt incurred by one partnership could propagate to another; and, in the usual case, harm a merchant who had nothing to do with that debt. At its most basic, the liability incurred by a partner *qua* partner only implicated the funds of the partnership in question, and usually in proportion to each partner's share in the partnership. There were additional refinements.

In the Maliki case, this meant that a partner engaging in legitimate transactions with partnership funds was first himself fully liable (pursuable for the full debt), to the extent of his net positive investment. At the end of the day, losses from legitimate trade would be deducted from overall gross and the remainder divided as agreed upon in setting up the partnership. In Hanafi law, liability in a *mufāwada* partnership approached the modern concept of corporate unlimited liability in that it implicated all partners to the full extent of the debt. In modern terms, it was several and joint: funds to cover a debt could in the interim be lost, and the debt still remain pursuable against the partnership funds of all members of the partnership.[72]

Generally, liability was not problematized in Islamic law because all types of partnerships had well understood liability. A *commenda* placed the risk on the investor, and losses that incurred in the legitimate practice of business were not owed by the partner providing the labor, they were owed solely by the partner providing the capital.

In the Maghrib, commercial law was shaped by *mālikī* versions of *shari'a* law, and it is on these variants that we will focus for the moment. There were three types of partnership under *mālikī* law. The first was the limited partnership or *'inān* (عنان) which placed severe limitations on partners' independence with regard to their use of joint capital.[73] Partners were obliged to have their co-partners' explicit approval for any use of the joint capital, except in situations of real emergency when consulting would jeopardize the capital.[74] Further, only the individual partner who interacted with particular third parties was held responsible for obligations or rights, for example, to return goods, resulting from that interaction.[75] Of course, in all partnerships, if the partner in question committed illegal acts the other partner(s) could not be held responsible.

In its mature development, the *'inān* partnership allowed partners to engage in a fairly wide range of activities with the concurrence of their partner. They could:[76]

a. use funds to buy or sell goods
b. sell goods for cash or credit
c. hire people to assist in transactions
d. appoint an agent
e. give goods as *ibdā'a*
f. travel with goods or funds
g. reinvest funds in other commodities

After the expiration of the partnership, each partner was to withdraw their initial investment, and split the profit or loss in the agreed upon shares.

In the second type of partnership, the *mufāwada* (مفاوضة) or unlimited partnership, the partnership was defined as involving only those assets and affairs specified as part of the pact, and so did not include extraneous matters or commitments. Thus, one partner could engage in commerce outside of the partnership without there being any implications for his partner(s); likewise, one partner could inherit money or find treasure, without his partner(s) having any claim on the money. Further, there was no requirement imposed for equality of investment or labor on the part of each partner. In fact, all that was required in this regard was a clear specification of the proportions of time and money each partner participating was investing; and, a clear specification of the proportions in which they were to share in any profits and risks (losses). An ideal partnership, however, should in addition have a one-to-one ratio of capital and labor, such that a partner investing 40 percent of the capital will be expected also to invest 40 percent of the labor, giving him an obvious moral right to share in 40 percent of the profit.

In Hanafi law, the main differences as far as these two types of partnership are concerned were that it strongly encouraged written contracts, encouraged unlimited partnerships specifically to use the term *mufāwada*, and emphasized that all partnerships should specify explicitly:[77]

a. the subject of the partnership
b. the names of the partners and their share of participation
c. the distribution of liability, profit and and labor

d. who had the right to deal in credit or conduct business and
e. the date / period of validity for the partnership.

Both the limited and unlimited partnership, had disadvantages for long distance trade in that they constrained to a significant degree the flexibility of a partner who might not be able to communicate quickly enough to avoid missing an opportunity. Also since a *mufāwada* was set up for a particular purpose, it inhibited ventures in new areas, however promising they might be.

The Commenda: *mudāraba / qirād*

A third type of partnership, the *commenda*[78] (the Italian term for the French *commandite* or the church Latin *accomendatio*, the German *Kommanditgesellschaft*, and the English silent partnership) had several major advantages over the *'inān* and the *mufāwada*. The most important might have been that by not requiring the joint ownership required by the *mufāwada* and the *'inān*, it facilitated the use of ambitious men, willing to travel and eager to make their fortune, by wealthy established merchants who preferred to stay put yet had more funds than they could profitably employ locally.

This favored long distance financial instrument, (also called the مضاربة *mudāraba* or قراض *qirād*) split the labor and the capital such that one or more partners (the sleeping partner(s) or financier(s) / *rabb al-mâl*) provided the capital to a partner who acted as an agent-manager who was given full right to trade with the capital, and took in return an agreed upon proportion of the profits (generally 50 percent or less). While this was in effect a partnership of profits, the agent-manager did not incur liability for loss except for criminal behavior or obviously negligent behavior (in the sense of it being outside the norms for sensible commercial behavior). This precluded, for instance, any spending on luxury consumption, but did not preclude the payment of normal expenses.[79] Losses were directly imposed only on the investors though, obviously, an agent who performed poorly, could not expect to see continued investments coming his way.

Maimonides treatment of partnership most resembled that of Shafi'i. He was concerned that there be at least a symbolic mingling of assets (they put their funds in a single purse *kis wahid*) or true joint ownership.[80] Maimonides similarly opposed the idea of an artisanal partnership of complementary skills, since their product is not yet realized, and is subject to fate - Shafi'i viewed this as akin to gambling, while Maimonides was troubled by the inability to properly assess the values brought to such a partnership. This concern for blending of assets into joint ownership was not one of the Roman requirements for *societas*, and, for Romans, joint ownership did not itself constitute a partnership.[81]

The Islamic and Jewish construction and use of commercial law seem to have been overwhelmingly motivated by ethics—a field that might be said to be under emphasized in Roman times or perhaps artificially narrowed to concerns with honor and trust more than fairness, *per se*. Romans fully understood the world was not fair at all and took few pains to change this reality.The *commenda* contract seems to have spread from the Mesopotamian area[82] to the Islamic world, and during the Islamic period into the Mediterranean world, where it came to dominate long distance trade. Scholars have reconstructed a full account of typical *commenda* operations as used by Jewish and Muslim merchants. Each of the four *madhhab* treated the *commenda* somewhat differently, though the differences are not as great as those for the limited and unlimited partnerships.

It has been suggested that the prominence of the *commenda* in the Iran-Iraq area, by contrast to its infrequency in Arabia, was due to high levels of urbanization in the former areas, and consequent greater opportunities for travelers to make profits.[83] Yet, a more plausible explanation may simply be that this was due to its long history of development in the Mesopotamian area since the second millennium BC. The earliest European use, by contrast, may have been in Venice ca.1072 AD.[84] As has been noted, the much earlier Roman *societas* could take the form of a sleeping partnership, in which the sleeping partner provided funds to another partner who did all the work, so that, in essence, it could be seen as a sort of *commenda* in embryo.[85]

By engaging in such *commenda* relationships, merchants established wide ranging commercial linkages that could bring goods of high value within their gambit of operations. Like other partnerships, *commenda* from its earliest instantiations in Mesopotamia allowed multiple investors to be involved. However, given that one agent made all the substantive decisions, and was liable only for clear irregularities, the *commenda* required a higher degree of trust than typical partnerships. Not all *commenda* relations involved the simple flow of goods and money back and forth between investors and agents, for agents were also free to set up their own networks and trade in their own choice of goods. Their real obligation was to split all profits in the agreed upon proportions, to keep careful accounts, and to maintain the *commenda's* affairs in a profitable vein.

As fully developed, a typical agent in an unrestricted *commenda* in Hanifī law could:[86]

1. Buy and sell all types of merchandise as he saw fit.
2. Buy and sell for cash and credit.
3. Give *commenda* goods as *ibdāʿa,*[87] leave *commenda* goods as a deposit or pledge.
4. Hire helpers as needed.

5. Rent or buy animals and equipment.
6. Travel with the capital.
7. Mingle *commenda* capital with his own resources.
8. Give *commenda* capital as a *commenda* to a third party.
9. Invest the *commenda* capital in a partnership with a third party.[88]

Some *commenda* were more restrictive, and might typically eliminate numbers (8) and (9), or define the commodities on which trade should be focused, or even the region in which trade was to be confined. In Maliki or Shafi'i law some of these options were not acceptable including all components of (3). More generally, Shafi'i seems to have developed his ideas on this with regard to legal theory alone, regardless of economic impact.[89]

The Hanafi legal version, which dominated in the lands that had been part of the Mesopotamian commercial center, was that any restrictions were moot if they rendered the *commenda* less profitable than it might otherwise be. Thus, if an agent infringed on restrictions and made a profit, or even could have normally been expected to make a profit in the activity pursued, then the prohibition would be seen as invalid by virtue of the overweening importance of the *raison d'être* of the *commenda*: to make a profit—to do what any reasonable merchant would be expected to do could not be wrong.[90]

Jewish merchants portrayed in the Cairo Geniza records (tenth to thirteenth century) also made extensive use of *commenda* (*qirād al-goyîm*) as it provided more flexibility than classical Jewish partnerships (*qirād betôrat 'isqā*). The latter typically gave the sleeping partner 2/3 of profits, along with full liability for losses; so, perhaps understandably, such contracts, being less attractive to the agent, are rare in the Geniza collection.[91] *Commenda* partnerships in the Islamic world might include several people, and involve both Muslims and Jews in the same partnership. Goitein notes, that *commenda* were to consider explicitly, and make provision for, a considerable number of issues, including:[92]

1. the number and status of contractees
2. object and purpose of the contract
3. specifics of partner contributions and privileges
4. share in profits and losses
5. conditions on expenditures and expenses
6. constraints on conflicts of interest (engagements in other partnerships)
7. who was exempt, as already a trustworthy witness, from an oath of partnership
8. the duration of the partnership
9. when accounts were to be rendered
10. any other special conditions

Actual *commenda* occasionally inform us not only about such considerations, but also about the justification for the specifics discussed which might include the purported benefit the prestige of one partner brings to the partnership, or even issues of demography. In a *commenda* dating from the last third of the eleventh century, a father in effect set up a trust for his two daughters by making a *commenda* with a merchant involving 50 dinar for his oldest daughter, and 25 for the youngest; specifying that the daughters' funds cover 5/12 to the merchant's 7/12 of any losses, while the merchant, the active partner, split profits between the girls and himself 50/50; and, invested only five dinars of his own up front. The apparent assumption was that the older daughter would reach her majority earlier and receive her share of the *commenda* at that point, with the remaining sum still invested on behalf of the younger for a longer period, expected to even out the total benefits accruing to each daughter.[93]

In order to allocate profit as specified, it was widely recommended that the initiation of a *commenda* be in currency because monetary profit was calculated at the end so interim inflation in the value of some goods would redound unfairly if two agents had not both invested the same goods in the partnership.[94] Of course, *pari passu*, currency could inflate in value, but it was less volatile than commodity prices and in the recommended case would affect each equally.

A *commenda* from 1080 AD involved an employee of the caliphal House of Exchange who invested 500 dinars (89.6 percent), along with his junior partner's 58 dinars, in a banking business where they were to share in profit and loss at 17/24 (70.8 percent) vs. 7/24. The senior partner had full control in signing or granting loans and took no oath, so we must assume the junior partner did most of the grunt work in return for a higher incentive structure: higher rate of profit on investment as well as higher rate of loss if things went poorly.[95]

Partnerships might last as long as the partners were satisfied, much like leaving funds these days with a broker, but less than satisfactory results would precipitate both an end to a partnership, and wrangles over how the assets should be divided. Many partnerships of all kinds were between family members. Agents in a *commenda* would normally share in profits, and receive operating costs and/or a minuscule salary having no relation to the amount for which they traded. This was quite suitable for a young family member with no capital of his own. *Commenda* declared invalid were deemed a contract for hire (*ijāra*), and the profits accrued to the investor who also bore the losses, while the putative traveling partner received whatever the courts deemed an equitable wage.[96]

STRATAGEMS: ETHICS AND REALITY

The difference between theory and practice, and the variations from our base cases, can most efficiently be broached by examining the literature on the standardized tricks or *hila* (حيلة) used across the Islamic world to make the practice of commerce more flexible. These were developed from the earliest times,[97] and saw perhaps their greatest development in the Hanafi tradition, under the rubric of "exits" (المخارج : viewed as ways out of a legal predicament). In principle, such exits were supposed themselves to be legal; and to conform to the spirit of the law. These tricks were legal ways to do things that might be illegal if done differently. Of course, some tricks involved circumlocutions of dubious legality or clear illegality, depending only in part on who was evaluating them.

In the Maliki tradition,[98] a slightly different metaphor was used (سد الضراء) that refers to blocking the evil consequences of legal acts. One of the justifications of these stratagems was to provide a means to remove oppression (ظلم) by the strong of the weak, for example, by allowing ambiguous expressions (otherwise illegal) when the weak person is forced to take an oath against his own interest by the strong. The Kufan authority, Sha'bī, referred to stratagems as "means by which one can escape from the unlawful to the lawful," and rejected only those "by means of which one seeks to prejudice another's right."[99]

In the context of debt, the standard legal procedure often involved a guarantor who was to stand in for the debtor (pay the debt), if the debtor defaulted. A stratagem benefitting the guarantor, attributed to Nasir b. Yahy al-Balkhi (d. 881–882 AD), was to ask a qadi to appoint an agent to negotiate with the debtor on behalf of the creditor if the creditor has disappeared deliberately before the due date in order to force the guarantor to pay.[100] While such a procedure clearly prejudices the rights of the creditor, to have the guarantor step up, the actual behavior of the qadi involves nothing explicitly illegal. Still since the intent is at least nominally to prejudice the interests of the creditor, Sha'bī might have deemed it illegal though an informal arrangement on the side, that is, negotiating new terms, might well address the creditor's disadvantage, and influence a qadi to approve the stratagem. Corruption might do the same of course.

A stratagem that was intended to save the creditor is attributed to Abu Hanifa in a argument with Ibn Abi Layla (إختلاف أبي حنيفة وإبن أبي ليلة). In this case, it involves first noting that there is a difference of opinion among authorities as to whether the creditor can pursue both the debtor and the guarantor. Some argue that once a guarantor comes into the picture the debt is transferred to the guarantor; others argue that if the guarantor fails to pay up *then and only then* can the creditor purse the debtor; and, yet others hold that the creditor can pursue either person as desired. The basic goal was to secure the latter option, regardless of the juridical venue, by specifying in the contract that the debtor and the guarantor stand guarantee for each other.

An extension of this stratagem involved the case of three guarantors and the legal principle that where there were three guarantors of a debt, the creditor could only pursue each for one-third of the debt. A stratagem suggested by ibn Qāsim was to stipulate in the initial contractual arrangement that each guarantor stands surety for each of the others. In this case the creditor could pursue any of them for as much of the debt as he wishes—as long as the total added up to the full debt.[102]

A more complex case might meet with quite varied opinions. One such example was the case of a creditor who claimed, without witnesses, that a debtor owed him 1,000 dirhams and a debtor who had, in previous dealings with this creditor, been defrauded of 1,000 dirhams. The question was whether the debtor could swear an oath that he owed the creditor nothing. Some authorities felt this was, though true, an illegitimate procedure because the oath that was required, even in this situation, was that the creditor had not loaned him the 1,000 dirhams in question (something not true); and, the oath proposed was intended to conceal the existence of the loan. Other authorities felt this was a legitimate stratagem to address an injustice.[103]

This raises the issue of the nature of an oath, and the possible difference between a divine perspective and a legal one. If lying before God is eventually catastrophic; and, in the short term dishonorable in the extreme; and, the forms of the oath are fixed and traditional then the law cannot condone a lie. On the other hand, the law by this time had already recognized the need to be flexible if it were to promote justice. It could be argued that it was the very rigidity of the oath that stood in the way of justice; and, so the oath had to be interpreted in the light of what would promote justice.

Islamic law dealing with selling real property also had to take into consideration the hidden interests of neighbors, who might preempt a sale in order to prevent strangers from moving into a neighborhood, by themselves offering the agreed upon sale price to the seller and exercising their right of preemption. A stratagem to get around this problem was to have the ratification of the sale by the potential preemptor stipulated in the sale itself—thereby nullifying the preemptor's claim. Alternately, a trick involving an artificially high sale price could be arranged. The buyer would agree with the seller on a price of say 1,000 dinar for a house worth 100, but, subsequent to signing the agreement, the seller in secret would remit 900 of the 1,000 dinar price to the buyer. The sale document would inhibit the potential preemptor from exercising a right to buy the property, and encourage him even to waive that right.

An archetypal stratagem that addressed Islamic concerns about prohibiting unjustified profit (ربا الفاضل) typically involved the sale of one quantity of gold now for a larger quantity later: in effect, lending at interest. For instance, one party might sell another 100 ounces of gold now for 110 to be repaid in a year. Disguised as an exchange, it could be gold objects of different gold content or even gold coins of different issues differing in weight by ten percent, this might appear legitimate initially, but on closer scrutiny it might turn out to be a way to guarantee one "seller" a ten percent profit at no (legal) risk. A variant was for the "borrower" to sell the gold items for 100 dinar (receiving the cash he needed); and, then immediately buy the items back on a promise of paying 110 dinar in a year to the initial buyer. These types of transactions were called *'īna* (عينة transactions that disguise an interest bearing loan), and were thought to be wrong by most authorities.

Yet, if several steps were introduced and sales consummated in different cities, it might be impossible to demonstrate prearranged market inequalities in the sequence of sales. The original meaning of *'īna* seems to have been simply selling on credit[104] where the delayed payment allowed the possibility (and obvious motivation on the seller's part) for a future higher return than that prevailing in the market at the time of sale. As mentioned above, the suspect nature of such a transaction recognized the hidden interest of the seller to receive an extra payment for delayed gratification. The *'īna* illustrates well the orientation of Islamic commercial law toward making explicit all interests and opposing opportunities for hidden interests that might give rise to hidden benefit from transactions.

The concern was not that speculation was unacceptable, on the contrary it was the norm; all investments in commerce are premised on buying cheap and selling dear. Rather, it was felt that contracts should not guarantee an uncertain benefit to only one party since this could not be explained as sharing risk; and it was this unfair advantage that motivated the concealment. In clear contrast, the *rahn* (hypotheque) of an agricultural property for a year carried a unclear benefit due to the hazards of climate, and since it could also be renewed, it could be said to resemble a loan at annual interest. While Islamic jurists would not tolerate unshared uncertainty due to human shenanigans, this form of contract was allowed, perhaps because credit was often needed in agriculture due to its uncertain returns, not attributable to human action, and the expected variation in return was a fraction of the probable return on the property so there were clear advantages to each party.

Even a *commenda* partnership contract such as a *mudāraba* / *qirād* might benefit from a stratagem. In principle, such a contract had to be between a working partner (who supplied labor) and an investor who supplied cash, because this facilitated the specification of the division of profits and risks.

If, instead, the investor wished to provide goods, such as grain, one solution, thought to clarify each partner's contribution, was to require a separate quantity of grain be first provided to the working partner, who would endeavor to sell it on salary. He, then, could trade with his own profits from that sale, but more importantly would share the risks and profits (as specified in the original *mudāraba*) based on clear knowledge of the value of the investors grain at the start of the partnership.

Alternately, the investing partner could first sell the grain to a third party, thus obtaining cash for the *mudāraba*, and his working partner would take this cash and repurchase the goods; and, viewing them as the embodiment of the fully specified cash loan (*qirād*) from the investing partner, the working partner would use the grain to make a profit in trade and share the profits and risks with the investing partner on the basis of the cash loan.[105] The intent of this lugubrious procedure was to prevent relationships (exploitative or not) between partners from being incompletely specified in advance. Since the value of the goods is unclear, running them first through the market clarifies their value; and, so allows the appropriate terms of the partnership to be scrutinized for fairness.

al-Ghazzālī noted in the eleventh century that merchants looked at anyone conducting commerce in accordance with the law as ridiculous.[106] Similarly, Maimonides (twelfth century), when consulted about whether the norm of selling goods on credit with payment collected months or years later was legal, since it opened the way for illegal collection of interest, replied that without sales on credit "most livelihoods would come to a standstill."[107]

It is highly probable that many merchants of the Islamic world must have taken a practical view, but specific deviations from the law would have still called for justification. In some cases, Islamic judges were forced by circumstances to accept that necessity is the mother of (temporary) invention. Thus, in eleventh century Cordova and Granada, shortages of supplies in a period of insecurity forced the inhabitants to engage in maritime trading that fell outside the legal norms.[108] When sailors could not be found willing to accept a fixed salary, presumably risks were too high, the judges ruled that the crew could both feed themselves from the supplies obtained and share in the profits by dividing what was left after consumption into agreed upon proportions going to the investors and the crew. This did not fit the standard model of maritime trade. The crew could not be defined as partners because no specified liability or legal partnership existed nor was it possible to imagine either that they were investors who stood to lose financially if the cargo was lost yet, rather than simply being on salary, they participated in the profits. The judge in this case explicitly noted that the Maliki position was capable of recognizing the public interest when necessary (مراعاة المصلحة اذ كانت كلية حاجية).

The classic notion that time is money was well understood in the Islamic world whose basic commercial principles included the admonition never to allow your funds to rest idle—something that was well represented in merchant concerns over delayed payment. One commercial letter between business acquaintances noted that the recipient of the letter had not only delayed the normal two months before paying 80 dinars, but had delayed a further five months, and had thereby "slaughtered me without a knife".[109] Given the slightly countervailing advice that profit was all about knowing what to buy and when to buy it, transactions on credit would be both normal and greatly facilitate trade, but excessive delays in receipt of payment were clearly recognized as representing financial loss. A frequent compromise involved partial payment in advance and delayed payment of the remainder—due once the goods had sold.[110]

On the assumption that al-Ghazzali and Maimonides correctly reported the norms, significant sums would have been earned in most areas of the Islamic world using less than impeccably legal strategies. The importance of earnings from funds on whose genealogy aspersions could be easily levied is borne out by a judgment about inheritance of such funds.[111] Attributed to Yahyā b. Ibrahīm, the judgment noted that while some thought funds earned in any illicit way were not rendered clean by inheritance, others thought they were, and an acceptable middle position restricted such cleanable "illicit" sources to dubious sales and usurious profits on transactions of grain, gold, or silver. These were rendered legal by inheritance (gains from theft or tax avoidance, most obviously, were excluded from the list). Nevertheless, it is likely as well both that the law significantly shaped the practice of commerce, and that the literature on clever ways of circumventing the strictures of the law may have been equal parts piety and utility; and, as al-Ghazzāli suggested, it may tell us a great deal about the practice of the law. The existence of the stratagem literature suggests that clever circumvention was required both if one was to abide by the spirit of the law yet prosper or if one wished, for good or dubious reasons, to escape the letter of the law.

THE RADHANITE AND MAGHRIBI MERCHANTS

The thirteenth century completion of the Reconquista in the Iberian peninsula, with the exception of the Nasrids in Grenada, the major expansion of Italian trade between the eleventh and twelfth century and a revitalization of the Byzantine empire began to transform the balance of power in the Mediterranean. Before this sea change, Jewish merchants played a more significant role in maritime trade.

In the ninth century, a group of Jewish merchants, the Radhanites flourished carrying trade from the northwestern shores of the Mediterranean to Egypt and the Levant. They traveled several commercial routes including overland through Gaul to the Byzantine Empire and then down the coast of the Levant, or used available shipping by sea from Provence to Egypt and from there down the Red Sea to India and China as well as east along the North African coast to Egypt. The northern of these routes even allowed them to buy slaves (eunuchs, slave boys, and slave girls) to bring south for sale in Muslim lands. Their prosperous trade connected the northwest of the Mediterranean world with India but our main account, from a ninth century writer Ibn Khurradadhbah, provides only basic trade information such as routes and goods traded.[112]

During a later medieval period, 1050–1250 AD, we have more information and can ascertain that trade across the Islamic side of the Mediterranean flourished commercially from the Iberian peninsula to the Levant and even east to India on the basis of the ideas and principles we have discussed in this chapter. One discrete implementation of these ideas, by what have come to be called a coalition of Maghribi merchants,[113] may illustrate some of the broader benefits of the institutionalization of such commercial norms. The Geniza records, and other sources, document this group of Jewish merchants who in the tenth century left the insecurity of Baghdad for Fatimid Tunisia; and, then moved with the Fatimids to Egypt (ca. 974).

Having, as a consequence, commercial contacts across the Mediterranean, they engaged in trade from one end of the Mediterranean to the other in the eleventh century, until the dominance of Catalan traders[114] in the western Mediterranean and Italian and Byzantine merchants in the eastern Mediterranean, beginning in the twelfth century, motivated the Maghribi merchants to move their base of operations to the Egypt-Indian Ocean arena. During their two centuries in the Mediterranean, the Maghribi merchants were a distinct minority with substantial sums to invest, a broad region of operations, and a relatively small membership. After this time they were assimilated into the broader Jewish community of Egypt.[115]

By maintaining strict norms of honor and trust among a coherent[116] group, the Maghribi merchants, as perhaps the Radhani before them, were able to look out for each others' merchandize on commercial ships and in ports, and so engage in long distance trade without ownership of ships or the development of corporations, guilds or legal structures of the sort subsequently developed in Italy to cover similar long distance trade. Their considerable and enduring success as a group depended on a tight imbrication of formal contracts and social norms of trust and honor providing a network of free services available to the entire group of merchants. The institutionalization of such norms of reciprocity via peer pressure was as critical to their long term success as the availability of legally binding financial arrangements such as the *commenda.*

The case of the Maghribi traders illustrates in finite form a pattern that was set in classical Athens in the maritime trade from the Piraeus and the networks of obligations standard in the early Republic of Rome in which trust, honor, and explicitly shared risk took institutionalized forms, and were keys to long distance trade and economic prosperity. Later developments on the north side of the Mediterranean including more radical innovations in finance set Europe on a distinct path, but these later institutions—though they provided some advantages—never dislodged the systems of honor and trust that undergirded Mediterranean commerce from its earliest days. Instead, they focused on addressing risk and liability in new ways that enhanced capital formation in commerce.

Of course it would be rash to focus on honor and trust without noting that piracy, enslavement, and guile played as important roles as ever. Though piracy was, briefly, almost eradicated under the early Roman Empire, piracy was common throughout the Middle Ages around the Mediterranean and was practiced by Christians and Muslims alike. Both groups only nominally justified their piracy on religious grounds, they often had mixed Christian and Muslim crews and pillaged with little regard to religious affiliation. Ships of either affiliation could buy assurances (e.g., "safe passage") from those whose ships engaged in piracy and these would, generally, be respected. Protection rackets were not invented by the mafia but have had a long Mediterranean genealogy.

The problem for pirates was that merchant houses in the major trading cities were on the lookout for goods lost to piracy and had the means to sanction theft at home. In the early medieval period we have been examining, this would have increased the cost of marketing stolen goods and limited options for profit. The much later (sixteenth century) establishment by the Medicis of Livorno as a free port in the Adriatic seems to have been directly motivated by the need for a clearing house for goods obtained through piracy.[117] The advantage of Livorno was that all goods could enter the port, merchants were granted rights, and the goods could be rapidly laundered and sent on to appropriate markets. Livorno was thus an early blueprint for Switzerland (where banking first appeared in the eighteenth century) and was created to conceal the evidence of crime in the spirit of free enterprise. In this sense, the Medici bank was in a long tradition of supporting what the Greeks called the *aphanes* (invisible) economic sphere. Not to be outdone, the Ottomans developed Izmir (Smyrna) in the seventeenth century to serve similar purposes.

CONCLUSIONS: AN ENVIABLE TRANSPARENCY IN LENDING

We have suggested in this chapter that the economic advantages gradually gained by Europe, beginning in the eighteenth century, should in no sense be attributed to the inadequacies of Islamic financial law. While no society fully empowers all of its people, economists concur that rents, elite capture, inequality, and corruption impair economic prosperity; and, that some degree of fairness is part of the package (opportunity is another part) that leads to prosperity and increased welfare. From this perspective, it is clear that the Islamic trajectory in commercial law must have contributed substantially to prosperity and welfare across the Islamic world. Those who insist on imagining that there must be an internal reason why modern industrial capitalism did not develop first in the Islamic world fail to understand the complexity of the "conjuncture" in Europe that led to industrial capitalism's success.

Economic productivity may be facilitated by financial institutions but many social and cultural factors influence the linkages between finance and production. Slavery in a society in which modern variants of citizen rights and individual empowerment are yet to be conceived meant something quite different than it did in nineteenth century America. Slaves in Sumeria contributed to the structure and prosperity of households, especially temple households, and then, later, to the prosperity of the state conceived as the greatest household. We may reasonably imagine the first millennia of the Christian Era as a period in which households initially held most rights over individuals followed by a gradual development of greater power over the individual by the state.

The notion that slaves largely did low status "domestic" or agricultural work must be resisted since the pattern established early by households to use slaves as household members in the most productive and suitable ways set a pattern that was the norm throughout the first millennium in the Islamic world. Slaves thus participated in the financial sector much as other people as well as being themselves objects of investment. In the second millennium AD, great networks of finance linking agricultural production and modern manufactures through the slave trade were developed but this will be examined in a second book.[118]

This chapter can neither do justice to the economic details across such a large area nor cover the full range of legal variation in commercial law across the early Islamic world. It does, we hope, illustrate the financial and economic sophistication of the early Islamic world, as well as the key role both ethics and justice played in Islamic finance. The long prosperity of the Islamic world owes as much to this foundation as to its receptivity to merchants from multiple ethnic and religious backgrounds. Prosperity across the Islamic world from Iberia to Indonesia owed much both to the intelligent elaboration of financial norms and to the elaboration of a tolerant and multi-ethnic society. While there are indisputable elements of continuity from the norms prevailing in the ancient world, there is also a core direction taken by the Islamic world which must, in its rational elaboration of ways to illuminate the hidden corners of finance by focussing on transparency and justice, be taken as extremely original and well considered.

Islamic commercial law refined instruments of credit built on a fairly exemplary system of ethics, but it also significantly supported the continued elaboration of informal networks of obligation (in which the *ibdāʿa* was a key institution). These informal networks in a mode similar to that found in the Early Republic, (epitomized there by common use of the *mandatum*) provided a broad range of free services that were as crucial to commerce as were financial contracts. While dishonesty within a partnership was naturally a problem for reputation, it was a private matter to which others, generally, had access only indirectly or through a rare court ruling. Public behavior, in terms of service to others free of charge, was much more open to scrutiny and of greater public concern, this scrutiny and concern provided significant advantages, in the form of free advertisement, given the high level of risk to which all commerce was subject.

Trust in others was a paramount concern for other reasons as well. Disregarding the difference between maritime and land transport, and focusing only on averages, in terms of both time and money, costs could be minimized by having goods travel as part of another merchant's baggage. Not surprisingly, reputation was everything; and, even if it was primarily gained within a fairly small community of peers, it could be widely known, and reputation would have been an essential part of identity, as the Geniza letters so eloquently testify. Critical loans as well as new commercial opportunities would accrue to those with impeccable reputations; and, avoid those less capable of avoiding aspersions of unreliability or, worse, unethical behavior.

At its most fundamental, Islamic financial law elaborated on the norms that Greeks inherited from Mesopotamia and Egypt and used in the Piraeus. By focusing on transparency and insisting on allocating risk, profit, and liability in proportion to investment (of labor or money), Islamic law at its best attempted to legislate justice and interdict hidden interests. The absolute refusal to countenance simple fixed interest rates surely owed something to Aristotle and Plato as well as to the instruments of credit developed specifically for long distance trade in Mesopotamia and subsequently used in the Nile. The extension of Islamic principles of commercial ethics to other subject matter such as endowments, *waqf*, rents, and all forms of investment provided an opportunity for jurists to elaborate a consistent ethics that may have owed as much to Ancient Egypt as to the Judeo-Christian legacy.

The extraordinary focus on a system of commercial justice that intended to treat everyone transparently and fairly is as admirable in its own way as the Ancient Egyptian concern with equality before the law. A similar argument is that the Islamic focus on transparency, and its prohibition of hidden advantages, was one of the roots of the long enduring commercial prosperity in the Islamic world — regardless of how perfectly such goals were attained.

We know far more about the practice of law for the early Islamic world than we do for early Mesopotamia, Egypt, or even the Roman Republic. This could empower us to be quite prolix but we have been parsimonious in our selections largely because enough material is available to give us some confidence that our selections are reasonably representative. The extensive literature on ways to avoid too literal application of Islamic law tells us both that there was considerable flexibility in practice and that the law did effectively preclude the most egregious examples of exploitation. As we have noted, Islamic law both looked poorly on theft or piracy and attempted to sanction those who obtained profits, even those inherited, from criminal activity.

Like the rest of the world, then and now, this did not mean everyone had similar opportunities, that piracy was not profitable, nor that the rich did not exploit the less advantaged (e.g., in this case, particularly slaves, servants, or the poor, and women to a lesser degree). Nevertheless, we have little doubt that Islamic commercial law did restrain the tendency for more general forms of social inequality to grow and that its focus on just allocation of risk, liability, and returns to investment of labor and capital had a significant role in stimulating stupendous economic growth across the Islamic world.

NOTES

1. Al-Muqaddasi, La meilleur répartition/*ahsan at-taqāsim,* 43. English translation from Horden and Purcell, *The Corrupting Sea*, 7.
2. Ibn Khaldun's reflection cited in Pirenne, *Muhammed and Charlemagne,* 166.
3. Goitein, *A Mediterranean Society* Vol. I, 285–305.
4. Many historical overviews are available, for example, Hourani, *A History of the Arab Peoples*, Lapidus, *A History of Islamic Societies*.
5. Horden and Purcell, 442.
6. Udovitch, *Partnership and Profit*, 228.
7. Mottahedeh, *Loyalty and Leadership in Early Islamic Society*, 72–84.
8. Einstein, "On the method of theoretical physics," 165 wrote, "It can scarcely be denied that the supreme goal of all theory is to make the irreducible basic elements as simple and as few as possible without having to surrender the adequate representation of a single datum of experience."

9. Kuran, *The Long Divergence*, cf in particular table 14.1, chapter 5, and pp. 129–38. See also, Rodinson, *Islam and Capitalism*.

10. Kuran, 129–30.

11. McChesney, *Waqf in Central Asia*, provides a scholarly review of the literature on *waqf* as well as an account of the shrine at Balkh (near Sammarqand).

12. Another example of this argument is, Bonine, "Vaqf and commercial land use." C. Geertz makes no distinction between rents and key right, and mentions only that *waqf* property usufruct is auctioned without drawing any positive or negative economic implications. Geertz, Geertz, and Rosen, *Meaning and Order in Moroccan Society*, 131.

13. In Morocco, the House of Iligh in the sixteenth to nineteenth centuries engaged in financing caravans, and a myriad of traditional business activities of great benefit to the economy. It also sold on credit to Jewish merchants, who left their families in the enclave as surety. Pascon, *La Maison d'Iligh*. Joseph notes that, in the seventeenth century Ottoman empire, lending at interest was in many, but not all, areas the norm even for charitable foundations. Inalcik, *An Economic and Social History of the Ottoman Empire 1300–1914*, chapter 17. "Trade: Regional, Inter-regional and International," 490. It is unclear how widespread or common this practice was in other areas or times but the cases cited are likely to have been influenced by exposure of the Ottomans to early modern European practice.

14. Marcus, "Rural Property and Social Structure." Mayer, *Property, Social Structure and Law in the Modern Middle East*, 123 provides numerous examples of this motivation for making endowments in Aleppo, Syria.

15. It is reasonable to assume that the enormous elaboration of personal and institutional endowments in Ancient Egypt had significant influence on the development of law regulating *waqf* in the Islamic world but a careful study of this has not yet been done.

16. McChesney, 7–15. McChesney (116) provides an example of a tax exempt *waqf* established (1618) from taxable land by surrendering to the government a significant portion of the original land, worth about one third of the total, in return for the remaining parcel being accepted as a tax exempt *waqf.*

17. Nevertheless, a tradition of favoring community granted the right of preemption to neighbors in the purchase of real estate as exemplified in the maxim, *jār al-dār ahaqq bi-dār al-jār*—the neighbor of the house is entitled to the house of the neighbor. Schacht, *The Origins of Islamic Jurisprudence*, 164.

18. An early Iraqi maxim known in Medina goes, *al-rahn bi-mā fīh* or the security takes the place of that for which it is given. Schacht, *Origins*, 186.

19. Park, "Essaouira: The Formation of a New Elite 1940–1980."

20. Such as the *hikr* and the *mursad* loan: Baer, "Hikr," Degeilhem-Schoem. "The Loan of Mursad on Waqf Properties." Kazemi and McChesney, *A Way Prepared.*

21. Udovitch, 80 points out that this differential was well known in the Islamic world and cites Sarakhsī's Mabsūt 22:38 on normally higher price for sales on credit. al-Sarakhsī was a Hanafi, jurist (d. 1090). Mālik himself (d. 796) taught that deferred sales were fine and that if the buyer went bankrupt and still had the goods the buyer

had first right to them but if the buyer died all creditors were of equal standing—Mālik cited by Shaybani, *The Muwatta of Imam Muhammad*, 345, #18.

22. Abu Hanifa, *319,* #295 provides these and other exceptions to zakat where levying the tax would harm productivity.

23. Arberry, *The Koran Interpreted*, 99. This passage from the beginning of Sura V., The Table, is one of three passages in the Koran forbidding gambling that serves as a key reason for Islamic concern with sharing risk transparently and forbidding a contract to put one party at risk and not another.

24. ash-Shaybani related that the Prophet said this to Abu Sa 'id al-Khudri who told Atiyyah al-'awfi as recounted by Abu Hanifa (699–767 CE). Abu Hanifa, *The kitab al-athar of Imam Abu Hannifah,* 450, #765. This and preceding passages in the sections on sales and loans emphasize that hidden benefit or unequal advantage from contracts and sales is usury and unacceptable.

25. Abu Hanifa, 453, #764. Even minor details of law need specification if transparency is to be achieved—by narrowing the right of pre-emption to only adjacent neighbors it precludes others using influence to an advantage.

26. The definition of the sunna (traditions) narrowed to its standard definition, traditions about the prophet Muhammed, at least by the time of Shafī'i (d. 820) who designated other tradition as mere *ra'y*–opinion (Schacht, *Origins*, 113. The sunna, as so conceived, is exemplified in the hadith about the Prophet Muhammad and the Qur'an. One might define Sunni's as those who confine their religious givens to the sunna but accept other authoritative interpretations of those givens while Shi'a allow the possibility of additional inspired sources (givens) such as the writings and actions of some of the descendants of 'alī.

27. Ess, *Prémices de la théologie musulmane*, 36.

28. The hadith provide the opinion and actions of the Prophet Muhammed accompanied by a chain of transmission (isnad) that allows scholars to evaluate the hadith in terms of its probable soundness. Thus if two adjacent links in the chain of transmission lived in different parts of the Islamic world and their biographers provide no evidence that they could have ever met the chain is not sound. Typically isnad are judged as fitting on at least three levels of probability and the top two levels are usually included in the major compendia of hadith where they are generally encountered by both scholars and the public. Many weak and hadith circulate as well.

29. Ess, 19.

30. Ess, 27–28.

31. Ess, 147.

32. al-Bukhari, Sahih al-Bukhari: Book 24, Hadīth 3. Translations online, Arabic: buliq, *minhāj al-Sālihīn*.

33. Ess, 33, 21.

34. Goitein, *Mediterranean Society,* 164–69, devotes a section to this arguing that merchants regularly devoted considerable time to unremunerated cooperation or commercial services to others.

35. Goitein, *Mediterranean Society*, 169.

36. Goitein, *Letters of Medieval Jewish Traders*, 36–77.

37. Ibid., 123.

38. Udovitch, 102.
39. Schacht, *An Introduction to Islamic Law*, 78.
40. Udovitch, 252–57.
41. Udovitch, 107.
42. Udovitch, 103 similarly cites Goitein with approval that *ibdā'a* are purely utilitarian. While reputation and honor have utility we would argue that they are more fundamental than instrumental.
43. Goitein, *Mediterranean Society*, 187, 178.
44. Ibid., 186.
45. Ibid., 250–51 also notes the frequent use of the term "*hujja*" for an acknowledgment of debt.
46. Islamic law gives clear precedence to current oral testimony, Wakin, *The function of documents in Islamic Law*, but documents were highly recommended in commerce with those most recent taking precedence over older documents: cf. Emile Amar, *L'Organisation de la propriété foncière au Maroc,* who studied this issue for Morocco at the beginning of the Protectorate when naive Europeans focussed on buying ancient (and invalid) titles to land.
47. Goitein, *Mediterranean Society*, 242. The Ottoman empire also used this term, Havala, for such a letter of credit: Inalcik, "Hawāla."
48. Ibid., 247.
49. Ibid., 243. In the example cited from Fustat the fine was six dirhams per day for delay in paying out 120 dinars. Goitein notes that in this period in Egypt 13 1/3 high quality dirhams exchanged for a dinar. This would make the fine about 0.375 (3/8ths) of a percent.
50. Ibid., 342.
51. The calculation for such transaction costs is that, at 3/8ths of a percent, 8 days delay will lose you 3 percent and 21 1/3 days delay will lose you 8 percent or the maximum premium that might be charged outside of exceptional times such as when the transport of goods was particularly risky.
52. Goitein, *Mediterranean Society*, 249.
53. Ibid., 250.
54. Shaybani, 357, #811.
55. Shaybani, 361, #823. In this passage, Shaybani is citing Abu Hanifa's approval of Ibn al-Malik's opinion.
56. Shaybani, 337, #768.
57. Goitein, *Mediterranean Society*, 262.
58. Lagardère, *Histoire et société en occident musulman au moyen âge*: Case #278, 174.
59. Lagardère, 341 #202.
60. Lagardère, 416, #184.
61. Lagardère, 341, #204.
62. The Qur'an, Soura 2: 282 suggests either two men or one man and two women make the minimal set of witnesses. The judge's specification of the latter choice undoubtedly has something to do with the subject matter of the case and probably also reflects the spirit of the Qur'an.

63. Lagardère, 198, #386.
64. Lagardère, 143, #136.
65. Lagardère, 170, #257.
66. Udovitch, 19-28 provides a discussion of this form of joint ownership.
67. Udovitch, 158.
68. Goitein, *Mediterranean Society*, 82.
69. Udovitch, 29–35.
70. Udovitch, 99 notes that even if two partners together engaged in a face-to-face transaction liability remained separate and unequal—in proportion to their shares in the partnership.
71. Udovitch, 41, 99, 240.
72. Udovitch, 100.
73. The term *'inān* is not used in the earliest sources. Udovitch, 145.
74. Udovitch, 40 ff, 146, note 28.
75. Udovitch, 136.
76. This is a summary of Tahawi's list intended to be compatible with Maliki, Hanafi and Shafi'i perspectives, Udovitch, 132–33.
77. Udovitch, 94.
78. As discussed in the chapter on Greek and Roman commercial thought, Andreau, *Banking and Business in the Roman World,* 151 remarks on the similarity between the medieval commenda and the Roman institution of *societas*. Udovitch, 17–39 suggests that the commenda, unlike the *mufāwada* and the *'inān*, does not fit into the Near Eastern and Judeo-Muslim tradition of joint property partnerships so it is possible the commenda in the Islamic world owes much to the Roman *societas*. Kohler, *Die Commenda Im Islamitischen Rechte*, noted that the prophet Muhammed used the commenda and traces the contract in its basic form to early Iraq.
79. Udovitch, 107, Schacht, *Introduction*, 156.
80. Goitein, *Mediterranean Society*, 170 notes that the Hebrew shuthafuth also insisted on joint ownership and suggests that this was the norm for partnerships other than the *qirād*: that is, the *mufāwada.*
81. *Corpus juris civilis, Digesta* 17:2. 31. C. H. Monro, Cambridge 1902: 19–20, extract cited in Udovitch, 36.
82. The chapter on Mesopotamia cites what is clearly an early form of the commenda dating to the Old Assyrian period (ca. fourteenth century BC), the *šipkātum* contract.
83. Udovitch, 209.
84. Constable, *Trade and Traders in Muslim Spain*, 71.
85. Andreau, 151.
86. This list is a synthesis of points made in Udovitch and Goitein, *Mediterranean Society.*
87. Entrusting commodities to outside parties in a limited partnership. Udovitch, 208.
88. Udovitch, 204.
89. Udovitch, 209.
90. Udovitch, 213.

91. Goitein, *Mediterranean Society*, 176.
92. Ibid., 171–72.
93. Ibid., 175–76.
94. Udovitch, 180-1.
95. Goitein, *Mediterranean Society*, 174–75.
96. Udovitch, 245.
97. Schacht, *Introduction*. 81.
98. Horii, "Reconsideration of Legal Devices (Hiyal) in Islamic Jurisprudence," 316.
99. Horii, 323.
100. Horii, 329.
101. Horii, 332.
102. Horii, 353.
103. Horii, 351.
104. Lane, 2217.
105. Horii, 354.
106. Hurgronge, Selected Works, 260, cited in Udovitch, 7.
107. Goitein, *Mediterranean Society*, 197.
108. Lagardère, 354, #273.
109. Goitein, *Mediterranean Society*, 196.
110. Goitein, Ibid., 199.
111. Lagardère, 207, #426.
112. Brief translated passages of Ibn Khurradadhbah's account can be found in Lopez and Raymond, *Medieval trade in the Mediterranean World,* 32–34. See also, Ashtor, "Aperçus sur les Radhanites," and Rotman, *Byzantine slavery in the Mediterranean*, 66–67, 74.
113. Greif, *Institutions and the Path to the Modern Economy*. Greif has published many studies of the Maghribi merchants but in this book he explicitly compares them with the Italian developments in Lisbon and makes a strong case for the late medieval period being a place where Europe began to follow a different path to long distance trade than the Islamic world.
114. Abulafia, *The Great Sea*, chapters III, 7–8 discuss the Catalan traders in some detail.
115. Greif, 61. Greif's extensive scholarly work develops a model he refers to as private-order contract enforcement institutions to describe this type of informal institutionalization of commercial norms not covered by options of legal enforcement. While we admire Greif's analysis we find his terminology which assimilates institutionalized social norms to contracts unpersuasive. In addition, as we have argued, the behavior has roots deep in antiquity, its character is more intrinsically tied to ethics and world view than the data on the Maghribi traders can illustrate, and its legacy is still with us.
116. Greif, 296 points out how the group imposed (ca. 1050) a year-long trade embargo on Palermo (Sicily) without recourse to any courts and were successful in getting a new tax annulled.

117. Molly Greene. Resurgent Islam: 1500–1700. Chapter 7 in Abulafia, *The Mediterranean in History*, 239–41. Greene cites a Venetian report from 1624 that explains that "Livornese, Corsican, Genoese, French, Flemish, English, Jewish, Venetian and other merchants are settled in Algeria and Tunisia. They buy up all the stolen merchandise and send it to the free port of Livorno and from there it is distributed all over Italy."

118. A good overview of slavery in the last three millennia across the Mediterranean can be found in, Youval Rotman, "Forms of Slavery," in Horden and Kinoshita, *A Companion to Mediterranean History*, chapter 17.

Conclusion

Hidden Interests and the Anthropology of Credit

As we have shown, understanding early finance requires a social and ethical conception of societies and insight into the imbrication of finance within those societies. Scholars have noted that "For the societies of the ancient Near East, social justice typically meant maintaining the existing social hierarchy."[1] Our research finds a myriad of evidence that supports this generalization we cannot summarize here. Yet, unlike culturally specific forms of social justice, which remained locked within these societies, their commercial notions of justice and rapid innovations in finance spread with their trade relations from urban areas to territories of city states, to larger nations or to empires in the Mediterranean, as well as across the fertile crescent and the Islamic world.

It is worth noting that an appealing way to define even a capitalist economy[2] is that it is transformational: that is, it transforms both itself and society over time and so changes in many ways. In capitalist societies, to a higher degree than in past societies, the driving force for change is competition, and in the modern era the key reason transformations are expedited is that to a closer degree than in earlier periods there is a price structure that values the factors of production at their economic value (e.g., their contribution to production). Significant social, financial, and technological changes then open opportunities that competition drives people and firms to pursue. Nevertheless, the other influences on the ancient societies we have examined in this book, for example, governmental or ethical or jural institutions (including institutionalized behaviors producing inequalities) continue to have their importance.

For the societies and periods we have examined, we take the position that although markets developed into significant institutions they were not yet pervasive, that is to say they were not in a position to price all the key factors of production at even approximately their productive value and so never attained the significance they have in a capitalist economy.[3] The factors of production were rarely priced efficiently enough to motivate purchase on the market; and, without other special advantages being added, such investments did not yield competitive levels of profit. Instead, the owners of the basic factors of production (e.g., labor, land, and capital) benefited from institutional arrangements that largely determined their profit levels even when some other inputs such as grain, copper, or bronze may at times have been relatively efficiently priced. As we have seen in the earliest sales documents the vast majority of buyers and sellers were elites and significant numbers of human beings were first captured then bought and sold as slaves. As a result, like land, labor was not priced at its productive value, and social connections shaped access to loans (capital) as well as what, if any, interest might be paid.

In our view the historical role of the state should be seen as a crude, and at best partially successful, response to market failures. It is rare, and recent, that competitive markets have even come moderately close to efficiently priced inputs for even basic production processes. Efficient pricing ought to be seen as something achieved by the economic system broadly conceived: requiring a competitive market, plus government provided legal support, plus a scientific enterprise that enables technological change as well as an ethical system conducive to incentives impacting the many not the few. Technological change is critical to competition that promotes efficiency: one signature trait of a capitalist market. Even today the value of many essential ecosystem services, such as water filtration in nature or replenishment of renewable resources are inadequately valued by capitalist markets. For instance, if the demand for particle board drives clear cutting of forests, many species that might potentially have enormous future value as botanical products may be ignored and improperly priced at zero.

In outlining the development of credit in the ancient world, we have focused on different elements in different civilizations, both to minimize redundancies and to take advantage of the differential preservation of ancient reflections on finance. The Mesopotamian region with its long and rich financial record preserved on cuneiform has provided an unmatched record for the development of credit instruments while the stupendous example of bureaucratic continuity in Ancient Egypt provides a source for studying the development of institutional systems of obligation. These systems motivated investment of a societal surplus accruing frequently due to the chaotic flood regime of the Nile. Classical Athens and the Early Republic of Rome explicitly introduced ethical claims focused on lending framed as honor and trust and thereby set the pattern for understanding the link between social networking and finance that was followed by the Christian and Islamic worlds.

Mediterranean Europe ended up incorporating a selection of ethical concerns from the Judeo-Christian tradition, which itself drew on both Egyptian and Mesopotamian concepts of justice. The Islamic world put a different spin on these traditions and emphasized the implications of transparency in finance—taking one tradition from Athens' Piraeus, while resolutely refusing the Agoran focus on hiding finances from others, in return for the fixed interest that played such a prominent role in Athenian citizens' financial strategies and those of their European heirs. We contend that it is likely that all ancient societies relied on free financial services rendered to others as part of the construction of honor and trust and, in consequence the acquisition of symbolic capital. It is at least noteworthy that in the modern world we are inclined to criminalize such services.

Although credit as a social institution may be an economic transaction, it is usually much more. Unlike cash deals that require only a brief relationship between buyers and sellers, credit is necessarily built on enduring commitments, as the Inupiac father cited in our introduction emphasized. An early religious sanction was the oath: an oath breaker risked not only sanction by the gods but also extreme social disgrace. As we saw in the second chapter on the Mesopotamian tradition, the oath was standard in many credit contracts between individuals until it disappeared during the Old Babylonian period (1894–1595 BC) as trade became more internationalized and the ability of community opprobrium to sanction oath breaking diminished.

One common way the need for trust in credit arrangements can be handled is to base them on personal, face to face relationships. Participants in credit may be kin, friends, neighbors, or coworkers. If they know enough about the other's moral character and economic assets they should be able to judge how far they can trust one another. The problems associated with trust were first clearly thought through in the Roman Republic. Willingness to trust each other does not address the issue of what to do if catastrophe strikes and ensuring repayment on a debt requires significant sanctions.

Where social relations are densely intertwined, any failure to uphold a bargain is quickly common knowledge, but to minimize risk a lender still needs some structure to treat all borrowers in, a socially perceived, just and predictable fashion. Where the social costs of being considered untrustworthy, or unjust, are high, loans may be quite informal; yet even in small communities there is often potential benefit in requiring formalities, documents, oaths, or witnesses. Such formalities insure that there is a social memory of transactions, and so may prevent conflicts over the nature of the original agreement. The development of instruments of credit in early Mesopotamian cities, whose populations were small, also speaks clearly to this point.

Although personal loans can be based on horizontal ties among social equals, they also may occur between persons occupying very different social, political, and economic positions However, in such cases, as significant sanctions may be entailed, these requirements may well have motivated the development of more formal sanctions and differential terms as a way to maintain the legitimacy of a social hierarchy. The ancient Egyptian legal system was unusual in stipulating equality before the law, regardless of social status, yet this nevertheless seems to have facilitated both adherence to a religious ideology and the practice of commerce.

In vertical relations between persons of very different statuses, or between institutions and individuals, loans commonly benefit one party more than the other. So, although I may borrow from a temple, it would be less likely to borrow from me. The careful calculations made for institutional lending of grain in ancient Mesopotamia and Egypt speak eloquently to the need to keep those loans profitable for the institution—which says nothing about their degree of utility to the recipient of the loan or the profitable or non-profitable (e.g., consumption) uses to which the loan was put. We know enough about grain compression to know that the rules were set to benefit the lender not the borrower. This should not be surprising.

Nevertheless, as we have seen, Roman elites lent to cities and organizations while across the ancient world countless religious institutions, based their long term finances on complex networks of obligations for labor, revenues from taxes or temple tithes as well as the mutual provision of services between the state, the religious infrastructure, and a host of individuals obligated in the form of long term prebends. We might, therefore, view these practices as being oriented toward the long-term prosperity of all parties even if the greater prosperity of those with power dominated the relationship.

The difference in directionality is not an issue of simply greater access to resources. Directionality plays an important role in communicating, affirming, and maintaining differentiations in social status, so individuals of high standing may be reluctant to borrow on the same terms no matter how great their need. As we saw, in Neo-Babylonian times a set of ten loans showed no relationship between rate of interest and amount of loan suggesting that other considerations were more likely paramount. We have suggested that regarding the ancient world as a place where market efficiencies in lending took priority over other considerations is anachronistic. Although there may never have been any society where economic efficiencies dominate all other considerations the fairly low value placed on economic efficiency relative to maintenance of social hierarchy may be seen as one of many issues particularly relevant in the ancient world.

As the ties between lender and borrower become increasingly remote, personal relations gave way to impersonal ones, and formal agreements replaced informal ones. The steps along this path we have documented for the Mesopotamian region include having such agreements made before witnesses, requiring trusted third parties to guarantee loans, demanding collateral, putting agreements in writing, keeping formal accounts and records, institutionalizing ways to trade or transfer debts, and using political authorities to sanction debts and enforce agreements. The rich record of Mesopotamian law cases provides ample evidence of the willingness of governments to provide guidance and sanctions for private and institutional lending.

The real complexities began when repayment could be in a different form than that in which the loan was rendered. The complications here are not so much that goods may be repaid with labor, or that one good or currency is repaid with another, but that the notions of equivalences become even more complex. The Mesopotamian cases, perhaps because the region relied heavily on channeling labor into productive endeavors, including captives from other lands, provided many examples of explicit accounting that packaged labor and other inputs into an advance (loan) in which both lender and recipient stood to gain.

Our analysis of the production of a group of female workers in the Ur III period suggested that an incentive structure in the loan of workers and outputs to the foreman provided benefits to the foreman both for efficient use of the labor or other inputs as well as costs for overwork leading to loss of labor. While lenders may have the upper hand in such negotiations, and such transactions offer a veritable maze in which "hidden" forms of interest can be concealed, the Ur III case suggests that practical considerations limited the disproportion in benefits between the two parties. The reliance of the Ur III state on such enterprises with explicit profit incentives and constraints also suggests that Ur III recognized both the benefits of efficient organization of labor and that overwork was unproductive.

As these elements coalesce into institutional forms, such as banking, credit relations can themselves sustain social projects in a way impossible for simple interpersonal credit. Thus, the Athenian state expected free services from its citizens in the form of liturgies and *eisphora* much as citizen peers in Athens expected friendly (no interest) loans. The obligations of citizens to the state not only harnessed the wealth of the elites for state projects but also motivated the secrecy of the Athenian banking sector and the competition, under threat of legal pursuit, to minimize public knowledge of wealth. This practice may well have a direct descendant in Swiss banking secrecy laws and the general western notion that such laws are acceptable—even when they clearly facilitate hiding criminal profits and the use of those illegally gained funds by banks in promoting national or international industries.

We have seen that by the early medieval period, Islamic scholars were already debating the ethics of using ill-gotten gains: concluding either that it was always unethical or that in some cases of inheritance no blame was to be attached to it—though this provided no defense against a claim for restitution by aggrieved parties to the extent the inherited funds allowed. This extrapolation from the Islamic emphasis on making hidden financial interests transparent fit into Muslim concerns over justice in commerce and finance. Both Mesopotamian and Egyptian civilizations benefitted from their efforts to institute justice in commerce and finance. The Egyptian focus on institutional finance and legal equality was quite distinct from the Mesopotamian concerns focused on taming arbitrary levels of exploitation in lending and on making some key terms, such as a rate of interest, more uniform while allowing a penal code that provided different sanctions depending on social status.

Aristotelian moral objections to lending at interest (it is unnatural) and Plato's view that it is socially destructive combined with Judeo-Christian concerns over exploitation to give usury its stigma—something that was entirely lacking in the Mesopotamian tradition from Sumerian times. It may be that the Sumerian language would have predisposed people to view cattle, grain or silver as equally agentive and thus made an Aristotelian argument unreasonable. Morality, inevitably, became part of the discourse about credit in the Mesopotamian area in the form of fairness in lending but it also touched the issue of reasonable expectations for yields for different commodities. Rates of interest seem to have been viewed as pragmatically determined; and, to the credit of Mesopotamian authorities, were not made dependent on the status of the parties to a loan even while punitive damages in criminal cases were directly tied to relative social status. Perhaps this is because, initially in Sumerian times, the "agent" producing the profit was the commodity, a status free object, and the trader merely facilitated that increase to occur.

Technical and social transformations in Mesopotamia provided further justifications for the emergence of new financial instruments and the refinement of older ones. The practical requirements of long distance trade clearly led to the development of early forms of the *commenda* (the *naruqqu*-contract in the Old Assyrian period) in which a person with funds partnered with (and empowered) an agent to trade for their mutual benefit. This extremely useful extension of older partnership contracts, documented in case law, was distinguished primarily by the agent sharing in profit and escaping some liabilities earlier required in partnership or employment contracts—the traveling agent thereby being more fully empowered by having his liability proportional to his own share of profit- greatly reducing his risk. The gradual development of private institutions run by merchants to regulate and adjudicate trade issues also enriched the financial policies of states in particular by avoiding the political issues that might have been associated with the infringement of local government authority by states who had no local suzerainty.

The Islamic effort to address the Greek and Judeo-Christian concerns over lending at interest *per se* was draconian, banning all lending at interest, as well as splendidly logical and innovative in taking this idea and generating a legal framework for inhibiting comparable forms of exploitation across the commercial and financial sectors. Muslim scholars felt, because commerce involved capital, labor, risk and liability, that justice in the financial sector required transparency and justice in all these areas. Clear specification of inputs, risks, and benefits in partnerships and loans could address the issue of transparency and the simplest way to address issues of justice was to evaluate inputs of all parties and insist that profits, risk, and liabilities all be fairly shared by each party. We noted that both Muslim and Jewish authorities, for example, al-Ghāzzalī and Maimonides, felt commerce required flexible interpretations of strictures against interest—allowing some "tricks" but neither argued against the key concerns about transparency or fair allocation of profit, risk, and liability.

Norms of commercial and financial behavior in the ancient world were increasingly constrained by a judicial structure that followed predictable and well-formulated rules and procedures that required explicit specifications in formal contracts. Yet, as in earlier and later societies, they were also constrained by customary expectations about honorable, not just legal, behavior. All authorities in the Islamic world concurred that as in Athens or Rome, honor and expectations of trust mandated the provision of free services which were viewed as an explicit component in the construction of social and cultural networks that was indispensable to economic success.

Islamic law explicitly protected such behavior from liability claims based on the ground that free services diverted resources from a partnership, even when explicit partnership assets were used. Jewish and Muslim merchants alike devoted significant resources to the provision of free services to each other. As in the Early Republic, it would be hard to imagine society having functioned without these activities. The idea that social beings behaved in exclusively self-centered ways was a figment of mid-twentieth century economic theory that, in the United States, was such a credo in economics that it gave rise to an unending critique from the other social sciences and the production of counter theoretical positions such as what was briefly called "post-autistic" economics.

Our analysis continues in a second book, *Hidden Interests in Credit and Finance*, which takes up the story beginning with the Byzantine and Ottoman Empires which took a pragmatic approach to lending; allowing interest at rates set by the state. The great European effort to rehabilitate lending and get around Christian concerns about usury was taken up by the Scholastics primarily in Italy, France, Germany and Spain, but as merchants developed new credit technologies and sophisticated banking, their ideas evolved in harness with the needs of commerce.

These European developments benefited from the great Islamic scholarship of the classical world which gave scholars in Spain and then elsewhere access to Greek thought. In this tragic, for what might have been, scenarios the reconquest of Iberia soon brought the Inquisition and a consequent failure to appreciate or to take up the challenge of transparency in lending so developed in the Islamic world. Our second book follows the many European developments on the continent and in England as well as the failure of the heirs of the reconquest of Spain and Portugal to benefit from the brilliant financial ideas which the multiethnic Iberian civilization had pioneered.

That book continues our examination both in Europe and North Africa to focus on private banking and state finance as well as the role of social capital, productive inequalities and ethical thought in financial systems. We look at the crucial role of credit in the Atlantic slave trade as well as the long shadow of colonial institutions and ethnic discrimination in market access in Morocco. Our final chapters of *Hidden Interests in Credit and Finance* deal with the development of consumer lending and the 2008 credit crisis: each of which in their own ways embody most of the issues that have proved important for millennia yet have assumed astonishing global reach only in recent decades.

NOTES

1. Wells and Magdalene, *Law from the Tigris to the Tiber*, 143.
2. Nell. *The General Theory of Transformational Growth.*
3. The issue is whether prices are conducive to investment. A simple way to look at the question is to ask whether a person could obtain finance at a reasonable cost, purchase a commodity such as land, labor, and other key inputs, and produce enough with those inputs to pay back the principle and finance costs as well as make a normal rate of profit on the investment. It is generally understood that efficient prices require the vast bulk of each potential input to be traded in a competitive market. In the absence of such conditions a capitalist economy does not exist even in the presence of a market. This in no way precludes the possibility of making profits by buying cheap in one place and selling dear in another or via free or subsidized access to productive inputs such as in a feudal economy.

Appendix

Technologies of Power and the Metrology of Grain Storage in the Ancient Near East[1]

It is not easy to address metrological issues in ancient Mesopotamia or Egypt for both epistemological and historical reasons. Leaving aside epistemological issues for the moment, we can note that in Europe it was only with the development of the meter that governments began to standardize measures geographically and substantively. In earlier centuries, even volumetric measure of grain differed from town to town and within towns the containers used for one grain were not the same size as those for another grain. It would be astonishing if the modern standardization in containers prevailed in the past. This has all been much discussed and carefully presented for premodern Europe but the same has not been done for the ancient world. The biggest obstacles to an understanding of such a complex issue may be the granularity of the admittedly numerous surviving tablets relative to the reality of myriad variations over time and space.

Witold Kula summarized the metrological understanding of premodern Europe under eight rubrics: the realism, symbolic, or functional character of measures, the role of measures in facilitating class and sovereignty, persistence and issues of unification or standardization of measures, role of measures within markets, social conditions for the evolution of measures, and the contribution of metrology to historical analysis. Kula[2] suggests that premodern measures usually not only vary by place, time, and material measured but also have social significance that in large part accounts for this variation. Sovereignty often imposes some degree of standardization at the level of central administration but until the modern period this standardization is unlikely to have devolved to the local level.

Kula's *Measures and Men* provides specific discussion of particular measures including those related to grain.[3] Among the "facts" well known to premodern Europeans were that grain settles in transit, compresses differently when poured into a container at waist height than at shoulder height or when poured into equal volume containers of different shape (e.g., wider diameters were conducive to more compression) or when placed in containers with different volumes (e.g., a bushel barrel or a granary). Mills might insist that the container be placed on their mill floor while other grain was being ground, which would cause settling, and then insist that the measure be topped off prior to being ground. Variations in the way grain was poured into a bushel container could itself make a difference of more than 8 percent. The difference between a heaped measure and a stricken one (leveled with the edge) could be between 6.5 percent and 13 percent of the total.

One unscrupulous Polish inspector revealed his estimate of the difference between compressed and uncompressed grain by noting that, although the "quarters" legally due were uncompressed and leveled off, to each eight gallon quarter assessed an additional two had to be added (a 25 percent increase) to make up for the fact that measures were uncompressed.[4] While empirical measures of ancient grains, in the spikelet form used to minimize insect damage, are difficult to estimate scientifically they would clearly vary depending on granary or heap size (Mesopotamians estimated the grain stored on quay side as well as in barges and granaries) as well as age in storage. We can assume that not only did measures differ by region, time, and substance but that they had to take a large number of factors into consideration if anything like rational accounting were to be followed.

Because grain has a tendency to deteriorate over time largely due to insect attack, throughout the grain producing world the practice was to put grain into the top of a granary and take it out from the bottom in order to ensure that old grain is consumed before new. This has the implication that typically grain removed from a granary both represents grain in its compressed state and is older grain. In this article we will begin with the situation in Mesopotamia and then follow with the Egyptian case where we have a clever instruction manual for estimating the amount of grain in a granary that clearly takes compression into account.

EVIDENCE FOR THE AWARENESS OF GRAIN COMPRESSION IN ANCIENT MESOPOTAMIA

Although we have considerable continuity of archaic terms in metrology lists in UR III (late third millennium BC) that continue through the sixteenth century BC, the lists already show a degree of discontinuity with the archaic period, such as lacking the term for *lidga* and list a *gur* as equivalent to 5 *barig* (not 8 *barig*) or 300 liters (not 480).[5] This quantitative difference could reflect a real metrological change due to the intervening Akkadian dynasty, or it may represent a desire to conform to some other constraint. Calculations of volume were well developed by archaic times, and having a granary be a simple multiple of a standard storage vessel would make accounting vastly simpler. If the storage vessel was large enough for the grain to be compressed, deposition of this pre-compressed grain would properly fill the granary without settling. If this is what is going on, two quite different *gur* measures may have been long in use—one for deposition of uncompressed grain and one for transfers of compressed grain—corresponding to the 3 barig difference between the two *gur*. The new definition of a gur might then imply a semantic switch from granary as receptacle to granary as source for distributions.

Support for the explicit recognition of grain compression in Mesopotamia can be found in sample problems for calculating the capacity of storage vessels, which being smaller than granaries might be far more widespread. Four such problems from the tablet referred to as Haddad 104 (ca. 1800–1750 BC) in the city of Me-turan of the Kingdom of Eshnunna (north of Baghdad) make this explicit. In each, the calculations involve what is called a *constant of storage* defined variously.[6] The variety of ratios used makes no sense outside of a recognition that grain compresses, and compresses differently depending on circumstances, for example, the size of a container, whether it has been allowed to settle, whether it is on a quay side in a heap waiting for transport, whether it has pre-settled due to having been transported, whether it comes out of a container already compressed, or whether the measures are of compressed grain from a granary.

An understanding of these examples requires some basic understanding of Mesopotamian sexagesimal notation. A typical notation is 6 (00 00), which in the numerology of the time, meant that the volume measures were to be multiplied by six to produce the grain capacity of that physical volume. Such a multiplier actually has to be understood in terms of a base calculation of five (5) *sila* per volumetric *sar* that would be appropriate when compression was not involved. Thus "6" meant that a volumetric *sar* that might be expected to hold "5" would hold an additional 20 percent or "6."

The instructions to scribes are to calculate the volume of the container and then multiply by the constant of storage to calculate the storage capacity. A simple example is the following (Haddad 104 problem one):

> following instructions on how to calculate area and then volume the instructions continue: "the volume will come up. Multiply [it] 0;00 18 45 by 6 00 00 (the constant) of storage, so that 1 52;30 will come up. The cylinder contains 1 (barig) 5 (ban) 2 1/2 sila of grain."[7]

While the math involves a simple sexagesimal multiplication the result, 1 52;30, is then converted to standard grain measures rather than the positional accounting scheme: 1 (*barig*) 5 (*ban*) 2 1/2 *sila*. More significant is the range of values in use for constants of storage when discussing grain. Haddad 104 provides eight problems of which six specify a constant of storage of "6 00 00," while two specify "5 00 00" which would seem to mean no compression. The full range for constants of storage in texts between 2100 BC and 1600 BC now appears to be from 4 48 00 (4.8) to 7 12 00 (7.2).[8]

While in many cases the relevant circumstances are not clear, and so we may never have a full explanation for why such different "constants of storage" were to be employed for grain, it is clear that a number of factors would be relevant including: type of grain, size of storage container, or size and shape of stack on loading dock, (calculations involve stack dimensions at bottom and height implying the angle of the heap), as well as whether the grain was pre-compressed or settled (e.g., transported or stored in a container) prior to the calculation. These considerations can easily explain a range of constants reflecting conversions from available physical volume to potential for storage of 96 percent to 144 percent (using 5 as the base). The default position must be that the "constant of storage" took into account compression otherwise their variable value in so many calculations remains a puzzle.[9]

Recognition of grain compression, in addition to being a recognition of reality, transforms the issue of hidden interest in grain lending. A simple equal exchange of compressed grain for uncompressed in a pre-harvest loan paid back at harvest could benefit the borrower 20 percent or more, if we exclude the issue of new grain for old. By contrast, recognizing that an adjustment for compression, due to having lent compressed grain and receiving less compressed grain in return, would mean an apparent advantage to the lender, ignoring the issue of old grain for new, was in fact only an exchange at parity or near parity.

With poor quality old grain, the borrower might be lucky to break even quantitatively even if the lent grain were compressed. The price differentials before and after harvest also need to be considered: even without a proper currency the key to obtaining an advantage is the relative terms of trade.

This in itself is a major puzzle for there is no reason to assume nonagricultural products go down in value at harvest relative to grain—rather they might be expected to be worth more grain when grain is plentiful. The loan of grain thus regularly had various forms of hidden interest: new grain for old, compressed vs. uncompressed, or more *sila* (e.g., +33 percent) after harvest for fewer *sila* loaned before harvest, and "expensive" grain before harvest vs. "inexpensive, low value" grain post-harvest. Similar issues arise in Egypt with similar solutions,. Acknowledgment of compression also contextualizes the modern obsession with interest rates as an anachronistic idea that obfuscates the important point that interest is merely one among many ways to extract benefits from lending.

EGYPTIAN ACCOUNTING TECHNIQUES AND THE RECOGNITION OF GRAIN COMPRESSION

The Rammesid *Instruction of Amenemope* (ca. 1295–1069 BC) includes a passage that makes it clear that Egyptians of the time were familiar with many of the issues discussed by Kula for Europe and the potential of measures to falsify:

> Beware of disguising the measure,
> So as to falsify its fractions;
> Do not force it to overflow,
> Nor let its belly be empty.
> Measure according to its true size,
> Your hand clearing exactly.
> Do not make a bushel of twice its size,
> For then you are headed for the abyss.
> The bushel is the Eye of Re,
> It abhors him who trims;
> A measurer who indulges in cheating,
> His Eye seals (the verdict) against him.[10]

Egyptian concerns with justice were acute and the importance of grain in the Egyptian economy can scarcely be exaggerated. While Egypt during the Roman Empire was often a net exporter of grain to the Mediterranean world, grain production in dynastic Egypt was a primary source of individual and institutional wealth. A frequent and recurring theme in Egyptian discussions of justice was about how fairness in measuring grain or land was fundamental to justice itself. When production is measured in grain, continued prosperity always depends to a significant degree on the storage, accounting, and internal distribution of grain and grain products. Accordingly, Egyptian administrations devoted major infrastructure and accounting effort both to the storage of grain and to baking of bread for distribution—as these were key elements of institutional salaries. Granaries and bakeries were critical institutions throughout dynastic Egypt, yet modern knowledge of metrology has not been adequately applied to ancient Egypt.

Though it has been little remarked,[11] Egyptian volumetric calculations recognized the compressibility of grain. Not to have done so would have caused problems. Typical cylindrical granaries (diameters typically averaged 2.5 meters but could be 3.5 meters or perhaps more) had grain poured in at the top and taken out at the bottom.[12] This would have ensured that old grain was sold before new grain. Egyptian measures for grain began with a simple *hekat* and a large, or quadruple, *hekat* which by volume was one-thirtieth of a cubic cubit. Accountants also used a *khar* of five quadruple *hekats* (twenty of the nominal thirty *hekats* of a cubic cubit). Since a key calculation required taking the amount of grain stored in a granary and turning it into a corresponding amount of loaves of bread,[13] Egyptian scribes had to be able to make volumetric measures of grain commensurate. The problem was that a given volume of compressed grain, such as in a granary, includes more grain than a similar volume of uncompressed grain poured into a simple *hekat* basket on the threshing floor. Scholars of ancient Egypt, strangely, have not usually accounted for this.

That this is implausible is clear if we examine the relevant problem from the Rhind papyrus, and keep the distinction between compressed and uncompressed grain in mind. The problem, which is intended to teach scribes, is how to calculate the capacity of a granary, and is stated as follows:

> A circular container of 10 by 10 cubits
>
> take away 1/9 of 10, thus 1 1/9; remainder 8 2/3 + 1/6 + 1/18
>
> Multiply the 8 2/3 + 1/6 + 1/18 by 8 2/3 + 1/6 + 1/18 (i.e., square it); result: 79 1/108 + 1/324
>
> Multiply the 79 1/108 + 1/324 by 10 (the height); it becomes 790 1/18 + 1/27 + 1/54 (i.e., in cubits cubed)
>
> *Add half to it*: it becomes 1185
>
> Multiply the 1185 by *1/20*, giving 59 1/4. This is the amount that will go into it in quadruple-*hekats*, namely 59 1/4 hundreds of quadruple *hekats* of grain.[14]

We know the dimensions of an Egyptian cubit (0.52035 m) from many sources so we can calculate the volume of a cubic cubit to be 0.140892 cubic meters. The granary in question was calculated by the Egyptians as having a volume of 790.11112 cubic cubits. but using a modern formula we would calculate it (pi times r^2 times a height of 5.2035 meters) as 110.6563 m^3 and therefore capable of holding 785.398 cubic cubits which we might convert directly to 5890.5 quadruple hekats. In the Rhind papyrus cited above, Egyptian scribes provide a similar calculation using a premodern formula. At first a volume of 790+ is calculated in cubic cubits. Half is added to this figure to get 1185. The final line uses this figure of 1185 and equates it to 5925 (59 1/4 hundreds), so in effect it multiplies 1185 by five. The 1185 units are actually converted to hundreds of quadruple *hekats* by dividing by 20 and multiplying by 100.

If we use the modern calculation of the volume of the excercise's granary and divide by the 5925 figure we have a hekat of 0.004669 m^3 which is 2.5 percent smaller than the 0.00478 m^3 standard used by most scholars. The agreement is close enough that we have to conclude that internal hekats are probably, volumetrically speaking, fairly standard.

We have ample evidence that grain does compress, clearly grain as spikelets should compress better than threshed non spikelet grain, and the Egyptians would certainly have discovered this. Although, we do not currently have experimental evidence in a granary of the size typical in ancient Egypt using spikelets of ancient grain.

The use of the new term *khar* does offer one simple possibility that would take into account the compressibility of grain. Within a granary any volumetric measure will be, in effect, leveled or "stricken" as it was termed in the middle ages even as all grain is compressed. "We need to keep in mind, therefore, both the difference between leveled and heaped measures and that between compressed and uncompressed grain. We may note that the citation above from *Instruction of Amenemope,* which presumably refers to the provision of rations, emphasizes the need for measures to be carefully leveled. Yet, outside such constrained circumstances a measure might more naturally be heaped. This extra grain would compress in volume once deposited in a granary and thereby enhance the weight of grain represented by any volumetric granary measure including those used to allocate rations.

The advantage of referring to grain in granaries by the terms *khar* and quadruple hekats would be to reference compressed grain made available as rations differently than heaped hekats entering granaries and mere volumetric measures of granary capacity (790 cubic cubits). It may be that the 20 hekats of a *khar* held approximately the same weight of grain as the 30 leveled and uncompressed hekats nominally making up a cubic cubit. The *khar* then would be a useful term if, as rations, leveled hekats always contained compressed grain and therefore as much grain as heaped but uncompressed hekats entering the granary.

It may be illustrative to examine Barry Kemp's analysis of the scribe's problem.[15] Despite citing the scribe's account from the Rhind papyrus, when he wishes to calculate diets, a few pages later Kemp borrows from the literature a figure for a simple *hekat* (4.78 liters or 0.00478 cubic meters) as well as the estimate that a ten-day ration included two-thirds of a simple *hekat* of barley, and one simple *hekat* of wheat (estimating 785 kg per m^3 for wheat and 705 kg per m^3 for barley). In this case it is clear Kemp's measure is uncompressed. This volume of a *hekat* is little different than the figure implied in the scribe's example. Kemp applies these figures to rationing, without considering whether different weights are appropriate at harvest vs. en route to bakeries and breweries or, more generally, in calculating conversion of granary volumes into bread or beer rations. In his subsequent calculations, Kemp provides no explanation for, or discussion of, the scribes mathematical detour through the *khar* and reaches a low calorie diet conclusion for laborers in dynastic Egypt based on an estimate of 0.6 kg of grain per day (comprising 40 percent barley and 60 percent wheat).

Kemp's calculation produces a figure that corresponds roughly with one estimate of Mesopotamian figures for Old Sumer grain rations (0.54 kg); and, possibly this similarity is viewed as a confirmation of the calculation. Yet, as we have seen, the archaic Mesopotamian records indicate a variety of items being rationed, multiple measures whose size is unclear, and almost certainly involve compressed grain as well, since multiple conversion rates are used to represent a sophisticated range of volumes and packing. It is far more plausible, in Egypt as in Mesopotamia, that workers also got other rations including beer which surely would have been brewed in bulk. Still we cannot ignore the simple reality that 0.6 kg of grain would provide at best 1650 calories, and if 40 percent of the ration was barley, there would have been even fewer calories. Half again as many calories would itself be inadequate for hard labor yet grain in some form provided the most significant source of calories.[16]

Not only should we, therefore, allow the possibility of grain compression, and the error in ignoring this, but we must also recognize that in many cases, there must have been some additional food consumed (e.g., oil, dates, or fish). The assumption of the *khar* as an accounting unit responding to compression in a granary clearly is compatible with reasonable dietary requirements and, equally importantly, justifies the etymological complexity of the Rhind Papyrus calculation.

Bread and other grain products provided as rations were traditionally compared within a scale of values based on how much grain they contained. Egyptians made careful calculations of grain content (noted as *pefsu* value) in grain products much as we found above in the archaic calculations from Mesopotamia. This centralization of nutritional calculations strongly suggests central provisioning of multiple types of rations as in Mesopotamia and a careful regard for nutritional requirements. A daily ration in dynastic Egypt for low status laborers was apparently ten loaves and some beer.[17] The actual pottery used to bake bread or brew beer turns out to have varied widely and reflects little evidence of standardization in Egypt: both because there were a variety of types of beer and of loaves of bread; and, because perishable materials were used to make baskets for grain transport. Since the volumetric measures Kemp uses to infer an inadequate diet are derived without recognition of grain compression, it is worth noting that had Kemp assumed that the *khar* implies compressed grain, his calculation for a daily consumption level by laborers in ancient Egypt might have been more in line with comparable figures for the Roman military of 0.94 kg of grain a day.[18]

From our perspective, the calculations we have reviewed are significant in that they establish the care with which Egyptian accountants kept track of grain receipts and expenditures. Many scholars have viewed grain as a reference currency in the ancient world because of the extraordinary importance paid to it, even though it could not assume many of the functions of a proper currency.

The weight adjustment possibly implied by the new term, the *khar,* should not be ignored as a mere etymological adornment; instead it may represent much more than an arcane terminology suited to mathematical exercises. More generally, if compressed grain is lent the lender requires more (uncompressed) grain returned just to break even, though lending old grain for new has its own advantages. That the Rhind Papyrus is an instruction manual for granary management dating to mid-sixteenth century BC suggests that the calculation is not esoteric knowledge, but rather widespread basic knowledge required of those responsible for keeping proper track of grain.

In Egypt, the original need to calculate in this way may have derived from inter-granary transfers as these required advanced knowledge of how much transport capacity would be needed to move the grain from one granary to the other. This might require calculating capacity ratios of the granaries themselves rather than simple volumetric ratios.

BROADER IMPLICATIONS

It is reasonable to suppose that the original proportions used in dynastic accounting became, overtime, a premium charged on loans to simplify accounting and facilitate the replacement of old stocks with new. There is some indication of a standardization in Mesopotamia during the early second millennium, the case law discussed in chapter 2 suggests that loans of grain were to specify 33 percent interest while loans of silver should specify 20 percent.

The simple explanation of this difference between acceptable interest on loans in silver and loans in grain is that it had to do with qualitative differences between grain and silver and this presumably included some role for grain compression and grain deterioration. The case law also suggests that profit is reasonable, given the 20 percent prescribed for loans in silver, which neither compresses nor ages. The Mesopotamian premium for grain loans (33/20 = approximately 65 percent) may easily be seen as encompassing both compression and issues of grain quality.

While Mesopotamians apparently took pains to incorporate compression into all their capacity measures for grain from quay side heaps, to shipping containers and granaries of various sizes by developing conversion to storage rations, the Rhind papyrus references only state granaries taking fairly standard proportions that may be appropriate for standard granaries.

This may have been because the key issue for clerks was twofold: how much could be fit in such a granary and how much compressed grain was needed for standard loaves or standard types of beer used in rationing. The simplicity suggested in the Rhind papyrus may have been due to the greater uniformity possible when Upper and Lower Egypt were unified and may perhaps not have been the case for less unified periods in dynastic history or necessitated by grain stored privately in the conditions.

Kula's eight rubrics suggest we need as well to consider a few additional issues. The role of measures in facilitating sovereignty is clear in the status attributed to the Mesopotamian legal compendia, the standardization of accounting of the Rhind papyrus and the role of authorities in evaluating lending practices in both Egypt and Mesopotamia. Although in most legal matters Mesopotamian practice was to differentiate based on class, it appears that in lending of silver or grain status was irrelevant when it came to the rates prescribed for private lending.

Kula also recommended that attention be paid to the evolution of measures and their linkage to historical analysis and in this regard a number of factors need to be considered including surety for loans and the evolution of the form of loan contracts. Where either debt bondage was impracticable or inadequate to serve as surety, once societies established adequate civil procedures then other forms of collateral, such as land titles or temporary usufruct of land, became alternate forms of potential collateral. Historically, once debtor-creditor relationships became institutionalized by temples or palaces, there appears to have ensued an evolution toward contracts providing, within a single document, similar social relations of dependency for the benefit of private parties. Individual parties could not assume repayment in the way temples and then palaces could so there were clear advantages to adding more conditionalities in the contracts.

NOTES

1. This appendix was presented as a paper at the Society for Economic Anthropology meetings in Lexington, Kentucky, in April, 2015.

2. Kula, *The Problems and Methods of Economic History*, 342ff.

3. Kula, *Measures and Men*, chapter 7, esp. pp. 43–70) In addition to the 25 percent compression figure provided by feudal historians, modern calculations for compacting "naked" wheats suggest that within modern silos barley might compress a further 12 percent and hulled hard wheat about 5 percent over normally settled wheat (Moya et al., "Mechanical properties of granular agricultural materials," 484). Ancient wheats such as Emmer were generally stored as spikelets since the hulls did not easily separate when threshed; Potts, "Weights and Measures," 62, and they would have been considerably more compressible. The spikelets and most of the hull was separated as a part of the grinding process for flour though ancient flour remained highly abrasive (Kemp, *Ancient Egypt*, 122). While I can find no modern figures for the compressibility of emmer spikelets, there is nothing unreasonable about the Egyptian calculation. If we were to use an expansion of 25–32 percent for aerated measures of modern grain, a 50 percent expansion is quite reasonable for comparing emmer spikelets in a basket with compressed emmer spikelets in a granary.

4. Kula, *Measures*, 134.

5. Nissen, Damerow and Englund, *Archaic Bookkeeping*, 142; Robson, "Mesopotamian Mathematics," 75. This indicates that from late fourth millennium two volumetric versions of a gur may well have been used at least through the early second millennium. Note that with a 300 liter gur rather than the 480 liter the granary would contain only 720,000 liters. As discussed earlier, in Uruk times granaries can be estimated to contain 2400 *gur* of 480 *sila* or 1,152,000 *sila* (one *sar* = 18,000 *sila* or liters).

6. Robson, Ibid., 123–27, 71. The numerological system used in the calculation appears to be sexagesimal place value (SPVS) see pp. 78–79. Thus, 18 45 is 18*60 + 45 or 1125, 6 00 00 is 6*360 + 0*60 + 0*1 or 21,600 (See also Chrisomalis, *Numerical Notation*, 250–51. Thus the multiplication says 1125 *sar* times 6*360 or 21600 give = 24,300,000 *sila*. This adds 20 percent to the figure you would get using 18,000 the normal volume of a *sar*.

7. Using the sexagesimal system of the time, this calculation is (18 45 = 18 + 45/60 = 18.75) * 6 = (1 52 30 = 112.5 = 1*60 + 5*10 + 2 + 30/60). The volume calculation in Haddad 104 (problem one) preceding this excerpt is a bit opaque to the general reader because the scribe is going from field level metrology to a volume metrology using scribal shortcuts that provide excellent approximations to modern algorithms but these mathematical details are not relevant to our discussion. The final phrase provides the conversion of total *sila* of grain (1 52;30 = 112.5) to appropriate terminology for stored grain: 1 (*barig*) 5 (*ban*) 2 1/2 *sila* using the equivalences of 1 barig = 60 ban, 1 *ban* = 10 *sila*. We should remember that this now refers to compressed grain in a granary which will stay compressed when it is measured out, *ceteris paribus* so its nutritional value per unit volume would be 20 percent higher.

8. Robson, *Mesopotamian Mathematics 2100–1600 BC*, 114–15 provides a table listing all known Mesopotamian constants of storage for grain specified between 2100 and 1600 BC.

9. Robson, "Mesopotamian Mathematics," 70–71 provides a table with volumetric measures culminating in a granary of 1,152,000 *sila* and the volumetric measure

of a *sar* as 18 m^3. Dividing 18,000 into 1,152,000 gives 64 *sar* and this cannot be a coincidence. If we take instead the later granary of 720,000 liters (the later *gur* contained only 300 liters rather than 480) then this granary would hold the same number of *gur* but only the contents of 40 volumetric *sar*. The ratios of 480/300 and 1,152,000/720,000 are both 1.6. Mesopotamians clearly liked their divisions simple so we might ask why complicate matters with a constant of storage if not because grain compresses. The granary was conceived as a multiple of a volumetric *sar* (or *sila*, i.e., liter) as was the storage container yet given the reality of compression grain capacities for the vessel and granary must be adjusted by a kludge factor: a constant of storage in Uruk times as in Ur III times. The original granary was, *in terms of volume*, built to contain the volume of 64 uncompressed *sar* of grain: although these *sar* each can contain 20 percent more than 18,000 uncompressed *sila* assuming a constant of storage of "6" is used (i.e., 21,600 actual *sila of grain*) they measure precisely 18,000 *sila* volumes (i.e., liters) but each is of compressed grain.

10. Roth 2006 II:157.

11. We know of no source that really takes grain compression into consideration but feel there must be one.

12. Kemp, 296ff.

13. Bread molds were exported at least as far as Palestine by as early as the first dynasty, Kemp, 77.

14. This problem appears on page 120 of Kemp and is problem 42 from the Rhind papyrus, a mathematical instruction manual for scribes dating to the fifteenth dynasty or Second Intermediate Period (mid-sixteenth century BC): year 33 of the reign of King Auserre / Apophis. The problem discussion by Robins and Shute, *The Rhind Papyrus*, 46 also passes over the *khar*.

15. Kemp, 120-7.

16. This calculation is based on the assumption that there are 3,300 calories in a kilogram of wheat but that one-sixth is lost in processing or is wasted leaving 2,750 calories. Sixty percent of this would be 1,650 calories. It is estimated that light labor expends 0.03 cal/lb/minute so a 150 lb man would minimally need 600*150*0.03 calories for ten hours of work and this is already 2,700 calories and a human must also live the additional fourteen hours in the day. In short, this 1,650 calorie ration is an implausible candidate for more than a portion of a worker's caloric requirements and so conclusions from this figure alone about a worker's diet shortfalls are entirely unwarranted.

17. Kemp 1989: 124–26.

18. Kemp, 127-8, cites Polybius (ca. 140 BC) for the Roman ration as 0.94 kg of grain per day. Kemp proceeds to use his much smaller figure throughout the remainder of the book with unfortunate results.

Bibliography

Abbott, Frank F. *A History and Description of Roman Political Institutions*. Boston: Elibron Classics, 1901.

Abraham, Kathleen. *Business and Politics under the Persian Empire: The Financial Dealings of marduk-nāṣir-apli of the House of Egibi (521–487 B.C.E.)*. Bethesda, MD: CDL Press, 2004.

Abu Hanifa. *The kitab al-athar of Imam Abu Hannifah*. London: Turath Publishing, 2007.

Abulafia, David. *The Great Sea: A Human History of the Mediterranean*. Oxford: Oxford University Press, 2011.

Abulafia, David, ed. *The Mediterranean in History*. London: Thames and Hudson, 2003.

Acemoglu, Daron, Simon Johnson, and James A. Robinson. "The Colonial Origins of Comparative Development: An Empirical Investigation." *The American Economic Review* 91, no. 5 (December 2001): 1369–401.

Akkermans, Peter M. M. G., and Glenn M. Schwarz. *The Archaeology of Syria. From Complex Hunter-Gatherers to Early Urban Societies (ca. 16,000–300 BC*). Cambridge: Cambridge University Press, 2003.

Allam, S., ed. *Grund und Boden in Altägypten*. Tübingen: Selbstverlag des Herausgebers, 1990.

Amar, Emile. *L'Organisation de la propriété foncière au Maroc*. Paris: Paul Geuthner, 1913.

Anderson, Siwan. "The Economics of Dowry and Bride Price." *Journal of Economic Perspectives* 21, no. 4 (2007): 151–74.

Andrade, E. N. Da C. Chapter 8. Isaac Newton. James R. Newman, editor, *The World of Mathematics*, vol. 1. (Mineola, NY: Dover Publications, 2000), 255–276.

Andreau, Jean. *Banking and Business in the Roman World*. Cambridge: Cambridge University Press, 1999.

———. *La vie financière dans le monde Romain: les métiers de manieurs d'argent (IVe siècle av. J.-C.- IIIe siècle AP. J.-C.)*. Rome: Palais Farnèsse Ecole Française de Rome, 1987.

Arberry, Arthur J., trans. *The Koran Interpreted*. Oxford: Oxford University Press, 1964.

Ashtor, E. Aperçus sur les Radhanites, *Revue suisse d'histoire*, vol. 27 (1977): 245–75.

Assmann, J. *Ma'at: Gerechtigkeit und Unsterblichkeit im Alten Ägypten*. Munich: Verlag C. H. Beck, 1990.

Baeck, Louis. *The Mediterranean Tradition in Economic Thought*. London: Routledge, 1994.

Baer, G. "Hikr" EI(2) supplement. Leiden 1982.

Bahrani. Zainab. *Rituals of War: The Body and Violence in Mesopotamia*. Brooklyn, NY: Zone Books, 2008

Bahrani, Zainab. *Women of Babylon*. London: Routledge, 2001.

Baines, John. *High Culture and Experience in Ancient Egypt*. Sheffield: Equinox, 2013.

Barjamovic, Gojko Thas Hertal, Mogens Trolle Larsen. *Ups and Downs at Kanesh. Chronology, History and Society in the Old Assyrian Period.* Leiden: Nederlands Instituut boor het Nabije Oosten, 2012.

Barlow, Charles T. "The Roman Government and the Roman Economy 92–80 B.C." *American Journal of Philology* 101, no. 2 (1980): 202–19.

Barnes, Jonathan. *The Complete Works of Aristotle*, Volumes I and II. The Revised Oxford Translation, Princeton, NJ: Princeton University Press, 1984.

Bell, Barbara. "The Oldest Records of the Nile Floods." *Geographical Journal* 136 (1970): 569–73.

Biddick, Kathleen. "People and Things: Power in Early English Development." *Comparative Studies in Society and History* 32, no.1 (1990): 3–23.

Boardman, John, Jasper Griffin, and Oswyn Murray. *The Oxford Illustrated History of Greece and the Hellenistic World*. Oxford: Oxford University Press, paperback edition, 2001 (originally published in 1986).

Bogaert, Raymond. *Banques et banquiers dans les cités Grecques*. Lyde: A.J. Sijthoff, 1968.

———. *Les Origines Antiques de la Banque de Dépôt. Une mise au point accompagnée d'une esquisse des opérations de banque en Mésopotamie*. Leyden: A.W. Sijthoff-Leyde, 1966.

Bongenaar, A.C.V.M., ed., *Interdependency of Institutions and Private Entrepreneurs*. Leiden: Nederlands Historisch-Archaeologisch Institute, Te Istanbul, 1998.

Bonine, Michael. "Vaqf and Commercial Land Use. The Bazaar of Yazd, Iran." Paper presented at the International Conference on Waqf, The Hebrew University of Jerusalem, June 1979.

Bottéro, Jean. *Mesopotamia, Writing, Reasoning, and the Gods*. Chicago: University of Chicago Press, 1992.

Braudel, Fernand. *The Structures of Everyday Life: The Limits of the Possible. Civilization and Capitalism 15th–18th Century*, vol 1. Translated by Sian Reynolds. New York: Harper and Row, 1985, 1992; first published in French, 1979.

Bringmann, K. *A History of the Roman Republic*. Cambridge, Polity, 2007.
Brown, Roger. *Words and Things*. New York: Free Press, 1958.
Brunt, P. A. *Italian Manpower, 225 B.C. AD–14*. Oxford: Oxford University Press, 1971.
al-Bukhari, Sahih al-Bukhari. www.sahih-bukhari.com.
buliq, 'uz al-din. Editor. minhāj al-Sālihīn min al-ahādith wa-sunna khātim al-anbiyā' wa-l-murasilīn. Beirut: Dar al-Fath, 1978.
Cashdan, Elizabeth, ed. *Risk and Uncertainty in Tribal and Peasant Economies*. Boulder, CO: Westview Press, 1990.
Chamboux, François. *The Civilization of Greece*. New York: Simon and Schuster, 1965.
Charpin, Dominique. "Marchands du palais et marchands du temple à la fin de la Ire dynastie de Babylone." *Journal Asiatique* 270 (1982): 25–65.
Chavalas. Mark W. *The Ancient Near East: Historical sources in Translation*. Oxford: Blackwell Publishing, 2008.
Chrisomalis, Stephen. *Numerical Notation: A Comparative History*. Cambridge: Cambridge University Press, 2010.
Clark, J. Desmond, and Steven A. Brandt, eds. *From Hunters to Farmers: The Causes and Consequences of Food Production in Africa*. Berkeley: University of California Press, 1984, 62.
Cohen, Edward E. *Athenian Economy and Society: A Banking Perspective*. Princeton, NJ: Princeton University Press, 1992.
Cohen, Joel E. *How Many People Can the Earth Support?* New York: W. W. Norton & Company, 1995.
Constable, Olivia Remie. *Trade and Traders in Muslim Spain*. Cambridge: Cambridge University Press, 1995.
Cooper, John M., ed. *Plato Complete Works*. Indianapolis: Hackett Publishing, 1997.
Cornell, Tim J. *The Beginnings of Rome: Italy and Rome from the Bronze Age to the Punic Wars* (c.1000–264 BC). New York: Routledge, 1995.
Coulanges, Fustel de. Numa Denis. T*he Ancient City: A Study of Religion, Laws, and Institutions of Greece and Rome*. Mineola, NY: Dover, 2006 [Originally published in 1864].
Cowell, Frank Richard. *Life in Ancient Rome*. New York: Penguin Putnam, [Originally published 1961].
Cox, Cheryl Anne. *Household. Interests: Property, Marriage Strategies, and Family Dynamics in ancient Athens.* Princeton: Princeton University Press, 1998.
Crawford. Harriet. *Sumer and the Sumerians*. Cambridge: Cambridge University Press, 1991.
Crocker, David A. *Ethics of Global Development. Agency, Capability, and Deliberative Democracy*. Cambridge: Cambridge University Press, 2008.
Daniels, Peter T. and William Bright, eds. *The World's Writing Systems*. Oxford: Oxford University Press, 1996.
David, Jean-Michel. *The Roman Conquest of Italy*. Translated by A. Nevill. Oxford: Blackwell Publishers, 1996.
Davidson, James. *The Greeks and Greek Love: A Bold New Exploration of the Ancient World.* New York: Random House, 2009.

Davies, Glen. *A History of Money: From Ancient Times to the Present Day.* Cardiff: University of Wales Press, 1994.

Davies, J. K. *Athenian Propertied Fymilies 600–300 BC*. Oxford: Oxford University Press, 1971.

Davies, J. K. *Wealth and the Power of Wealth in Classical Athens*. New York: Ayer Co Pub, 1981.

Descat, R. "L'économie antique et la cité grecque; un modèle en question," *Annales* HSS 50 (1995): 961–89.

de Vaux, Roland. *Ancient Israel: Its Life and Institutions.* Translated by John McHugh. Grand Rapids, MI: Erdmans Publishing Company, 1997.

Dobb, Maurice. *Theories of value and distribution since Adam Smith. Ideology and economic theory*. Cambridge: Cambridge University Press, 1971.

Douglas, Mary. *In the Wilderness: The Doctrine of Defilement in the Book of Numbers*. Oxford: Oxford University Press, 1993.

Durand, J. M., ed. *La Femme dans le Proche-Orient antique*. Paris: Editions Recherche sur les Civilisations, 1987.

Edgerton, William F. "Amêlu and Mushkênu in the Code of Hammurabi." *The American Journal of Semitic Languages and Literatures* 41, no. 1 (October 1924).

Einstein, Albert. "On the Method of Theoretical Physics." The Herbert Spencer Lecture. Oxford, June 10, 1933, *Philosophy of Science* 1, no. 2 (April 1934): 163–69.

Engels, Friedrich. *The Origin of the Family, Private Property, and the State.* New York: International Publishers, 1972 (Reprint of fourth edition printed in 1892).

Englund, R. K. "Administrative Timekeeping in Ancient Mesopotamia." *Journal of the Economic and Social History of the Orient* 31, no. 2 (1988): 121–85.

Erdkamp, Paul. *The Grain Market in the Roman Empire: A Social, Political and Economic Study*. Cambridge: Cambridge University Press, 2005.

Ess, Josef van. *Prémices de la théologie musulmane*. Paris: Albin Michel, 2002.

Faulkner, Raymond O., trans., comment by Oden Goelet J. *The Egyptian Book of the Dead: The Book of Going Forth by Day—The Complete Papyrus of Ani Featuring Integrated Text and Full Color Images*. San Francisco: Chronicle Books, 1998.

Ferguson, Everett, ed. *Encyclopedia of Early Christianity*. New York: Garland Publishing, Inc. 1990.

Feyerabend, Paul. *Against Method: Outline of an Anarchistic Theory of Knowledge*. London: Verso, 1975.

Fine, John V. A. *The Ancient Greeks: A Critical History*. Cambridge, MA: Harvard University Press, 1983.

Finley, Moses. *The Ancient Economy*. London and Berkeley: University of California Press, 1973.

Finley, Moses. *Ancient History: Evidence and Models*. London and New York, Elizabeth Sifton Books, 1985.

Finley, Moses. *Studies in Land and Credit in Ancient Athens, 500–200 B.C.: The horos inscriptions*. Oxford: Transaction Books, 1985 (revised from 1951 edition).

Firth, Raymond and B. S. Yamey. *Capital, Savings and Credit in Peasant Societies: Studies from Asia, Oceania, the Caribbean and Middle America*. Chicago: Aldine Publishing Company, 1964.

Foster, Ben. "Ebla and the origins of Akkadian accountability." *Bibliotheca Orientalis* 40 (1964): 298–306.

Foucault, Michel. *Dits et Ecrits* I & II. Paris: Gallimard, 2001.

Frayne, Douglas R. *Ur III Period (2112–2004 BC)*. Toronto: University of Toronto Press, 1997.

Freedman, David Noel, ed. *The Anchor Bible Dictionary*, Vol. 6. New Haven, CT: Yale University Press, 1992.

Friberg, J. *Reallexikon der Assyriologie* 1990 Band 7: 570.

Friedman, Milton. *Money and Economic Development*. New York: Praeger, 1973.

Geertz, Clifford, Hildred Geertz and Lawrence Rosen. *Meaning and Order in Moroccan Society*. Cambridge: Cambridge University Press. 1979.

Gelb.I. J. "Ebla and Lagash: Environmental Contrast." *The Origins of Cities in Dry-Farming Syria and Mesopotamia in the Third Millennium B.C.* edited by H. Weiss. Guilford, CT: Four Quarters Publishing Co., 1986.

Gelb, Ignace J., Piotr Stenkeller, Robert M. Whiting Jr. *Earliest Land Tenure Systems in the Near East: Ancient Kuddurus*, Volume I Plates, Volume II text. Chicago: The Oriental Institute of the University of Chicago, 1991.

Gibson, McGuire and Robert D. Biggs, eds. *The Organization of Power: Aspects of Bureaucracy in the Ancient Near East*. Chicago: The Oriental Institute of the University of Chicago, 1991.

Goitein, S. D. *A Mediterranean Society, Volume I: Economic Foundations*. Berkeley: University of California Press, 1999.

———. *A Mediterranean Society, Volume IV: Daily Life*. Berkeley: University of California Press, 1999.

———. *Letters of Medieval Jewish Traders*. Princeton, NJ: Princeton University Press, 1973.

Grajetzki, Wolfram. *The Middle Kingdom of Ancient Egypt*. London: Duckworth, 2006.

Greenberg, James B. *Santiago's Sword: Chatino Peasant Religion and Economics*. Berkeley: University of California Press, 1981.

Greif, Avner, *Institutions and the Path to the Modern Economy: Lessons from Medieval Trade*. Cambridge: Cambridge University Press, 2006.

Gunderson, Lance H. and C. S. Holling. *Panarchy: Understanding Transformations in Human and Natural Systems*. Washington, DC: Island Press, 2002.

Harris, J. R., ed. *The Legacy of Egypt*, 2nd Edition. Oxford: Clarendon Press, 1972.

Hassan, Fekri A. "The Dynamics of a Riverine Civilization: A Geoarchaeological Perspection on the Nile Valley, Egypt." *World Archaeology* 29, no. 1, Riverine Archaeology (June 1997): 51–74.

Hayes, John L. *A Manual of Sumerian Grammar and Texts*, 2nd Edition. Malibu, CA: Undena Publications, 2000.

Hecht, N. S., B. S. Jackson, S. M. Passamaneck, D. Piattelli and A. M. Rabello, eds. *An Introduction to the History and Sources of Jewish Law*. Oxford: Clarendon, 1996.

Herodotus. *The History*. Translated by David Grene. Chicago: University of Chicago Press, 1987.

Hickman, Benjamin Studevent. *The Organization of Manual Labor in Ur III Babylonia*. Ph.D. diss. Harvard University, 2006.

Hock, Ronald F. "Lazarus and Micyllus: Greco-Roman Backgrounds to Luke 16:19–31." *Journal of Biblical Literature* 106, no. 3 (September 1987).

Horden, Peregrine and Sharon Kinoshita. *A Companion to Mediterranean History*. Oxford: Wiley Blackwell, 2014.

Horden, Peregrine, and Nicholas Purcell. *The Corrupting Sea: A Study of Mediterranean History*. Oxford: Blackwell, 2000.

Horii, Satoe. "Reconsideration of Legal Devices (Hiyal) in Islamic Jurisprudence: The Hanafis and Their "Exits" (Makharij)." *Islamic Law and Society* 9, no. 3 (2002): 312–57.

Hornblower, Simon, and Anthony Spawforth. *The Oxford Companion to Classical Civilization*. Oxford: Oxford University Press, 1998.

———. *The Oxford Classical Dictionary*, 3rd Edition. Oxford: Oxford University Press, 1996.

Hourani, Albert. *A History of the Arab Peoples*. Cambridge: Harvard University Press, 1991.

Houston, Stephen D., ed. *The Shape of Script: How and Why Writing Systems Change*. Santa Fe, NM: SAR Press, 2012.

Hudson, Michael. "How Interest Rates Were Set, 2500 BC–1000 AD: *Más*, *tokos* and *foenus* as Metaphors for Interest Accruals." *Journal of the Economic and Social History of the Orient* 43 (2000): 132–61.

Hudson, Michael, and Marc Van De Mieroop, eds. *Debt and Economic Renewal in the Ancient Near East*. Bethesda, MD: CDL Press, 2002.

Hudson, Michael and Cornelia Wunsch. *Creating Economic Order: Record-Keeping, Standardization, and the Development of Accounting in the Ancient Near East*. Bethesda, MD: CDL Press, 2004.

Hurgronge, C. Snoucck. *Selected Works*, edited by G. H. Bousquet and J. Schacht. Leiden, 1957.

Hurst, H. E. "Long-Term Storage Capacity of Reservoirs." *Transactions of the American Society of Civil Engineers* (1951), pp. 116, 770 and "Methods of Using Long-Term Storage in Reservoirs." *Proceedings of the Institute of Civil Engineers*, part I, p. 319.

Huskinson, Janet. *Experiencing Rome: Culture, Identity and Power in the Roman Empire*. New York: Routledge, 2001.

Hymes, Dell, editor. *Language in Culture and Society*. New York: Harper and Row, 1964.

Inalcik, Halil, ed. *An Economic and Social History of the Ottoman Empire 1300–1914*. Cambridge: Cambridge University Press, 1994.

Inalcik, Halil., Hawāla, EI(2), III, 283–85 (1969).

Jeffrey, Richard. *Subjective Probability: The Real Thing*. Cambridge: Cambridge University Press, 2004.

Johnson, Justin Cale, and Steven J. Garfinkle. "The Growth of the Early State in Mesopotemia: Studies in Ur III." *Proceedings of the First and Second Ur III Work-*

shops at the 49th and 51st Rencontre Assyriologique Internationale. London: July 10, 2003; Chicago: July 19, 2005.

Kamm, Anthony. *The Romans*. London: Routledge, 1995.

Katary, Sally L. D. *Land Tenure in the Ramesside Period*. London: Kegan Paul, 1989.

Katz. Victor J., ed. *The Mathematics of Egypt, Mesopotamia, China, India, and Islam: A Sourcebook*. Princeton, NJ: Princeton University Press 2007.

Kazemi, Farhad, and R. D. McChesnay, eds. *A Way Prepared: Essays on Islamic Culture in Honor of Richard Bayly Winder*. New York: New York University Press, 1988.

Kemp, Barry. *Ancient Egypt: Anatomy of Ancient Civilization*. London: Routledge, 2006.

Keynes, John Maynard. *A Treatise on Probability*. Aberdeen, WA: Watchmaker Publishing, 2007 (orig. 1920).

———. Chapter 9, "Newton, the Man." in James R. Newman, editor, *The World of Mathematics*, vol. 1: 277–85.

Khalidi, Tarif, ed. *Land Tenure and Social Transformation in the Middle East*. Beirut: American University, 1984.

Kitto H. D. F. *The Greeks: A Study of the Character and History of an Ancient Civilization, and the People Who Created It*. Baltimore: Pelican, 1951.

Kohler, Josef. *Die Commenda Im Islamitischen Rechte. Ein Beitrag zur Geschichte Des Handelsrechts*. Würzburg: Stahelschen Universitäts-Buch & Kunst-Handlung, 1885.

Kopytoff, Igor, ed. *The African Frontier: The Reproduction of Traditional Societies*. Bloomington: Indiana University Press, 1987.

Kramer, Samuel Noah. *History Begins at Sumer*. Philadelphia: University of Pennsylvania Press, 1988 (orig. 1956).

Kula, Witold. *An Economic Theory of the Feudal System*. London: Humanities Press, 1976 (orig. 1962).

———. *Measures and Men*. Princeton, NJ: Princeton University Press, 1986. London: Allen and Unwin, 1956.

———. *The Problems and Methods of Economic History*. Aldershot: Ashgate, 2001.

Kulauran, Timur. *The Long Divergence: How Islamic Law Held Back the Middle East*. Princeton, NJ: Princeton University Press, 2011.

Kuznets, Simon Smith. The Doctrine of Usury in the Middle Ages. MS. Transcribed by Stephanie Lo. An Appendix to Simon Kuznets: Cautious Empiricist of the Eastern Jewish Diaspora, p. 14. Downloaded October 1, 2013. home.uchicago.edu/weyl/Usury_appendi.doc.

Lagardère, Vincent. *Histoire et société en occident musulman au moyen âge. Analyse de mi 'yar d'al-wanšarisi*. Madrid: La Casa de Velazquez, 1995.

Lambert, W. G. *Babylonian Creation Myths*. Winona Lake, IN: Eisenbrauns, 2013.

Lane, E. W. *Arabic English Lexicon*. The Islamic Texts Society, 1984 (orig. 1863).

Lapidus, Ira M. *A History of Islamic Societies*. Cambridge: Cambridge University Press, 1988.

Larsen, M. T. "Partnerships in the Old Assyrian Trade." *Iraq* 39 (1977): 119–45.

Le Claire, Edward E. Jr, and Harold K. Schneider, eds. *Economic Anthropology. Readings in Theory and Analysis*. New York: Holt, Rinehart and Winston, Inc., 1968.

Lefkowitz, Mary R., and Maureen B. Fant. *Women's Life in Greece and Rome: A Source Book in Translation*, 2nd Edition. Baltimore: Johns Hopkins University Press, 1992.

Le Glay, Marcel, Jean-Louis Voisin, Yann Le Bohec. *A History of Rome*. Chichester: Wiley-Blackwell, 2009.

Leveau, Philippe. "La ville antique, 'ville de consommation'? Parasitism social et économie antique", *Etudes Rurales* 89–91 (January–September 1983): 275–83.

Lichtheim, Mirriam. *Ancient Egyptian Literature*, Vols. I–III, Berkeley: University of California Press, 2006.

Lichtheim, Miriam. *Late Egyptian Wisdom Literature in the International Context: A Study in Demotic Instructions*. Göttingen: Vandenhoeck & Ruperecht, 1983.

Liverani, Mario. "Political Lexicon and Political Ideologies in the Amarna Letters." *Berytus* 31 (1983).

Lopez, Robert S., and Irving W. Raymond. *Medieval Trade in the Mediterranean World. Illustrative Documents*. New York: Columbia University Press, 2001.

Lorton, David. "The Treatment of Criminals in Ancient Egypt," 20 *Journal of the Economic and Social History of the Orient* 2, 43 (1977).

Maine, Henry Sumner. *Ancient Law*. Tucson: University of Arizona Press, 1986 [Originally published 1864].

Maloney, Robert P. "Usury in Greek, Roman and Rabbinic Thought." *Traditio* 27 (1971): 70–109.

Mandelbrot, Benoit B., and James R. Wallis. "Noah, Joseph, and Operational Hydrology." *Water Resources Research* 4, no. 5 (1968): 909–18.

———. "Some Long-Run Properties of Geophysical Records Water Resources Research." 5, no. 2 (1969): 321–40.

Marcus, Abraham. "Rural Property and Social Structure." In Ann Elizabeth Mayer, *Property, Social Structure and Law in the Modern Middle East*. Albany: SUNY Press, 1985, 123.

Matthiae, Paolo and Nicolo Marchetti, eds. *Ebla and Its Landscape: Early State Formation in the Ancient Near East*. Walnut Creek, CA: Left Coast Press, 2013.

Mayer, Elizabeth. *Property, Social Structure and Law in the Modern Middle East*. Albany: SUNY Press, 1985.

McChesney, R. D. *Waqf in Central Asia: Four Hundred Years in the History of a Muslim Shrine, 1480–1889*. Princeton, NJ: Princeton University Press, 1991.

McKeon. Richard, ed. *The Basic Works of Aristotle*. New York: Modern Library Classics, 1941.

Mcelduff, Siobhán. *Cicero in Defense of the Republic*. London: Penguin, 2011.

Meadows, D., et al. *The Limits to Growth*, 2nd Edition. New York: Universe Books, 1974.

Meislin, Bernard J., and Morris L. Cohen. "Backgrounds of the Biblical Law against Usury." *Comparative Studies in Society and History* 6, no. 3 (April 1964).

Midant-Reynes, Béatrix. *The Prehistory of Egypt: From the First Egyptians to the First Pharaohs*. Translated by Ian Shaw. Oxford: Blackwell, 2000 (orig. 1994).

Mieroop. Marc Van de. *Cuneiform Texts and the Writing of History*. London: Routledge, 1999.

———. *A History of the Ancient Near East: ca. 3000–323 BC*. Oxford: Blackwell, 2004.

Millett, Paul. *Lending and Borrowing in Ancient Athens*. Cambridge: Cambridge University Press, 2002 (orig. 1991).

Morris, Ian. *Burial and Ancient Society: The Rise of the Greek City-State*. Cambridge: Cambridge University Press, 1990.

Morstein-Marx, Robert and Nathan Rosenstein, eds. *A Companion to the Roman Republic.* West Sussex: Blackwell Publishing, 2007.

Mottahedeh, Roy. *Loyalty and Leadership in Early Islamic Society*. Princeton, NJ: Princeton University Press, 1980.

Mousourakis, George. *The Historical Institutional Context of Roman Law*. Burlington, VT: Ashgate Publishing, 2003.

Moya, M., M. Guaita, P. Aguado, and F. Ayuga. "Mechanical Properties of Granular Agricultural Materials, part 2. *ASABE* 49, no. 2 (2006): 484.

Al-Muqaddasi, Muhammad ibn ahmad Shams al-Din. *La meilleur répartition pour la connaissance des provinces / ahsan at-taqāsim fi ma'arifat al-aqālīm*. Translated from Arabic by A. Miquel. Damascus: Institut Français de Damas 1963, 37.

Nam, Roger S. *Portrayals of Economic Exchange in the Book of Kings*. Leiden: Brill, 2012.

Napier, David. *Masks, Transformation, and Paradox*. Berkeley: University of California Press, 1986.

Nell, Edward J. *The General Theory of Transformational Growth.* Cambridge: Cambridge University Press, 1998.

Nell, Edward J. and Karim Errouaki. *Rational Econometric Man: Transforming Structural Econometrics*. Northampton, MA: Edward Elgar, 2013.

Neufeld, E. "The Rate of Interest and the Text of Nehemia 5:11." *The Jewish Quarterly Review*, New Series 44, no. 3 (January 1954): 194–204.

Nevett, Lisa C. *House and Society in the Ancient Greek World.* Cambridge: Cambridge University Press, 1999.

The New American Bible. (An official Catholic translation) or the New American Standard Bible. Iowa Falls: World Bible Publishers, Inc., 1991.

Newman, James R, ed. *The World of Mathematics*, vol. 1. New York: Dover Publications, Inc., 1956.

Nissen, Hans J. *The Early History of the Ancient Near East: 9000–200 B.C.* Chicago: University of Chicago Press, 1988 (orig. German 1983).

Nissen, Hans J., Peter Damerow, and Robert K. Englund. *Archaic Bookkeeping: Early Writing and Techniques of Economic Administration in the Ancient Near East*. Chicago: University of Chicago Press, 1993.

Ouyang, Xiaoli. *Monetary Role of Silver and Its Administration in Mesopotamia during the Ur III Period (c. 2112–2004 BCE): A Case Study of the Umma Province*. Madrid: Consejo Superior de Investigaciones Cientificas, 2013.

Park, Thomas K. "Early Trends toward Class Stratification: Chaos, Common Property, and Flood Recession Agriculture." *American Anthropologist*, New Series 94, no. 1 (March 1992).

———. "Essaaouira: The Formation of a New Elite 1940–1980." *African Studies Review* 31, no. 2 (1989): 11–132.

———. *Risk and Tenure in Arid Lands: The Political Ecology of Development in the Senegal River Basin*. Tucson: University of Arizona Press, 1993.

Park, Thomas K., and Aomar Boum. *Historical Dictionary of Morocco*, 2nd Edition. Lanham, MD: Scarecrow, 2006.

Park, Thomas K., and James B. Greenberg. *Hidden Interests in Credit and Finance: Power, Ethics, and Social Capital across the Last Millennium*. Lanham, MD: Lexington Books, 2017.

Parker, Robert. *Polytheism and Society at Athens*. Oxford: Oxford University Press, 2005.

Pascon, Paul. La Maison d'Iligh et l'histoire sociale du Tazerwalt. Rabat: Société Marocaine des Editeurs Réunis, 1984.

Patch, Blanche. *Thirty Years with G.B.S.* New York: Dodd, Mead & Company, 1951.

Peck, Harry Thurston. *Harper's Dictionary of Classical Literature and Antiquities*, 2nd Edition. New York: Harper & Brothers, 1897.

Pestman, P. W. *Recueil de textes démotiques et bilingues. II. Traductions*. Leiden: E.J. Brill, 1977.

Petersen, David L. *The Prophetic Literature: An Introduction*. Louisville, KY: Westminister John Knox Press, 2002.

Pettinato. Giovanni. *Ebla: A New Look at History*. Baltimore: Johns Hopkins University Press, 1991.

Piketty, Thomas. *Capital in the Twenty-First Century*. Cambridge, MA: Harvard University Press, 2014.

Pirenne, Henri. *Muhammed and Charlemagne*. Translated by Bernard Miall. Cleveland: Meridian Books, 1957.

Pirenne, Jacques. *Histoire des institutions et du droit privé de l'ancienne Egypte. III. La VIe Dynastie et le Démembrement de l'Empire*. Bruxelles: Edition de la fondation Egyptologique Reine Elisabeth, 1935.

Poe Yu-Ze Wan *Reframing the Social. Emergentist Systemism and Social Theory*. Farnham: Ashgate Publishing, 2011.

Polanyi, Karl. *The Great Transformation*. New York: Holt, Rinehart and Winston, Inc., 1957.

Pontin, Clive. *A Green History of the World*. New York: Penguin, 1991.

Popper, William. *The Cairo Nilometer*. Berkeley: University of California Press, 1951.

Porten, Bezalel with J. J. Farber, C. J. Martin, G. Vittmann, and contributions by Simon Hopkins and Ranon Kastzoff. *The Elephantine Papyri in English: Three Millennia of Cross-Cultural Continuity and Change*, 2nd Revised Edition. Leiden: Brill, 2011.

Postgate, J. N. *Early Mesopotamia: Society and Economy at the Dawn of History*. London: Routledge, 2004 (1992).

Potts, D. T. *Mesopotamian Civilization: The Material Foundations*. Ithaca, NY: Cornell University Press, 1996.

Potts, D. T., and Marvin A. Powell. "Weights and Measures." *The Anchor Bible Dictionary*. Edited by David Noel Freedman, Volume VI Si-Z. New Haven, CT: Anchor Bible, 1992, 897–908.

Powell, Marvin A. "Weights and Measures." *The Anchor Bible Dictionary*. Edited by David Noel Freedman, Volume VI Si-Z. New Haven, CT: Anchor Bible, 1992, 897–908.

Putnam, R. Bowling Alone: *Making Democracy Work: Civic Traditions in Modern Italy*. Princeton, NJ: Princeton University Press, 1993.

Renger, Johannes. "Institutional, Communal, and Individual Ownership or Possession of Arable Land in Ancient Mesopotamia from the End of the Fourth to the End of the First Millennium B.C." *Chicago-Kent Law Review* 71 (1995): 269–319.

Richards, E. G. *Mapping Time: The Calendar and Its History*. Oxford: Oxford University Press 1998.

Robbins, Gay, and Charles Shute. *The Rhind Mathematical Papyrus: An Ancient Egyptian Text*. London: British Museum Publications, 1987.

Robson, Eleanor. *Mathematics in Ancient Iraq: A Social History*. Princeton, NJ: Princeton University Press, 2008.

———. *Mesopotamian Mathematics*. Chapter 3 in Katz, 2007.

———. *Mesopotamian Mathematics: 2100–1600 BC. Technical Constants in Bureaucracy and Education*. Oxford: Clarendon Press, 1999.

Rodinson, Maxime. *Islam and Capitalism*. New York: Pantheon, 1973.

Roover, Raymond de. "The Scholastics, Usury, and Foreign Exchange." *The Business History Review* 41, no. 3 (Autumn 1967).

Roth, Martha T. *Law Collections from Mesopotamia and Asia Minor*, 2nd Edition. Atlanta: Scholars Press, 1997.

Rotman, Y. *Byzantine Slavery and the Mediterranean*. Cambridge, MA: Harvard University Press, 2009.

Rüpke, Jörg. *The Religion of the Romans*. Cambridge: Polity Press, 2007 (Originally published in German 2001).

Sandys, John Edwin. *Aristotle's 1912 Constitution of Athens: A Revised Text with an Introduction by Sir John Edwin Sandys*. London: MacMillan and Co., 1912.

Schacht, Joseph. *An Introduction to Islamic Law*. Oxford, Clarendon, 1982 (orig. 1964).

———. *The Origins of Muhammadan Jurisprudence*. Oxford: Clarendon Press, 1950.

Scheidel, Walter, and Sitta von Reden, eds. *The Ancient Economy*. New York: Routledge, 2002.

Scheidel, Walter, Ian Morris, and Richard Saller, eds. *The Cambridge Economic History of the Greco-Roman World*. Cambridge: Cambridge University Press, 2007.

Schumpeter, Joseph A. *History of Economic Analysis*. New York: Oxford University Press: 1974.

Schwartz. Glenn M., and John J. Nicols. *After Collapse: The Regeneration of Complex Societies*. Tucson: University of Arizona Press, 2010.

Sen, Amartya. *The Idea of Justice*. Cambridge, MA: Harvard University Press, 2009.

Sen, Amartya. “Rational Fools.” *Philosophy and Public Affairs* 6, no. 4 (Summer 1977): 317–44.

Seyffert, Oskar. *A Dictionary of Classical Antiquities, Mythology, Religion, Literature, and Art*. Translated from German and Revised and Edited by Henry Nettleship and J. E. Sandys. London, Swan Sonnenschein and Co, Ltd., 1894.

Sharlach, Tonia M. *Provincial Taxation in the Ur III State*. Leiden: Brill, 2004.

Shaw, Brent D. and Richard P. Saller, eds. *Economy and Society in Ancient Greece*. London: Chatto and Windus Ltd., 1981.

Shaw, Ian, ed. *The Oxford History of Ancient Egypt*. Oxford: Oxford University Press, 2000.

ash Shaybani. *The Muwatta of Imam Muhammad*. London: Turath Publishing, 2004.

Siegel. Bernard J. “Slavery during the Third Dynasty of Ur.” *American Anthropologist* New Series, 49, no.1 (January 1947): Part 2.

Simon, Herbert A. “Organizations and Markets.” *Journal of Public Administration Research and Theory: J-PART* 5, no. 3 (July 1995): 293–94).

Simon, Herbert A. “Altruism and Economics.” *The American Economic Review* 83, no. 2 (May 1993): 156–61).

Skaist, Aaron. *The Old Babylonian Loan Contract*. Ramat Gan: Bar-Ilan University Press, 1994.

Smith, William. *Dictionary of Greek and Roman Antiquities*. Boston: Little Brown and Co., 1870.

Snell, Daniel C., ed. *A Companion to the Ancient Near East*. Oxford: Blackwell, 2007.

Sraffa, Piero. *Production of Commodities by Means of Commodities*. Cambridge: Cambridge University Press, 1960.

Ste Croix, G. E. M. de. *The Class Struggle in the Ancient Greek World: From the Archaic Age to the Arab Conquests*. Ithaca, NY: Cornell University Press, 1981.

Strassler, Robert B. *The Landmark Thucydides: A Comprehensive Guide to the Peloponnesian War*. New York: Free Press, 2008 [First published 1996].

Szpakowska, Kasia, ed., *Through a Glass Darkly: Magic, Dreams and Prophecy in Ancient Egypt*. Llandysul: Classical Press of Wales, 2006.

Taylor, Charles. *Sources of the Self: The Making of the Modern Identity*. Cambridge, MA: Harvard University Press, 1989.

Termin, Peter. *The Roman Market Economy*. Princeton, NJ: Princeton University Press, 2013.

Toynbee, Arnold. *A Study of History*. Oxford: Oxford University Press, 1934–1961.

Trigger, B. G., B. J. Kemp, D. O’Connor, and A. B. Lloyd. *Ancient Egypt: A Social History*. Cambridge: Cambridge University Press, 1983.

Udovitch, Abraham. “At the Origins of the Western Commenda.” Speculum 37, no. 2 (April 1962).

———. *Partnership and Profit in Medieval Islam*. Princeton, NJ: Princeton University Press, 1970.

Vansina, Jan. *De la Tradition Orale. Essai de Méthode Historique: Annales du Musée Royale de l’Afrique Cnetrale, 1961.*

Veenhof, Klaas R. "'Modern' Features in Old Assyrian Trade." *Journal of the Economic and Social History of the Orient* 40, no. 4 (1997): 336–66.

Veenhof, Klaas R., and Jesper Eidem. *Mesopotamia: The Old Assyrian Period*. Fribourg: Academic Press, 2008. Orbis Biblicus et Orientalis 160/5.

Verboven, Koenraad.. *The Economy of Friends: Economic Aspects of Amicitia and Patronage in the Late Republic*, Bruxelles: Editions Latomus, 2002.

Versteeg, Russ. *Law in Ancient Egypt*. Durham, NC: Carolina Academic Press, 2002.

Veyne, Paul. *The Roman Empire*, 3rd Edition. Cambridge, MA: The Belknap Press of the University of Harvard, 2002 (orig. 1987).

Von Reden, Sitta. *Der Pirāus im 5. und frühen 4. Jahrhundert: Eine Hafenstadt in einer Agrargesellschaft*. Unpublished dissertation. Berlin. 1987: 66–72.

Vööbus, Arthur. "The institution of the Benai Qeiama and Benat Qeiama in the Ancient Syrian Church." *Church History* 30, no. 1 (March 1961).

Wakin, Jeannette. "The Function of Documents in Islamic Law." Tahawi's *kitāb al-shurut al-kabir*. Albany: SUNY, 1972, the chapters on "Sales."

Warburton, David A. *State and Economy in Ancient Egypt: Fiscal Vocabulary of the New Kingdom*. Göttingen: University Press Fribourg, 1997.

Ward, Allen M., Fritz M. Heichelheim, and Cedric A. Yeo. *A History of the Roman People*, 4th Edition. Upper Saddle River, NJ: Prentice Hall, 2003.

Waterfield, Robin. *Xenophon's Retreat: Greece, Persia, and the End of the Gold Age*. London: Faber and Faber Ltd., 2006.

Wells, Bruce, and F. Rachel Magdalene. *Law from the Tigris to the Tiber: The Writings of Raymond Westbrook*, Vols. I and II. Winona Lake, IN: Eisenbrauns, 2009.

Westbrook, Raymond, and Richard Jasnow. *Security for Debt in Ancient Near Eastern Law*. Leiden: Brill, 2001.

Wilkinson, Richard H. *The Complete Temples of Ancient Egypt*. New York: Thames & Hudson, 2000.

———. *The Complete Gods and Goddesses of Ancient Egypt*. New York: Thames & Hudson, 2003.

Wittfogel, Karl A. *Oriental Despotism: A Comparative Study of Total Power*. New Haven, CT: Yale University Press, 1963.

Wolff, Jonathan, and Avner De Shalit. *Disadvantage*. Oxford: Oxford University Press, 2007.

Yoffee, Norman. "Aspects of Mesopotamian Land Sales." *American Anthropologist*. 90, no. 1 (March 1988).

———. "The Decline and Rise of Mesopotamian Civilization: An Ethnoarchaeological Perspective on the Evolution of Complexity." *American Antiquity* 44, no. 1 (January 1979).

———. *Myths of the Archaic State: Evolution of the Earliest Cities, States, and Civilizations*. Cambridge: Cambridge University Press, 2005.

Zelnick-Abramovitz, Rachel. "Did Patronage Exist in Classical Athens?" *L'Antiquité Classique* T. 69 (2000): 65–80.

Žižek, Slavoj. *Less Than Nothing: Hegel and the Shadow of Dialectical Materialism*. London: Verso, 2012.

Index

About the Authors

Thomas K. Park has taught in the School of Anthropology at the University of Arizona since 1986. He received a joint PhD in anthropology and comparative world history from the University of Wisconsin–Madison in 1983, an MA in agricultural economics in 1982, and a BA with Joint First Class Honors in anthropology and philosophy from McGill University in 1974. His first publication to deal with ancient Egypt, "Early Trends toward Class Stratification: Chaos, Common Property and Flood Recession Agriculture," appeared in the *American Anthropologist* in 1992.

James B. Greenberg is professor of anthropology, and a senior research anthropologist in the School of Anthropology at the University of Arizona. He received his PhD from the University of Michigan in 1978. His areas of expertise lie in economic anthropology, political ecology, globalization, law and development, violence, urban anthropology, migration, peasant and working class livelihoods, Latin America, and borderlands. His books include *Neoliberalism and Commodity Production in Mexico* (University of Colorado Press, 2012); *Reimagining Political Ecology* (Duke University Press, 2006); *Blood Ties: Life and Violence in Rural Mexico* (University of Arizona Press, 1990); and *Santiago's Sword: Chatino Peasant Religion and Economics* (University of California Press, 1982).

Lightning Source UK Ltd.
Milton Keynes UK
UKOW01n0735080218
317556UK00012B/532/P

9 781498 545815